Personal Development and Discovery Through Leisure

THIRD EDITION

Ernest G. Olson, Ph.D.
California State University—Sacramento

KENDALL/HUNT PUBLISHING COMPANY
4050 Westmark Drive Dubuque, Iowa 52002

ISBN 978-0-7575-4879-6

Printed in the United States of America
10 9 8 7 6 5 4

Contents

Foreword

Dr. Ernie Olson has written an important book. It is a unique combination of theory, practice, philosophy and personal experiences. Dr. Olson brings a unique perspective to the field of leisure education. His academic work stems from the strong theoretical traditions of the University of Illinois, Champaign-Urbana. This, coupled with a rich professional and experiential background, allows him to speak from experience as well as theory. His work in the field of general education has provided him with unusual insight into the pedagogical needs of college age students. This insight is reflected in both his writing style and content. He writes in a relaxed and informal manner. He writes in first person and often speaks directly to the reader.

The book begins with a discussion on discovery. The notion that discovery is an important ingredient in the leisure lifestyle is a theme that soon becomes familiar to the reader. Dr. Olson presents a convincing argument that growth and development are promoted through leisure discovery. He encourages the reader to develop a philosophy that promotes not only leisure discovery, but exploration in all aspects of life. He even suggests that by developing a discovery philosophy formal learning can take on the dimensions of leisure experience.

Dr. Olson is a strong voice for the value of play. Following a discussion on the meaning and characteristics of play, Dr. Olson presents a convincing argument that play is essential for growth and development, not only during the formative years of life, but also during adulthood. He effectively dispels the idea that play has no value for adults.

Early in the book Dr. Olson discusses the epistemology of leisure, both from a philosophical perspective and a scientific perspective. He carefully describes the philosophical process and explains how one's philosophy of leisure contributes to one's growth and development. He contrasts philosophy with the scientific method and demonstrates how both fields are essential to one's understanding of leisure, play, and recreation.

The book looks closely at many important areas of life experience. The discussion on leisure motivation examines leisure from a social, psychological and physiological perspective. In his chapter on human development and leisure, he looks closely at the relationship of leisure to physical, social, cognitive, and personality development. Conversely, he also looks at the relationship of developmental phase to leisure choices. He presents chapters on such important areas as successful aging, leisure and work, the relationship of leisure to health, love and leisure, stress and distress, humor, and how to create a discovery lifestyle.

The book has a distinctly personal tone. It generally doesn't address global, historical, or social issues. That is not the purpose of the book. The reader will soon learn that it is written with the reader in mind and addresses issues that have personal value to the reader. The book also has a pragmatic theme to it. Throughout, the reader will find suggestions on how to enrich one's life through expanding one's understanding, appreciation and application of leisure. It offers practical suggestions to help one make meaningful behavioral and attitudinal changes. In addition, the book is laced with humorous anecdotes and fun exercises.

In short, Dr. Olson has written an academic but practical book, an enlightening but motivating treatise. It is a book the reader will not only find educational, but enjoyable.

Carol Stensrud, Ph.D.

Introduction

At one time I thought of calling this book "Discovering Leisure in a Chaotic World" but for now the book is simply entitled *Personal Development and Discovery Through Leisure*. The image of a "chaotic world" reflects the idea that the pressures of contemporary society make it increasingly important for people to learn to relax, chill, kickback—in other words, to discover leisure. The "development" idea suggests the relationship between leisure and human development. Both titles are appropriate for the content of this book—neither is adequate. The book advances a collection of ideas and research findings about the relationship of leisure to physical, social, psychological, and cognitive development. But there is more. It also tries to go one step further. It suggests ways and means of incorporating leisure into one's life. The fundamental goal of *Personal Development and Discovery Through Leisure* is to help you hang loose in a chaotic world and in the process reach toward your physical, social, cognitive, and psychological potentials.

On occasion you will note use of the word "pleisure." The spelling is correct. It was Dr. Carol Stensrud who coined this term. It is the product of combining the words "leisure" and "pleasure." Pleasure refers to something which produces enjoyment or in which one finds delight. Leisure can refer to a state of mind characterized by perceived freedom and intrinsic satisfaction. It can also mean "free time." Pleisure refers to finding joy in leisure or taking delight in leisure. A "pleisurist" is one who finds joy in the leisure lifestyle.

"Discovery event" is another term occasionally referenced in this book. I am not certain as to the original source for this term, but I am going to credit Professor Bill Finch. A discovery event refers to an activity that is new to you. By engaging in a new activity, you discover not only something about the activity, but you discover something about yourself. Generally, the process of discovery yields gains in personal growth and feelings of life enrichment. Many of us avoid new activities like the plague. The fear of not fitting in, the fear of failing, the fear of the unknown are all fears that keep us from discovery. By adopting the "discovery event philosophy" we overcome such fears, and find our lives characterized by increased pleisure, growth, and development. The joy of discovery is a quiet theme throughout this book.

And, now just a short note of appreciation for people who have made this book possible. My Mom and Dad played a role in this book. (In part, I wrote it so they would know what I teach.) My three children have made a contribution by teaching me the most important concepts of what I know about play and its relationship to growth and development. My thanks go out to the many students I have taught who have in turn motivated me to continually learn. There are many colleagues who have contributed to this book in subtle and ways unknown to them—too many to name. However, I must thank Gail Ma and Edrak Thomas for their careful proofreading; graduate students Soo Bazzano and Lillian Leong for their research assistance; and Susie and Trang Le for their word processing skills, patience, and good humor.

Ernie Olson, Friday, May 6, 2003

How To Use This Book

As you will soon learn, this is not only a textbook, but it is also a workbook. Whether you are reading the book on your own, or are reading it as part of a course of study, you are encouraged to participate in the exercises included in this book. Most of the exercises are found in the back, a few are included within the text. They are designed to give an interactive component to the text, to allow you to participate on a personal level. One of my goals in writing this book is to share with you some ideas that might help make your life a little more enjoyable and your leisure more meaningful. The exercises are designed to take you out of reading-mode and into action-mode. I think you will like the ideas presented in this book, but as I often tell my students, "A good idea is just a good idea until it is put into action." In other words, I'm hoping you will feel sufficiently motivated by the material in the book that you will want to put some, if not all, of the ideas presented here into action. The worksheets found in the appendix are all designed to help bring that about. So, I know this sounds like an oxymoron, but take your study of leisure seriously. By so doing, it may have a profound impact on the quality of your life.

One of the exercises included in the appendix is the Leisure Profile Packet. This exercise consists of several scales that will enable you to construct a leisure profile. You might want to complete the LPP before you begin your reading to see where you are right now. You can use it as a basis for comparison for where you are once you have completed the reading and engaged in the other exercises.

CHAPTER 1

A Short History of Leisure, Recreation, and Play

A Big Bang In the Night

Astronomers tell us that the universe was born in an immense explosion spewing hot gases into previously empty space. As the gases cooled, some of the resultant matter took the form of planets, one of which was planet earth. For billions of years, the earth was inhospitable to life. But, eventually it cooled, took its present form and provided a fertile environment for the simple life forms that began to form. The life forms gradually and over millions of years became increasingly complex, and eventually the planet was dominated by giant lizard-like reptiles. Today we call them dinosaurs.

I'd love to have a complex thought, but if I did, my body would stop working!

Dinosaurs came to dominate planet earth, but in spite of their size and complexity it appears that their evolution did not include cognitive development. While their bodies, in many instances, grew to great proportions, their brains remained disproportionately small. For example, it is estimated that the modern day rabbit had more brainpower than a giant brontosaurus. With such limited intelligence, dinosaurs functioned on an instinctive level. As creatures of instinct, they lacked the capacity to engage in even the simplest forms of problem solving. It is equally unlikely that dinosaurs had the capacity to engage in anything resembling play.

Their lives were characterized by eating, sleeping, and feeding. Play was beyond their capacity and absent from their agenda. However, their lack of intelligence did not seem to adversely affect them, for they thundered across the planet for millions of years. Then, an amazing phenomenon occurred, about 65,000,000 years ago something when terribly wrong for Earth's giant reptiles. Almost overnight, most of them became extinct.

With the demise of dinosaurs, mammals emerged. Evolving both intellectually and physically, mammals became "smart" animals, and over millions of years evolved into the upright standing, creatively thinking, and emotionally feeling species known as *homo sapien*. Human's, unlike their reptilian predecessors had all of the tools to engage in **playful behavior**, and to organize that behavior into increasingly complex forms of structured play that came to be known as recreation. In addition, humans also had the intellectual capability to conceptualize and ponder abstract ideas, including the phenomenon now referred to as **leisure.**[1]

I started to have a complex thought, then I laid down and it went away!

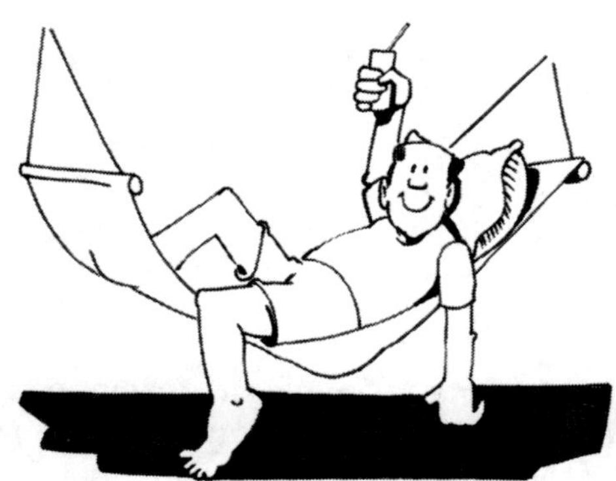

Primitive Peoples

To primitive people, magic and religion were powerful forces. All aspects of their lives were influenced by mysterious forces that instilled awe and wonderment and often fear and anger as well. To modern people, lightning and thunder, the changing seasons, rain and snow, and other natural phenomena are easily explained through the application of scientific principles. But to primitive folks, these same phenomena were only understandable when explained in religious or magical terms. Consequently, the mind set of early humans must have largely been directed at bringing some degree of order to what no doubt appeared a frightening and chaotic world. In order to do this, primitive people resorted to prayer and supplication, which often took the form of dancing, chanting and singing. Storytelling played an important role among primitive peoples, as did crude drawings and symbols. Even though one may look at these activities as being recreational, among primitive peoples, these activities were primarily engaged in to influence the mysterious forces that constantly appeared intent on disrupting their lives. Early primitive people traveled in small bands, hunting and foraging, often passing whole lifetimes without crossing the path of other groups, but as the planet became more populated and as people became more learned in ways to manipulate their environment, play and recreation became an increasingly important part of tribal life. Play became a primary means of education and socialization, and provided a way of practicing important survival and battle skills.

Nearly 10,000 years ago in what later became known as Mesopotamia, a major transition in the lifestyle of *Homo sapiens* began to occur. People settled in fixed villages and cities, a written language was developed, an aristocracy was created, and an economic interdependence between social and vocational classes emerged. Civilization had come to planet Earth.

1. **Want to know more?** See Carl Sagan's book *The Dragon's of Eden.*

Pre-Christian Civilization

Human beings have been described as "animals that like to figure things out."[2] The productivity, complexity, and advances of early civilizations attest to that notion. Ancient Egyptians were masters of astronomy, engineering, agriculture and construction. And they appeared equally adept at entertaining themselves. Modern nightclubs find their roots in ancient Egypt; the bullfight, music, drama, and dance were important sources of recreation and worship. During the latter part of its history, many of these activities lost their religious significance and were participated in primarily for their recreation value. Even prostitution became a licensed leisure occupation.[3]

It was the Ancient Greeks, however, who placed the greatest value on leisure, particularly those living in the period known as the "Golden Age of Pericles" (500-400 B.C.). Because of the value accorded organized leisure activities, this period is referred by some scholars as the "First Recreation Revolution" (Chubb and Holly 20). Competitive sports were a frequent form of entertainment, even such formal events as weddings featured sports for the amusement of the guests. The modern Olympics find their origin during this period. Music and drama play an important role. Although the relationship between leisure and other social values was recognized, leisure was viewed as having value in and of itself. To the ancient Greeks, leisure was an end to which all free people aspired. As Aristotle said:

> *Nature requires that we should not only work well, but to use leisure well; ... for the first principle of all action is leisure (Kraus 134).*

Regrettably, and this is an important point, not all of Greece was free to enjoy the benefits of a leisure oriented society. The leisure enjoyed by the free citizens of Greece, came at the expense of those who were enslaved. It is often stated that in Athens there were four slaves to every free male. It was this underclass that did the chores that liberated a minority of free citizens from obligations that would have otherwise interfered with their recreational pursuits. Ironically, the very people who made leisure possible for the free citizen were unable to engage in leisure themselves. Leisure was unavailable to slaves and members of the lower class, and was, to a very large extent, available only to the male members of upper class society. Even free-women were considered second-class citizens whose function was primarily to tend to the home and attend to family matters.

The Roman view of leisure was not nearly as idealistic as the Greeks. The Roman hierarchy viewed recreation in pragmatic and utilitarian terms. Initially, leisure was looked upon as being essential to good health, useful in teaching correct values, and of economic value. But as the empire began to sag with its own political burdens and excesses, and as free Roman citizens found themselves with increasing free time, the prevailing leisure philosophy was one of entertainment and distraction. By the First Century A.D., sports and games had become commercialized and professionalized. By the year 93 A.D., there were 159 public holidays. The famous Roman baths provided endless amusement and recreational opportunities. By the end of the Fourth Century it is estimated that there were approximately 856 such facilities, capable of accommodating over 60,000 people at one time. And, of course, there were the arenas, the largest of which (the Circus Maximus) could accommodate 350,000 people. Arenas throughout the empire became known as the sites of increasingly bloody entertainment. During the reign of Caligula and Nero, recreation took monstrous forms, and the glory which had been Rome descended into the depths of human deprivation and prepared the way for the Mongolian hordes that ultimately crushed the greatest of empires.[4]

2. I heard Carl Sagan say this on *The Johnny Carson Show,* (January 20, 1986).
3. Many recreational activities lost their religious significance, and became solely recreational.
4. The Ancient Romans sensationalized leisure and used it politically. Could that happen today?

The Roman empire spanned nearly 1,110 years. It's recreation and leisure evolved from simple pastimes to orgies of blood and sensation. Early in its history, Roman recreation was similar to that of the Greeks, but increased unemployment, free-time, and social unrest led to increasingly colorful and extreme forms of leisure entertainment. This, the "de-evolution" of leisure among the Romans was in part the result of a political and philosophical system that failed to recognize that the human spirit needs not to be fed a diet of escalating entertainment, but rather needs to be nourished on opportunities to grow and develop. History might have taken a different course had the prevailing philosophy of Ancient Rome been more akin to that of Ancient Athens. *To see the extent that contemporary society has come to embody some of the values that led to the destruction of the Roman Empire watch television for 30 minutes, change channels every 60 seconds. Count the number of times you see violence, sex, or sensational images. You will quite likely see that we have quite a bit in common with Ancient Rome.*

The Middle and Dark Ages

With the **fall of the Roman Empire**, a period of great social stagnation and decline emerged. Warring tribes and unreliable coalitions shattered the central authority once held by Rome, leaving Europe in chaos. With time the Catholic Church arose as the dominant and unifying force throughout Europe, and with its ascendance to power came a decline in any behavior, object, or idea that had characterized the Roman lifestyle. Many of the commonly accepted leisure activities of ancient Rome, were viewed by Catholicism as sinful. In addition, it is well to remember that under the Romans, Christians had been severely persecuted. Consequently culture and Roman developments were generally despised by Catholic Church leaders.

The antagonism felt by the Church for things Roman resulted in a severe backlash against anything reflective of Roman culture. Consequently, many of the advancements made by the Romans (and Greeks as well) were lost. For example, the art of soap production was lost making the Dark Ages not only dark but dirty. It is believed that much of the disease associated with this period could have been prevented had the knowledge of soap making not become a forgotten art. Critical thinking generally suffered during this time, as well. Music, arts, sciences and philosophy were inhibited during this time. It is fair to assess this period as a time characterized by limited opportunity and strong religious and political sanctions against play and entertainment.[5]

To characterize the **Dark and Middle Ages** as a period of time devoid of recreation and leisure would be an unfortunate overstatement. One of the defining characteristics of humanity is a universal need for play and relaxation. Certainly, this need was not eliminated by the circumstances of this period. Rather, the form that recreation and play took was influenced by the social circumstances of the time. Society during the Middle Ages was stratified along social-economic lines. At the top of the order were the nobility and the clergy, then came the peasants who were further ranked as freemen, villeins, serfs, and slaves. Men dominated all levels, and women were generally viewed as inferior to men. Play and recreational opportunities were influenced as much by rank as by the inhibiting influence of the Church.

The nobility had more opportunities for leisure than the lower classes. The peasant classes were extremely poor and relatively defenseless against the demands of the nobility. The nobility had more free time for leisure pursuits than the downtrodden lower classes. Not only did the nobility have more time for leisure, they engaged in more sophisticated forms of recreation than those of lower rank. For example, hunting was a favored sport among the nobility; whereas, among the peasant classes, hunting was an essential means of procuring food. Music, dance, and sports were popular among the nobility; whereas among the peasants cockfighting, bull-baiting, and wrestling were popular. During the Dark Ages, the Church even orchestrated leisure opportunities through religious celebrations and festivals.

With the passage of time, the backlash of the Church against the depravity of Rome lessened, and for that matter, the controlling influence of the Church diminished as well. With these changes, the people of Europe began to experience a rebirth in their interest in recreation and leisure.

5. Renaissance essentially means "rebirth."

The Renaissance Period

There is no magic date on which one can say the Renaissance began, but historians indicate that the Renaissance began in Italy sometime during the 14th century. Unlike the Dark and Middle Ages, this period was marked by a renewed interest in secular things as opposed to the religious obsession that characterized the preceding 1,000 years. Although the Catholic Church remained a powerful influence throughout Europe, it's political influence had diminished and its increasingly liberal stance permitted a new sense of freedom among populations that had once been seriously oppressed by the Church. Consequently, people began to explore science, art and philosophy. Music and dance became important forms of creative expression. A philosophy celebrating the unity of the mind and body developed and thus championed a holistic perspective toward life and learning. It was in this new environment of freedom that many great thinkers, scholars and artists emerged. Perhaps the spirit of the Renaissance is best typified by Leonardo Da Vinci, who during his 67 years on the planet became known for his expertise and accomplishments in art, anatomy, engineering, architecture, music, science and was well respected as an inventor.

Recreation during the Renaissance became increasingly specialized. Musicians, visual artists, thespians and actors slowly acquired professional status. Sports and athletic competitions became popular. Leisure and recreation assumed proportions somewhat similar to that of the Ancient Greeks, but the forces opposed to human freedom and expression were not to be denied.[6]

The Reformation

During the **Renaissance**, Catholicism lost a great deal of its political power. Furthermore, doctrinal shifts representing an increasingly liberal religious philosophy occurred as well as growing corruption in church ranks. These two factors combined to stimulate criticism of the church and a call for reformation among Catholic conservatives. Chief among these critics were Martin Luther, John Knox and John Calvin. The protestations of these and others led to the formation of several apostate religious organizations referred to collectively as **Protestants.** Not known for their tolerance, these religions made attempts to curtail public amusements, sports, arts and other pleasurable pastimes. The emphasis clearly was on work, indeed a grim dedication to work. Where Protestant religions became dominant, dissenters were ruthlessly suppressed and some, in the name of Jesus, were even burned at the stake. In England, Protestants themselves were repressed by the State Church, thus encouraging many "Puritans" to emigrate to the New World. Consequently, recreation in Colonial America was greatly influenced by Protestant philosophy. For example, early laws in most of the colonies legislated against any form of idleness, which was viewed as the source of all vices. Dancing, public entertainment and other amusements were condemned as the tools of Satan.

In Other Parts of the World...

- While Europe was going through the Dark and Middle Ages, **India** was experiencing a lifestyle filled with leisure and recreation. The wealthy created ornate gardens and lakes. Those who had leisure time, mainly the rich, spent it attending literary parties, writing poetry, and engaging in amorous adventures (Cordes and Ibrahim 26) Sports were also widely played. This included marbles, swimming, wrestling, boxing, javelin, and various ball games.

- Like India, **Japan** did not have a "Dark Age" that was going on in Europe at this time. Public bathhouses became very popular in Japan during the 6th century C.E. Dancers and singers entertained the people who frequented these places. Japanese society enjoyed listening to music and having poetry readings in their homes. In the 7th century, Japanese drama emerged. Their plays brought together

6. Reformation means to *reform*.

dance, music, and drama. Comedy was also very popular for the Japanese. During the 16th and 17th centuries, puppet shows, or **kabuki,** developed[7].

- Between 500 and 1500 B.C.E., the **Muslim World** intertwined leisure with their religion. The works of the Greeks, Romans, Persians, and Eastern Indians heavily influenced their culture (Russell 26). During the holy month of Ramadan, where they fasted from sunrise to sunset, the evenings were spent playing card and table games like chess and backgammon. Women, who had to stay in separate quarters, were entertained by female belly dancers.

- **China** has a rich cultural history and recreation has always been a part of it. Competitive archery appeared around 110 B.C.E. and soccer was developed in China during the Han Dynasty (206 B.C.E-25 C.E.). According to Ruth Russell, professor at Indiana University, the Tang Dynasty (618-907) marked "the beginning of leisure in Chinese society" (Russell 25). Chinese estates had many buildings devoted to leisure activities such as listening to music, entertaining with writers, painters, storytellers, and admiring the moon. When Europe was going through the Renaissance, so were the Chinese in some respects. Many novels as well as plays were written in the 14th century. Since the 1800's, China has had to deal with Western influences on their culture although the old ways were much preferred. Men still enjoy going to teahouses. Drama is also popular. Peking Operas are favored as well as old Chinese plays. Old Chinese books are still read in leisure time and painting in the old style (flowers, birds, trees, landscapes) is preferred. Western sports like baseball and tennis are now played by the Chinese youth (Lang 27).

The Reformation was not a bright chapter in the history of recreation and leisure, but the human need for play and recreation could not be repressed for long. By the beginning of the 19th century, prohibitions against play and recreation had been somewhat relaxed, a trend which continued until the early stages of the Industrial Revolution.[8]

The Industrial Revolution

Industrialization in Europe increased the average work day from 12 hours in the early 1700's to 14 to 18 hours by the middle 1800's (Kraus 159). During this period, the Protestant ideals were reinforced, producing the **Protestant (Puritan) Work Ethic**. Work was viewed as man's self-justification, the purpose of life. By the 1850's, laws were passed protecting workers and the escalation of the average work day was reversed.

It was, however, the **Civil War** that had the greatest positive impact on recreation during this period. Army camps provided young men with an opportunity to meet men from other parts of the country and to share with them ideas and activities regarding leisure and recreation. In an effort to escape the horror of war and boredom of camp life, many soldiers sought relief through recreation, free from the puritanical influence of home and family. Consequently, following the war, soldiers returned home with a broader view of leisure and recreation and tended to promote recreation in their home communities.

During the late 1800's, commercial amusements prospered, including the development of amusement parks. Professional baseball was established (1869). Tourism increased. Basketball was invented in 1891. Several volunteer youth serving agencies were founded, which provided opportunities for children and teenagers, and in 1896, the Olympic games were reopened.[9] Conservation of recreation resources became an issue

7. You can find the "Japanese Drama" in the *Microsoft Encarta 98 Encyclopedia*.
8. Religious leaders who protested against the liberal thinking of the Church were called *Protestants*. Recreation was viewed by Protestants as sin.
9. 1869 Professional baseball is begun. 1891 Basketball is invented. 1896 Olympic Games are reintroduced.

during this time.[10] It was in 1864 that Congress set aside the Yosemite Valley and eight years later declared Yellowstone a National Park.[11]

An important leader in the Recreation Movement during the late 1800's was Frederick Law Olmstead, Sr. (1822-1903). Olmstead was a visionary, artist and technician. He was one of the principal designers of New York's Central Park. His commitment to providing quality leisure environments for the public led him to design and develop many urban parks, regional, state and national parks. In addition, his work influenced the direction taken by other designers and park planners.

Additional important developments regarding municipal parks during this period include:

- Place D'armes Square, Canda's first major public park, founded in Montreal Quebec, Canada in 1821.
- Central Park founded in New York City, 1850.
- Enabling legislation enacted in New Jersey to permit communities to establish municipal parks, 1885. This was the first of such legislation in the U.S.
- The Boston Sand Gardens are established, 1885.
- Metropolitan Park Commission founded in Boston, Massachusetts, in 1892.
- John Muir, naturalist, established the Sierra Club, 1992.
- Resource Driveway and Park District Act passed in Illinois, 1893 permitted unincorporated areas the authority to establish park systems.[12]

It was also during the 1800's that various Christian religions began to take an enlightened perspective of recreation and leisure. The Muscular Christian Movement and the YMCA set the church stamp of approval on sports. It was also during the late 1800's that intercollegiate sports became popular. The recreation movement in the United States was clearly underway.

The Recreation Movement

We often hear recreation and leisure scholars speak of the "**recreation movement**." What are they talking about? Social movements are said to involve a number of steps or stages. Movements begin in respect to some compelling social need. This need is initially addressed by an organization or groups of organizations which then set out to create fundamental changes in the way that government and society address the need. So in reference to the **recreation movement** *we are talking about a series of events that grew out of a perceived need relating to organized recreation and which taken together resulted in significant growth and development in the way that recreation was viewed by society and the manner in which recreational services were delivered.*

The recreation movement in the United States began in response to conditions associated with urban growth and industrial development (Kelly 148). Children had few places to play, they were increasingly at risk as they tried to find play opportunities in busy streets and industrial areas. Progressive thinkers took note

---

10. 1864--Yosemite established, 1872--Yellowstone National Park established.

11. Yellowstone National Park has to be one of the true wonders of the world. Its geysers, hot springs, raging rivers, giant gorges and enchanting waterfalls make it a truly national treasure. It was first seen by explorers in 1870, whose first inclination was to lay claim on the area and use it for commercial purposes. Ultimately, their sense of perspective won over their greed, and they petitioned Congress to set aside this area upon discovering this wondrous land (Carlson, Deppe, Maclean, 123).

12. For more on enabling legislation see the chapter dealing with the legal foundations of leisure service.

of this and began to provide limited play areas for city children. One of the most notable developments occurred in Boston. Most historians give credit to the **Sandgardens of Boston** as the inception of the recreation movement. The Sandgardens were really nothing more than large piles of sand made available to urban Boston's children for supervised play. Developed in 1885 for the children of Boston, similar play areas soon appeared in other cities. In 1892, Jane Adams established the first model playground at the Hull House, one of the nation's first settlement houses. Park systems soon began to appear across the United States, many modeled after **Central Park** of New York City which was dedicated in 1853.

Of particular prominence during these formative times was a man by the name of Joseph Lee. Known as the "father of the playground movement," Lee was a lawyer and philanthropist who came to view recreation and play as having great value to society. He wrote extensively on the subject and was a popular orator. He was the president of the American Playground Association from 1910 until his death in 1937.

The recreation movement was not limited to urban areas. In many respects it became a national phenomenon. There were factors at work across the fabric of the nation that had far reaching consequences. Industrialization, urbanization, commercialization of recreation, increasing crime and concern about the environment are examples of these factors. Carlson, Deppe, Maclean and Peterson identified nine such points that they believe led to the first formal efforts to initiate professional recreation and leisure services on a national scale (Carlson and MacClean 42-44).

1. By the early 1900's, it was clear our national resources would eventually be depleted unless protected.
2. The Industrial Revolution had led to unpredicted free time and also had a dehumanizing effect.
3. People began moving to the cities.
4. Crime was steadily increasing.
5. Population was steadily increasing.
6. Mental health problems were steadily increasing.
7. "Unwholesome" recreation was increasing.
8. People were increasingly mobile.
9. Many cities and special interest groups began to demonstrate the need for a resource network.

Several organizations serving the recreation field were started at the turn of the century. People began to move into the cities and the demand for leisure services increased. Many men and women were concerned about "the provision of proper environments for play and the wise use of leisure" (Sessoms 45). This meant having regulations that would ensure the parks and playgrounds that people used would be safe. Many cities and special interest groups began to demonstrate the need for a resource network. The first playground commission was established in 1904 by the city of Los Angeles. In 1906, a group of socially conscious leaders met in Washington D.C. to resolve some of the recreation and leisure problems of the day. This led to the founding of the American Playground Association. It was later changed in 1911 to the Playground and Recreation Association to reflect a broader area of interest (now it is called the National Recreation and Park Association). They advocated for increased opportunities in music, drama, and the arts in school. Laws were passed in many states mandating physical training classes and areas for recreation in school system (Carlson, Deppe, and MacLean 43). The purpose of this group remains to be the "promotion and development of leisure services that will bring a better quality of life not only for children but for all people" (Ball and Cipriano 13). As a result of this **Playground Movement** at the turn of the century, the National Education Association recognized the importance of recreation by including "education for leisure" as one of the Seven Cardinal Principles of Education in 1918.

Another important organization that was started at the beginning of the twentieth century was the National Park Service. In 1906, Congress passed the Antiquities Act, giving the President the power to designate national monuments and protect them from being destroyed. In 1916, Congress decided that a federal agency needed to be formed to regulate this and the Bureau of National Parks, thus the National Park Service, was formed.[13]

World War I and the Roaring 20's

> *U.S. involvement in the War to End All Wars lasted from October 17, 1917 to November 11, 1918. The war itself lasted only four years. Ten million people died during this time and another 20 million were wounded. This was, however, not to be the last war. . . .*

As a result of the recreation resources made available for the Military, World War I brought an upsurge in public appreciation for public recreation, and set the stage for a period of unprecedented license. In answer to both the financial needs and the emotional/social needs of this period, the Federal Government instituted several emergency efforts. The result was a dramatic increase in public recreational facilities and leadership training. It is interesting to note that it was during the Depression that the 18th Amendment (Prohibition) was repealed. Federal programs which contributed to the recreation movement included the Federal Emergency Relief Administration (FERA), the National Youth Administration (NYA), the Works Progress Administration (WPA), the Civilian Conservation Corps (CCC). These agencies administered and funded many outdoor recreation developments. The arts received a boost from the Federal Arts Program. It was during this time that college training first became available for recreation workers (1937).[14]

World War II

Just as with World War I, World War II, in spite of its carnage, in the long term had a positive impact on the recreation movement. The Special Services Division of the U.S. Army, the Welfare and Recreation Bureau of the Navy, and the Recreation Service of the Marines provided organized recreation for thousands of men and women serving in the Armed Services. The Red Cross, USO and the National Recreation Association and countless community recreation programs contributed to meeting the leisure needs of military personnel, their families and those working in war industries. Following the war they brought their interest in organized recreation back to their communities. Just as servicemen and women had been exposed to organized recreation in the military, home-front recreation increased to provide recreational support to those working in the war industries. As a consequence of this dramatic increase in recreational opportunities, by the time the war ended, millions of Americans had become accustomed to enjoying government sponsored recreational activities and programs. Naturally, many of these people wanted to continue to enjoy organized recreation and encouraged their communities to further develop such programs. People with recreational training found employment opportunities serving those who had come to value organized recreation and leisure. In addition, many cities erected "living monuments" in the form of parks, stadiums, and other recreational facilities.[15]

The 1950's, to Present Day

Upon conclusion of World War II, a healthy economy brought an increase in leisure activity. Transportation and entertainment flourished. The 50's became appropriately, "The Fabulous 50's." Bill Haley and the Comets

---

13. 1906--The American Playground Association of America was founded.
1911--Changed to Playground and Recreation Association of America
1926--Changed to National Recreation Association

14. National Education Assn. included "worthy use of leisure" as a basic goal of education--1918.
PRAA requested to help develop recreational services for the military. War Camp Community Services established.
The Great Depression led to many projects which provided infrastructure for recreation.

15. Army Special Services established to provide recreation for the military USO established.

and Elvis Presley started a revolution that "rocks on" even today. And then came the Beetles, long hair, hippies and the birth control pill. The 60's was a decade of social conscience, experimentation, and conflict. From a recreational standpoint, people experienced more freedom and variety; social programs sponsored by the government provided services for the disabled and minority groups. The Civil Rights Movement touched the social conscience of the U.S. and great strides were made toward racial and gender equality. But Vietnam and racial strife made for shaky times and conflict.[16]

During the early 1950's international travel expanded dramatically, and with that expansion came an awareness among recreation and leisure professionals that leisure and recreation issues had global implications. In 1956, the first international association for recreation professionals was established. Initially known as the **International Recreation Association**, it later changed its name to the **World Recreation and Leisure Association.**[17]

In 1966, five separate professional recreation and leisure organizations--the American Association of Zoological Parks and Aquariums, American Institute of Park Executives, American Recreation Society, National Conference on State Parks, and the National Recreation Association--merged to form the **National Recreation and Park Association.**[18]

The Outdoor Recreation Review Commission (ORRC) and the Bureau of Outdoor Recreation (BOR) was established during this time in the Department of the Interior. The BOR was established by executive order in 1962. The Bureau of Outdoor Recreation was given the mission of unifying and promoting federal programs concerned with open space, natural resources, and outdoor recreation. It was responsible for managing the **Land and Water Conservation Fund** established in 1965. It also served to coordinate the services of the **National Wild and Scenic Rivers System** and the **National Trails System.** The bureau also worked closely with state and local agencies that provided recreation services. It is known for developing the first Nationwide Outdoor Recreation Plan. Renamed the Heritage Conservation and Recreation Service in 1978, this bureau was dismantled and its functions absorbed by the National Park Service 3 years later as a cost-cutting measure.[19]

The "Stressful 60's" were replaced by the "Sane 70's." With the end of the Vietnam conflict came a period of relative calm, the social unrest of the 60's was replaced by an urgent need to heal the scars of the previous decade and resolve the economic problems created by the energy crisis and runaway inflation. In addition, the sexual freedom of the 60's appeared to have spawned genital herpes, a venereal precursor of things to come. The sexual license of the flower children was suddenly challenged.[20]

One notable advancement during the 60's and 70's was the increase in the number of universities offering professional preparation for careers in leisure services. This was, in part, a function of society's increasing acceptance of recreation and leisure service as a legitimate and important governmental function.[21]

But the picture was not all positive. During the latter part of the 1970's the economy took a down turn. By the early 1980's park districts and municipal recreation agencies began cutting back on services. Several cities took severe hits in terms of programs and facilities. Some have never fully recovered. This period had a profound impact on recreation and leisure service management. The public service model of recreation service gave way to a more business, "pragmatic" approach to recreation programming. Programs became more entrepreneurial with fees and charges becoming an important part of their funding schemes. Furthermore, many agencies found value in subcontracting programs and services to private businesses. Some of the gains made on the university level for recreation and leisure study programs were lost during the late 1980's. Usually in the name of economizing, several university programs were severely reduced and in some cases completely eliminated.

16. International Recreation Association formed--1956.
1962 John Glenn orbits earth.
The most popular movies during the 60's: *Thunderball* and *The Graduate*.
17. Want to know more? Visit the WLRA home page at http://www.worldleisure.org/
18. For more on NRPA visit their website: http://www.nrpa.org/
19. The BOR was short-lived. It was phased out of existence in 1978.
20. Educational Amendment Act of 1974 (Community Schools Act) encouraged use of schools for after-hours recreational use.
21. A period of austerity: Late 1970's and 80's.

In the 1980's, the natural environment became a concern for a large number of Americans. Many people saw that the land set aside for parks was dwindling, that wildlife was being endangered, and that the environment was threatened on various fronts. The public increasingly called upon government to take steps to protect our natural resources and environment. In a poll conducted in 1988, seventy percent of those questioned wanted better environmental protection even if it was at taxpayer cost or personal sacrifice (Opie 417). There was a corresponding movement among the public to simplify their lifestyles supported a more conservation oriented ethic. This was in startling contrast to the Reagan-Bush administration, which not only cut back money for recreational programs, but also sold thousands of acres of wildlife for business interests. President Reagan said in 1981 "when you've seen one redwood, you've seen them all" (Opie 417). Hundreds of thousands of Americans joined environmental groups, such as the Sierra Club and Greenpeace, in opposition to the government's position toward wildlife areas. The National Recreation and Park Association published pamphlets and magazines to educate the public about the tenuous state of park facilities during this time. The National Park Service, as well as many park districts, had to struggle to maintain the land under their control. The National Parks and Conservation Association fought on behalf of the National Parks against a government that placed industry above preserving wilderness areas. Ironically, in a time where most Americans knew the importance of having land for recreational use, the government had an agenda that seemed ignorant of the social, spiritual, and recreational value of the nation's natural wild-lands and open spaces.

A period of austerity: Late 1970's and 80's.

While tax-funded programs were being reduced, there was a more positive picture emerging in the field of commercial recreation. Generally speaking the past three decades have been favorable to the commercial recreation industry. Travel, tourism, theme parks, hobbies, entertainment, and professional sports have continued to grow and innovate.

On other fronts, It was in the 1980's that Halley's Comet came back for a visit, but was so faint that it was barely visible. Terrorism continued to expand, making no corner of the world safe from its evil reach, religion experienced a revival, arcades gave way to home video, and physical fitness, and the fitness industry boomed. AIDS became an international problem, making sex a scary proposition. Movies remained as popular as ever with a new emphasis on machismo and patriotism.

Although the 1980's made huge strides in technological development, it was the 1990's that showed just how remarkable technology was becoming. Home computers became indispensable and the internet made access to information and communication unbelievably convenient. Entertainment took an interesting turn, making home entertainment more attractive than ever before. Sitting in front of the computer no longer was equated with work. One of the risks of the new technology is that it will turn society into a less friendly and social place.

Once I got on line with the internet, I became an urban hermit. --Derek Jones

There is some concern that computers may not be having the best influence on our children. The manner in which children process information may be impaired by spending too much time in front of the computer. One of the professional recreation's challenges is to provide opportunities for children to engage in normal developmental play activities. In addition, it seems that instead of unparalleled free time, contemporary society is burdened with longer work days and fewer discretionary days. This poses a problem for those children whose parents must work through the afternoon leaving children unsupervised.

Some issues that plagued the recreation field in the 1980's were resolved in the 1990's. The government set aside huge amounts of land for recreational use. As an example, in 1996, President Bill Clinton set aside $6.4 million dollars to create the Grand Staircase-Escalante National Monument in Utah. Thousands of acres were conserved from any kind of development.[22] The importance of having parks and open areas for public

22. For more on this go to www.doi.gov (October 7, 1999)

use was being reinforced. The environment became a hot topic as many people found out the effects that pollution and toxic waste had on recreational areas.

An example of the environmental conscience that developed in the 80's and grew throughout the 90's is Julia "Butterfly" Hill. Starting in 1997, Hill took up residence in a giant redwood tree in the Headlands Forest of Stafford, California. She lives 180 feet above ground on a platform to protect an ancient redwood tree from being cut down by a lumber company. She does her cooking on a propane stove and communicates with others via a cellular phone. Hill has said that love is her motivation for living in a tree[23]. She is truly dedicated to the protection of the ancient forest. Because of her efforts, the Department of Forestry withdrew the logging permit pending a review of their logging practices.

The 1990s and the New Millennium

In addition to outdoor recreation, Ruth Russell believes that the major categories for leisure in the 1990's are in the areas of "relaxation, mass media, sports, tourism, and volunteerism"(146). Television is the major way that most relax. In a survey conducted in 1992, 92.8% of Americans stated that they watch television an average of two hours and fifty-one minutes a day (Russell 147). In an article for LIFE magazine, journalist Todd Brewster states that television has become "the most powerful instrument of social transformation in the latter half of the 20th century" (Brewster 71). This is no surprise considering that the vast majority of people choose to spend their leisure time watching various dramas, comedies, sporting events, and current news events unfold before them on their television. Going to the movies is also more popular than it has been in 40 years. According to the Motion Picture Association, 1.48 billion tickets were sold in the United States in 1998, the highest since 1958. On average, each American is viewing 5.5 movies per year[24]. In addition to mass media, the most popular venues of recreation presently are going to sporting events, traveling, and volunteering services to organizations and people who are in need of it.

Now in the New Millennium, we see technology playing an increasing role in providing people with recreation and leisure opportunities. The computer and computer technology has altered the recreational landscape. Even dating has changed. As the writer JC Canon says, "Today if you see an attractive person at the market, you rush home and hope you will find him or her on the Internet." In spite of technological changes, the world is not a safer place today, nor is it a happier place. It seems the same technology that enables us to play on the Internet, is the same technology that enables terrorists to wreak havoc throughout the world. And there is another downside to the technology boom. We are finding that children are less active and more likely to be obese. Learning effective social skills requires human interaction, but computers and cell phones place an artificial barrier between one another. As a consequence of these types of problems, there is an increasing awareness that leisure and recreation services can play an important role in meeting the needs of the future. Among these are the developmental needs of children, the social needs of the aged, the conservation of our national resources and improving the environment, as well as helping society achieve greater racial and gender equity.

23. For a full account go to "Environment News Service, "Julia 'Butterfly' Hill's Year Atop Giant Redwood", (http://ens.lycos.com/ens/dec98/1998L-12-10-02.html), 2.
24. For more go to www.mpaa.org

Looking Ahead

We have come a long way since the beginning, since the Big Boom. But, in spite of our intelligence and ability to solve problems, the problems persist, and one of the great challenges of the future will be to develop social and personal strategies and values that ensure all people a quality life. In our next chapter, we will look at the present and how leisure can help you make your personal history an exciting and meaningful adventure.

References

Ball, Edith and Robert Cipriano. *Leisure Services Preparation.* Englewood Cliffs, NJ: Prentice-Hall, 1963.

Brewster, Todd. "How TV Shaped America." *LIFE,* April 1999.

Butler, George D. Introduction to Community Recreation. New York: McGraw-Hill Book Company, 1976.

Carl Sagan on *The Johnny Carson Show* (January 20, 1986).

Carlson, R.E., and J. Maclean, T.R. Deppe. *Recreation and the Changing Scene.* Belmont: Wadsworth Publishing Company, 1979.

Carlson, Reyold, Theodore Deppe and Janet MacLean. *Recreation in American Life.* Belmont: Wadsworth, 1963.

Chubb, Michael and Holly R., One-Third of Our Time? And Introduction to Recreation and Behavior and Resources. (New York: John Wiley & Sons, 1988) p. 20.

Cordes, Kathleen and Hilmi Ibrahim. *Applications in Recreation and Leisure.* New York: McGraw-Hill, 1999.

Environment News Service. "Julia 'Butterfly' Hill's Year Atop Giant Redwood". (http://ens.lycos.com/ens/dec98/1998L-12-10-02.html) (December 10, 1999).

Foster, Rhea Dulles, *A History of Recreation: America Learns to Play.* New York: Appleton-Century-Crofts, 1965.

"Japanese Drama". *Microsoft Encarta 98 Encyclopedia.* (CD-ROM)(1998).

Kelly, John R. *Leisure.* (Englewood Cliffs: Prentice Hall, 1992) p. 148.

Kraus, R. *Recreation and Leisure in Modern Society.* Santa Monica: Goodyear Publishing Co., Inc., 1978. Moris, D. *The Human Zoo.* New York: Dell, 1969.

Lang, Olga. *Chinese Family and Society.* (New Haven, CT: Yale University Press, 1950)

Lee, Robert. *Religion and Leisure in America.* New York: Abingdon Press, 1964.

Opie, John. *Nature's Nation: An Environmental History of the United States.* New York: Harcourt Brace, 1998.

Roberts, J.M. *History of the World.* New York: Alfred A. Knopf, 1976.

Russell, Ruth. *Pastimes*. Madison, WI: Brown and Benchmark, 1996.

Sessons, Douglas. *Leisure Services*. Englewood Cliffs, NJ: Prentice-Hall, 1984.

Weiskopf, Donald C. Recreation and Leisure: Improving the Quality of Life. Boston: Allyn and Bacon, 1982.

www.doi.gov (October 7, 1999)

www.mpaa.org (September 19, 1999)

CHAPTER 2

On Exploring Leisure

The *Random House Word Menu* defines exploration as "traveling in an unknown region for educational purposes" (616). I like that definition. It's the "educational purposes" part that I find attractive. From this perspective, the purpose of exploration is *learning*. I suppose many folks associate exploration with economic gain or adventure and excitement. Although I am all in favor of economic gain, and having an exciting time, I am much more impressed with the idea of engaging in a new activity for the sake of learning. *Learning implies growth, enrichment, enhancement, awareness and a whole host of other attributes which are desirable to both individuals and society.*

Leisure is a little more complicated to define, in fact there are numerous definitions for this very familiar word. *It can be thought of as an activity, state of mind, or free time.* Most people think of it as a period during which one is free to engage in relaxing or playful activities. For others it refers to discretionary time, unscheduled time. Within recent years, more and more people have come to view leisure as a *state of mind*, a subjective state of being where the intensity of pleasurable experience obviates awareness of competing stimuli. Some definitions take elements from all of these perspectives and combine them together in a *holistic* definition. The free-time notion or activity notion of leisure views leisure as a block of time during which one is free to choose from a constellation of available options. Many of these options take the form of personal expression through music, drama or art, outdoor adventure, hobbies and crafts, intellectually stimulating activities and other forms of recreation. *In the state of mind definition, one is free from perceptual awareness of ideas, events or things that generally interfere with one's feelings of pleasure or satisfaction.*[1]

So what is a leisure explorer? Most of us follow familiar paths when it comes to our recreation and leisure pursuits. Some of us even find ourselves in some very deep ruts. As we get older the path seems to narrow and the side roads get fewer. It is when we leave the road in pursuit of new recreational or leisure experience that exploration occurs. It is when we defy the recreational mundane and ignore leisure convention that we become explorers. We can theorize and speculate as to what value we might find in a new recreational experience. We can image what growth and development might occur, but it isn't until we experience the new activity that we learn what value it actually affords us.

I believe that most people are leisure explorers. Some people are more direct in their exploration than others. Some constantly seek new diversions, and throw themselves into one adventure after another. Some

1. Exploring the etymology of the word "leisure" and words related to leisure is very important. Consequently, Chapter 3 is devoted to a discussion on the meaning *of leisure, play, recreation, work, and games.*

people find great satisfaction in activities fraught with danger. For these intrepid explorers, recreation is found in activities like mountain climbing, sky diving, and spelunking. Some of us explore our potential as artists, musicians, writers, and poets. Others explore collecting, model building, and hobby crafts. Many of us are rather good at spectating, and most of us find more leisure in our daydreams than in our realities. Regardless of the extent, it is fair to say that most people value leisure, and when given the opportunity and resources they gladly seek out some type of leisure experience. It is equally fair to say that most of us fall short of our potential for leisure exploration.

True Leisure Exploration Involves Striking Out to Experience Something New, Not Just Changing Channels

In exploring leisure activities, in a sense we are really exploring ourselves. Leisure becomes a laboratory wherein we can test ourselves against numerous challenges, practice social skills, develop our physical capabilities, express ourselves creatively, and redefine our self-definitions. Leisure exploration is more than just having fun, it is learning about life, about others, and ourselves.

As people get older, as they become more set in their ways, it becomes increasingly difficult for them to try new activities, more difficult to explore. Furthermore, you don't have to be a "seasoned citizen" to suffer from this kind of problem. You can suffer from a "leisure activity rut" even when you are relatively young. It seems that only very young children are truly spontaneous and uninhibited. As we get older, a definition of self begins to emerge. Included in that definition is a description of what we do and don't do as part of our leisure activities.

> *To encourage continued leisure exploration, I have my students participate in what Bill Finch calls "discovery events." My particular application of this concept calls for my students to engage in four new activities, or perhaps better stated, activities with which they have little or no experience.*
>
> *When you look at the vast number of recreation and leisure activities from which one can choose, you can't help but wonder why we do so few, and why the few we do are so similar. The answer lies in who ultimately is in control. Who do you have to ask permission from in order to go to an opera? Who determines whether you go skiing? Who determines whether you write a letter in poetry form, or draw a cartoon, or go on a nature hike? You and I, either deny permission or give the go-ahead. We make the decision, others might influence us, but we are the ones in control. Sometimes we give ourselves permission, sometimes we disqualify ourselves. The concept of the discovery event is based on the premise that as explorers we don't have to be good at something, we don't have to even enjoy it; all we have to do is give ourselves permission to learn about the event and how it affects us. Once you catch on to this concept, it has a profoundly freeing effect. When I am faced with an activity that seems intimidating, I simply give myself permission to explore, to experience a discovery event. This simple mental act causes me to perceive the threatening event in a completely different light. Usually after experiencing the event, I find my fears were exaggerated and that my experience was generally positive.*[2]

Look at the following list of activities. I'll bet you will look at some of them and say, "yes, that's me." You will look at others and probably say, "You couldn't pay me enough to do that–that's just not me!"

Aerobatic Flying
Dirt Biking
Aerobic Dance
Ballooning
Parasailing
Bull Riding
Flying Ultralights
Racing (autos, bikes, motorcycles)
Survival Games
Windsurfing
Gymnastics
Tandem Skydiving
Whitewater Rafting
Downhill Skiing
Rock Climbing
Scuba Diving
Ropes Course
Spelunking
Hang Gliding

River Climbing
Water Skiing
Cross-country Skiing
Wilderness Camping
Rock Climbing
Mountaineering
Roller Coasting
Orienteering
Martial Arts
Snowboarding
Surfing
In-line Skating
Standup Comedy
Dance Performance
Painting
Public Speaking
Inventing
Sculpting
Musical Composition
Problem Solving

Social Dancing
Theatrical Performing
Teaching a Skill
Ballroom Dancing
Stimulating Conversation
Playing Cards
Playing
Table Games
Sexual Intimacy
Attending the Opera
Visiting an Art Gallery
Traveling to a Different Country
Learning a Foreign Language
Spectating at Court
Meeting Someone for the First Time
Flower Arranging

This is certainly not a comprehensive list, but it gives you a sense of the kinds of leisure activities people explore. It provides a chance to evaluate your own leisure interests. But, being active in leisure pursuits is

2. Philosophers place emphasis on free-will, the capacity to make a conscious decision irrespective of contraindicating factors, this idea is considered in a subsequent chapter, and is the basis of this statement. Also in a subsequent chapter we examine some of the factors that explain leisure motivation. These factors include psychological factors such as values, personality, and attitudes; social dimensions such as socialization, status, culture, education and economics; and physical factors such as age and fitness level.

only one dimension of the leisure experience. Being a leisure explorer involves a lot more than just experiencing recreational activities, but this is a good place to start.

What Value Is There in a Scholarly Exploration of Leisure?

"You teach a college class in leisure?" This is a question, asked with an incredulous tone, I hear frequently. While walking to the library not long ago, I was stopped by a foreign language professor who wanted to introduce me to a visiting scholar. He began the introduction by saying, "Just wait until you hear what this guy teaches–tell him what you teach." When I revealed that I was a recreation and leisure professor, the visiting scholar laughed and said, "You must be joking!" Experiences such as this suggest to me that many people understand neither the nature nor value of leisure.

There is always the implication that what we teach in leisure courses is fluff, easy, trivial etc. But what we teach is far from fluff, far from trivial. At the heart of leisure education are two fundamental goals. Mundy and Odum describe these goals in this way:

1. The essence of leisure is freedom; therefore, leisure education must, above all else, facilitate individual self-determination in leisure.
2. The leisure experience is uniquely individual . . . therefore, the individual should be the primary focus of the process, recipient of the values, evaluator of the outcomes, and agent of the leisure education process (4).

Another way of describing the goal of leisure in education is found in the term *effective leisure functioning*. This refers to an individual's ability to do the following:

1. Operate from a mind-set characterized by *perceived freedom.*
2. Experience *intrinsic satisfaction.*
3. Demonstrate *competence* in leisure activities.
4. Make choices that produce a generalized *positive affect* (feelings).
5. Make choices that contribute to *growth and development.*

Having taught other subjects (research, legal liability, management, statistics, programming) I am of the opinion that teaching a leisure education course is much more difficult than most people imagine. This is because there is a fundamental contradiction between the goals of leisure education and the traditional approach to education. Kelly (1990) even goes so far as to suggest that teaching leisure in a traditional manner is not the best approach. Leisure is based on self-direction and intrinsic satisfaction; education is typically based on a system of extrinsic rewards and external direction. He says ". . . if the functions and the structure of the institution are in contradiction to the basic meanings of leisure . . . then how can the school educate for leisure?" (314). In leisure education we encourage self-determination, but the traditional model allows for little self-determination. In leisure education, we applaud intrinsic rewards, but in a classroom, motivation is largely based on extrinsic reward. The professor has to work particularly hard to conform to institutional requirements and still demonstrate the principal goals of leisure education. The student must also work hard to find ways to incorporate leisure principles in the learning process. Furthermore, the student is often challenged to re-evaluate some of her most cherished beliefs, as well as apply diverse concepts from other fields to the leisure experience. A course in leisure should be interesting, even fun, but it definitely isn't easy.

Leisure education can be thought of as a process which increases the awareness of the student regarding the value of leisure, as well as ways and means of enhancing the role of leisure in one's life. This process is based on cognitive and affective learning experiences which produce an increased level of awareness of the value of leisure, and increased level of understanding of leisure concepts, and an increased capacity to utilize leisure in one's life for increased life satisfaction. This concept is illustrated in the following diagram:

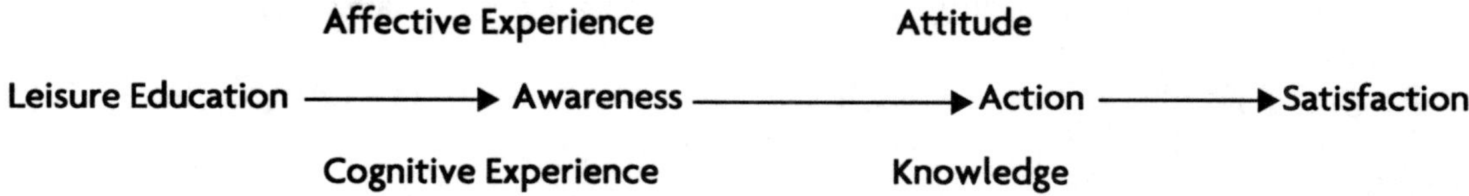

Leisure Education in the Public Schools

Our school systems are particularly good at achieving cognitive goals—reading, writing, and arithmetic learning goals. Unfortunately, schools are much less adept at promoting affective goals—goals relating to emotional responses and attitudes. And, equally unfortunate is the trend in the U.S. away from kinesthetic goals (physical skills).

The result is that formal education is producing people who are not particularly well equipped to cope with either the challenges of leisure or the demands of living in a complex and often chaotic society.

It is not enough to learn how to perform in the workplace. True, it is absolutely essential that people acquire marketable skills and a respect for the work ethic. As that wise philosopher, *Anon Y Mous*, once said, "If all you do is put your nose to the grind stone, soon all you have left is a bloody nose." Put in less graphic terms, the same wise person said, "All work and no play makes Jack a dull boy." (A more politically correct version of that saying would be, "All work and no play makes a person really boring.") Dullness is not a particularly good *affec*t.

It is affect that makes life worth living, and yet very little attention is given to dance, music, drama, visual art, tactile art, expressive readings, or poetry in our school systems—the very areas of study that are most likely to produce positive affect in our children.

Individuals who spend their time operating within narrow scholastic or career parameters are people who often find their lives characterized by "treadmill" living. Repeating the same behaviors day in and day out, they live lives bereft of the kinds of affect that recreation and play offer. Their free time lives are apt to be characterized by a limited repertoire of interests. For them leisure holds less promise than for the person who has a wide array of interests, and enjoys a degree of balance in their free time. I call this type of leisure "meaning less leisure." Within recent years there has been increased talk about educating the whole person, "educating for leisure." It appears that little is being done in the way of leisure education in the primary and secondary levels, but there is movement on the college level. It is not uncommon now for recreation and leisure studies departments to offer general education courses focused on helping students to learn how to get the most out of their leisure time.

Because of the profound importance of the early years of development, early childhood education should include a leisure education component. Such a component would provide a foundation for subsequent learning. By high school, students would have a basic set of leisure skills, values, and concepts to assist them as they prepare to enter into the adult world.

Ruskin and Sivan in their book Leisure Education in School Systems identify three areas that a leisure curriculum should include:

1. **Knowledge and Understanding of Leisure.**
    - To understand the meaning and culture of leisure.
    - To have a positive and socially acceptable mind toward leisure.
    - To understand and be aware of the role and importance of leisure.
    - To expand knowledge of the variety of leisure activities, of the risks involve in harmful activities and the learn to avoid them.

- To recognize the criteria for choosing and valuing leisure activities.
- To learn to appreciate Creative expression in art.

2. **Attitudes**
   - To create a balanced and healthy lifestyle which includes both work and leisure?
   - To foster self expression.
   - To develop positive attitudes toward learning within formal informal frameworks.
   - To develop positive attitudes toward culture and country.
3. **Practical Skills**
   - To learn different skills such as those for sports, culture, health, music etc.
   - To be able to set objectives for his/her own satisfying leisure.
   - To contribute to his/her personal growth and development through leisure.
   - To acquire physical aesthetic and cultural skills for his/her leisure involvement.

They go on to make a very important point, leisure education is a broad umbrella that can encompass all other curricula. For example, a biology class can include reference to things to look for when visiting a national park or special outdoor environment. An English class can promote the recreational value of personal writing or reading for pleasure. Indeed some instructors will do this on their own. What Ruskin and Sivan are calling for is a formal effort by school systems to promote leisure across the curriculum.

Unfortunately, learning to use leisure in ways that produce positive outcomes is generally left up to the individual.

CONTRIBUTIONS OF LEISURE EDUCATION Current research argues eloquently that leisure education can make a powerful contribution to the life of the leisure student. Simply put, for people who learn to make leisure an important part of their lives, the potential for self-actualization and life satisfaction is far greater than for those who do not (Wade, 1985; Iso-Ahola and Weissinger, 1987). **It has been demonstrated that students of leisure experience an increased appreciation for leisure and an increased probability of developing *effective leisure functioning*.[3] This is important because there is evidence that people who demonstrate adequate leisure functioning experience an array of impressive benefits.** Witt and Ellis, the authors of the *Leisure Diagnostic Battery* state:

> Adequate leisure functioning may provide the individual with such benefits as a positive self-concept, mental health, enhancement of creative ability, and physical, emotional and social growth and development. Deficiencies in leisure functioning may lead the individual to depression, isolation or social deviant behaviors (2).

In addition to those benefits identified by Witt and Ellis, there are other benefits that appear to be associated with effective leisure functioning. For example:

- Smith, Snyder, Trull and Monsma showed a strong correlation between leisure functioning and **marital satisfaction** (1988). People who enjoy an active leisure lifestyle seem to have happier marriages than those people who don't have satisfying leisure.
- Roberts, Lamb, Dench and Brodie showed a direct relationship between **physical health** and leisure involvement (1989). People who participate in physical recreation experience a number of health benefits including enhanced immune systems, low body fat, and cardiovascular health.
- Carolyn Bradley demonstrated that leisure skills correlate with **job search skills** (1989). Presumably, people who function well in leisure have the skills requisite to success in the pursuit of employment.

3. For a sampling of the studies that relate to the value of leisure education see Weissinger and Caldwell, 1990, 41; Backman and Mannell, 1986; Searle and Mahon, 1990; Shinew and Blaukamp, 1996.

- DeCarlo showed that recreational involvement was a good predictor of aging with minimum inconvenience (1975). **Successful aging** is correlated with not only physical recreation, but also recreation that is intellectually stimulating. As for longevity, intellectually stimulating recreation may be just as important as physical activity.
- A number of studies show that play can contribute to **learning in children** (Lee, 1971; Burner, J. 1974; Feitlson and Ross, 1973; Ellis, 1973). Play is common to all mammals, and is essential for successful growth and development. children deprived of normal play can experience social, mental, emotional, and physical retardation.
- Iso-Ahola, following an extensive review of leisure, concluded that leisure involvement is significantly related to **psychological adjustment** (1980). The term psychological adjustment relates to sense of balance in one's life. Leisure involvement seems essential for a balanced lifestyle.
- Tinsley and Howard found that leisure tended to meet a person's need for **life enrichment** through enhancing such variables as self-actualization, companionship, power, compensation, security, social service, intellectual aesthetics, and autonomy (1981). That participation in leisure activities that fit one's personality leads to feelings of well-being, including feelings of satisfaction and increased self-esteem, has been demonstrated by Melamed, Meir and Sampson (1995).
- Leisure activities may be thought of as "freely chosen" activities. Such activities have value because they **produce a generalized positive affect**—good feelings. Mannell, Zuzanek and Reed (1988) found that freely chosen activities may also lower tension, and enhance concentration.
- **Leisure involvement may help prevent depression**. In a study of the leisure patterns of senior citizens and measures of affect, it was found that among men, low physical leisure activity was related to a probability of depression. Among women depression was linked to low levels of leisure satisfaction (Lomraz, et al, 1988).
- Leisure has **therapeutic value**. It has long been recognized that recreation and leisure have a positive impact on one's physical and mental health. Within recent years, the therapeutic value of leisure and recreation among **special populations** has been recognized and carefully studied. (D'Antonio, 1988; Crawford, 1986). One of the reasons that recreation has therapeutic value may be due to the capacity of leisure experiences to generate within participants feelings of self-determination as well as provide a network of social support (Coleman and Iso-Ahola, 1993).
- **Outdoor recreation** offers special opportunities for people. Ulrich and Addoms (1981) found that a residential park provided the following values to users: aesthetic value, environmental contact value, and social experiences.
- Leisure, particularly outdoor recreation, may provoke a **spiritual experience**. (McDonald and Schreyer, 1991). When faced with wonders of nature, people often find themselves contemplating metaphysical questions of existence and purpose as well as reflecting on the nature of beauty. An awareness of a divine purpose often occurs during such moments.

The concept of effective leisure functioning is central to a *leisure lifestyle*. And since effective leisure functioning can be encouraged through leisure education, the thrust of this book is to acquaint you with concepts and ideas that will lead to a better understanding of leisure and an increased appreciation for the role that it can play in your life. Throughout this book, ideas, study findings, philosophies, anecdotes, and exercises are presented—all designed to help you develop leisure knowledge, skills and attitudes. Throughout, you will note a tone of advocacy. I believe that play, recreation, and leisure make an important contribution to the quality of one's life. In addition to being familiar with some of the research findings focusing on the value of leisure, I know from personal experience about the value of leisure in my own life and the impact it has had on my continued growth and development. What's more, over the years I have heard the testimony of countless students, who following their study of leisure, have told me about remarkable changes that occurred as a result of having learned to appreciate leisure more fully and apply it more effectively. As one of my recent students put it, "Leisure works, it's the bomb!"

And speaking of students and effective leisure functioning, let me tell you a brief story . . .

A few years ago, I had a delightful student who I believe typified adequate leisure functioning. She was neither chronologically nor physically young. She was 83 years old, but her spirit was that of a much younger woman. She demonstrated social, psychological, and physical health. Even in her "old age" she retained the enthusiasm and zest for life generally reserved for children. She was creative, coped effectively with stress, demonstrated good health practices, had a good self-esteem, and had a great sense of humor. She had a love for learning, and was a good student. She was also adventurous. On one occasion, during one of my lectures on discovering leisure activities, she raised her hand and reported that she had recently had a new discovery. I asked for a report and she replied that she had been bungee jumping for the first time! When asked how she enjoyed it, she responded, "I loved it, and it was great for the osteoporosis."

Life is nothing more than a great "leisure laboratory." If you choose to make leisure an important part of your life, you will find there is much to discover and in the discovery your life will be richer.

REFERENCES

Backman, S.J. and R.C. Mannell. "Removing Attitudinal Barriers to Leisure Behavior and Satisfaction: A Field Experiment among the Institutionalized Elderly." *Therapeutic Recreation Journal* 20.3 (1986): 46–53.

Blauwkamp, J. and K.J. Shaw. "The Effects of Leisure Education on Leisure Attitudes." *Abstracts from the 1996 Symposium on Leisure Research*. Arlington VA: National Association for Recreation and Parks, 1996.

Bradley, C. "Integrating the Search for Work and Leisure." *Journal of Employment Counseling* 26.2 (1989): 70–76.

Bruner, J. "Child's Play." *New Scientists* 62 (1974): 125–128.

Coleman, D. and S.E. Iso-Ahola, "Leisure and Health: The Role of Social Support and Self-determination." *Journal of Leisure Research* 25.2 (1993): 111–128.

Crawford, M. "Development and Generalization of Lifetime Leisure Skills for Multi-handicapped Participants." *Therapeutic Recreation Journal* 20.4 (1986): 48–60.

Dattilo, J. and W.D. Murphy. *Leisure Education Program: A Systematic Approach.* State College, PA: Venture Publishing, Inc. 991.

DeCarlo, T.J. "Recreation Patterns and Successful Aging." *Gerontology* 29 (1974): 416–422.

D'Antonio, I.J. "The Use of Humor with Children in Hospital Settings." *Journal of Children in Contemporary Society* 20.1–2 (1988): 157–169.

Ellis, G.D. and P.A. Witt. *The Leisure Diagnostic Battery: Background, Conceptualization, and Structure.* Division of Recreation and Leisure Studies, North Texas State University, Denton, 1982.

Ellis, M.J. *Why People Play.* Englewood Cliffs, New Jersey: Prentice-Hall, 1973.

Feitelson, D. and G.S. Ross. "The Neglected Factor." *Play and Human Development.* 16 (1973): 202–223.

Glazier, S. *Word Menu.* New York: Random House, 1994.

Iso-Ahola, S. *The Social Psychology of Leisure and Recreation.* Dubuque, Iowa: Wm. C. Brown, 1980.

Krain, M.A. "Policy Implications for Aging Well: Employment, Retirement, Education, and Leisure Policies for the 21st Century." *American Behavioral Scientist* 39.2 (1995): 131–151.

Lomraz, J., S. Bergman, E. Simon, and N. & S. Dov. "Indoor and Outdoor Activities of Aged Women and Men as Related to Depression and Well-Being." *International Journal of Aging and Human Development* 26.4 (1988): 303–314.

Mannell, R.C., R.C. Zusanek, Jiri & Larson, Reed. "Leisure States and 'Flow' Experiences: Testing Perceived Freedom and Intrinsic Motivation Hypotheses." *Journal of Leisure Research* 20.4 (1988): 289–304.

Martin, L.Y. "The Role of Play in the Learning Process." *Educational Forum.* 43.1 (1971) 51–58.

Melamed, S, E.I. Meir, and A. Samson. "The Benefits of Personality Leisure Congruence: Evidence and Implications." *Journal of Leisure Research.* 27.1 (1995) 25–40.

Mundy, J. and L. Odum. *Leisure Education*: Theory and Practice. 1971.

Roberts, K.; Lamb, K.L.; Dench, S. & Brodie, DA. (U Liverpool, England) "Leisure Patterns, Health Status and Employment Status." *Leisure Studies* 8.3 (1989): 229–235.

Weissinger, E., and L. Caldwell. "Antecedents of Leisure Boredom in Three College Samples. In Abstracts from the 1990 Symposium on Leisure Research." *Abstracts from the 1990 Symposium on Leisure Research.* Arlington, VA: National Association for Recreation and Parks, 1990.

Roberts, K.; Lamb, K.L.; Dench, S. & Brodie, D.A. (U Liverpool, England) "Leisure Patterns, Health Status and Employment Status." *Leisure Studies* 8.3 (1989): 229–235.

Ruskin, Hillel and Atara Savin. *Leisure Education In School Systems.* Jerusalem, Israel: Magnes Press of the Hebrew Univesigty of Jerusalem

Smith, G.T.: Snyder, Douglas K.; Trull, T.J. & Monsma, B.R. "Predicting Relationship Satisfaction from Couples' Use of Leisure Time." *American Journal of Family Therapy* 16.1 (1988): 1–13.

Tinsley, H. and R. Kass. "The Latent Structure of the Need Satisfying Properties of Leisure Activities." *Journal of Leisure Research* 11.4 (1979): 278–291.

CHAPTER 3

Notes on Knowing about Leisure

Questions regarding human behavior have been around for a long time. Answers historically have come from philosophers and common sense. Within recent years, science has developed an increased interest in unraveling questions and issues regarding human behavior. One area which has long been a concern of philosophers, and has recently become an area of scientific investigation, is that area of human endeavor referred to as "leisure."

Philosophy

> Being a philosopher, I have a problem for every solution.
>
> —Robert Zend

Someone once said that philosophizing is the process of making sense of experience. In other words, philosophers attempt to answer questions that are the result of natural human curiosity. Throughout history humans have been curious about the elements that comprise our realm of existence—our world, solar system, and universe. We are also curious about *events* that defy understanding. Death is a mystery that philosophers have tried to explain. Our purpose for existence is another mystery that philosophers have long pondered. Another question that philosophy tries to answer is whether God created man or did man, in his desperate search for understanding in a sometimes frightening and unpredictable world, create God.

The word **philosophy** in its literal (Greek) sense means "love of wisdom." Wisdom can be thought of as the ability to use knowledge in a logical fashion. *Thus, a philosopher is one who seeks knowledge and proposes logical applications of such knowledge.* In their attempts to acquire knowledge, philosophers rely on two sources for information:

1. sense perceptions
2. logic and reason

Sense perceptions enter into philosophy in a very direct fashion. Every question asked, every mystery investigated by a philosopher, first began with an observation. The observation may have dealt with a question of physical reality or of metaphysics, but without the awareness of a problem, a philosopher would have no inclination to apply logic and reasoning to its solution. Unlike the scientist who relies heavily on testing and measuring a phenomenon, a philosopher attempts to solve problems through use of logic and rational thought. Through the use of logical reasoning, philosophers weave a comprehensive collection of interrelated concepts which give meaning to the issues, events, and problems observed. Such a collection of interrelated concepts is referred to as "a philosophy." When philosophers "philosophize" they normally apply methods of logical induction or deduction. Both of these processes are primarily subjective, and as such require careful, creative and insightful thought by the philosopher:

> Philosophy: unintelligible answers to insoluble problems.
>
> —Henry Adams

Deductive reasoning involves predicting a logical consequence following some general assumption. *Deduction is the inference from the general to the specific*. The process used by philosophers is often referred to as syllogistic reasoning. In this type of logic, one begins with a major premise which is related to a minor premise which leads to a logical conclusion. An example of deductive reasoning is as follows:

Major Premise: Only humans engage in recreation.
Minor Premise: Turtles are not humans.
Conclusion: Turtles do not engage in recreation.

Inductive reasoning on the other hand works from the specific to the general. For example:

Major Premise: My turtle does not engage in recreation.
Minor Premise: A turtle is a reptile.
Conclusion: Reptiles don't recreate.

Philosophies based on this type of reasoning are only as good as allowed by the logic used in their creation. For example, if a philosopher accepts an incorrect major premise, or fails to draw the correct inference from two correct premises, then the philosophy will be flawed. The following is an example of the latter problem.

Major Premise: George W. Bush is tall.
Minor Premise: George W. Bush is a politician.
Conclusion: All politicians are tall. (Any vertically challenged politician would protest this conclusion.)

Many of us use this type of logic in our own personal philosophies with equally illogical results. We look at professional basketball players and infer that in order to play basketball one must be tall, or at artists and assume that one must be gifted to be a painter, or at creative writers and infer that in order to write successfully one must have studied writing, etc. Making correct observations, identifying logical relationships, and drawing correct inferences are as important in a personal philosophy as a formal philosophy.

A personal philosophy can be thought of as a statement of one's beliefs and values. *Thus, a leisure philosophy is a statement of one's beliefs and values regarding leisure. Not all of the relationships that make up one's philosophy are likely to be founded on logic.* Many of our values and beliefs are based on folklore and myth. These values are often viewed as valid in our attempts to understand and explain leisure, and as a consequence, may become the basis for a philosophy including inferences drawn from the incorrect premises. Inasmuch as the primary function of philosophy is to discover truth, it is important that in our personal philosophizing we try to utilize the best information about leisure available. Science is one source for such information, but there are other sources as well. Many of us make judgments about leisure on the basis of what we learn from religion, formal philosophies, tradition, and personal experience. As Dr. Pete Rombold puts it, "One's personal philosophy is a combination of formal philosophy, science, religion, folklore, myth and whatever else it takes to help make sense out of things" (1989).

The Questions of Philosophy

The ultimate questions of philosophy relate to the nature of reality. At one time, philosophy applied principles of logic to almost all observable and speculated phenomena. The subjective nature of philosophy permitted examination of such diverse phenomena as the underlying nature of the solar system and the nature of God. The vocabulary of philosophy gives you an idea of the kinds of questions philosophy has historically dealt with.

Metaphysics

In common terms it might be said that metaphysical questions relate to the supernatural. From a more objective point of view, metaphysics is a branch or concern of philosophy that deals with questions of reality with particular reference to that which is not readily discerned by the senses.

Epistemology

In its root form, the word means the study of knowledge. Essentially epistemology is a branch of philosophy that is primarily concerned with examining the validity of that which we call knowledge.

Axiology

This is the branch of philosophy which deals with the nature of values. It is often divided into two categories: ethics and aesthetics. Ethics is concerned with questions of right and wrong. Aesthetics is concerned with the study of beauty.

The domain of philosophy once knew no limits, but with the development of science, has come a reduction in the scope and depth of philosophical inquiry. Today, philosophy is largely concerned with axiological issues and to a lesser extent, metaphysical concerns. Science has answered many of the early questions of philosophy and has largely relegated modern philosophy to determining the value of such findings.

Philosophy is important to leisure practitioners because it helps structure one's approach to the leisure experience. It is philosophy that ultimately has to answer questions of quality and value regarding leisure experiences. It is the philosophical process that deals with right and wrong, good and bad, pleasure and pain. As prominent thinkers attempted to unravel the mysteries of the universe, they attracted followers, became teachers, and often developed elaborate philosophies to support their teachings. Over time, these philosophies

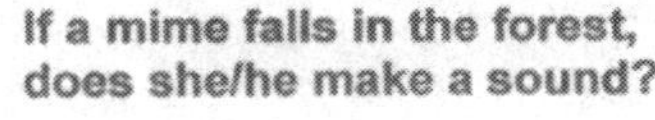

became the basis for formal systems of thought. Such systems are often referred to as "formal philosophies" or "schools of thought." Many such formal philosophies have emerged over the years, some of which seem to be particularly enduring and influential. It would be impossible to fully examine these philosophies due to the limitations of time and space; however, I have selected several that I think are representative, and which have had a significant influence on Western thinking. These philosophies can loosely be divided into two categories: classical philosophies and modern. In the section that follows, four classical and three modern theories are summarized.

Naturalism

As the name applies, naturalism comes from the word **nature**, and as such has a broad perspective. All aspects of the physical world fall within the province of this philosophy. Naturalism from an ontological (relating to the nature of existence) viewpoint argues that there is no reality except that found in nature. As Randolph Webster states, "Naturalism, from the standpoint of metaphysics, is the theory that all reality is nature. Nothing exists beyond, above or apart from it. There is no God, no soul other than that which is found in Nature" (18).

Early philosophers associated with naturalism include Leucippus and Democritus who lived in Thrace around 500 B.C., Epicurus who lived between 341–270 B.C. and by Lucretius who lived from 96–55 B.C. Each of these philosophers viewed physical matter as clusters of infinitely small, indivisible units called **atoms**. Hence, nature consisted of substances and things composed of atoms organized in such a manner as to give them form and identity. Inasmuch as atoms were highly mobile, these things dissolved or dissipated when the atoms moved apart.

Epicurus taught that pleasure was the basis of the happy life. He emphasized the importance of moderation in all things. He contended that excess leads to pain and fear which he viewed to be evil. He advocated both passive and active pleasures, but favored mental activities because he viewed them as more enduring and less likely to lead to pain or fear. Sexual activities were viewed as far less desirable than friendship. Although he did not disbelieve in God, he viewed religion and fear of death as the two most devastating sources of unhappiness. The philosophy he taught became known as Epicurianism, and today we honor his memory in our use of the **epicure**, which has come to refer to a person of fastidious taste.

Later naturalist philosophers focused on the importance of functioning in natural patterns and rhythms. Consequently naturalism provided a philosophical framework for the leisure lifestyle. For example, Rousseau, a philosopher who lived from 1712 to 1778, believed that schools confined children too much, and warped their natural development. He argued that children should be allowed to develop in a natural manner, and that their education should include those activities to which they were most naturally predisposed. He believed in the importance of political freedom as well as freedom from religion. From his perspective, religion was a manifestation of man, and nature was a manifestation of God.

Herbert Spencer was a 19th Century philosopher and writer (1820–1903) who is known for his attempt to develop a unitary theory of all natural phenomena. This theory was based on the premise that all matter was affected by two processes:

1. evolution
2. dissolution

His philosophy explained change as a function of natural forces which were the manifestation of the Supreme Being, present in all things. Because of the role that force played in Spencer's ontology, he became known as an "energist." He, like Rosseau, was an advocate of a leisure oriented lifestyle. He was a strong advocate of physical education and recreation as part of a healthy lifestyle and requisites to sound thinking.

Idealism

Unlike naturalism, idealism argues that existence cannot occur outside of the mind, i.e., reality is ultimately an *idea*. Two early philosophers subscribing to this notion were Socrates (469–399 B.C.) and his student,

Plato (427–347 B.C.). Plato was a writer and thinker. To him ideas were more real than physical forms, which were viewed as imperfect copies of real and perfect ideas.

Rene Descartes was born in 1496 and died in 1650. During his relatively short life, he made many important contributions to philosophical thought. He has been referred to as the "father of modern philosophy" (Webster 32). Webster goes on to describe Descartes' philosophy as follows:

> Descartes believed that all knowledge is uncertain and the way to find truth is to doubt everything, the only undoubtful thing being one's ability to doubt. This ability to doubt he reasoned, makes man a thinker. Thinking has to be done by someone. Since he was doing the thinking he was someone. Hence, he drew the inference, "I think, therefore I am . . . ." He reasoned that an imperfect being cannot originate a perfect idea. He was an imperfect being because he doubted. Therefore, he could not initiate a perfect idea. This perfect idea had to come from some place. Since it could not have come from nothingness, it must have come from some perfect Being. If this be true, a perfect being exists (33).

Immanuel Kant (1724–1804) is associated with idealism because of his philosophy regarding the acquisition of knowledge. He argued that an individual's understanding of the physical world is a function of sensory perceptions. These impressions are limited in scope and accuracy; consequently, it is impossible for an individual to fully understand the nature of physical reality. However, he believed that through reason an individual could develop a model of reality, which if not wholly accurate, could serve to explain the nature of perceived phenomena.

Webster identifies three types of idealism: subjective, objective, and personal. **Subjective idealism** argues that physical things would not exist were there no one to see them. You have heard the question, "If a mime trips and falls in the forest, does he make a sound?" To the subjective idealist, the question only has meaning if there is someone in the forest to listen. **Objective idealism** accepts the idea of reality independent of perception, but underlying all physical reality lies a spirit or ideal reality. **Personal idealism** is related to leisure in that it focuses more on personal freedom than the previous two points of view. To the personalist the awareness of quality, sensations and feelings are very important. Similarly freedom is highly valued. Personalists believe that the function of society and government is to provide everyone an abundant life (39).

Regardless of the specific point of view, idealism has made an important contribution to leisure and recreation by encouraging intellectual and spiritual development. Of particular importance was the early Athenian philosophy of developing the whole person, where beauty, harmony, excellence, virtue, and fitness were equally valued. To the ancient Greeks, leisure was a highly valued state of being, for it was through leisure one was able to engage in intellectual pursuits.

Realism

Unlike the subjective idealist, the realist doesn't believe a perceiver need be present in order for a falling mime to make a sound. Material objects are believed to exist without being perceived. Consequently, ideas are viewed as imperfect reflections of reality, and thus empiricism is seen as a more valid way of developing knowledge than **a priori** reasoning (deriving solutions independent of experience). As Hocking states, "Realism . . . is a disposition to keep ourselves and our preferences out of our judgment of things, letting the objects speak for themselves" (45).

Realism is closely related to empiricism, which itself is not a philosophy but rather an approach to solving the problems raised by philosophy. This approach argues that the only way to acquire information is to do so through sense perception. It is empiricism that the method of scientific inquiry is based upon. Realists believe that it is through empiricism that one can achieve happiness by learning how to function effectively in the real world. Representative of the realist philosophy in leisure are the philosophies of J.B. Nash and Allen Sapora.

Pragmatism

Of more recent origin than the previous three philosophies, pragmatism is less concerned with the metaphysical than it is with the epistemological. In pragmatism, the focus is on knowledge, not abstract theories of reality. As Webster puts it:

> "It is not concerned with what exists outside of experience, only with experiences. . . . (it) is concerned with both knowledge and practice and interprets experience in terms of its practical consequences" (64).

Although the originator of pragmatism is usually considered to be William James, John Dewey is also closely connected to the early development of this relatively modern philosophy. It is from Dewey that we get many of our ideas regarding education. The type of learning advocated by pragmatic philosophy involves individual initiative, interdisciplinary study, and the application of the experiment in problem solving. This type of education calls for the education of the whole person, and as such legitimizes training in recreation and leisure-related areas. Similarly leisure is looked upon as providing individuals with opportunities for personal growth and development.

Modern Philosophies

Logical Positivism

Attributed to the work of Ernst Mach, this philosophy was the outgrowth of a group, active in the 1920's, known as the Vienna Circle. Essentially they argued that although most philosophers believed a premise had to be either true or false, a third possibility existed: the premise could be meaningless. To the logical positivists, a premise was meaningless if it could not be tested by sense experiences. Consequently, a premise regarding life after death has no utility in this philosophy. For that matter, metaphysics has no place in logical positivism. The extent to which one's perception of leisure as a valuable experience can be validated through the senses is the extent to which leisure is important.

Existentialism

Unlike logical positivism, this philosophy requires a metaphysical orientation, that permits the individual to perceive the world as a purposeless, hostile and uncertain environment. The individual is viewed as a free agent, faced with determining his/her purpose and destiny in life. This philosophy argues that life has significance to the extent to which one becomes involved in seeking meaning. Leisure has meaning only to the extent that it contributes to one's sense of self.

Dialectical Materialism

Dialectic to the ancient philosophers meant a type of dialogue through which conflicts were resolved. The dialectic process involved the examination of contesting points of view stated as theses and antitheses. The differences ultimately gave way to a new point of view referred to as simply "synthesis." Marx and Engels adapted this idea to their philosophy of social change. They argued that ideas are generated by social and economic factors which are a function of materialistic forces. Marxism argues that feudalism is displaced by capitalism which in turn is displaced by socialism and a classless society. According to this philosophy "true" leisure cannot be achieved in a capitalistic society; a socialist society is the only system capable of providing leisure for society.

Religion

Religion: A daughter of Hope and Fear, explaining to Ignorance the nature of the Unknowable.

—Ambrose Bierce

Before philosophy there was religion. When faced with answerable questions primitive man turned to fanciful and hopeful explanations. Natural events were interpreted in terms of daily experience and common knowledge; thus, lightning came to be thought of as a supernatural spear, and thunder the tramping of the spear thrower's giant feet. That which could not be understood was viewed as a manifestation of some form of supernatural power. These primitive explanations of natural phenomena provided the basis for early belief systems that we refer to as religions. Although philosophy and religion are both concerned with metaphysical and ethical issues, there remains one major difference: *Philosophy attempts to answer questions through logic, whereas religion demands its adherents to accept answers by faith.* In fact, philosophy was born when ancient Greek thinkers refused to be bound by the theologies of their time and set out to explore the world independent of the inhibiting influence of religion.

Religion like philosophy consists of principles, beliefs, and values integrated in such a manner as to provide a pattern or model for living. Modern religions tend to base their systems of belief around the idea of one or more gods who are viewed as powerful, all-knowing, and caring. Furthermore, in most religions, these gods are viewed as superhuman, and as such entitled to obedience, worship and reverence. Most religions teach that the source of their theology is from a single or multiplicity of gods. However, some religions such as Buddhism, Taoism and Brahmanism began as philosophies, but later acquired the attributes of religion. Most religions develop relatively complex rules and rituals. Good is defined in absolute terms, and is associated with some supreme deity. Evil is equally defined in absolute terms and is often associated with an evil deity such as the Christian's concept of Satan.

Religion is a pervasive force upon the planet. There is not a society on earth that is not in some way influenced by religion. For example, the conflict between the West and Iran is largely a matter of religion. Similarly the ongoing conflict in Northern Ireland breaks down on religious lines. The United States is not immune from religion in politics. The presidential campaign of 1988 included a Protestant fundamentalist who claimed that his nomination came directly from God. (Incidentally, he may have had God's nomination but he didn't get his party's, he lost the election.) *The Information Please 1989 Almanac* identifies 14 different major religions, accounting for over 4,000,000,000 people. The largest and most influential is the Christian faith with over 1,600,000,000; the next largest group is the Muslim faith at nearly 1,000,000,000 followed closely by the Hindu religion at 836,000,000.

We must respect the other fellow's religion, but only in the same way that we respect his theory that his wife is beautiful and his children smart.

—H.L. Mencken

Different religions view recreation and leisure differently. Early religions tended to be more tolerant of recreation than those of modern times. For example, music, dance, drama, social entertainment, and at certain times a form of temple prostitution played important roles in the religion of ancient Egypt. Contrast this view with the theology of the early Catholic Church which viewed play and recreation suggestive of pagan ideals and as such viewed all forms of pleasure as evil and a threat to one's spiritual salvation (Kraus 64). At the same time the Catholic Church was suppressing play in Western Europe, the metaphysical doctrines of China had given rise to a culture that placed great value on recreation and entertainment. Kraus describes the recreational practices of the Sun Dynasty as follows:

> Hangchow was filled with places for social gatherings, such as gardens for pleasure outings, teahouses where rich people took music lessons, or boats on the lake where guests were entertained. The pleasure grounds were huge covered markets where lessons were given in dramatic art, singing and dance, and various types of theatrical societies, including societies for football and polo, poetry and puppetry enthusiasts, archery and crossbow experts, and a host of other pastimes (Kraus 68).

The Reformation which occurred in the 1500's resulted in the establishment of Protestantism and set the stage for the emergence of the Puritan Ethic. Austere and solemn, the practitioners of Puritanism, in the name of God, waged a solemn war against many forms of pleasure seeking, even, under some circumstances, to the point of imprisoning or killing dissenters.

> The time you enjoy wasting, is not wasted time.
>
> —Bertrand Russell

Unlike early Christian religions, it must be pointed out that many modern Christian religions show no antagonism toward recreation. Rather than condemn recreation and leisure, most Western religions have come to assume responsibility for providing leisure services for their members. The Mormon Church for example, as early as 1926, established a church recreation program which included such goals and purposes as:

> . . . making the joys of recreation a vital part of the life of each member; developing better brotherly feeling through wholesome social contacts; promoting opportunities for leadership, bettering physical and mental health; maintaining an environment for the cultural and social refinement of youth and developing the power of self-expression through such activities as drama, music, and debating (Carlson, Deppe, and MacLean 203).

This is representative of the approach that many Western religions now take regarding recreation and leisure. When faced with the alternative of allowing their members to be tempted by worldly recreation, they offer activities which conform to their particular theology. Few religions today are as vigorously opposed to recreation as were the early Catholics or Protestants. Although, for many people the saying of Heywood Brown still applies, "The pursuit of happiness belongs to us, but we must climb around or over the church to get to it" (Peter 428).

Creating Your Own Philosophy of Leisure

It should be clear by now that you have a personal philosophy of leisure, a philosophy which in many respects determines how you spend your free time as well as how much leisure you bring into other aspects of your life. The unfortunate thing about many personal philosophies is that they are allowed to develop at random, they evolve without the benefit of critical and logical thinking. Such philosophies, rather than contributing to the quality of one's leisure may in fact have the opposite effect. Similarly, there are those of us who embrace religious beliefs that place leisure in a negative light, glorifying work and placing recreation in the category of sinful behavior. If leisure is to become a positive force in your life, if it is to become a significant part of your lifestyle, it is essential that you develop a philosophy that supports the value of the leisure experience.

Following are four suggestions for developing a leisure philosophy:

1. **Learn to Think Critically and Logically.** At the heart of an effective philosophy is thinking. Not just any kind of thinking, but rational and critical thinking. To develop an effective philosophy you must learn how to evaluate philosophical ideas and concepts. Not all ideas are equal, and to discern the truly good ideas from the mundane you need to polish your ability to think critically and logically.

2. **Acquire Knowledge**. Read and study. Don't be afraid of new or different ideas. Constantly be on the lookout for new information, and, when you acquire it, evaluate it for relevance to your personal philosophy of leisure.
3. **Express Your Philosophy**. Don't be afraid to test your philosophy on others. The process of sharing your ideas will serve to clarify your philosophy; the feedback you receive will assist you in evaluating your ideas.
4. **Don't Be Afraid to Change Your Philosophy**. One bad thing about adopting someone else's philosophy is that most religions and formal philosophies are not geared for change. One very nice thing about a personal philosophy is that it is not as rigid as formal schools of thought. Consequently, as you grow and develop, your philosophy can change and grow too.

Science

Aristotle could have avoided the mistake of thinking that women have fewer teeth than men by the simple device of asking Mrs. Aristotle to open her mouth.

—Bertrand Russell

It can be argued that philosophy and science are different sides of the same coin. If philosophy is largely the subjective, the qualitative side, then science is the objective, quantitative side. Scientific research is systematic, controlled, empirical, and critical. Science rests its case on observations and measurements, and then only if such data meets certain rigorous tests. Philosophy applies reason and logic to generate a network of principles and hypothesized relationships. It is at this point that science and philosophy interface most strongly, for it has become the task of science to test the presumed relationships inferred by philosophy.

Science is what you know, philosophy is what you don't know.

—Bertrand Russell

The scientific approach to knowing is best demonstrated in the so-called "scientific method." Though presented differently in different texts, the scientific method normally contains the following elements:

- **Identification of a Question**. Before science can begin an investigation, there first must be a clear and precise problem. Identifying the problem is one area in which philosophy can contribute to science.

Using the philosophical methods of logic and reasoning, problems can be isolated and posed as research questions. Research questions usually take one of two forms: *basic* or *applied*. Basic research deals with problems associated with the development of scientific theory. Applied research tries to use science to solve practical everyday problems. Experiments designed to contribute to our understanding of the universe's origin is an example of basic (or pure) research. An experiment designed to contribute to building a better mousetrap is an example of applied research. Research studies often have both theoretical and practical value.

- **Hypothesis Formulation**. Hypothesis comes from the Greek word for **suggestion** and, essentially that is precisely what a hypothesis is—a suggestion regarding the relationship between two or more variables. Here again, philosophy contributes to science. By postulating a presumed relationship between variables, philosophical reasoning can provide the basis for a controlled and systematic evaluation of the presumed relationship.
- **Testing**. Science places great value on observation and measurement. Over the years, science has developed elaborate and elegant strategies to measure the extent to which an independent variable can influence a dependent variable.
- **Evaluation**. Science is its own most vigorous critic. Before any research findings can be accepted as "probable fact," the underlying assumptions, research design, analysis, and conclusions are all carefully examined. In evaluating research, science demands reliable and valid methods.
- **Communication**. Once a study has been completed, it is incumbent upon the researcher to communicate the results to others who might be interested in the results. In recreation and leisure studies this usually is done through an article submitted to one of the professional journals serving the recreation and leisure profession.
- **Theory**. At the heart of leisure science lies theory. As hypotheses are tested and understanding of some phenomenon grows, science acquires the ability to explain the nature of the causal basis of the phenomenon in question. With such understanding, science then is able to predict relationships with other variables. This understanding may be thought of as theory—theory leads to subsequent hypotheses, and the process is self-perpetuating.

The Language of Leisure Science

> The chief virtue that language can have is clearness, and nothing detracts from it so much as the use of unfamiliar words.
>
> —Hippocrates

The process and language of leisure science is the same as with other social sciences; it is only the content that differs. Following are some of the principal terms and phrases used by researchers. By understanding the language of science you can get a better picture of what leisure research involves.

Nominal Fallacy

A nominal fallacy is the erroneous belief that just because something has been named, it has also been explained. To say a person seeks leisure to avoid boredom really tells us nothing about the conditions, circumstances or antecedents of boredom. It is akin to saying that people seek recreation because of an instinct. Researchers try to avoid the nominal fallacy by carefully looking for underlying explanations.

Operational Definition

An operational definition is a statement of the operations used in a study to determine the relationship between an independent and dependent variable. For example, an operational definition for leisure satisfaction could be a score on a test designed to measure satisfaction.

Reliability

In research terms, reliability refers to consistency. A test or method must be capable of replication. A test that is inconsistent (unreliable) is of little value.

Validity

A test or research project must measure or study what it purports to study. Sometimes a scientist will unknowingly measure something other than the variable in which he is interested. This can lead to invalid results.

Generalizability

A study is normally conducted in order to enable a researcher to generalize the findings from the research subjects to a larger population. For example, the Gallup Poll carefully selects its subjects so that there is a high probability that their opinions reflect the opinions of the country as a whole. The small group with whom the researcher works is called a *sample*. In order to ensure that the sample is representative of the population at large, the sample is drawn using a random-sampling procedure. It is impossible to draw a perfect representation of the population. There will always be some degree of difference between the sample and the parent population, this difference is referred to as *sampling error*. Researchers attempt to keep sampling error as low as possible by using techniques that give every member of the population the same chances of being selected for inclusion in the sample. The extent to which the sample population is representative of the parent population is the extent to which the study findings are generalizable.

Variables

In common terminology, a variable is something that is "free to vary." Science makes an attempt to understand what causes variables to change. In research terminology, a variable that is the presumed cause for some change in another variable is referred to as the *independent variable*. The variable believed to be affected by the independent variable is called the *dependent variable*. In other words, the outcome variable is dependent upon the independent or causal variable. There is a third class of variables that scientists are concerned about. These are variables which might have an unknown or unexpected influence on a dependent variable. These are referred to as *confounding* variables. For example, it has long been known that almost any type of change in a research situation will bring about a change in the dependent variable. In fact, it is quite conceivable that much of the "variance" measured in a study could be due to the fact that subjects in the study altered their behavior, not so much because of the independent variable, but because they wanted to please the researchers. Fortunately, science has developed several research designs which help prevent the intrusion of extraneous or confounding variables. Some variables cannot be observed. They must be inferred. Such variables as perception, motivation, arousal etc. can only be inferred. These are referred to as *organismic or intervening variables*.

Research Designs

Everyone is familiar with at least two research designs used by behavioral scientists—the experiment and the survey. Although important and useful designs, these are only two methods out of many available to leisure behavior researchers. These two approaches are quantitative in nature, i.e., they rely heavily on statistical principles. There are other less quantitative approaches, which also are frequently used in the study of leisure behavior. These include descriptive methods which emphasize description and subjective judgments rather than quantitative analysis. These types of studies are often referred to as qualitative designs. You can visualize research designs as forming a continuum ranging from the highly analytical, or quantitative, to the highly subjective or qualitative. Representing the analytical extreme is the experiment, where a study is structured to control for confounding variables, thus making it possible to clearly identify the relationship between an independent and dependent variable. On the other extreme, there are studies where a researcher makes a careful observation of a behavior and tries to describe it as accurately as possible. The qualitative side of the continuum can be thought of as a transition space between philosophy and science. In cases where the intent is to develop a hypothesis amenable to further testing, the activity can be thought of as scientific research.

Qualitative	**Continuum**	**Quantitative**
Descriptive	**Observational/Correlational**	**Experimental**

Early studies in recreation usually fell on the qualitative side of the continuum; however, by the 1930's there were those in the profession who were advocating the use of scientific research to address some of the problems and questions associated with play, recreation, and leisure. J.B. Nash, in *The Organization and Administration of Playgrounds and Recreation* advocated the use of scientific surveys to assist in determining what a community recreation program should include (230). In 1934, Mason and Mitchell called for the scientific appraisal of the claims that play builds character.

> Since organizations promoting play wear the label of character building agencies and set forth a program toward this end, the assumption has followed that they are accomplishing their objectives . . . Casual observation by leaders has seemed to indicate that they are being benefited. Merely labeling an activity as character building does not make it that. . . casual observation is no adequate appraisal of results. There has been a growing tendency, therefore, to seek adequate measuring devices which will determine scientifically just what the character results of any given play activity are (272).

By the 1940s, most management textbooks in recreation and leisure were advocating the use of survey research to determine community needs and interests, but aside from this "applied research," little systematic investigation as recommended by Mason and Mitchell was being done. In 1948, Meyer and Brightbill had this to say about the state of research in recreation and leisure:

> In comparison with the physical sciences, and in fact many of the social sciences, the field of recreation is relatively untouched by research. Recreation requires increasingly critical and exhaustive investigation and experimentation in order to improve and revise currently accepted conclusions in the body of newly discovered facts. Research is based upon scientific study that brings about creative activity, generating new ideas and practices (71).

In 1954, the Research Council of the American Association for Health, Physical Education and Recreation listed the following pertinent suggestions for research studies in recreation:

1. The development of an instrument which may be used to predict the success of prospective recreation leaders.
2. A study of the age levels of readiness of children for the development of basic recreation skills.
3. A study of those leadership techniques which have proven most successful in the conduct of various activities.

4. Origin of established recreational interest.
5. Collecting hobbies of the residents of a small community.
6. Longitudinal study of the effects of recreation.
7. Analysis of therapeutic values of recreation.
8. Study of the motivational factors in sports.
9. Longitudinal studies of changes in recreational interests and patterns.

By the 1960s, university recreation and leisure departments began to participate in increasingly sophisticated research projects including the application of experimental design to leisure problems. But, even as late as 1974, one prominent leisure scholar had this to say about the research of leisure related topics in university settings:

> Only persons who wish to avoid promotions would consider doing research on such interdisciplinary topics as pollution, natural resources development, the energy crisis, let alone leisure and recreation (Neulinger 72).

In spite of this cheerless observation, the field of recreation has continued to devote increasing attention to the scientific study of leisure and leisure related areas. One of the milestone accomplishments in the area of recreation research was the decision of the National Recreation and Park Association in 1969 to begin publishing *The Journal of Leisure Research.* Modeled after similar journals in other disciplines, this journal provides a means of communicating the findings of scholarly research to members of the profession. In 1979, Donald Peligrino published *Research Methods for Recreation and Leisure: A Theoretical and Practical Guide*. In 1983, the American Academy for Park and Recreation Administration was founded. In order to encourage the publication of scholarly reports and research it began publishing the *Journal of Park and Recreation Administration.* In 1984, *Leisure Sciences: An Interdisciplinary Journal* was begun.

A review of the content of contemporary recreation research journals and texts tend to support the notion that leisure research has made a rather dramatic shift from a philosophical qualitative approach to a more scientific and quantitative design. However, it should be noted that during the mid-90's, recreation and leisure researchers showed a renewed interest in qualitative methods.

Using Research to Know about Leisure

It is generally accepted that leisure is a central component to a quality lifestyle. Hence, if one is to optimize the probability of quality in his/her life, an understanding of leisure is essential. By increasing one's understanding of leisure, one's ability to facilitate and experience leisure is increased, and with an increase in leisure an increase in the overall quality of one's life is likely to follow. In order to increase one's understanding of leisure, we need two types of information: (1) we need to know what causes leisure, and (2) we need to know what leisure causes. In other words, we need to look at leisure as both an independent variable and a dependent variable. Neulinger supports this notion:

> The implications of leisure are most directly reflected in what has come to be known as "the quality of life." Irrespective of what one feels is the definition of leisure, be it of free time, activities or state of mind, the nature of that leisure will affect the person's quality of life which will in turn affect one's leisure. Leisure can either be the cause or the effect, the independent or the dependent variable. Since leisure as a state of mind comes about as a function of the myriad conditions of one's life, its investigation and advancement require as complete a picture of the overall quality of life as possible, including such matters as health, public safety, education, employment, incomes, housing, and general trends. . . (72).

Current research is being done in all of the areas listed by Neulinger and more. Within recent years, researchers have been investigating the formation of leisure attitudes, the effect of leisure on development, the relationship of self-esteem to leisure involvement, the therapeutic uses of leisure, the healing power of play and laughter, the relationship of family leisure and family cohesion, and even the role of play in the classroom. Many of these studies flow both ways, allowing us to understand what leisure causes and what causes leisure. Both kinds of information are essential to our ability to make decisions regarding how to facilitate leisure and enhance the quality of life.

In reading reports about research findings regarding leisure, it is important to remember that not all research is equally good. Not every scientist employs the rigor and dedication called for by the scientific method. Researchers make mistakes too. Unfortunately, too many people assume that science is perfect, and that findings of science are an accurate reflection of the relationship between the variables studied. This blind faith in science can lead some people to accept incorrect information. In order to be an effective consumer of leisure-related research, it is essential that you know what to look for in a research report. Here are some rules to help you use research in making decisions regarding leisure in your life:

1. **The Findings of a Research Study Cannot Be Generalized to Your Life**. Science generalizes from samples to larger groups. Science determines the probability of relationships existing between variables within a certain population. But just because there is a high probability that a relationship exists between certain variables within a population to which you belong, does not mean that the findings pertain specifically to you. For example, it may be found that people who score high on a playfulness scale also tend to live longer than those who are less playful. This can be alarming news if you tend to be on the serious side of things. However, it's conceivable that a person can be "deadly serious," but live far longer than the average—even though the research indicates that there is a relationship between play and longevity.
2. **Not All Studies Meet the Test of Validity**. If a study fails to measure what it claims to measure, the results may be useless or even damaging. In reading a scientific study, pay attention to what a writer says about validity. Quite often researchers report evidence of reliability, but say very little about validity. This can be misleading, for even the most reliable test or research instrument can be invalid. Although reliability is a prerequisite for validity, it alone does not guarantee it.
3. **Understand the Theory**. Competent researchers describe the theoretical basis for the hypotheses they are researching. This is usually done through a review and summary of other studies that are related to the theoretical underpinnings of the hypotheses being tested. By carefully reading the literature review presented at the beginning of a study, you should be able to see the logic underlying the research design. This is helpful to understanding both the concepts being tested, as well as evaluating the validity of the study. If you see a flaw in the flow of the logic of the study, you would be wise to accept the research findings with caution.
4. **Put It in Your Language**. Sometimes understanding a research study is difficult because of the special language used by behavioral scientists. What may at first glance look like a complicated concept, may in reality be quite simple, once you get past the scientific jargon. A good dictionary is helpful in demystifying scientific reports. Once you understand the key words, summarize the study by using your own words.

Closing Note...

In this unit, we have looked briefly at two ways of knowing about leisure: the philosophical and the scientific. We have looked at some of the key words and concepts related to both fields and outlined some ways in which both can contribute to our understanding of leisure. In developing a leisure lifestyle, it is important that we learn how to utilize the findings of science, but think like philosophers.

REFERENCES

Carlson, N.R. *Psychology.* New York: Allyn Bacon, Inc., 1987.

Carlson, R.E., et al. *Recreation and Leisure: The Changing Scene.* Belmont, California: Wadsworth Publishing Company.

Carlson, Reynold, Teodore R. Deppe, and Janet MacLean. *Recreation in American Life.* Belmont, California: Wadsworth Publishing, Inc., 1974.

Journal of Leisure Research. Washington, D.C.: National Recreation and Park Association.

Journal of Park and Recreation Administration. Bloomington, Indiana: American Academy for Park and Recreation Administration, January, 1983.

Kraus, R. *Recreation and Leisure in Modern Society.* New York: Scott Foresman Company, 1986.

Leisure Sciences: An Interdisciplinary Journal. New York: Crane, Russak and Company, Inc.

Meyer, H.D. and C.K. Brightbill. *Recreation Administration: A Guide to Its Practices.* Englewood Cliffs, NJ: Prentice-Hall Inc., 1948.

Mitchell. E.D. *The Theory of Play.* New York: A.S. Barnes and Company, 1937.

Nash, J.B. *The Organization and Administration of Playgrounds and Recreation.* New York: Barnes and Company, 1931.

Neulinger, J. *To Leisure: An Introduction.* Boston: Allyn & Bacon, Inc., 1981.

Pelegrino, D.A. *Research Methods for Recreation and Leisure: A Theoretical and Practical Guide.* Dubuque, Iowa: Wm. C. Brown Company, 1979.

Persig, R. *Zen and the Art of Motorcycle Maintenance.*

Peter, L.J. *Peter's Quotations: Ideas for Our Time.* New York: William Morrow and Co., 1977.

Plutchik, R. *Foundations of Experimental Research.* New York: Harper and Row Publishers, 1968.

Simon, J. *Basic Research Methods in Social Science: The Art of Empirical Investigation.* New York: Random House, 1969.

Rombold, C.P. *Personal Communication.* March 15, 1989.

Webster, R. *Philosophy of Physical Education.* Dubuque, Iowa: Wm. C. Brown, Publishers, 1965.

CHAPTER 4

Coming to Terms

For some words, their meanings are clear. Unfortunately, that isn't the case with the word **leisure**. It seems that there is no one universally accepted definition for this seemingly simple term. Indeed, John Neulinger (1982) has identified 14 separate definitions for this capricious word. A careful reading of these different definitions suggests that most of them can be categorized in one of two broad categories: (1) those that are **quantitative** in nature, and (2) those that are **qualitative**. It can be argued that there is also a third class of definitions, those that attempt to combine both dimensions. These so-called **holistic** definitions bring nothing new to our understanding of leisure—they merely rearrange the parts presented by other authors representing differing viewpoints.

Quantitative definitions attempt to define leisure in terms of discretionary time or by activities engaged in during free time. From a research standpoint, quantitative definitions are particularly useful in studying the economics and sociology of leisure because of the ease with which they can be operationalized for research purposes. As DeGrazia says:

> "The word leisure has always referred to something personal, state of mind or a quality of feeling. It seemed that in changing from the term leisure to the term free time, we . . . now had something that could be measured with ease" (59).

By viewing leisure as merely time or activity, we are subtly led away from the personal and most significant aspects of leisure, and the further we are led away from the personal nature of the experience, the less capable we are of understanding it. The second category of definitions address these deeper issues and as such can be thought of as qualitative because they tend to view leisure as a complex of emotions, attitudes, and personal values. Leisure according to this view, is entirely subjective, a state of mind. Of this, Neulinger states:

> "To the degree the mind, or more appropriately, experiences, is the scientific domain of psychology, this view may also be called a psychological one" (22).

The Quantitative Point of View

The quantitative point of view is generally considered the most pervasive, the one most commonly used by the general population. Referring to this point of view, Charles Brightbill in his book, *The Challenge of Leisure*, defines leisure as:

> Time beyond that which is required for existence, the things we must do to stay alive. . . and subsistence, the things we must do to make a living (4).

Murphy views leisure as ". . . that time available to be used at the individual's discretion" (15). Robert Lee, a contemporary of Brightbill said:

> Leisure is most commonly viewed in relation to time—free time, time not devoted to paid occupation or time off from work (26).

This point of view is further supported by Richard Kraus (1980), recognized authority on recreation and leisure, who defines leisure as:

> . . . that portion of an individual's time which is not devoted to work or work-connected responsibilities or to other forms of discretionary or unobligated time (44).

The *Webster Dictionary* lends support to this point of view by defining leisure as "Opportunity or time afforded by freedom from immediate occupation or duty; free of unoccupied time. . ."

Although the most common definition, the **free time** definition has often been criticized as too simplistic. One of the early critics of this point of view was Robert Lee

> . . . . an attempt to define leisure by putting the stress on the time element free time, spare time, left-over time, unobligated time—is bound to be misleading. This is basically a quantitative view of leisure, an arithmetic approach which simply subtracts the time devoted to work, sleep and other necessities from the 24-hour day to derive the surplus time. To be sure the time focus is necessary, yet it is not a sufficient condition of leisure. At best this is a minimal view, and at worst a distortion, for it fails to capture the depths of the meaning of leisure, the essentially inner and subjective quality of experience (27).

The **discretionary time** view ignores a fundamental truth, free time in and of itself is value free. Free time can lead to a curse or a blessing; what gives a period of time value is the activity that one experiences during such time. Time is nothing more than the period during which **something** occurs. It is the **something** that determines the value we place on the time in question. Values can be thought of as the "rating and significance given certain things" (Webster 209). The rating and significance that one places upon leisure is largely a function of his or her philosophical frame of reference. For many, leisure is regarded in positive terms, yet for others leisure is viewed as a threat or in some religions as a sin.

Free time may provide the context for the activity, but until one has entered into the leisure activity the temporal context remains only a **potential for some activity**. It acquires value only when behaviors are set into operation. Activities possessing positive value produce responses such as "Wow, time sure flies when you are having fun." Bad choices are reflected in statements such as, "What a waste of time!" Such evaluations only occur after the fact. Free time provides the opportunity for choice, but it is the nature of the activity chosen that determines the value of any given block of time. Robert Lee supports this criticism thusly:

> Free time is not really synonymous with leisure. The unemployed or the confined may have free time but not necessarily leisure. Not everything one does qualifies as leisure. Of course free time may be converted into leisure time. Hence, free time is only potentially leisure time. Noncommitted or free time may well be idle time. The mood of leisure is affirmative, whereas the

mood of idleness is negative. Idleness must not be confused with leisure, for idleness renders leisure impossible. . . (28).

Although, consensus as to definition may be lacking, it is generally accepted that leisure is not a value-free concept. And, if it can be argued that **if leisure is something of value** and **free time is value free**, leisure and free time simply cannot be one and the same.

Another criticism of the free time idea pivots on the meaning of the word **free**, which is defined as "**Not subject to physical or moral restraint; nor bound by adherence to form or rule**" (*Webster's Encyclopedic Dictionary* 368). Once you make a choice, once you commit yourself to a course of action, a block of time ceases to be ***free time*** and becomes **scheduled time**. Free time exists only when your options remain before you; once you make a choice your actions are dictated by the structure inherent in the activity you schedule. Even the most simple of leisure pursuits will possess some degree of structure, even idleness, for every condition of life is bound to physical and social influences. As Bennet Berger states, "If sociology has taught us anything, it has taught us that no time is free of normative constraints" (In Lee 27). Certainly, every activity engaged in for recreational reasons is laden with social expectations and constraints. Once you make a decision on how to fill a block of unscheduled time, a set of appropriate behaviors is activated. These behaviors are governed by social expectations relative to the activity chosen and can be viewed as a form of structure. Berger supports this notion by saying that free time may be more obligated because where commitments are voluntary they tend to carry with them a sense of responsibility (In Lee 27).

With responsibility and structure comes constraint, which is the antithesis of freedom. And, if freedom is the essence of the discretionary time definition, it is clear that free time can only exist in the abstract. In addition to social influences, one must consider the constraining influence of the physical laws of nature. Only in the abstract, i.e., conceptually, can one be free of the impositions of biological needs and functions and the constraints and inconveniences of the physical environment. Even during periods of idleness, one must attend to biological needs as well as cope with environmental factors. Consequently, free-time activities are limited not only by social but by physical forces as well, and the extent to which such forces operate is the extent to which one is incapable of being free. The ever-present demands of the present, even during periods of idleness, are so limiting that it is obvious that free time is something that can only exist in the minds of philosophers and dreamers. Consequently, as a definition for leisure, it is ill-conceived as well as misleading.

Another quantitative point of view argues that leisure is nothing more than an activity into which one freely enters. Representing this point of view are Neumeyer and Neumeyer who state that leisure is, ". . . any activity carried out freely without restraint or compulsion. . . ." (15) Dumazedier is of a similar mind, he says, "Leisure is activity. . . apart from the obligations of work, family and society to which an individual turns at will . . . ." (16). This definition is similar to the free time definition in that it contrasts leisure to commitment or restraint. The emphasis, however, is upon the behavior rather than the time frame. One problem with looking at leisure as an activity freely entered into is that such a definition fails to deal with the fact that not all free time behaviors are of equal value. Indeed, many of the behaviors people engage in during their discretionary time have clearly negative value. The harmful consequences of recreational drugs, the mind-deadening influence of modern television and movies, the environmental damage done by heavy user loads on recreational lands are examples of free time activities gone awry. If leisure is neither positive nor negative, then this approach is perhaps adequate, but modern thinking, energized by scientific research (Neulinger, 1971, 1981, Ellis, 1983, Kaplan, 1975) suggests activities normally associated with leisure possess social and personal value. If this is true, then perhaps it is an inaccurate representation of the facts to refer to harmful or negative activities as leisure. The axiological issues inherent in this perspective pose serious questions relative to the validity of this class of definitions, a problem that didn't exist in the more qualitative orientation of the ancient Greeks.

The Qualitative Point of View

This point of view dates back to Ancient Greece, where leisure was highly valued for its educational and personal developmental values. It was believed that through leisure an individual could come closest to achieving his/her intellectual and spiritual potential. In fact, it was Aristotle who said, "The aim of education is the wise use of leisure." The connection between leisure and education can be demonstrated in another way. The Greek word for leisure is **scola**, the word from which we derive the English word **school**. Again reinforcing the idea that leisure was associated with the cognitive activities involved in the process of personal growth and learning. Here there is no argument with the value component of leisure. It was not merely time, not just an activity engaged in without compulsion, but rather an activity leading to self-improvement and personal growth. Socrates viewed leisure as "the best of all possessions."

> Liberty is being free from the things we don't like in order to be slaves of things we do like.
>
> —Ernest Benn

Our English word leisure comes from the Latin **licere** which means to be permitted or to be free. The words liberty and license share this same root. In the classical view, leisure then involved being sufficiently free from constraints to engage in contemplative and educational pursuits. Robert Lee puts it this way:

> "If freedom and learning are twin attributes of leisure, then it is apparent why leisure should be considered the basis of culture. The choice of leisure time activities can give shape and meaning to our cultural configurations. The spirit of leisure is the spirit of learning, of self-cultivation. In a sense, the world of leisure is a great laboratory for learning. Leisure provides the climate for the growth of man's whole being, for contemplation of man's ultimate concerns, for activities which enrich the mind, strengthen the body, and restore the soul" (33).

This early view can be criticized on two points. (1) The emphasis on the intellectual was too limiting and too narrow in scope. To the ancient Greeks the ideal condition of being was contemplation of artistic pursuits. There is more to life than these activities and should be accounted for in a philosophy of leisure. This view tends to be too narrow in that respect. (2) This philosophy required that an individual have sufficient free time to enable him or her to pursue desirable activities. Among the Greeks, this was facilitated through slave labor, and from that perspective is morally reprehensible.

Within recent years a more modern definition has emerged. This definition, like the classical notion, places emphasis on the individual, but rather than stressing certain activities, it focuses on the emotional response produced by the activities engaged in. This approach is superior to the other points of view because it recognizes that leisure potential not only differs from activity to activity, but from person to person. Pieper represents this point of view when he argues that leisure does not necessarily follow free time. Instead he points out that leisure is a ". . . mental and spiritual attitude—it is not the result of external factors, it is not the inevitable result of spare time, a holiday, a weekend or a vacation" (40). To Pieper leisure is a "higher order than the active life. . . it involves the capacity to soar in active celebration, to overstep the boundaries of the workaday world" (41).

Of more recent origin is the conceptualization of John Neulinger. Neulinger views leisure as a function of two psychological constructs: **perceived freedom** and **intrinsic motivation.** This psychological perspective deals with the free time question by arguing that freedom is relative to one's capacity to view one's self free from external or internal constraint. Neulinger describes perceived freedom as a "state in which a person feels that what he is doing, he is doing by choice and because he wants to" (15). Thus, neither time nor activity are viewed as important from this perspective. Neulinger goes on to say, "Leisure has one and only one essential criterion, and that is the condition of perceived freedom" (Ibid). He goes on to point out that in addition to perceived freedom, leisure has two additional dimensions. In Neulinger's words, "These dimensions are the motivation for the activity (extrinsic to intrinsic), and the goal of the activity (instrument to final)" (16). Later (1981) he modified this model to include only perceived freedom and intrinsic motivation. He summarizes the revised model thusly:

> The model then, distinguishes between leisure and nonleisure states on the basis of the variable perceived freedom. It further qualifies these states in terms of a second variable, namely motivation. The behavior involved is categorized as either intrinsic or extrinsic (or both). If the satisfaction gained stems from the activity and not from a payoff or consequence therefrom, the behavior is judged to be intrinsically motivated. If the satisfaction comes from a payoff—if the activity itself is not the reward but only leads to a reward—then the activity is seen as extrinsically motivated. . . . On the other hand, outcomes are phenomenologically irrelevant for intrinsically motivated behavior. Since most real life behavior has components of both intrinsic and extrinsic motivation, the model provides for mixed conditions, thus leading to six cells.
>
> 1. **Pure Leisure**. A state of mind brought about by an activity freely engaged in and done for its own sake.
> 2. **Leisure-Work**. A state of mind brought about by an activity freely engaged in and providing both intrinsic and extrinsic rewards.
> 3. **Leisure-Job**. A state of mind brought about by an activity freely engaged in, but providing satisfaction only in terms of its consequences or payoffs.
> 4. **Pure Work**. A state of mind characterized by an activity engaged in under constraint, but providing intrinsic rewards only.
> 5. **Work-Job**. A state of mind characterized by an activity engaged in under constraint providing both intrinsic and extrinsic rewards.
> 6. **Pure Job**. A state of mind characterized by an activity engaged in under constraint with no rewards. (29–32)

Although well respected, Neulinger's model is not without criticism. One problem rests with the term **perceived freedom**. The word "perceived" is defined as "to have or obtain awareness by the senses." Freedom is defined as the "state of being free; exemption from constraint." Thus, the implication is clear, in order to be at leisure one must be aware of his or her state of being exempt from constraint. However, in practice, perceived freedom only seems to be an important awareness during the time that a potential leisure activity is being considered. Once an activity has been engaged, perceived freedom only becomes an issue if the activity proves less than satisfying. In that case, the participant evaluates the activity and its attendant circumstances and makes a determination as to whether he or she should stay with the activity or abandon it. In highly satisfying situations, the issue of freedom becomes irrelevant because the intensity of the activity causes one's perception to be limited to the dynamics of the experience. In other words, there may be times when constraining situations are not perceived as such because the satisfaction inherent in the activity overshadows the participant's awareness of constraint. This phenomenon might be referred to as *perceptual freedom* and may be a better criterion than "perceived freedom" for identifying leisure.

Some people are capable of experiencing the presumed effect of perceived freedom in situations normally thought of as constraining, such as the student who becomes so enthralled with his/her studies that he is freed from awareness of external noise or biological needs. A student who studies nonstop for hours without raiding the refrigerator might be manifesting the kind of freedom produced by involvement in a highly stimulating experience. A painter who can't put his brush down because of the exhilaration of the creative process or the employee who enjoys her work so much that she works well past closing are examples of people so involved in the activities that they are freed from awareness of external or biological constraints. According to Neulinger, these people could not be construed as being at leisure, rather according to this conceptualization they would be involved in **pure work**.

Another criticism with Neulinger's model is that it fails to account for the tendency of people to build constraints into their pleasurable activities. Indeed many of the activities that we cherish most are replete with

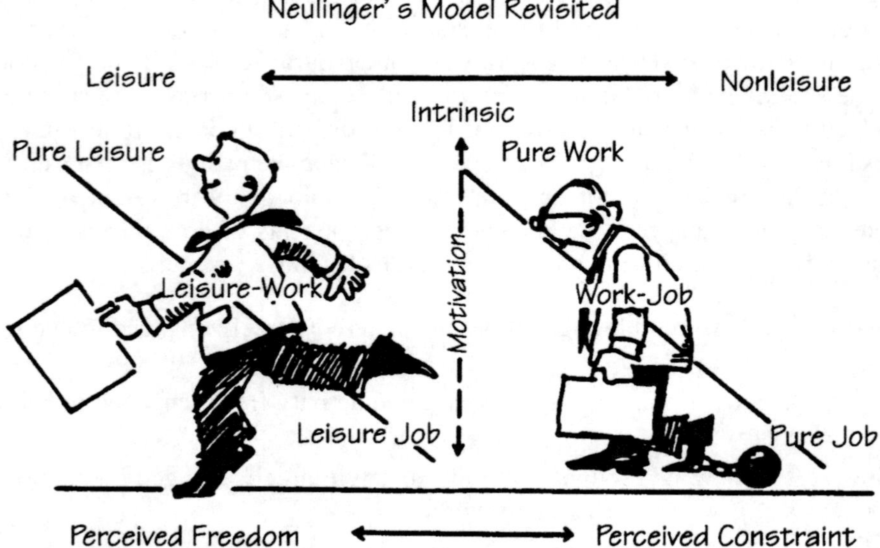

constraints and limitations. Once an individual has made a decision to participate in an activity, he or she must abide by the rules, policies and to a less extent, social mores regarding the activity. Neulinger argues that "... to leisure implies being engaged in an activity as a free agent of one's own choice" (15). And yet, once at leisure are there constraints that one would prefer not to have to deal with? This conceptualization fails to account for situations freely entered, but not free from perceived constraint. Again, it can be argued that freedom only occurs when one is sufficiently satisfied by an experience to lose awareness of any external or internal real or imagined constraint. Neulinger's simplistic explanation of perceived freedom may be rooted in his training as a researcher, where a premium is placed on operational definitions. However, a more phenomenological viewpoint expands the role of freedom, in our understanding of leisure, to include freedom from external and internal conditions which detract from the satisfaction yielded by some activity. Rather than perceived freedom being the "primary dimension of leisure," it would appear that Neulinger's second dimension, "intrinsic motivation," or stated in terms of an outcome, intrinsic satisfaction, might well be the most important single dimension in distinguishing leisure from other states of being.

Although Neulinger acknowledges that leisure is primarily viewed as a positive condition, he fails to examine the question of values. Consequently, from his perspective, an activity potentially harmful to an individual or society could be construed as leisure if it were intrinsically satisfying and engaged in freely. This viewpoint differs dramatically from other qualitative points of view in that it fails to limit leisure to activities that yield socially valued outcomes. Thus, from this point of view, even the most heinous activities could technically be referred to as leisure as long as they met Neulinger's criteria. Most people would take exception to the idea that vandalism, drug use, drive-by shootings, and other criminal activity are examples of leisure.

Given the criticisms and limitations of Neulinger' s model, his research and creative theorizing regarding leisure marks an important milestone in the field of leisure studies. His notion that leisure is marked by a sense of freedom when expanded to mean an absence of awareness of constraint, coupled with the idea of intrinsic motivation provides a sound basis for an understanding of the experience we call leisure. This conceptualization can gain further credibility by appending the idea that leisure, as in the Greek formulation, is neither harmful to the individual nor to society, and at its very best is personally and societally enriching.

Mike Ellis made a major contribution to our understanding of leisure by examining the biological basis of play. In his book, *Why People Play,* (1973) he presents an insightful explanation of the interplay between physiology and psychology as related in the tendency of neophilic animals to seek arousing, nonutilitarian activity. He argues that people, and many animals, have a biological need to seek "an optimal level of arousal." This notion relates to what Desmond Morris refers to as the "stimulus struggle." An optimal level of arousal was shown by Ellis to be highly correlated to feelings of satisfaction (and performance). This fits nicely with Neulinger's notion of leisure as intrinsically satisfying. Furthermore, it can be argued that it supports the expanded freedom conceptualization in that one can only function optimally when unaware of real or fancied constraints.

By melding together elements from the work of Neulinger, Ellis and the early Greeks, an attractive and intellectually tenable definition arises. This definition focuses on (1) the personal and social value of the experience; (2) the psychological dimensions of the experience and (3) the physiological nature of the experience. In its most succinct form it can be stated as follows:

> Leisure is an activity which produces a state of being, physiologically characterized by optimal arousal, psychologically characterized by perceptual freedom and intrinsic satisfaction, and associated with positive value for both the individual and society.

Serious and Casual Leisure

Sociologist Robert Stebbins, suggests that leisure can be viewed as taking two forms: casual and serious. This model provides a useful tool in furthering our understanding of the role that leisure play's in our lives, and the impact that it has on society.

Casual leisure typically requires no special learning or significant skill and as the name implies is done in an informal and laid-back manner. It's the kind of leisure that is characterized by activities that can occur with ease and spontaneity: conversation with a friend, watching television, playing on the computer, going out for dinner. Even activities requiring some measure of skill may fall under the casual heading, provided they are only engaged in rarely, and primarily for intrinsic reasons. In other words, casual leisure isn't taken very seriously. It doesn't require a particularly great investment in time, resources, education, or energy. However, some casual leisure can be the most expensive. For example, a stay at a fancy Caribbean resort, a trip to outer space via that Russian agency that offers such, a dinner at Maxim's.

Serious leisure involves greater intensity than casual leisure. Serious leisure involves engagement in what is generally thought of as a leisure activity, but to the level that it begins to possess the characteristics of a career in that leisure role. In other words, in serious leisure people approach an activity with far greater intensity and commitment than is demonstrated in casual leisure. In a serious leisure career, people *seriously* seek the special skills requisite to success in the leisure activity; they take courses on related subjects; they invest both time and, sometimes, money in the activity; and they tend to define themselves by their serious leisure activity. Serious leisure in turn can be categorized as **amateur** level involvement, **volunteerism**, and **hobbies**. Seemingly related to serious leisure, but lacking the long-term commitment demonstrated by serious leisure is **project-based leisure.** Dr. Stebbins describes project-based leisure in this way:

> *Project-based leisure is a short-term, moderately complicated, one-shot, or occasional, though infrequent, creative undertaking carried out in free time. It requires considerable planning, effort and sometimes skill or knowledge, but is for all that neither serious leisure nor intended to develop into such* [4].

One of the characteristics of serious leisure is that *social worlds* emerge to support and socially frame the leisure activity. In a sense, the activity becomes a hub, or focal point for a constellation of supporting and related activities. Special locations emerge where the activity occurs, organizations develop around the activity, special mechanisms of communication come into being to enable practitioners to stay in touch, special tools are produced, and special products are manufactured. In short, a *serious leisure social* world is very much like the world that revolves around one's work career, or an academic discipline.

4. For more on project-based leisure, read Dr. Stebbins article: "Project-based Leisure: Theoretical Neglect of a Common Use of Free Time" found in *Leisure Studies,Vol. 24, No. 1, 1–11, January 2005*

In conceptualizing the notions discussed here, it might be beneficial to substitute the term "recreation" for the term "leisure." Serious leisure then becomes "serious recreation," casual leisure becomes "casual recreation" and project-based leisure becomes "project-based recreation." For some readers, this perspective may be more compatible with their perception of the term "leisure."

As an example, consider the social world that supports and frames my interest in political cartooning. Not only do I enjoy viewing the work of others, I enjoy producing my own political cartoons. I have taken classes on the subject, volunteered to teach others, acquired all of the equipment and tools necessary to produce comic art, and invest hours in studying the political climate. No matter where I go I carry a sketchpad. On occasion I will submit cartoons to various publications for consideration, but mostly I do them for my own enjoyment and the enjoyment of my friends and family. I have found a portal into a social world that is filled with like-minded characters, and I have made lasting friendships with many of these folks. It is fair to say that political cartooning is my hobby, and that my status is that of an amateur. I've even volunteered to caricatures for fund raisers and donated numerous cartoons to colleagues and friends. For me comic art and particularly political cartooning is serious leisure. What got me started? The following cartoon tells it all.

Take a moment and look at your own leisure profile, can you find an example of serious leisure in your own life? Do you engage in any hobbies, have amateur standing in a certain field, or regularly practice volunteerism? What benefits do you think might accrue to people who engage in serious leisure? What problems might associate with serious leisure?

"Pleisure"

If you have been following along, you will have already discovered this word and its meaning. I introduced its origin in a footnote in an earlier chapter. But, let me explain it a little more fully here. Dr. Carol Stensrud, my friend and colleague, is a very clever woman. She coined this term by combining the words "pleasure" and "leisure." Pleasure means to find "delight in something." Leisure can mean either "free time" or "a state of mind characterized by freedom and satisfaction" Consequently, "pleisure" is either a block of time characterized by opportunities to experience delight, or a state of mind delighting in feelings of satisfaction and freedom. It is a pleasant term, and one that keeps popping up in this book.

One of the characteristics of the pleasurist is that he or she knows how to view life from a balanced perspective. Every so often you meet someone who seems to have it all together, seems to have *developed a balanced lifestyle. Years ago (1961), I met a pleasurist by name of Roy Crouch. I was only eighteen, just starting college, and impatient with things that I didn't understand. (Of course, I didn't view Mr. Crouch as a pleasurist, rather I saw him as the kindly old man who dispensed gasoline and sagacious virtues at Roy's Service Station.) One Fall morning when I pulled in to Roy's Service Station for $1.25 of gasoline, I was particularly impatient, particularly serious, and particularly stressed. I had a twenty-mile drive to the university ahead of me and a stern math professor waiting to administer an exam to me and my fellow classmates. My mind was filled with binomial expressions, my vision was focused on immediate tasks, and my patience was limited. Roy ambled over to my car. He wore a smile that seemed as comfortable as an old pair of shoes, and his eyes twinkled like a new chrome bumper. He looked like he had just stepped out of the universe for a short visit among mortals, liked it and settled in. In conversation with Roy, I mentioned how I wished that the week were over. He paused for a moment and looked at me from a temporal perspective of 75 years and said, "Never wish your life away. . . because that's one wish that can easily come true." He then made a few observations about the weather, the clean smell of Autumn and the brilliance of the golden hued leaves making their last statement before winter. I paid Roy and then raced down Highway 91 to face the awful hand of fate as only a math test can manifest.*

Years have passed quickly, and today I can't so much as tell you even the name of my former college algebra instructor or how I did on that exam, but I can still see, as though it were yesterday, kindly Roy Crouch looking through playful eyes, admonishing me to expand my values and broaden my perspective. "Never wish your life away. . . because that's one wish that can easily come true."

Play

It was Dr. Ellis who coined the term "Play as Arousal Seeking." In this notion, play is viewed as the product of the organism to generate interactions, with the environment or self, that elevate arousal towards the optimal for the individual. When this occurs during nonutilitarian activities, some would argue that this is play. Others go beyond this limitation and suggest that leisure occurs when one achieves his/her optimum level of arousal, regardless of the form or nature of the activity.

Play is normally regarded as an activity engaged in spontaneously and driven by intrinsic motivation. It may be of very short term duration, but it is always marked by a sense of freedom, frivolity and fun. Play may occur during work or recreation. It may produce leisure. It is nicely characterized by the word "playfulness."

Play is central to so much of the good things in life, so much a part of a leisure lifestyle, that I have devoted an entire chapter to it. I take play very seriously. More on this later.

Recreation

Kraus tells us the term recreation stems from a Latin word "recreation," which means "that which refreshes or restores" (32). Consequently, recreation is generally viewed as activity engaged in for the fun and restorative value associated with it. In distinguishing recreation from play, the following points should be considered:

1. Play is usually spontaneous; recreation is usually planned for.
2. Play is usually of a short term; recreation usually involves more time.
3. Play usually requires no special equipment or facilities; recreation frequently involves both.
4. Play is engaged in for intrinsic reward; recreation frequently employs extrinsic motivation.
5. Play is seldom organized or sponsored; recreation is often organized and sponsored by either a public or commercial agency.
6. Play is often goal free; recreation frequently involves very specific goals.

Games

When we think of games, we often think of the social games of childhood. These types of recreational games are close relatives of the more complex games that provide endless hours of entertainment for millions of Americans. Games form the heart of many recreational programs throughout the country. A game is defined as:

> "... a transaction between two or more people in which there exists a sought after goal which can be achieved only in certain prescribed ways, and which is generally performed because of recreational values" (Berne 48).

Other characteristics associated with games are:

1. They involve two or more people.
2. They require rules and prescribed behaviors.
3. They usually require certain equipment and activity sites.
4. They involve a certain degree of competition.
5. They are played for fun; they are not taken too seriously.

Interpersonal Games

Eric Berne, in his book, *The Games People Play* (1964), defines games somewhat differently from our definition of social recreation games. Dr. Berne states:

> A game is an on-going series of complementary ulterior transactions progressing to a well defined, predictable outcome. Descriptively, it is a recurring set of transactions, often repetitious, superficially plausible, with a concealed motivation; or more colloquially, a series of moves with a snare or "gimmick" (48).

Dr. Berne points out other important characteristics of interpersonal games:

1. Games differ from other social pastimes and recreation in that they possess an ulterior quality.
2. The nature of the payoff differs.
3. Social games involve contest; interpersonal games involve conflict.
4. Social games are often exciting; interpersonal games are always dramatic.
5. Social games are honest; interpersonal games, for the most part, are dishonest.

Understanding interpersonal games is important in learning how to be at leisure because in many respects interpersonal games and leisure are mutually exclusive. Game playing, according to Berne, is done by people who suffer from an imbalance resulting from a disproportionate influence by one of the three basic ego states. When these three ego states, referred to by Berne as the **parent**, **adult**, and **child** egos, are in a healthy balance, the probability of game playing is very low. Seriously disturbed individuals not only have a strong inclination toward game playing but also tend to play intensely. As Berne puts it:

> "Many games are played most intensely by disturbed people; generally speaking, the more disturbed they are, the harder they play" (173).

Critical to our understanding of the relationship between interpersonal games and leisure is the notion that most games are unconsciously motivated. That is not to imply that people cannot consciously engage in games, indeed they do, but it is important to note that they do so willingly; they choose to create and act out a game scenario. For example, there is the story of the young woman who sent flowers to herself hoping that her erstwhile suitor might respond by giving her more attention. As the story goes, she consciously designed this ploy, with one outcome clearly in mind. From start to conclusion she was consciously aware of what she was doing and viewed her actions as rational and appropriate to her situation. But, many interpersonal games are a function of the unconscious mind. Games entered into unknowingly and under the control of the unconscious mind are basically beyond the awareness of the player. As Berne states:

> "What we are concerned with here, however, are the unconscious games played by innocent people . . . of which they are not fully aware and which form the most important aspect of social life all over the world" (49).

Behaviors directed by the unconscious mind are often powerful interventions into the attempts of the conscious mind to organize behavior in productive and pleasurable patterns. Such an intervention seriously dampens an individual's ability to experience personal satisfaction. The victim of this type of disorganization feels burdened and rather than perceiving himself or herself free, they long for freedom. The greater the imbalance, the less capable the individual is to experience the key dimensions of leisure—perceived and perpetual freedom and intrinsic satisfaction. Rather than being optimally aroused, the game player is often supra-optimally aroused. Furthermore, the behaviors demonstrated by the game player are generally destructive and of little or no positive value to the individual or society. Interpersonal games clearly fall outside the domain of leisure.

As pointed out earlier, common to all games is the motivation to manipulate another person into a situation where the game player experiences some type of payoff. This payoff is designed to meet some unexpressed ego need. For example, an individual who has a disproportionate child ego is likely to consistently manipulate other people into catering to his/her "childish" whims and desires. On the other hand, a person who is over influenced by a parent ego is likely to be controlling and dogmatic in his/her dealings with others, often manipulating others into subordinate behaviors through the use of guilt or praise. A classic example is the person who ensures that he/she will remain in control of significant others by being so concerned about other people's welfare that he/she worries himself sick. Certainly, at some point in your life, you have heard someone say, "I was so worried about you that I couldn't sleep. In fact I called every hospital in the state, the highway patrol, and everyone you know." That person was likely your mother.

Dr. Berne argues that each of the egos play an important role in our daily activities. Certainly there are times when it is appropriate to be childlike, at other times authoritative, and yet at other times contemplative and rational. However, game playing leads to ego-related behaviors that are **inappropriate** to a given situation. The elimination of inappropriate behaviors is a goal of the well-adjusted human being, and is referred to as **autonomy**.

Autonomy according to Dr. Berne, is characterized by three capacities, all of which are closely connected to leisure. They are: awareness, spontaneity and intimacy. In reference to awareness Dr. Berne states:

> "Awareness means the capacity to see a coffee pot and hear the birds sing in one's own way, and not the way one was taught. . . . A few people, however, can still see and hear in the old way. But most of the members of the human race have lost the capacity to be painters, poets or musicians, and are not left the option of seeing and hearing directly even if they can afford to; they must get it second hand. The recovery of this ability is called 'awareness'. . . . The aware person is alive because he knows how he feels, where he is and when it is. He knows that after he dies the trees will still be there, but he will not be there to look at them again, so he wants to see them now with as much poignancy as possible" (178).

Spontaneity to Berne means "option, the freedom to choose and express one's feelings from the assortment available. . . . It means liberation. . ." (180). There are times when it is entirely appropriate to spontaneously lapse into silly behavior and to be playful and childlike. There are times when it is entirely appropriate to express your opinion, to be assertive or self-indulgent. Spontaneity implies a freedom to self-expression without having to resort to manipulative and deceitful behaviors.

Intimacy is the ability to express, and equally important, to receive affection. The comfort provided by a game-free intimate relationship is rich in leisure potential and one of humankind's most powerful needs.

The steps necessary to eliminate game playing from one's life go beyond the scope of this unit; however, it should be clear by now that interpersonal games are the antithesis of leisure and deserve one's careful attention. It is far easier to learn how to deal with games when played by others than to reapportion our respective ego loadings. The elimination of games from our interpersonal relationships is very important. By learning how to cope with game playing in others there will quite likely be a side benefit in the increased sensitivity to our own tendencies for such behaviors. Dr. Berne suggests two strategies to be used when you become the focus of someone's game. The simplest strategy is to simply withdraw from a game. When you sense that you are being manipulated, take yourself out of the game situation. Tell the other person, "I sense that you are trying to manipulate me, and I like you too much to allow it to happen." The second alternative is to expose the game. Here you have the benefit of opening the door to adult ego based interaction. A lead into such a discussion might be, "I sense that underlying what you are saying is a feeling or a need for. . ." If a rational discussion fails to ensue and the game continues, then withdraw. Your ability to demonstrate awareness to what is going on in such situations is a good indicator of the extent to which you have achieved autonomy and likewise a good measure of the extent to which you understand and value leisure.

Furthering Adult Behavior

In considering the three different ego states described by Berne, it is clear that the parent and child ego states are often in opposition: the child wants, the parent gives; the child whines, the parent comforts; the child demands, the parent disciplines. When one ego state dominates an individual, there is a tendency for the individual to seek out a partner whose behavior is dominated by the opposing ego. In simplistic terms, this is the basis of what many people are now calling *co-dependence*. Such a relationship might seem like a match made in heaven—a child ego state driven individual being lovingly cared for by a parent ego driven partner. Rather than to promote healthy behavior, these types of relationships produce what is referred to as "enabling behavior." The childish needs of one partner support the other partner's needs for control and dominance. And similarly, the behavior of the dominating partner supports the ego needs of the childish partner. These types of relationships are generally unhealthy and are characterized by a great deal of game playing. Rather than dealing with issues directly, people in co-dependent relationships resort to old scripts that have proven effective in pushing the partner's buttons. The tendency of these manipulations work to reinforce the game playing behavior and the result is the relationship becomes further dysfunctional, and rather than generating leisure, results in appearances on the *Jerry Springer Show.*

I am acquainted with two individuals whose lives unfortunately demonstrate co-dependence and its harmful effects in an all too familiar way. She clearly is the parent ego in the relationship. It is "her way or the highway." But, on the other hand, she can be very nurturing and loving. Her love and nurturing, however, come at a price. Her husband, in order to be the recipient of affection, must have done something very pleasing. As an individual driven by a child-ego, he has a high need for affection. Consequently, in order for him to meet his need for affection he is constantly doing her bidding. Occasionally he resorts to a typical child strategy in his bid for affection—he resorts to seeking pity for some real or imagined pain. This only works when he completely emasculates himself. Sometimes he pouts, sometimes she shouts. What a life!

In discussions with my students, and in workshops, I often ask people to describe the characteristics of an adult. The responses have been surprisingly consistent. Most people seem to see adult behavior as possessing at least five characteristics. So, in addition to those identified by Berne, I am including what I call the 5 R's of Being an Adult. They are as follows:

An adult is responsible. I learned about this word from an old hippie. He gave me a wonderful definition. He said, "It means that you have the ability to respond." Most of us have more ability to

respond to situations than we realize. An adult responds, doesn't just react, but logically and clearly acts to resolve problems in a reasonable manner. If you have the ability to respond and don't, you are being irresponsible. Sometimes irresponsibility is a manifestation of a game. If you demonstrate enough irresponsibility, eventually others will start compensating for you. They may even start doing your work. I once had an irresponsible secretary. It worked well for her, I ended up doing my own work rather than entrust it to her. She did her nails and talked on the phone instead. Yes, go ahead and say it—I lost the game! However, later on, she lost her job.

An adult is reliable. At the heart of a healthy relationship is trust. In an adult relationship (work, social, or marital) the participants can be relied upon, they can be trusted. When you can't trust a person to keep his word or be on time, it makes for an uncomfortable relationship. This is particularly true when the person is actually playing a game such as, "Let's See if I Can Make Her Uncomfortable Enough to. . . ." Unreliability may mark an individual's inability to sustain a relationship, but unwillingness to end it in an honest fashion. "By consistently being inconsistent I can eventually displease her enough to get her to leave me—something I want, but don't have the courage to address honestly."

An adult is rational. An adult doesn't make snap judgments. Too often people make judgments on the basis of an ego need. "I know she didn't mean to spill the milk, but I can get more ego-mileage by making her feel bad." An adult is objective and logical in drawing conclusions and making decisions. "She didn't mean to spill the milk, she already feels bad enough."

An adult is reasonable. In legal settings you frequently hear reference to "the reasonable person test." For some legal questions, it is important to determine how a typical, reasonable person would react to some set of circumstances. The assumption is that among reasonable people there are certain standards of acceptable behavior. A person operating as an adult is generally in touch with such standards and behaves accordingly.

An adult is realistic. An adult is able to see the world as it is. Some people are constantly practicing what psychologists call denial. They refuse to accept the reality of some situation. An unwillingness to accept reality is characteristic of both parent and child ego-states. I once had a student who insisted on being a rock climber. The only problem was that he was terribly obese and relatively weak. He simply couldn't rock climb, but he insisted that he could. He purchased the latest gear, took classes, and repeatedly set out to climb various rock faces. He never succeeded, and he never faced reality. Although he always failed, he could say, "Look how hard I am trying."

An adult is respectful. An adult shows respect to other people. This means allowing others to be themselves, to withhold judgment, and to accept another person to the degree that its reasonable to do so.

In assessing your behavior, you might want to consider the 5 R's next time you sense you are involved in an unhealthy interpersonal transaction. Ask yourself, "Am I being reasonable, rationale, realistic, responsible, and reliable?" The more one operates from an adult-ego, the greater the probability of experiencing leisure. Adult behavior is consistent with the leisure lifestyle because it fosters behaviors that are perceptually freeing and intrinsically satisfying.

Good Games, Bad Games

There are several arguments that can be made for minimizing interpersonal games.

One argument that relates to the theme of this book is that the more one engages in interpersonal games, the less one engages in reality. As the deceit compounds, precious time, energy and other resources are directed away from dealing with real issues and instead used to carry on the game and the numerous games that stem from the original game. These efforts to maintain "a cover" lead to layer upon layer of deceit and artificiality. The more one's life is layered by deceit, the more difficult it is for a person to be free to engage in authentic, meaningful experience.

> One of my friends had been going to an expensive hairstylist for years. One day, her niece who had been attending cosmetology school offered to cut her hair for free. When she returned to her original stylist, and was asked where she'd been, she responded, "My niece is in cosmetology school and needed a guinea pig." Even though her niece went into real estate, she still uses "the niece cut my hair" to explain the long gaps between visits to the original stylist. The truth is that she frequently goes to a much less expensive stylist. She says that she feels guilty every time she goes into the original stylist, or even worse, when she bumps into her accidentally at the market or mall—particularly just after getting a haircut. If she sees the stylist line public, she feels like she has to dodge and weave to avoid the awkward moment when the stylist says, "Oh, looks like you have been to your niece." This deception began with a simple white lie.

Little white lies are easy to generate. For many of us, it is easer to tell a little white lie than to face the truth. For example, how many times do you hear yourself making an excuse to terminate a telephone call? "Oh, my goodness, my cell phone battery is just about exhausted." Or, "Oh, my goodness, I think there is someone at the door." Or, "Oh my goodness, I'm right in the middle of studying for a big exam." If it's not convenient to have a conversation at the time of the call, why not simply say so: "It's not convenient for me to talk just now. May I call you later?" If you don't enjoy talking to someone, and prefer not to talk to them, why not say so? "I'm not interested in having this conversation, it would be better if you called someone else." That may sound Dr. Phil-like, but if you honestly express yourself in a reasonable and respectful manner, three things happen

1. You are perceived by others as a person of integrity.
2. It prevents the downward spiral of game playing.
3. It allows you to demonstrate respect to the most important in your life—you.

And, in general it minimizes your tendency to play games and in short gives you a better grasp on reality. It makes it more likely that you will operate from the adult ego-state.

You may ask, are there no good games? Dr. Berne acknowledges that are some games that are designed primarily to manipulate a person in a positive way: increase self-regard, engender joy/pleasure, motivate to accomplish, and nurture. These games tend to occur with less frequency than more negative variety. In a good game, the manipulation is designed to produce a positive outcome, without the recipient of the outcomes realizing that a manipulation has occurred. For example, a person is feeling a little down, and so a friend sends her flowers from an anonymous admirer. If the intended effect is to cheer the friend up, and it works, then the sender and the receiver both win.

Some games might be considered "marginal" in that they may have both positive and negative outcomes. These games tend to have limited consequences. For example, "the low battery ruse" may help curtail unwanted conversations, without having to tell the caller that his/her call is unwanted. This usually occurs between friends, and as long as the ruse remains hidden, most likely there will be no harm. However, there is always the risk that the ruse will be discovered. Discovery then leads to the inevitable question, "Gosh, if you would lie about your cell phone battery, what else are you lying about." Even if the question is never overtly expressed, the seed of doubt, the eroding influence of suspicion will likely taint the relationship. Again, in short, it is probably better to simply stick with the truth. "Can't talk now, how about later?"

Dr. Berne talks about five different categories of interpersonal games (pastimes, levels 1,2,3 and good games). Another way to view interpersonal games is to view them as falling on a continuum:

An example of a good game: An old gentleman had suffered an atrial fibrillation. Even though his physician had assured him that it was not life threatening and that he had nothing to worry about, the old guy couldn't help but worry. After hearing of the old guy's concerns, one of his friends told him, "Heck, I've had that for twenty-years, you've got nothing to worry about." The truth was the friend was telling a white lie, but it made the old gentleman feel much better.

The Sacramento State of Mind

When asked what attracts them to Sacramento, many people say it is Sacramento's proximity to both the mountains and the sea. Drive two hours to the east and you are in the Sierra Mountains. Drive two hours to the west and you are at the beach. The adult ego is sort of like Sacramento. From the adult ego, whenever it's appropriate, you can access the child or parent ego. Sometimes it's highly appropriate to be childlike, and other times more controlled and authoritative. If you are psychologically balanced, it is always easy to return to the adult ego. It's a very short drive. For this reason, I sometimes refer to the adult ego as the Sacramento State of Mind.

Classifying Leisure Activities

No discussion on leisure would be complete without looking at some of the systems used to classify leisure activities, events, and behaviors. Classification systems contribute to the language of recreation and leisure and help us communicate ideas about leisure involvement. But, how does an activity classification relate to you? I like to think of classification systems (some people call them taxonomies) as leisure menus.

By being familiar with the rich array of activities available to us, we can make better decisions when it comes to partaking of the leisure lifestyle.

Classification of Activities by Form

MITCHELL AND MASON (1934). Mason and Mitchell designed a three-fold classification system wherein activities were divided according to whether they were primarily "motor, sensory, or intellectual" (101). This classification system can be diagrammed as shown below.

This early classification system possesses a certain theoretical elegance, which lends it credibility even in this era of technology and scientific sophistication.

MEYER AND BRIGHTBILL (1948). Meyer and Brightbill argued that classifying recreational activities in broad categories such as mental, physical, cultural, and social was unsatisfactory (364). It was their contention that every activity possessed all of these characteristics in some degree. Identifying the most predominant attribute could be very challenging in the case of most activities. Consequently, they argued for a classification system based on the outward form of the activity. As they put it, "When one studies the field. . . definitely established areas appear which lend themselves to classification. . . (364)." Alphabetically, the areas they identified are as follows:

- Arts and crafts
- Dancing
- Dramatics
- Literary activities
- Music
- Nature and outings
- Social events
- Sports and organized games

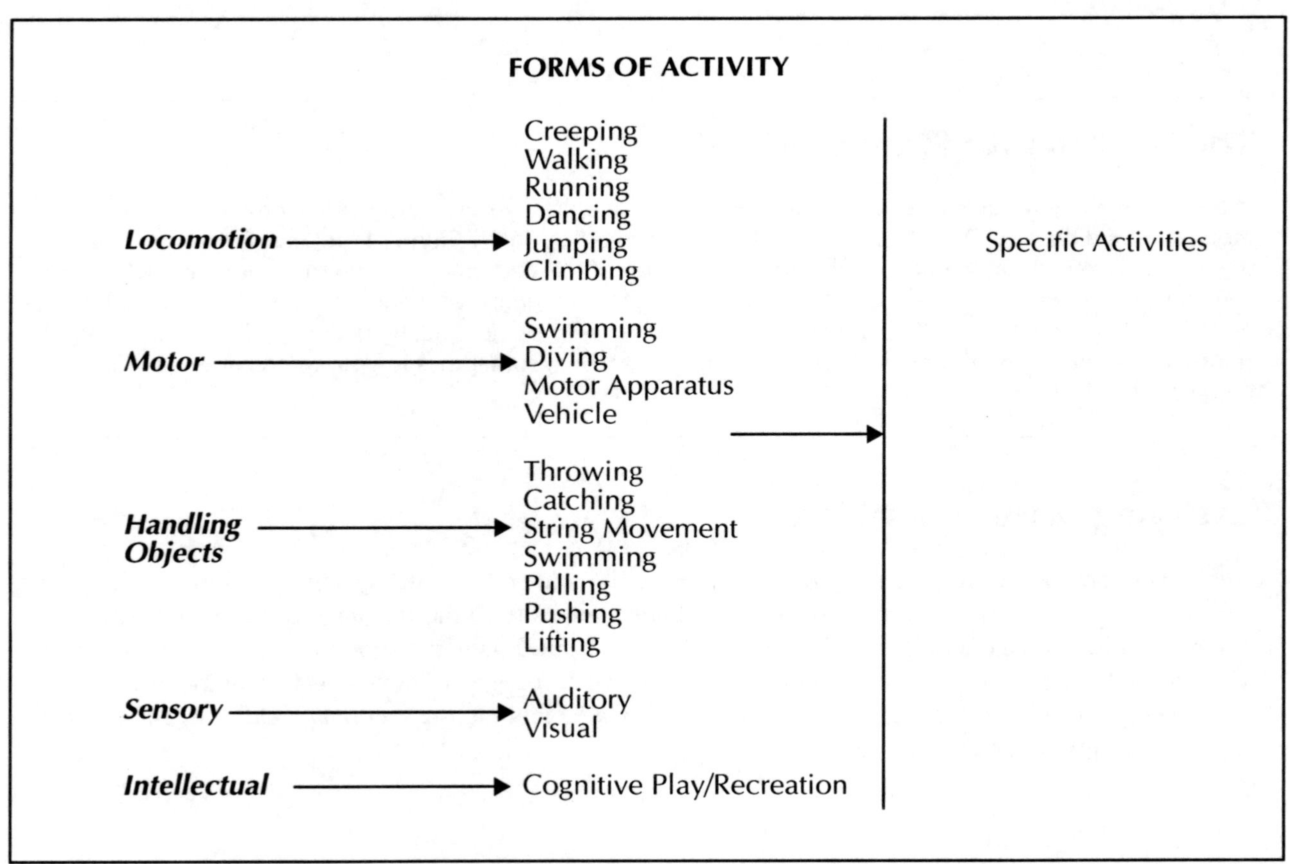

ROGER CAILLOIS (1961). French sociologist Roger Caillois directed his analysis to the classification of games, but even so, this system has application to the broader category of general leisure activities. Caillois suggests there are four basic types of activities: *agon, alea, mimicry and ilinx.* (Kraus 26–27).

1. *Agon* refers to activities that are competitive in nature. Winners are determined through skill, strength, creativity, etc. Activities of this sort involve risk and reward and are typified by most sport and athletic contests and many card and table games.
2. The second category, *alea*, refers to games of chance. The Great California Lottery is an example of such an activity.
3. Illusions or imaginary play or entertainment based on imitation is the basis for the category referred to as *mimicry*. It even includes such activities as movies and theater.
4. Finally, Caillois suggests a fourth category which consists of play activities based on the pursuit of vertigo or dizziness. This category includes all games and activities that affect the physiological sense of balance. Popular *ilinx* activities include some forms of dancing, amusement park rides, skiing, hang gliding, etc. Drugs and alcohol are included under this category.

The English equivalents to the Latin terms used by Caillois are Competition, Chance, Imitation, and Vertigo (Bammel and Bammel 72).

CARLSON, DEPPE AND MACLEAN (1963). In their book, *Recreation and American Life*, these authors identify 11 categories of leisure activities. They are as follows:

Arts and crafts
Dance
Drama
Mental, linguistic and literary
Music
Outdoor recreation
Social recreation
Sports and games
Hobbies
Service activities
Special events

OVERS, TAYLOR AND ADKINS (1968). No doubt, the most complete of the classifications systems, the *Avocational Index Inventory*, classifies 999 separate activities. It utilizes a three-level, triple-digit system. On the first level, nine major categories are identified; each category is assigned a single-digit designation:

100 Games
200 Sports
300 Nature Activities
400 Collection Activities
500 Craft Activities
600 Art and Music Activities
700 Educational, Entertainment and Cultural Activities
800 Volunteer Activities
900 Organizational Activities

The activities are then further divided into second-level divisions using a second-digit designation. For example, under Category 100–Games, you see:

100 Games
110 Active Games
120 Target and Skill Games
130 Table and Board Games
140 Card Games
150 Knowledge and Word Games
160 Puzzles
170 Model Racing Games
180 Miscellaneous

The third level adds a third digit which can be illustrated by looking at 110 Active Games:

110 Active Games
111 Running Games, e.g., tag, hide-and-seek, flags, pom-pom, etc.
112 Throwing Games, e.g., catch, frisbee, keep away, etc.
113 Indoor Games, e.g. musical chairs, Simon says, dunking, etc...and on to 119.

One attractive aspect of this approach is that it tends to be somewhat dynamic, flexible enough to accommodate new activities as they are developed. The author points out that since the first version, many new activities have been added.

RICHARD KRAUS' CLASSIFICATION (1978). Prominent recreation educator, and leisure scholar, Richard Kraus, classifies recreation by the following categories (Kraus, 1978):

1. popular sports, including both participant and spectator,
2. outdoor recreation, including activities such as fishing, camping and boating,
3. travel and tourism,
4. other forms of commercial entertainment and cultural activity,
5. various forms of recreation centered around real estate, residential communities and shopping centers,
6. gambling,
7. television,
8. technologically-based activities, and
9. miscellaneous hobbies.

MARKETING RESEARCH (1983). The leisure classification system used in market research tends to define leisure in terms of a specific market. Guided more by pragmatic than philosophical concerns, this type of classification is designed to be used in the acquisition of reliable and valid data to assist in marketing decisions. The Opinion Research Corporation leisure activities classification is illustrative of this approach to leisure activity classification.

1. Active Sports
   —swimming
   —fishing
   —camping
   —jogging
   —bowling
   —tennis
   —hunting
   —rollerskating
   —skiing
   —golf
   —ice skating
   —racquetball
2. Volunteer Activities
3. Home Oriented Activities
   —exercise
   —gardening
   —cooking
   —woodworking
   —needlework
   —sewing
   —coin collecting
   —stamp collecting
4. Social Events
   —movies
   —sporting events
   —live performances
   —museums
   —cafes/discos

BIPOLAR CLASSIFICATION. Loesch and Wheeler in their book, *Principles of Leisure Counseling* (1982), suggest that it is "helpful to look at leisure activities in terms of their various potential dynamics." A convenient way to do this is to elaborate on some possible bipolar dimensions of leisure activities (38). In this type of classification system, activities are placed on a continuum, where the opposite ends of the continuum are represented by descriptions viewed to be bipolar or consisting of diametrically opposed attributes.

Loesch and Wheeler identify 12 bipolar dimensions:

1. Individual vs. Group
2. Intellectual vs. Non-intellectual
3. Competitive vs. Non-competitive
4. Active vs. Passive
5. Physical vs. Non-physical
6. Short Terms vs. Continuing
7. Vocation Congruent vs. Vocation Incongruent
8. Self Oriented vs. Other Oriented
9. Person Centered vs. Product Centered
10. High Risk vs. Low Risk
11. Expensive vs. Inexpensive
12. Essential vs. Optimal

BOLLES LEISURE MAP (1981). Richard Bolles in his *Three Boxes of Life and How to Get Out of Them* presents an interesting way to organize one's leisure. He divides leisure activities into two broad categories: Those you do alone, and those you do in the presence of or with others. A second dimension is included in this model: activities are classified by energy expenditure. For example, sitting watching television is a rather passive activity requiring little energy; a fast game of racquetball is a real energy consumer. He sees activities as falling on a continuum of low energy use to high energy use. This continuum is viewed as having four basic activity groups: (1) killing time, (2) celebrating, (3) achieving something, and (4) competing against self or others. The following chart illustrates this model:

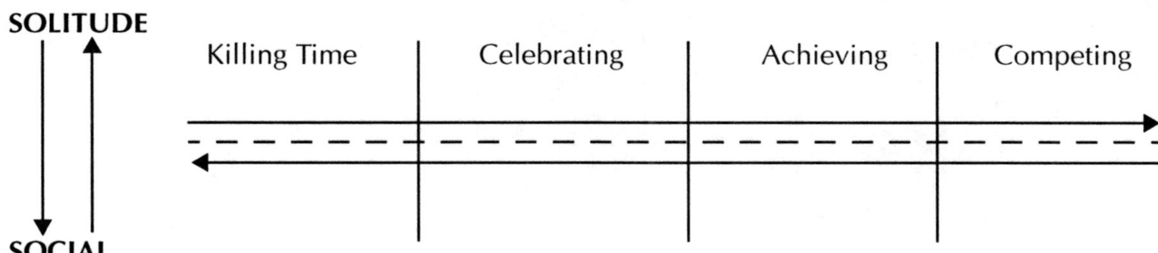

Bolles uses this model as a means of getting people to analyze the kinds of activities that they can do during leisure. Rather than provide them with a list, they are encouraged to identify activities that they enjoy and then fit them somewhere on the leisure map. Bolles uses an octagon for the actual mapping exercise, but this gives you an idea as to how a leisure map is created. Note, the vertical line between activities done in solitude and those done socially is also a continuum (380–390).

Classification by Development Value

Recreation activities gain importance to the extent to which they help people grow.

—Sarah Louise Williams

J.B. NASH. This is one of my favorites. Nash was a philosopher and educator, particularly prominent during the 1950's. He argued that recreation activities could be categorized by the extent to which they contribute to personal growth. He believed that recreation/leisure activities were by their very nature positive. Activities which produced negative outcomes consequently could not be construed as recreation. He realized, however, that not all free time activities would be of "worthwhile nature" and although not deserving classification as leisure activity should be accounted for nonetheless. He handled this problem by viewing non-recreational, free time activities as representing the mirror image of his leisure classifications.

Essentially, Nash saw leisure activities as occurring on four levels. These he portrayed as a pyramid not only because such a diagram suggested ascending value, but also due to the quantity of human energy believed directed toward each. At the base, Nash placed watching activities for distraction or mild entertainment. This is the spectator level. The next level shows more intense involvement and is marked by emotional intensity. Active participation is the next level, followed by the highest level, which Nash refers to as the creative level. The following diagram is my interpretation of Nash's conceptualization (89). Note, I have indicated the degree of positivity and negativity with the greatest of either falling at the extremes of the continuum. Although some spectator experiences might be very positive, Nash would be inclined to argue that the most positive yields come from creative activity.

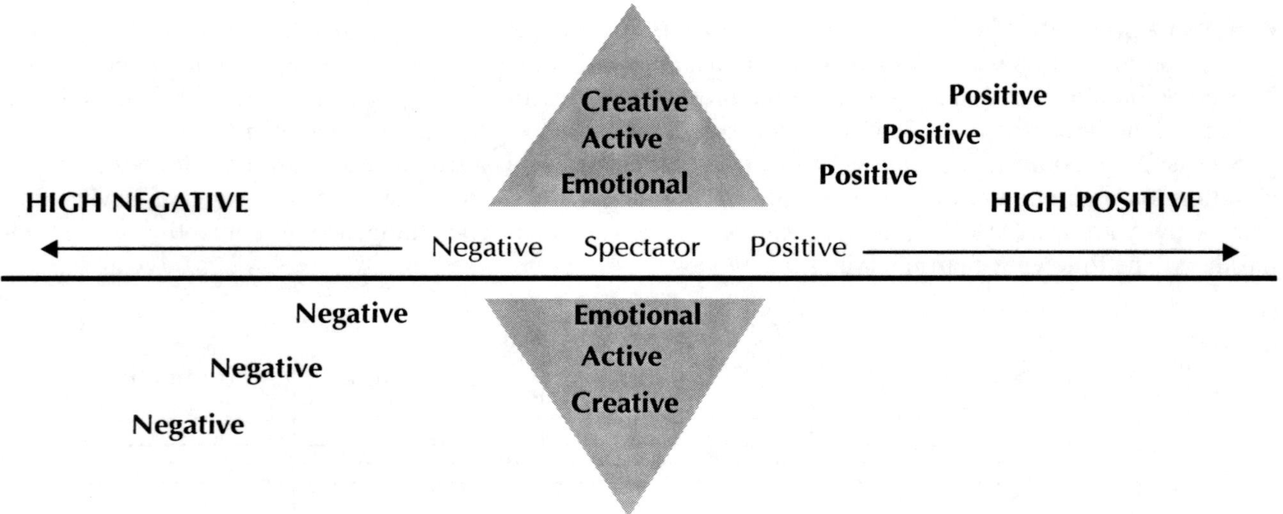

Classifying Activities By Motivation

Some activities can be linked with specific motivations. For example, people strongly motivated by a need for physical risk may seek involvement in such activities as hang gliding or sky diving. A collection of activities categorized by degree of physical risk might be of heuristic value for the person motivated by such a need. Consequently, there may be utility in classifying activities according to the motivations they serve.

> If the outcome is good, what's the difference between motives that sound good, and good sound motives.
>
> —Laurence J. Peter

As early as 1934, Mitchell and Mason recognized the value of using motives as a means of classifying recreation activities. Although they also advocate classifying activities by "outward form," they point out that it is the "motives of the players that determine the character of the play" (114). They identified six general motives, or as they called them, "types of wishes," believed to be common to all people. These six wishes formed the basis for their classification system. This system is summarized as follows:

Motives	Activities
A wish for new experiences	Fighting Competition Hunting Curiosity Roving Speed Creativeness
A wish for security	Flight and avoidance of danger Acquisition Imitation Religion
A wish for response	Sociability Courtship and mating Parental love Boon friendship Altruism
A wish for recognition	Desire for membership in groups Desire for affiliation with causes
A wish for the aesthetic	Desire for beauty in color Desire for beauty in form Desire for beauty in sound Desire for beauty in motion Desire for rhythm in general

In 1979, Tinsley and Kass (in Beard and Ragheb, 1983) undertook a study of the need dimensions met by involvement in leisure activities. They factor analyzed undergraduate students on 45 need dimensions. Following a factor analysis of their data, they discovered ten factors or motivations believed to be met through involvement in leisure activity. They named these motivations as follows:

Self-Actualization
Companionship
Power
Compensation
Security
Social service
Intellectualism
Aestheticism
Exercise
Self-Esteem
Self-Control

In 1983, Beard and Ragheb identified 49 "reasons" for engaging in leisure activities. These reasons were the basis of the items comprising a survey instrument that was administered to 1,205 subjects. Four factors were extracted: (1) an intellectual motive, (2) a competence/mastery motive, (3) a social motive, and (4) a stimulus avoidance motive.

In 1985, students in a recreation class at California State University (n = 40) were asked to complete the statement, "I participate in leisure activities that. . ." The results of the survey were content analyzed and 20 motives identified (Olson, 1985). This study suggests that college age students seek activities for the following reasons.

entertainment	novelty	solitude	social
competition	risk	intellectual	physical
skill	play	sexual	creativity
attention	outdoors/nature	sensuality	rhythm
emotional	self-enriching	philanthropic	familiar/safe

These 20 motives cross activity boundaries, thus allowing several specific activities to be related by motive. Some activities are clearly social whereas others tend to be of a solitary nature, but in selecting an activity other less dominant motives must be considered. One might be seeking a solitary, but novel, activity in the outdoors which is self-enriching. By understanding one's motives for selecting an activity, activity selection itself becomes a more objective and rational task.

Specific activities may change, but it is believed that motives are relatively enduring. Motives may be positive or negative, thus accounting for negative behavior during recreational activities. Although some motivations may be categorized as negative, most people are prompted to engage in recreation for positive reasons. This is demonstrated in the above list of leisure activity motivations. All twenty can easily be construed as being of a positive nature.

The question must be raised as to what extent leisure activity motivations are known to the leisure participant. It is quite likely that a goodly portion of leisure behavior is influenced by subconscious factors. Other behavior may be influenced by masked motivations, i.e. motivations not clearly seen or understood by the doer. An individual may engage in competitive behavior because of a high need to demonstrate dominance, but is unable to verbalize this motivation because of a lack of self-understanding and motivational awareness. Similarly, an individual may avoid competition because of a lack of confidence or an inability to cope with losing. One of the principal limitations of using a motivation based system is the inability to detect hidden motives.

To have personal value to an individual, a classification scheme must contribute to self-enlightenment regarding one's leisure activity potential. By merely looking at the kinds of activities one prefers, some idea as to the underlying motivations may be suggested. In this scheme, specific activities are ignored and the individual is asked to focus his/her *perceived motivations*. Activities are then fitted to the motivational pattern.

Closing Notes. . .

In this unit we first looked at the meanings of the words recreation, play, leisure, and games. Leisure was presented from two basic perspectives. The quantitative perspective presents leisure as a measurable block of obligation-free time. The qualitative point of view describes leisure as a state of mind characterized essentially by perceived freedom and intrinsic satisfaction. Play was described as a nonutilitarian expression of one's need for optimal arousal. Certain characteristics were identified as attributes of play. Recreation was explored using the same attributes, and shown in many respects to be just the opposite of play. For example, play is spontaneous, recreation is planned. Games were viewed from the recreation perspective and the interpersonal perspective. Whereas recreational games contribute to the leisure lifestyle, it was shown that interpersonal games can have the opposite effect.

This unit also looked at ways professional recreators classify recreational activities. Most classifications categorize activities by the form that the activities take. J.B. Nash classifies activities by how they contribute to an individual's personal development. Some leisure scholars, including Mitchell and Mason, advocate classifying activities by the motivational needs they meet in the participants.

In 1963, Carlson, Deppe and Maclean said that any approach to recreation program classification is "arbitrary and will meet with conflict" (362). Of course, that is partly due to the dynamic nature of leisure activities. Technology and social change are forever producing new activities, thus making only the broadest categories viable for any period of time. Of course, the broader the category, the least likely it will be much value. It is believed that human motives may be relatively stable, and hence serve as a useful basis for classifying activities.

REFERENCES

Bammel, G. and L.L. Burrus-Bammel. *Leisure and Human Behavior.* Dubuque, Iowa: Wm. C. Brown Company, Publishers, 1982.

Beard, J.G. and M.G. Ragheb. "Measuring Leisure Motivation." *The Journal of Leisure Research* 16.3 (1984): 219–227.

Berne, E., M.D. *Games People Play.* New York: Ballantine Books, 1964.

Bolles, R.J. *The Three Boxes of Life and How to Get Out of Them.* Berkeley: Ten Speed Press, 1981.

Brightbill, C.K. *The Challenge of Leisure.* Englewood Cliffs, NJ: Prentice-Hall, 1960.

ibid.

Carlson, R.E., T.R. Deppe and Janet R. Maclean. *Recreation in American Life.* Belmont, CA: Wadsworth Publishing Company, Inc., 1963.

De Grazia, S. *Of Time, Work and Leisure.* New York: Anchor Books, 1962.

Dumazedier, J. *Toward a Society of Leisure.* New York: Free Press, 1967.

Ellis, M.J. *Why People Play?* Englewood Cliffs, NJ: Prentice-Hall Inc., 1973.

Kaplan, M. *Leisure: Theory and Policy.* NY: Wiley and Sons, 1975.

Kraus, Richard. *Recreation Today: Program Planning and Leadership.* Pacific Palisades, CA: Goodyear Publishing Company, Inc., 1966.

Kraus, R *Recreation and Leisure in Modern Society.* NY: Appleton-Century-Crofts, 1980.

Lee, R. *Religion and Leisure in America: A Study in Four Dimensions.* New York: Abingdon Press, 1964.

Meyer, H.D. and C.K. Brightbill. *Recreation Administration: A Guide to Its Practices.* Englewood Cliffs, NJ: Prentice-Hall, Inc., 1948.

Mitchell, E.D. and B.E. Mason. *The Theory of Play.* New York: A.S. Barnes and Company, 1937.

Murphy, J.F. and D. Howard. *Delivery of Community Leisure Services: A Holistic Approach.* Philadelphia: Lea and Febiger, 1977.

Nash, J.B. *Philosophy of Recreation and Leisure.* St. Louis: The C.V. Mosby Company, 1953.

Neulinger, J. *The Psychology of Leisure.* Springfield, Illinois: Charles C. Thomas, 1974

ibid.

Neumeyer, M.H., and E.S. Neumeyer. *Leisure and Recreation* (rev. ed.). NY: The Ronald Press Company, 1958.

Overs, R.P., S. Taylor and C. Adkins. *Avocational Counseling Manual.* Washington D.C.: Hawkins and Associates, Inc., 1977.

Olson, E.G. "Motivations of Leisure Behavior among College Students." California State University, Sacramento: Unpublished Manuscript, 1985.

Peter, L.J. *The Humor Prescription.* NY: Ballantine Books, 1986.

Rombold, P. Personal communication. Sacramento, September 16, 1989.

Stebbins, R. 1992. Amateurs, Professionals, and Serious Lesiure. Montreal, Quebec: McGill-Queen's University Press.

Stebbins, R. "Project-Based Leisure: Theoretical Neglect of a Common Use of Free Time." Found in *Leisure Studies,* Vol. 24, No. 1, 1–11, January 2005.

Webster's New Collegiate Dictionary. Copyright 1975, by G. and C. Merriam Co.

Webster, R. *Philosophy of Physical Education.* Dubuque, Iowa: William C. Brown Co., 1976.

CHAPTER 5

On Play and Being Playful

In the play of children you can get a glimpse at life's greater purpose.

—Sara Louise Williams

> We were in Hawaii. My son, Trevor, was only ten. He was all eyes and action. He was filled with curiosity mixed with the innocence of childhood. He was enthusiastic about everything and seemingly powered by an endless supply of energy. My daughters were there as well; however, they were older, calmer, and in comparison to Trevor, much easier to manage. I could generally count on the girls not getting into trouble. As for Trevor, I could count on him doing his best to avoid trouble but finding it anyway.
>
> We were spending the day at Hanauma Bay. My oldest daughter had proved a fearless snorkeler, but it seemed she found sun tanning more appealing. My second daughter had frightened herself from out of the water when she caught a glimpse of one of her own fins and thought she was being stalked by a shark. Trevor on the other hand viewed the bay as a great, wondrous, aquatic playground. He snorkeled with great abandon. A fogged lens didn't slow him down. He swam past the breakwater out into the deep water. He caught cresting waves and rode them as far as they would take him, then paddled back for more. And, when my own exhaustion compelled me to go in, he cheerfully swam along, all the while asking when he could go back out again.
>
> I recently visited Hawaii again. I again swam in Hanauma Bay, but this time the little boy was not at my side. I couldn't help but reflect on that earlier time, and how I would like to visit not just the bay but that day in 1984 when Trevor and I rode the waves and swam with tropical fish.

The government ought to require that on every calendar sold in America, the following words should appear: WARNING! The dates on this calendar are closer than they appear.

Bringing Play into Perspective

I recently spoke to a student who confided in me that she didn't know how to play. From her perspective play was frivolous, unproductive and undesirable. Her day was devoted to "productive" tasks. She looked at the world through serious eyes, and lived within a body wracked with stress. She was only 25. That was two years younger than a friend of mine, who subscribed to a similar work ethic. At twenty-two my friend was in her first year of medical school. She worked hard, graduated and entered her internship. By the time she became a resident, at age 27, she was deeply disturbed, very unhappy and convinced that she was inadequate to the tasks of her profession. One day she left the hospital and drove her Volkswagen from off a cliff near Santa Cruz, California. She too was unable to play.

In our quest for success, we are told to work hard, to sacrifice, to struggle, to focus and in the process we become narrow in our scope, and like a tightrope walker, the more narrow our path the more difficult it is to find a balance point. As human beings we are more than just our work, more than just the things the money produced by our work enables us to buy, more than the status accorded us by our work. A unidimensional individual has nothing against which he can achieve a balance. It is only when you embrace your multidimensionality that you can begin to develop a balanced perspective. As a human you have a potential for love, for creativity, for compassion, for rhythm, for movement, for passion and yes, even play. Unfortunately, for many of us these very human qualities have been sacrificed to the God of Mammon. In our quest for all that money can buy, we have traded a treasure trove of pleasure for material possessions. And, so we enter into the adult world, knowing that something is missing from our lives and thinking that we'll find it if we work a little harder, narrow our focus, strive with a single minded purpose, make more money.

When our middle child was three years of age, we enrolled her in a university laboratory school. Everyday after my work, I would stop by and watch her through the one-way glass. The children in the lab were wonderful to watch. They were so in touch with their humanness. They were a sea of motion, until their little bodies called out for rest, and then they were a sea of tranquillity as they napped. When they were happy they laughed, when they were unhappy they cried. They touched, and hugged and kissed, and ate and drank with exuberance. They danced and acted, climbed and fell, chased and were chased. They drew marvelous pictures of worlds that I on a clear day can dimly remember. They were as Persig would say, "At the head of the train of their own awareness." They were alive, and they were in touch with life's well spring. The were explorers and pleisurists.

There have been countless times, when reflecting on the joy of my childhood, that I have heard my conscious mind say, "Gee, I wish I could be a kid again." And, when I reflect on my college days, I often hear myself say, "Oh to be twenty-one again" And, with few exceptions, when I think back on pleasant times, I often long for yesterday.

> Time is sure fun when you're casting flies.
>
> —C. Garth Olson

When I reflect on pleasant memories, I see a commonality. As a child I had great adventures, riding imaginary ponies, exploring wonderful hideouts, and flying intricately hand-crafted space craft. I remember playing touch football on the hospital lawn, playing tag on the school ground, raiding the girls' slumber party, having snowball fights, and playing catch on the roadway in front of my house. I remember my first date, my first kiss, my first dance with a girl who seemed to like me. I remember summers spent playing in the band and working at a supermarket. In all of the memories, whether passionate, sexual, social, athletic, or artistic, there was a special element that did much to make the activities memorable. Common to all of those pleasant moments was play, the spontaneous, supercharger of emotions and maker of memories.

As we get older there seems to be forces at work to minimize our ability to generate memorable experiences. It starts when we are very young and usually at the hands of well meaning parents who have grown to believe that work is the ultimate good to which one should strive, and play being the antithesis of work is something that, although tolerated in children, must ultimately be suppressed if one is to be successful. So consequently, it is not uncommon for parents to admonish children to, "stop acting like a child," "to stop playing around," or "to grow up." In some families the fine line between adulthood and childhood is the line beyond which play no longer exists. To extinguish one's capacity for play is to eliminate an important part of the life equation, a part that can never be filled by some other factor. When play is eliminated, the capacity for pleisure is compromised and discovery stifled. Few pleasant memories for future reflection can be generated by one who cannot play. Without play, a balanced life is no more possible than flight is for a bird with only one wing.

Within recent years modern science has turned its attention to play. Without exception, the scientific investigation of play has revealed that play is both natural and learned, is linked with feelings of pleasure, satisfaction and well-being, and essential to one's physical and emotional health. In scientific terms, play can be thought of as a nonspecific attempt to achieve optimal physiological arousal through behaviors for which there is no apparent utilitarian value. (A poet might argue that there is great utilitarian value in a joyful memory.) Furthermore, it can be viewed as a state of mind characterized by a sense of freedom and an abundance of positive feelings. In other words, during play we are free from external issues and concerns and plugged into our most basic human feelings. It is during play that we biologically function best. Harmful stress and play are mutually exclusive conditions. During play we are like the children in the lab school; we can focus on the experience of the moment, free from external interference. It is play that allows us to find rapture during sex, laughter during humor, thrill during movement, and self-expression during art. And, it is play that makes the memories of many of those times to which we wish we could return.

Reclaiming and Preserving Your Birthright to Play

Perhaps you haven't lost it, but the older you are the greater the probability that your capacity for playful behavior has been whittled away by social and biological forces. There will always be those around you who criticize your penchant for play, there will always be authority figures to admonish you to be more serious, and there will always be someone admonishing you to work harder and produce more. And, if that weren't enough, disregarding the protests of the ego, the body slowly succumbs to the aging process. Hearing and sight diminish, skin loses its flexibility (as do the joints), strength and endurance decrease, taste buds lose their discriminatory powers, and centers of gravity shift lower. Although at the root of play, in the long term, our biology is no more its friend than the antiquated philosophies of the Puritan Work Ethic.

A person who embraces play, who makes it an important factor in his/her lifestyle tends to age more slowly than less playful people. This has been demonstrated empirically, and on a personal level by my Aunt Christa who, in spite of being robbed of her physical vitality by the aging process, never lost her sense of playfulness. She often said, "I may be old, but I haven't grown up and don't intend to." Aunt Christa believed that inside everyone was the "child-self" just waiting to get out. My last conversation with her occurred just after she had been released from the hospital. Glaucoma had robbed her of her sight, a stroke damaged her coordination, and thus, unable to see or move effectively she was further disabled when a fall broke her hip. I called to see how she was doing, with a chuckle tickling her voice she responded, "Well, I'm not dead yet." Up to the end she maintained her sense of humor and playful perspective.

How does one keep in touch with the child within? Unfortunately, I know of no formula guaranteed to access your potential for play. Nor do I know of a formula to guarantee that you won't lose your inherent potential for play. I do know that if you don't use it you will lose it. And, I do know that as you get older your probability of engaging in playful behavior diminishes. I also believe, that as you get older, the value that play can hold for you increases. That is, the more factors arise which fight the play experience, the more important it is that we stimulate play behaviors.

Discovering the Dimensions of Play

The word play is derived from an Anglo Saxon word ***plega***, meaning a game or sport, a skirmish or battle. Similarly, it is related to the Latin word ***plaga***, which means stroke or thrust. Today the word play has come to have several meanings. On one hand, it is viewed in much the same way as its ancestral terms—the "course or conduct of a game," but it is also viewed as to frolic, to have sexual relations, to appear in the press, to operate on the basis of a hunch, to perform on a musical instrument, to act out in a dramatic manner, even to "discharge as from a hose." As an example of the ways that we use the word play, examine the following sentence.

> *The musician played his instrument, while the gambler played out his hunch that the local team would not play well. Meanwhile, downtown a fire roared, upon which the fireman played a stream of water. Before it had played out, the fire had caused the cancellation of a Broadway play, and had caused the lovers in the balcony to stop playing around. Unwilling to play along, the newspaper gave the story full play. Later the gambler made a play for the musician's girl. As for the girl, she played her stereo, while the light from a neon light played on her face.*

Play from the standpoint of the leisure explorer is all of this, but much more. For the pleasurist, play is primarily a self-directed activity, usually of short duration, but capable of producing intense feelings of satisfaction. More specifically play can be thought of as any activity possessing the following characteristics:

Spontaneity. Play is rarely planned. It normally just happens, and it happens at the strangest times. It happens when you are at work, when you are recreating, when you are having lunch, when you are making love. Play just seems to happen. I recall one time sitting in a very solemn meeting with two of my friends. We were in high school. Sam Moore started pulling faces at Richard and me. This triggered a playful response, mirth set in and the meeting was spent trying to conceal our playful mood.

Transient. Play doesn't usually last very long. It suddenly emerges, swelling like a wave, and then, rapidly dissipates or merges into another behavior or emotion. Love making is a wonderful example. Frequently, a sexual encounter begins with tickling or some other playful behavior only to give way to a more intense and satisfying behavior. Play emerges during boring stretches of work, provides a brief release from drudgery and then subsides. Even during times of trauma, great stress or illness we find play emerging to momentarily free us from discomfort and boost our spirits.

Independent of Things. Play needs neither equipment nor facilities. All play requires is a creative mind, nothing else is essential in order for play to occur. Some of our best play occurs in our minds. Fanciful trips, amazing adventures, amorous encounters, can all be generated by the cerebral cortex. And, of course, when two or more people find themselves sharing a playful mood, joyous conversations ensue, flirting, teasing and humor all follow.

Intrinsically Rewarding. Play is self-nurturing. Something happens during play that makes us feel good about ourselves, it makes us feel healthier, happier, smarter, more physically capable and even better looking. We engage in it not because of some external reward, but rather because we enjoy the feelings produced by it.

Goal Free. We live in a goal oriented world. And, even though much of our life revolves around goals and objectives, play is amazingly goal free. When it happens, it is usually so captivating that we lose track of the goals and objectives that direct much of our behavior. We forget about our worries and our fears. We get caught up in a wonderful stream of emotion, which for a short period of time frees us from the burdens we bear and the heaviness most of us carry.

Suspends Reality. During play one's focus narrows. The relevant becomes irrelevant and for a time all that matters is the moment. During play, one's cares and worries are forgotten; one's social roles give way to imaginary roles; and the only reality that really matters is the activity at hand.

Provokes Laughter. It is usually easy to spot a person at play, because people at play invariably smile and laugh. In fact, next time you are at play try to suppress this natural tendency. I once watched two my of students, caught in a playful mood attempt to suppress their giggles. Unfortunately, they were unable to, and since smiles and laughter tend to be contagious, most of the class (including the professor) soon found themselves in the same condition. One of the nicest attributes of play is its capacity to generate a sense of humor. And of course, without a sense of humor life can be a very dreary proposition.

A person without a sense of humor is like a wagon without springs, jolted by every pebble in the road.

—Henry Ward Beecher

Play Always Produces Leisure. Play invariably is associated with the two principal characteristics of leisure: intrinsic satisfaction and perceptual freedom. It is the ability of play to generate leisure that makes play so valuable in lessening the harmful effects of living in an uptight world.

Some Other Facts about Play

PLAY IS UNIVERSALLY FOUND AMONG MAMMALS. Recently, during a visit to the Sacramento City Zoo, my attention was caught by noise coming from a crowd gathered in front of the bear exhibit. There must have been 50 people crowded along the guard rail along the mote which kept the bears protected from the spectators. The crowd oohed and awed and applauded. I was puzzled by their behavior. Normally zoo spectators are much quieter, more like museum visitors, but clearly these folks were being entertained. I finally found a position from which I could observe the bears in action. And in action they were. They were having a wonderful time—playing. As humans we have a special sense of appreciation for animals that tend to play freely. Indeed one of the major reasons that dog is man's best friend is the canine's playful nature.

PLAY IS VOLUNTARY. You cannot force someone to have fun. Neither can you structure or organize play into your schedule. Play occurs only after we give ourselves permission—to play.

PLAY COVERS A WIDE RANGE OF BEHAVIOR. Play is not limited to one type of behavior, rather it is a behavior that can occur in other behavioral contexts. Consequently, we find play in the classroom, in the courtroom, in the kitchen and even in the operating room. In many respects play seems to play a cathartic role, allowing people in relatively serious situations to release tension and pressure. Its transient nature allows this to occur in a rather brief period, thus enabling the principal task to continue without significant interruption. In addition the release provided by play usually contributes to a more effective completion of the dominant task.

I think the next best thing to solving a problem—is finding some humor in it.

—Frank Clark

PLAY IS CARRIED ON BY BOTH CHILDREN AND ADULTS. Unfortunately too many people believe that play is only acceptable for children. The fact is that it is as acceptable and important for adults as it is for children. Play has therapeutic and developmental value. Within recent years, we have seen the emergence of the field of therapeutic recreation. This field has as its basic purpose the application of play, recreation, and leisure to clinical settings. Furthermore, thanks to the research of people such as Piaget and Erikson, we have come to understand that play is essential for satisfactory cognitive, affective, psychological, physical, and social development. As children, play helps us learn about our world, strengthen our bodies, and help us learn to relate to others. As adults, play helps us maintain our physical health, our mental well being, and social relationships.

Play is a self-nurturing activity, a self-initiated kind of therapy.
Not everything that is faced is changed, but nothing is changed until it is faced.

—James Baldwin

Personal Leisure Laboratory Activities to Promote Play

At your next party or social event, see if you can promote playful behavior among your guests by using the following activities:

COURAGEOUS CLOTHESPIN GRAB. Guests are each given ten clothespins and told to wear them in such a manner that it would be difficult for another guest to steal one. The object of the game is to steal as many clothespins from others while trying to prevent the theft of your own. Naturally the guest with the most clothespins is considered the winner. An alternative is to try to get rid of the pins by attaching them to other guests.

SLAMMERS AND CREEPERS. Played at a table, this game is always a hit. No props are necessary, aside from one coin per team. Players are divided into two groups with a spokesperson for each team. Teams sit across from one another at the same table. One team passes a coin from hand to hand under the table while trying to conceal its movements from the other team. The other team tries to discover who has the coin. The spokesperson of the guessing team starts the guessing procedure by saying to the team with the coin, "Elbows on the table." The coin passers must respond by putting their elbows on the table with their closed fists raised in full view of the opposing team.

The spokesperson of the guessing team then commands either "Slammers" or "Creepers." When "slammers" is called, the coin passers must clap their hands onto the table. The noise of the slapping hands usually conceals the sound of the coin. When "creepers" is called, the coin passers place their fists on the edge of the table and slowly extend their fingers, again being careful to conceal the coin. The guessing team may then consult with one another as to who has the coin. The spokesperson then points to the hand that the team believes conceals the coin. If they are right, they trade roles with the other team. If they are wrong, the person puts his empty fist on his lap and the game continues. Each hand placed on a lap counts as one point for the coin-passing team.

How Playful Are You?

Here is a little exercise for you. It is designed to measure the extent to which you can be described as a playful person. And, in a sense, since play is such an important aspect of pleisure, you might think of this scale also as an indicator of the extent to which you are a pleasurist.

Olson's Playfulness Scale

This questionnaire is designed to help you assess your current level of playfulness. Read each statement carefully and then enter the most appropriate response from the following scale:

STRONGLY AGREE=5 AGREE=4 UNDECIDED=3 DISAGREE=2 STRONGLY DISAGREE = 1

1 _______ I rarely take things too seriously.

2 _______ I can generally find a funny side to most things.

3 _______ I am pretty creative.

4 _______ I seldom get bored.

5 _______ I enjoy teasing my friends.

6 _______ It is easy for me to talk to strangers.

7 _______ People view me as a fun person.

8 _______ I can express myself in novel ways.

9 _______ I find it easy to have fun in public places.

10 _______ It is easy for me to be silly.

11 _______ I enjoy being teased.

12 _______ I enjoy solving problems in creative ways.

13 _______ I enjoy pulling little pranks on my friends.

14 _______ I enjoy the reactions I get from other people.

15 _______ I think it is fun to dress in a creative and playful manner.

16 _______ I often enjoy being around strangers.

17 _______ It is easy being around strangers.

18 _______ People seem to like to be around me.

19 _______ I think of myself as a playful person.

20 _______ Being playful makes me feel good.

To determine your score add the numerical values you chose for each item.

The sum of these is your playfulness score.

Write your score here:__________

What did you learn?

And So How Playful Are You?

An average score on this scale is 65. If you scored between 60 and 70 points, you are within the average range. Most people who have used this scale fall in this range. People scoring between 70 and 80 points are considered more playful than the average, and those scoring in the 90's are viewed as generally very playful. Those who score below 60 and above 50 are considered less playful than average, whereas those scoring lower than 50 are considerably below average. And, so where do you fall on this scale?

This scale does not measure actual incidents of playful behavior, but rather the extent to which one likely possesses a playful attitude. You can think of an attitude as the degree to which an individual is emotionally drawn toward or repelled from a certain object, in this case—play. Inasmuch as attitudes tend to precede behavior, it can be said that people scoring high on this scale are people who possess a relatively positive attitude toward playful behavior. Hence, if you are a high scorer on this scale, you are likely to demonstrate more playful behavior than someone who scored low on the scale. And, inasmuch as a sense of freedom as well as an appreciation for intrinsic rewards are characteristic of this type of a playful attitude, it is conceivable that the high scorer also tends to be less subject to stress, less likely to be inhibited, and more likely to view life from a balanced perspective. However, it should be pointed out, that although most of us could benefit from a more playful attitude, it is important that play be balanced against other important life variables (work, fitness, finances, family, education, marriage, friendships etc.). An overemphasis on play can have deleterious effects, and consequently, in some instances, the play prescription might wisely be directed at lessening play behaviors in order to bring about a better balance in an individual's life.

Implicit in much of what has been said earlier in this unit about play, is the notion that play has something to do with the extent to which an individual develops a balanced personality, physical and emotional wellness, and a satisfying lifestyle. What has not been pointed out is the idea that in order for play to make this contribution it must occur in proportion to other equally important factors. It, in and of itself, is not likely to lead to these important outcomes. In fact, it should be remembered that excess in any area is likely to subtract from other and perhaps equally important areas that contribute to human growth and development. In order for play to produce its optimum effect, it must be expressed in a balanced way. All play and no work may not yield as much satisfaction as a balance of play and work. A person who treats serious financial matters in a playful fashion, or who has difficulty taking interpersonal relationships in a responsible fashion, or who is cavalier about his responsibilities to others, runs the risk of creating a lifestyle rife with problems and unhappiness; the solution to life's problems cannot be found in playful behavior. A person who plays to the extent that he or she is rendered dysfunctional when faced with critical, traumatic or serious issues, is clearly a person who has failed to achieve balance in his or her life. Play is an important part of the life prescription, but it must be prescribed in the right proportions.

In prescribing play, and ultimately this is your responsibility, it is important to follow this axiom:

> Play should be encouraged to the extent to which it contributes to feelings of harmony between the various parts of one's personality as well as the extent to which one functions harmoniously with the elements that make up one's environment.

In other words, play is important as long as it contributes to the physical, psychological, emotional, and social well-being of an individual. When play distracts from one's ability to solve important problems, relate effectively with other people, or complete important tasks, then it can be said that play is dysfunctional, i.e. it is play behavior which does not help the individual function in an effective and healthy fashion. Play which contributes to the quality of one's life can be referred to as **functional play**, whereas play behavior which is counterproductive can be referred to as **dysfunctional play**. Similarly attitudes about play can be designated as functional or dysfunctional. The thrust in this book is to assist people in developing functional attitudes regarding play, and thus contribute to one's life by encouraging functional play. Although it may be a problem for some, few people are dysfunctional because of too much play. The majority of people can benefit from increasing their propensity and capacity to play. Consequently, in the this book the focus is on ways and means of increasing functional play attitudes and behaviors.

Play As Recess

A functional attitude toward play enables a person to use play as a means of coping with stressful situations, as a means of recharging one's energy or discharging tension. In addition, a functional play attitude contributes to an individual's ability to view life's circumstances, problems, and even crises in rational and when appropriate, in humorous ways.

> You grow up the day you have your first good laugh—at yourself
>
> —Ethel Barrymore

Recess Is an Opportunity for Discovery

In fact, it was during recess that some of my most memorable experiences occurred. Regardless how difficult a class was, I always had recess to look forward to, that break in the day when I could slip from the clutch of my teacher and race freely about the playground with my little colleagues. During recess a child can interact with his/her friends, release tension and stress, and for a short time suspend reality while the cognitive batteries are recharged. In many respects play behavior can serve the same function as recess, but because of its spontaneous nature and limitless boundaries, no bell need sound to legitimize its occurrence. Thus, play can occur at anytime or place to discharge tension, minimize stress and suspend reality for a few moments, resting the mind and recharging the spirit. Even during the most critical situations, play can be appropriate. I remember talking to a surgeon who related some of the jokes he had heard during surgery. He viewed humor (which is a verbal form of play) during surgery as very important in that it alleviated some of the stress and tension present during a serious operation. During boring or intensely serious meetings, I often find myself drawing humorous illustrations (another form of play) to help me minimize the boredom or cope with the intensity of the situation. Sometimes, the play behavior can be fleeting, lasting only for a few seconds, at other times it can last for hours, and in rare circumstances—days. I refer to those play experiences of very short durations, measured in minutes and seconds, as **microplay**. Those that extend beyond a few minutes I refer to as **macroplay**.

Microplay

Recently I attended a rather boring meeting. During this meeting I decided to record what I perceived to be examples of microplay. During the 2 hours that the meeting was in session I recorded 137 incidents of microplay distributed among the 37 people in attendance. I included behaviors which I viewed as spontaneous, non-task oriented, entertaining and of short duration. Granted this is not very scientific, and calls for conclusions strictly on *prima facie* evidence; nevertheless, the point is that during the two hours in which I observed the behavior of my colleagues, I witnessed behaviors that appeared to be entered into not because they contributed to the task at hand, but rather because they freed participants from boredom.

Among the behaviors observed were: doodling, playing with one's hands or other body parts (hair, nose and chins were particularly popular), playing with one's pencil or pen, staring at various objects about the room, closing eyes with head bent, closing eyes with head lifted, making humorous comments to the group, making humorous comments to nearby people, modeling with paper (one person was observed making a paper airplane), and one person was even observed playing with a rubber band.

Macroplay

Unlike microplay, macroplay can last for hours and even days. Due to the fact that in order for this to occur several conditions must be present, the probability of macroplay occurring is considerably less than the probable occurrence of microplay. The principal factors required for macroplay are: (1) adequate time and other resources to sustain the play experiences, (2) the appropriate attitude to generate and sustain the play experience, and (3) a social and physical environment conducive to play.

A friend once told me that she and her lover had difficulty sustaining play during the week. On weekends, however, when they were able to leave town and seek refuge at a bed and breakfast on the coast of Northern California, they were able to maintain play for hours at a time. By leaving their home environment and embarking on a weekend vacation, they symbolically were rejecting the forces and factors which impinged upon their ability to be playful. Once away from their home environment, they allowed their playful attitudes to surface, and sustained by a leisure environment engaged in playful activities for long periods of time. As she put it, "We could barely get along during the week, but our weekends were wonderful; we were so spontaneous and uninhibited, it is hard to believe we were the same people."

Examples of macroplay can be found in such activities as dancing, playing table games, flirting, foreplay, conversation, team and individual sports, entertainment events, and creative arts. The principal criteria for this type of play can be summarized thusly: (1) primarily spontaneous and uninhibited, (2) changes or suspends reality, (3) is engaged in for intrinsic reasons, (4) is characterized by feelings of energy, (5) seems to pass quickly and (6) is narrowly focused. Such events may in reality be a collection of individual play events, each of which feed into the larger event and thus give the appearance of a sustained or long term play activity. Regardless of the underlying structure of the event, the net result tends to be an intense feeling of satisfaction and pleisure. Such an event makes for an excellent recess.

Deciding in Favor of Play

Do you want more play in your life? Do you feel the quality of your life would be enhanced by more play behavior and a more playful attitude?

Before you offer a definitive answer, answer the following questions.

For each question, answer using the following five point scale:
Strong Yes = 5, Yes = 4, Undecided = 3, No = 2 and Strong No = 1.
After answering the questions total your points and multiply by 2.

1. Do you suffer from hypertension?
2. Do you feel that you have too much to do?
3. Is stress a problem in your life?

4. Are you dissatisfied with the quality of your interpersonal relationships?
5. Is your job a source of dissatisfaction?
6. Do you often feel bored or anxious?
7. Do you feel that others get more breaks (opportunities) than you?
8. Are you frequently worried about the ills and problems of society?
9. Does money pose a problem in your life?
10. Do you feel you never have enough time to do what you really want to do?

If you scored in the 90's you are in dire need of more play. You are under a great deal of stress, and although not a solution to the problems that contribute to such a high score, play can help you cope with those problems and simultaneously bring more joy and "pleisure" into your life. A score in the 80's is better, but still suggestive of a situation into which more functional play attitudes and behaviors is an important need. Similarly scores falling in the 60's and 70's suggest a need for additional play. Scores falling in the 50's indicate a lifestyle in which the role of play has not been clearly defined. Scores falling below 40 are indicative of a lifestyle in which one's play needs are adequately met, and where the emphasis should be on maintenance not necessarily change.

Reflect back to your score on the playfulness scale. Do you see a relationship between the score on this scale and the earlier score? If you scored high on the playfulness scale but low on this scale, the indication is that although you have a positive attitude toward play, your life's circumstances have caused you to suppress your natural tendency to play. Shame on you. The prescription here is clear—let your natural tendencies come to the surface. Let yourself play more. If you scored low on both scales, then the indication is that you need to develop a more functional play attitude, which then logically will contribute to a more playful lifestyle. In the next section we focus on ways and means of enhancing one's functional play attitude.

> Allowing yourself to be playful is the wisest thing you can do.
>
> —Jones Williams

On Becoming More Playful

> To stay healthy, you must prevent hardening of the attitudes.
>
> —Patsy Edwards

What ultimately determines one's ability to play is locked somewhere in the cerebral cortex and goes by the name attitude. An attitude can be described as a feeling or emotion toward some fact or thing. In psychological terms, we might say that attitude is the tendency to respond to some stimulus object in a predictable way. Inasmuch as the human mind can entertain countless attitudes, and inasmuch as attitudes are antecedent to behavior, we can argue that one's behavior is an indicator of the relative strength of one's attitudes. In other words, what determines whether or not we engage in a playful activity is determined by a complex of attitudes which we unconsciously weigh against one another. In individuals where the play attitude is strong, the probability of play is greater than in an individual where play is viewed in less positive terms. Consequently, in helping a person become more playful, a good starting point is at the root of the problem—one's attitudes.

Attitudes and interests (and behaviors) are basically learned. It is true that some people may exhibit behaviors that are the result of physiological imbalances caused by disease, diet or congenital problems, but these are the exception. For most people, the behaviors and attitudes that disrupt one's leisure are the product of prior experiences, the product of learning. Thus, assuming the absence of any physiological problems, to become a more playful person you will have to learn some new attitudes and perhaps unlearn some others. If one wishes to change some behavior, it is important to examine the attitude that predisposes one toward such behavior. Similarly, if one wishes to engage in certain behaviors, it follows that necessary antecedent attitudes need to be developed. Take the man who says that he is interested in learning to be more social with women, but has a strong prejudice (negative attitudes) about men who engage in social dance as a recreational activity. This poses a problem, because one of the favorite social pastimes of most women is social dancing. What is our man to do? In order for him to become a more social individual, he must learn the appropriate social skills, and of course this means that he must unlearn certain attitudes and replace them with attitudes that support his desire for increased sociability. He must alter not only his attitude about dance, but also about masculinity, and any other attitude which mitigates against the dance experience. How does one do this?

Wife: *My husband is taking me dancing again tonight.*

Wife's Friend: *Oh, I didn't know your husband knew how to dance.*

Wife: *Well, he isn't very coordinated, and his sense of rhythm is awful, but he has a great attitude!*

In some instances our most salient beliefs about an object may be incorrect. An individual who has incorrectly learned that play is an unnecessary and perhaps even harmful behavior, must unlearn these incorrect notions and replace them with a more accurate representation of the facts. Of course this can only occur when an individual recognizes that his/her attitudes are preventing him/her from having experiences that are deemed desirable, and commits him/herself to a program of change. One of my closest friends during college is now a very successful businessman. During college he was known as a very serious student. When we would invite him to participate in some college mischief or recreation, he would dismiss us as immature and reprimand us for not being more serious. Over the years, he has become very successful as a businessman, but has proved a dismal failure when it comes to play. Although, still a relatively young man, he recently suffered a heart attack. His doctor prescribed medication and a change in lifestyle. His doctor's admonition was to learn to take things less seriously—to learn to be more playful. For the first time in my friend's life he is looking at play as having some utility. Instead of being viewed as a waste of time, he now looks at play as essential to his well-being. It took a heart attack and his physician's advice to motivate him to enter into a program which involves, among other things, changing his attitude about play.

Another way to bring about a change in attitude is to change one's beliefs about the characteristics or attributes of an object. Some of the attributes of play for example, include laughter, smiling, spontaneity, a suspension of reality, and disinhibition. For some people, to smile is to show weakness, to suspend reality to be impractical, and to be disinhibited or spontaneous to risk the ridicule of significant others. I recently attended a workshop on play and humor. One of the participants was reluctant to wear a humorous name tag. When asked why, she replied, "Because it is undignified." She was unwilling to wear the name tag because the principal attribute of the name tag was its humorous content. Her attitudes about humor were far less positive than her attitudes toward what she viewed as proper decorum. Needless to say, this person had a relatively negative attitude toward play. Given time and inclination she could alter her orientation toward play by learning to value the characteristics (attributes) of playful behavior. Unfortunately two days weren't enough to affect a change in this person. At the end of the program she still wouldn't wear a name tag!

> Attitudes are like tools, for example, if all you have is a hammer
> it is amazing how many things look like nails.
>
> —Kevin Williams

Case Studies in Play

MICROPLAY 1. The minister in a small suburban church had carefully prepared his text for his sermon. The ten page manuscript was typed in double space and neatly stapled together. About one-half hour before the church service began, he placed the manuscript on the pulpit and then retired to his office. Noticing this, one young parishioner slipped up to the pulpit and secretly removed the final page. When it came time for his sermon, the minister delivered his prepared address with verve and passion. He finally read the last line of what had become the last page. It read, "And so, Adam spoke to Eve and said. . ." He turned the page and to his dismay the final leaf was missing. Undaunted and with a twinkle in his eye he said aloud, "And so, Adam spoke to Eve and said. . . there seems to be a leaf missing." Following the laughter from the congregation, he then explained his ad lib.

MICROPLAY 2. Traffic was a snarl on a ribbon of irritation. Wendell B. was dutifully observing the distance between his car and the one in front of him, when he noticed an opening in the line of faster moving traffic in the center lane. He was not alone in coveting the open space, but being closer than anyone else, it was Wendell that was able to occupy it. The driver who also wanted the space was a wild haired woman who became noticeably irritated at Wendell. As Wendell moved away from her, he could see her baring her fangs and making hostile gestures. Wendell was struck by the similarity between the woman's appearance and the pictures of baboons competing for dominance. The thought assuaged his initial displeasure at being the object of insult gestures, and in fact, brought a moment of humor to a hot, smoggy afternoon on an LA freeway.

MICROPLAY 3. The Victorian was a classic motion picture theatre. It had footlights and a curtain that raised just prior to showtime. I'll never forget watching two playful people do their impromptu imitation of Fred and Ginger on that stage. Just prior to the curtain going up, silhouetted against the curtain, these two playful people waltzed across the stage, at first to the amazement and then applause of the audience. The irony was that I had always wanted to do that, but couldn't muster the nerve. Now the old theatre is gone, and so is my chance.

MACROPLAY 1. The meeting was very boring, but social niceties demanded that Phyllis D. remain until its tiring conclusion. Phyllis was not the only one bored. Some folks were clearly having difficulty remaining awake, others fidgeted and some just looked pained. Phyllis, a budding cartoonist, saw the meeting from an opportunistic perspective. She pulled out her sketchpad and began to do cartoons of the speaker and anyone else within her visual range. To those around her, she seemed immersed in the meeting. The speaker appreciated her interest. After the meeting concluded, Phyllis was heard to comment on how quickly it had ended.

MACROPLAY 2. Charlene and Bill M. both felt they needed a vacation. Married for five years and with three children they really didn't have much time to themselves. Bill was a little reluctant to take time off when Charlene made reservations for them at Eva's Sierra Bed and Breakfast. Once at the resort, they had some difficulty getting adjusted to their new environment and relative free time. After dinner, they retired to their room. What ensued can't be described in complete detail, but rumor has it that it began with Charlene tickling Bill. This escalated to a pillow fight and from there you are invited to speculate. The rest of the weekend was spent in numerous play activities. When they returned, they both reported that they both had felt and acted like kids for the first time in years.

Becoming More Playful: A Strategy

> He that aims at nothing is bound to hit.
>
> —Larz Bishop

If you have come to a point where you recognize that playfulness is desirable, and you want more of it, then you have already taken the first step toward developing a more playful lifestyle. You have a goal, and you have already begun to strengthen your attitudes toward play. If you are at this point, or close to it, then the following steps might be helpful:

1. **Clarify Your Goals.** Yes, he who aims at nothing is bound to hit. Make certain that your goals are realistic and achievable. Remember to achieve one major goal you are going to have to first achieve many smaller objectives. Try: This week, I am going to engage in one playful behavior with my husband. Try: Today, when I feel bored, I am going to do one silly or playful thing.
2. **Collect Some Baseline Data.** It is a good idea to collect some data about what you want to change before you undertake your self-directed change program. Keep a diary for a week or two describing the extent to which your daily patterns include playful behavior.
3. **Use Contingencies.** By attaching playful behaviors to activities or events that you normally do, you can increase the probability of bringing more play into your life. It is important that you systematically try to experience more play for a very basic reason. By increasing the number of play experiences that you have, the probability of strengthening your attitudes regarding play is increased. Commit yourself to attaching a playful behavior to normal routines. For example, if you drive to work daily, what can you do during your drive that would be playful? For many of us a daily commute is a source of stress; however, for a playful person it can be a source of amusement. By learning how to make a commute playful you will make great strides in developing a playful attitude which can generalize to all other aspects of life. A personal note: When I commute, I find great pleasure in conducting my own radio talk show and singing spontaneous songs about the folks I pass in the commute. I have even been known to sing the "Peanut Butter Song" in a traffic jam.
4. **Work on Being More Creative.** Creativity and play go together, you simply cannot be playful without demonstrating some degree of creativity. Pay attention to the creativity of others, learn about creativity, and practice being more creative. I view creativity as such an important factor in leisure discovery that I have devoted an entire chapter to it.
5. **Reinforce Your Playful Behavior.** When you do something that you view as playful, reward yourself. Literally give yourself a pat on the back. I mean it. Reach right up there and pat yourself on the back and say, "Good for you, you are becoming more playful!" The giving of positive reinforcement to one's self is referred to as an affirmation. Write little notes of congratulation to yourself, give yourself a daily debriefing pointing out your humorous coups, and tell others about your progress. Tell your friends things like, "I used to be deadly serious, but it was killing me, now I am becoming a much more playful person. . . and I like it."
6. **Keep a Play Diary.** Earlier I suggested that if you embark on a self-directed program to increase playful attitudes, you should begin by collecting some baseline data. This gives you a basis for evaluating your progress, but of course in order to make such an evaluation, it is important to maintain a record of your success and failures. I personally do this by keeping a cartoon diary, but you might want to use a different approach. What is important is that you systematically record your progress. As you become more playful this will serve to reinforce further change, but in order for that to occur you need to be able to demonstrate that you are indeed making progress.
7. **Try Being More Spontaneous.** Try to listen to your inner yearnings a little more clearly. Don't evaluate every desire in terms of what others are expecting from you, rather give yourself a chance to be expressive. If you find humor in something—express it. If you feel like being silly, be silly (silliness might just possibly become you). If you feel like dancing in the street, do it! It was Halloween and I had brought a trick or treat sack with me to school. After passing some treats out to my students, I spontaneously attached the sack to my office door. At the end of the day it was full of candy and money. Some people were putting things in, others were helping themselves. It made for great fun and conversation.
8. **Assemble a Playfulness File.** Begin to collect articles, books, records and other information relative to playfulness. You might even want to do as my friend Carol Severin does. She collects toys

and novelty items. These go into her playfulness stimuli kit. Personally I think everyone, adults and children alike, should have a toy box—a collection of playful objects.

9. **Maintenance.** Just by reading this chapter, you should feel more playful, but unless you make a concerted effort to maintain this current level, you run the risk of losing even this small gain. It is sort of like dieting. A friend of mine who had been dieting for some time once said to me, "I can hardly wait until I reach 120 pounds, I'm going to really pig out then." It was clear to me that she had failed to make a significant change in her underlying attitudes and values regarding weight and fitness. She viewed a diet as a means to an end, not as an end in itself. In order to maintain her desirable weight, she would have to alter her values so that her lifestyle promoted her ideal weight; otherwise, her life would be an endless battle with her weight and marked by endless diets. Change required a commitment, a full commitment, and that simply means that it is a never-ending process. The whole point of change is to grow, to get closer to our ultimate goals, to continually improve and to continually identify new short term and mid-range goals. Maintenance is perhaps a misnomer, because in order to maintain we must continually adapt to the ever-changing conditions in which we live. And, so it is with play, as we go through life our circumstances will continually change. Some of those circumstances will be more conducive to play than others. The true test comes when adversity taps us on the shoulder and says, "Play with this!" It isn't what happens to us in life, but rather how we choose to view it. A person with a playful attitude will handle moments of adversity and come out smiling.

> Playfulness and wisdom are not mutually exclusive, in fact
> under many circumstances being playful Is the wisest thing you can do.
>
> —Jones Williams

REFERENCES

Bammel, G. and L.L. Burrus-Bammel. *Leisure and Human Behavior.* Dubuque, Iowa: Wm. C. Brown Company, Publishers, 1982.

Brightbill, C. *The Challenge of Leisure.* Englewood Cliffs, NJ: Prentice-Hall, 1960.

Csikszentmihalyi, M. *Beyond Boredom and Anxiety.* San Francisco: Josey-Bass, Inc. Publishers

De Grazia, S. *Of Time, Work and Leisure.* New York: Anchor Books, 1962.

Dumazedier,I. *Toward a Society of Leisure.* New York: Free Press, 1967.

Ellis, M.J. *Why People Play.* Englewood Cliffs, NJ: Prentice-Hall Inc., 1973.

Kraus, R. *Recreation and Leisure in Modern Society.* NY: Appleton-Century-Crofts, 1980.

Levy, J. *Play Behavior.* New York: John Wiley and Sons, 1989.

Mitchell, E.D. and B.D. Mason. *The Theory of Play.* New York: A.S. Barnes and Company, 1937.

Nash, J.B. *Philosophy of Recreation and Leisure.* St. Louis: The C.V. Mosby Company, 1953.

Neulinger, J. *The Psychology of Leisure.* Springfield: Class. C. Thomas, 1974.

O'Morrow, G. and R.P. Reynolds. *Therapeutic Recreation.* Englewood Cliffs, NJ: Prentice-Hall, Inc., 1989.

Stebbins, R. Amateurs, Professionals, and Serious Leisure. Montreal Quebec: McGill. Queen's University Press.

Reilly, M. *Play as Exploratory Learning.* Beverly Hills: Sage Publishing, 1974.

Webster, R. *Philosophy of Physical Education.* Dubuqe, Iowa: William C. Brown Co., 1976.

CHAPTER 6

Motivational Basis of Leisure

Talk about motivation for leisure, I am full of it. But nevertheless, here I sit at the keyboard of my ancient Smith-Corona, my aching back wondering why it has been condemned to this uncomfortable orange swivel chair. The answer is simple. My need hierarchy has condemned me to postpone my recreation in lieu of communicating my understanding of leisure motivation to countless, faceless, nameless students who might benefit from this manuscript. And, so in my best work ethic manner, I will now return to the task at hand, mindful that tomorrow I will play.

Theories of Leisure Motivation

In Western Culture, the first attempts to explain why people engage in leisure related behavior (play, games, or recreation) can be traced back to the 19th Century to the efforts of German writer and philosopher, Frederich Von Schiller. Since Schiller's "Surplus Energy Theory," there has arisen a multitude of theoretical explanations of why human beings engage in the activities of leisure.

A theory, as described earlier, *is a collection of information verified through research to the point that reliable predictions can be made regarding the phenomenon in question*. Theories differ from philosophy by the degree to which the assumptions fundamental to the theory have been empirically evaluated.

The quality of theory can be tested by evaluating its fundamental assumptions and by examining the theory's ability to predict the relationships suggested by the theory. In the following section, you will be presented with several theories which have been advanced over the years. This historical perspective will provide you with insight into the evolution of leisure theory. It will also provide you with an exercise in critical thinking, for as you review each theory, pay particular attention to its ability to explain and predict. One of the problems associated with reviewing theories of leisure is found in the lack of universal agreement as to the definition of leisure. Consequently, in describing each theory, the presentation begins with a definition of leisure. You will notice that each theory views leisure in a slightly different way; however, as pointed out earlier, theories will usually fall into two broad categories: those which view leisure in qualitative forms and those viewing leisure in quantitative forms.

Theories selected for inclusion in this unit are summarized in the following chart (adapted from Ellis, 1973). Some of them have already been discussed earlier, some will be discussed in this chapter, others are not discussed beyond this summary.

Author/Date/Name	Definition	Theory	Criticism
Schller/1800/ Surplus Energy I	Free Time Activity	Leisure activity/play is the result of surplus energy	Stored energy does not correlate with activity
Spencer/1896/Surplus Energy II	Free time activity determined by response deprivation	All bodily systems required expression when response is deprived need to respond is increased	What about "use it or lose it?"
McDougal/1823/Instinct	Free time activity is a function of instinct, i.e., an unlearned response	Genetic encoding presupposes one to certain behavior	Much leisure activity is learned behavior
Groos/1898/Preparation	Free time	Play behavior is the result of one's need to prepare for a new activity	Explains leisure play in utilitarian terms; whereas all leisure is not utilitarian
Gulick/1902/ Recapitulation	Free time	Leisure behavior is a function of developmental reenactment of the history of the species	Leisure behavior does not follow evolutionary sequences
Patrick/1916/Relaxation-Recreation	Free time	Leisure occurs in response to the body's need to recover from work	Not everyone works
Mitchell/Mason/1934/ Self-expression and Sapora and Mitchell 1961	Free time	People seek to express themselves according to physical and psychological limitations. Such self-expression produces intrinsic rewards and hence is self- motivating	Doesn't explain why people seek activities that go beyond their limitations
Escatona/1943/ Compensation	Free time	Leisure activities compensate for psychological needs not met during work	Doesn't account for nonwork related behavior
Breer/Locke/1945/ Generalization	Free time	Leisure activities are a carryover from satisfying work experience	Doesn't account for nonwork related behavior
Berkowitz/1964/ Catharsis	State of mind	Harmful emotions drive one to express them through socially acceptable activity	Not all leisure activity is motivated by harmful emotions
Walder/1933/Erickson/ 1950/Psychoanalytic	State of mind	Leisure activity is a response to the need to reduce negative past or future experiences through playful stimulation	Not all leisure activity is motivated by negative emotion
Erickson/1950/Piaget/ 1962	State of mind	Leisure activity is a function of intellectual and physical development	Activity decreases even though intellectual growth may continue
White/1959/ Competence-Effectance	State of mind	Leisure activity is a function of a person's need to demonstrate competence and thereby achieve a feeling of effectance	Fails to explain the underlying motivation for competence and effectance
Ellis/1973 Arousal	State of mind (biological)	Leisure is a function of an organism's inherent need to structure behavior so as to produce optimal physiological arousal	Fails to explain the underlying motivation for competence and effectance
Csiksentmihalyi/1975/ Flow	State of mind	Intrinsically motivated behavior which produces flow or total involvement, peak experience	Similar to Ellis

An understanding of these theories gives us some insight into what motivates people to seek out and engage in leisure activities. Nevertheless, no one theory adequately explains the value people place on leisure or the reasons underlying their leisure choices. There are numerous factors that influence our leisure choices, and in order to understand what motivates people to leisure, these different factors must be examined. It is to that end this chapter is directed.

A Conceptual Framework

Sepho Iso-Ahola, renowned leisure social psychologist, developed a model to help explain what accounts for our leisure choices (228). This model makes it clear that there are a number of factors that influence leisure behavior. Some of these differences are "hidden" to our awareness while others are "open" to our perception. In addition, there are situational influences that result from the specific situation in which the leisure behavior occurs, and broader social/cultural influences that reflect societal norms and expectations. Furthermore, he identifies four different "causal factors" which must be considered in considering the motivational basis of leisure activity. Hidden factors include biological factors and early socialization, as well as one's need for optimal arousal. Open factors include intrinsic motivation, perceived freedom, and competence, and of course, one's leisure needs (and values). This model provides a useful conceptual framework from which to view the information presented in this chapter. In this chapter, we will address the factors presented in this model, as well as other related ideas. My interpretation of Iso-Ahola's model is as follows:

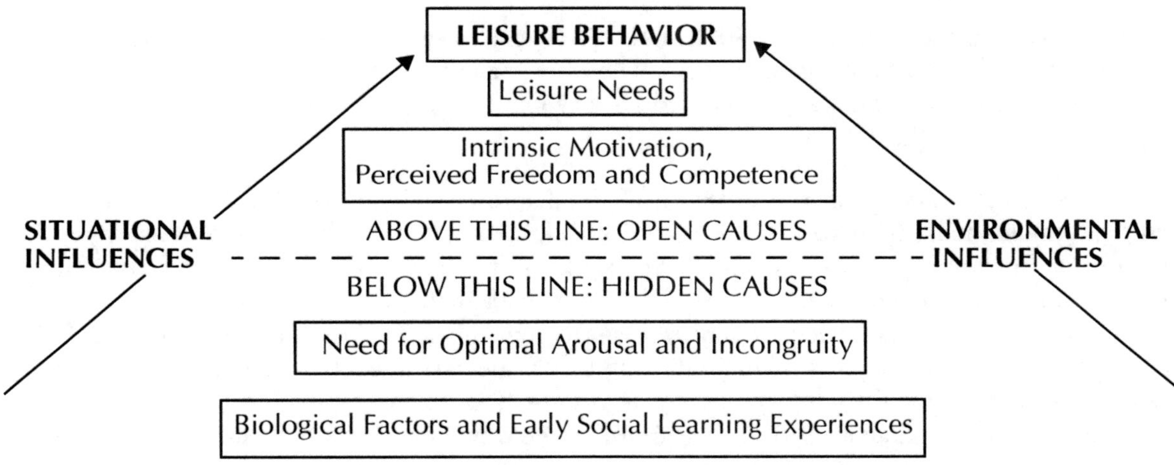

Physiological Needs

Much of human behavior is a function of physio logical needs. These are characterized by such behaviors as eating, drinking, sex, self-protection, and the like. Psychologists refer to the physiological conditions responsible for such behaviors as *physiological drives*. Such drives are seen as a function of the organism's need to reduce the deprivation which gives rise to them (Munn 141). It is believed the physiological drives are activated when the organism experiences disequilibrium, and that the organism is motivated to behavior which contributes to physiological balance, a condition called *homeostasis* (Munn 142).

These physiological drives explain, in biological terms, why people "need" to eat, drink, and mate, but fail to explain why there is such great variability in the form of such behaviors. This is important in examining the motivation of leisure, because as we have illustrated, perceived freedom is at the heart of leisure and is the element in leisure which permits such great variability in behavior. The drive to reduce hunger may take one person to McDonald's, another to a picnic, and yet another to a five-star restaurant. What motivates one person to dine while another snacks cannot be explained fully by the notion that behavior is directed by a need to reduce some form of internal biological imbalance.

Stimulation Seeking

In 1954, Bexton, Heron and Scott conducted a unique and often cited study of sensory deprivation. In this study, subjects were required to live in a situation devoid of as much external stimulation as possible. The subjects suffered from hallucinations and trance-like conditions. J.C. Lily took stimulus deprivation a step further by immersing naked subjects in tepid water, depriving them of light and minimizing sound. Subjects reported that normally, within an hour or two in the tank. they experienced an intense desire for stimulation. This usually produced a variety of methods of self-stimulation. Continued participation in the experiment often led to hallucinations (Lily, 1956).

These early studies demonstrated something most people know intuitively. We often engage in activities because they arouse us. Deprived of stimulation, we, much like Lily's subjects, attempt to increase stimulation in whatever ways seem appropriate and available. This need for stimulation is referred to by anthropologist Desmond Morris as the **stimulus struggle**. Morris suggests that the "object of the struggle is to obtain the optimum amount of stimulation from the environment" (Morris 147).

This notion is supported by research surveyed by Ellis in his book *Why People Play* (1973). Citing D.D. Schultz, Ellis refers to the process directing an organism's need for optimal arousal as "sensoristasis" (93). This concept is analogous to homeostasis. Schultz describes sensoristasis as follows:

> Sensoristasis can be defined as a drive state of cortical arousal which impels the organism (in waking state) to strive to maintain an optimal leve l of sensory variation. There is in other words, a drive to maintain a constant range of varied sensory input in order to maintain a cortical arousal at optimum level (in Ellis 93).

Ellis goes on to point out that in order for a stimulus to provide an individual with adequate cortical arousal the stimulus must be perceived as unique, novel, complex, or possess information which leads to uncertainty. On the other hand, when a stimulus presents information which leads to supra-arousal, the individual seeks stimuli which reduce uncertainty and returns cortical arousal to optimal levels (94).

It is important in a discussion of sensoristasis to remember that there is a considerable difference between **optimal** and **maximal**—maximal referring to the greatest quantity of something that is possible. *Optimal refers to the most satisfactory or most desirable.* Too much arousal for a given circumstance is referred to as **supraoptimal arousal**. Too little arousal aside from being referred to as boredom. is referred to as **suboptimal arousal**. Supraoptimal arousal is usually attended by feelings of anxiety, rapid pulse rate, gastrointestinal disturbances, and other physiological distress signals. Suboptimal arousal is also stress producing. In either event, the effects are detrimental. When one achieves optimal arousal, one normally experiences feelings of satisfaction, physical well-being, and is relatively free from the disturbing effects of anxiety. So consequently, when one is over aroused, the tendency is to reduce arousal. When one is under aroused, the tendency is to increase arousal. Morris has identified six strategies that people employ in an effort to maximize the probability of achieving optimal arousal.

1. If stimulation is too weak, you may increase your behavior output by creating unnecessary problems which you can then solve.
2. If stimulation is too weak, you may increase your behavior output by over-reacting to normal stimulus.
3. If stimulation is too weak, you may increase your behavior output by inventing novel activities.
4. If stimulation is too weak, you may increase your behavior output by performing normal responses to sub-normal stimuli.

5. If stimulation is too weak, you may increase your behavior output by artificially magnifying selected stimuli.
6. If stimulation is too strong, you may reduce your behavior output by limiting responsiveness to incoming sensations (Morris, 1976).

Support for the idea that neophilic animals have an inherent need for optimal stimulation finds further support in the work done by Marvin Zuckerman on risk taking.

Sensation Seeking and Risk Taking

Why are some people motivated to seek recreation in activities that are clearly dangerous while others carefully avoid such activities? This phenomenon has been the subject of several research studies (see Zuckerman, 1979 and 1983) the findings from which provide us with some important insight into understanding why we choose the recreational activities that we do.

Marvin Zuckerman, perhaps the foremost authority on risk-taking behavior, began his research in the 1960's. Initially he was concerned with understanding why human beings and other neophilic animals seek change rather than adapting to it. He was interested in understanding why human beings show such a great interest in playful nonessential behaviors. As he puts it:

> Why do we risk upsetting our stable, comfortable, and predictable social arrangements to make personal and collective revolutions? Why do we ski and race our cars at excessive speeds, fully aware of the risks in these unnecessary activities? Why do we disturb the healthy homeostatic balances in our bodies with the drinking of alcohol, ingestion of drugs, jogging and other potentially addictive and physically stressful activities? Why can't subjects be content and happy lying for a few hours or days in a comfortable, dark, soundproof room. . . ? Why do some persons engage in these activities whereas others behave like 'normal' tension reducing fear-avoidant persons should? Is there a generalized trait that can subsume various kinds of risk taking, sensation seeking and intolerance of constancy? (Zuckerman 2)

Zuckerman's research on risk taking in humans has centered around "sensation seeking" as the presumed general trait underlying play and novelty seeking. Zuckerman hypothesized that the principal motive for seeking new and sometimes risky experiences was a need for sensory stimulation. To test his hypothesis he developed an instrument referred to as the **Sensation Seeking Scale**. This instrument was designed to measure the extent to which an individual values and seeks external stimulation. During the course of his research, he discovered four subfactors of sensation seeking that became the basis for a more reliable and valid instrument (Form V). These four subfactors are as follows:

1. Thrill Adventure Seeking (TAS): Items on this scale reflect a desire to engage in physical activities involving elements of speed, danger, novelty, and defiance of gravity (parachuting, hang gliding, etc.).
2. Experience Seeking (ES): Items here reflect the seeking of novel experiences through travel, music, art, and spontaneous, nonconforming lifestyles with similarly inclined persons (membership in special interest organization and groups).
3. Disinhibition (DIS): Items here describe the need to seek release in uninhibited social activities with or without the aid of alcohol.
4. Boredom Susceptibility (BS): Items reflecting an aversion to repetitive experience, routine work, or predictable people with a reaction of restless discontent when unavoidably exposed to such experience (42).

Zuckerman's research has demonstrated that high sensation seekers tend to engage in behavior that most persons appraise as moderately risky where low sensation seekers tend to avoid such situations; Sensation seekers in college are inclined to volunteer for research studies involving hypnosis or sensory deprivation and to participate in encounter groups and other similar novel activities. In regards to sports recreation, high sensation seekers tend to prefer sports that are generally viewed as dangerous. These include skydiving, scuba diving and skiing. Sensation seekers are drawn to gambling and tend to prefer poorer odds than low sensation seekers. Sensation seekers are more inclined to travel, even to exotic and dangerous locales than low sensation seekers (217).

Sensation seekers have been shown to have an attraction toward mental activities that produce vivid images, daydreams or fantasies. Consequently high sensations seekers may be more inclined toward the recreational use of drugs or alcohol. Similarly, sensation seekers may find greater recreational value in adventure films, "X-rated" movies and fictional writing (250). Low sensation seekers tend to favor musicals, comedy and drama (Schierman and Rowland, 1985). The tendency for high sensation seekers to find value in stimulating reading and other external forms of stimulation may prove counterproductive in the classroom. In educational situations where little opportunity for creative or imaginative work is allowed, high sensation seekers may perform below their potential (Zuckerman 249). This may be particularly true of students who score high on the Boredom Susceptibility or Disinhibition Scales.

In the area of attitudes, Zuckerman reports that there is a strong correlation between liberal philosophy and sensation seeking. He further points out that the "traits and cognitive styles of the authoritarian personality seem to be characteristic of the low-sensation seeker (267)." These findings are consistent with his findings regarding sexual attitudes. Sensation seekers of both sexes are more inclined to permissive attitudes regarding sexual behavior (*Ibid*).

It is not surprising to learn that high sensation seekers view risky situations as less dangerous than low sensation seekers (217). What might be optimally stimulating to a high sensation seeker could produce supraoptimal arousal in a low sensation seeker. Consequently, activities which may be viewed with disinterest by high sensation seekers may hold optimal arousal potential for a low sensation seekers. Conversely recreational activities that may be avoided by low sensation seekers, because of their high arousal potential, may yield optimal arousal to the high-sensation seeker. Clearly, leisure can only occur when congruity between one's arousal need and the arousal potential of an activity occurs. When faced with supraoptimal arousal one seeks to be free from excessive stimulation; when stimulation is too little, one seeks escape from boredom. Furthermore, either situation is relatively devoid of intrinsic motivation. Hence, it can be argued that leisure occurs only when an individual is at his/her optimal arousal level. During supraoptimal or suboptimal arousal, leisure can not occur.

It is important that students of leisure be clear on the relationship of sensation seeking to leisure. An incomplete understanding of this relationship can produce unfortunate misconceptions. This was illustrated to me recently when one of my students told me that she had taken the "Zuckerman Sensation Seeking Scale: Short Form" and scored very low. She was devastated. Her score fell within the low-sensation seeker range. She said, "I just couldn't believe it. I wanted to be a high-sensation seeker, after all, doesn't everyone?" Her concern reminded me that in our media-conscious society, there is a great deal of emphasis placed upon taking risks, being adventuresome and challenging the odds. This however, does not mean that sensation seekers are inherently better than those who prefer a quieter mode. It tells us more about what it takes to sell newspapers and television programs than it does about the values associated with sensation seeking. What is important is not what Hollywood or Madison Avenue tells us to value, but rather finding out what works for us. If activities generally viewed as having a low risk element produce a pleasurable response, then by all means do them, and enjoy them. To try to force yourself to adapt to high-risk leisure, when your preference is toward safer activities will only yield frustration and dissatisfaction.

Pleasure Seeking

Dr.'s Ornstein and Sobel view pleasure seeking as the motivational basis for much of human behavior. They argue that human beings possess ". . . an effective internal health maintenance system, one guided by pleasure" (25). They have drawn this conclusion from a number of sources, perhaps the most remarkable of which is the work of psychologist James Olds. While exploring the relationship of different parts of an animal's brain to alertness, Olds made an interesting discovery. He found that when electrical stimulation was applied to different parts of the limbic system, the animal seemed to experience pleasure.

In a now famous series of experiments, electrodes were implanted in the limbic region of laboratory rats. The limbic system is composed of several structures generally believed to be associated with primitive urges such as eating, fighting, and sex. The cages in which the rats were kept were each equipped with a small lever that the rat could push to trigger a burst of electrical stimulation. Once the rat discovered the correlation between pushing the lever and the pleasurable sensations the electrical stimulation produced, the rat would push the lever repeatedly. Rats would self-stimulate as many as 5,000 times in one hour. Deprivation of other needs such as food or water didn't seem to affect their desire for self-stimulation (Vander, Sherman, Luciano 698).

Although, the early work of Olds seemed to suggest that the brain contained a clearly defined pleasure center, subsequent research suggests a different conclusion. It appears that there are several areas of the brain which can produce pleasurable responses. This led to the belief that pleasure is not necessarily found in fixed structures of the brain, but rather found in various electrochemical pathways. One pathway in the brain which may be part of what Olds calls "the river of rewards" is the *medial forebrain bundle*. This is a large tract of ascending and descending axons passing from one end of the brain to the other, and which have particularly powerful affect on the hypothalamus (Vander, Sherman, Luciano 698). The idea that there may be pleasure pathways in the brain is supported by research on neurotransmitters. Vander, Sherman and Luciano present evidence that ". . norepinepherine and dopamine (both of which belong to the family of catecholamines) are transmitters in the pathways which underlie the brain reward systems and motivation" (699).

Ornstein and Sobel tell us that in addition to electrical implants, there are other less artificial means of stimulating pleasure pathways. They refer to these natural means of stimulating pleasure response as *pleasure channels* (31). Common pleasure channels include good tastes, sounds, smells, and sights. These are the *sensory channels*. In addition there is the *mental channel*. It is possible to stimulate a pleasure response by thinking pleasurable thoughts. Similarly, it is possible to produce a negative response by entertaining negative thoughts.

It is easy to understand how people are motivated to seek pleasure through food, smells and sights. It is more difficult to understand why people aren't more motivated to think positive thoughts, particularly if negative thinking produces negative emotional responses. Part of the answer is found in the simple, direct link between sensory stimulation and pleasure. The taste of a cookie has an immediate impact on the pleasure pathways. Whereas, the mental channel is far more complicated. The mental channel resonates with values and expectations, and as such introduces a judgment component into any attempt to entertain pleasurable thoughts. Unreasonable fears or low self-image mediate against positive thinking. Furthermore, thoughts can be fleeting and transitory, shifting from positive to negative.

The Autonomic Nervous System and Leisure

Healthy organisms have an amazing capacity to keep their internal environments in balance. Fluctuations in fluid pressure, balance, and chemical composition vary between rather narrow limits. The control of this internal balance is largely a function of the **autonomic nervous system (ANS)**. The ANS, as its name implies is basically automatic, and largely beyond conscious or voluntary control. For example, you have very little direct control over the functioning of your heart, or over the secretions of your endocrine system. Fortunately, our brains are smart enough to keep conscious meddling out of homeostatic functions.

The ANS is viewed as being composed of two sub-systems: the *parasympathetic nervous system* and the *sympathetic nervous system*. The parasympathetic nervous system conserves bodily energy, attends to such matters as digestion, salivation, intestinal functions, and permits sexual activity. On the other hand, the sympathetic nervous system does largely just the opposite—it activates the body for emergency situations, inhibits sexual activity, digestion and bowel functions. It prepares the body for maximum conversion of energy. As you can see these two systems are opposite sides of the same biological coin. Both of these systems are primarily controlled by a portion of the brain referred to as the *hypothalamus* and to a lesser extent by the so-called "master gland," the *pituitary*.

The arousal of the body is generally a function of the sympathetic nervous system. This occurs when the hypothalamus is stimulated by either impulses originating from the cortex or from some external source. When presented with something frightening, the body responds immediately, but a mere memory or imaginative thought can have a similar effect. Merely thinking about an impending examination or long-awaited date can activate the sympathetic nervous system. The hypothalamus is bordered and anatomically related to what is referred to as the limbic system, which is believed to be primarily associated with emotional reactions to situations that call for fight, defense, or flight. The following chart describes the functions of the parasympathetic and sympathetic systems.

FUNCTIONS OF THE AUTONOMIC NERVOUS SYSTEM[A]

Organ	Sympathetic Stimulation	Parasympathetic Stimulation
Eyes	Accommodates for distance vision Dilates pupil Lens flattens	Accommodates near vision Constrict pupils Lens bulges
Lacriminal Glands	Not innerated by this system	Secretion of tears
Sweat Glands	Copious sweating	Also stimulates sweating
Heart	Increases rate and force of contraction	Decreases rate and force of contraction
Lung	Bronchi dilates producing increased ventilation	Bronchi constricts
Stomach	Sphincter contracts Glandular secretion inhibited	Sphincter dilates Glandular secretion permitted
Intestine Wall	Inhibition	Increases tone of muscles Decreases muscle tone
Anal Sphincter	Contraction	
Pancreas	Diminishes enzyme secretion Stimulates glycogen secretion which leads to increase in glucose	Stimulates secretion of pancreatic enzymes (aids in digestion)
Kidney	Decreases output	Not known
Urinary Bladder	Relaxation	Contraction
Penis	Ejaculation due to sympathetic stimulation of prostate	Erection through vascular dilation
Arterioles in Skin	Constriction	Not innervated by this system
Skeletal Muscle	Vasodilatation	Not innervated by this system
Arrector Muscles of Hair Follicle	Constriction causing hair to stand erect	Not innervated by this system

[a]It should be noted that the sympathetic nervous system is activated not only in recreational situations where some real or perceived threat exists, but also in any form of physical exercise. For example, during an aerobic workout the sympathetic nervous system will have greater involvement than the parasympathetic nervous system. Furthermore, it should be noted that in most recreational situations both systems will be activated to some extent; however, one will always have more involvement than the other, depending upon the body's immediate needs. For example, it is through the parasympathetic nervous system that penile and clitoral erection occurs, but it is through sympathetic stimulation that orgasm occurs.

Just as the hypothalamus and limbic system stimulate bodily responses to situations and thoughts, the reticular arousal system (RAS) serves to arouse the cerebral cortex. Located within the brain stem and connected to other regions of the brain by small processes, this system is responsible for *alerting the cerebral cortex* to any form of *neural stimulation*. For the most part, much of this comes from external sources and is dependent upon sensory receptors. However, the RAS doesn't interpret the nature of the stimulation, only alerts the cortex to its presence in order that the cerebral cortex can then respond in whatever manner is appropriate. Once alerted, the cortex can deal directly with the input from the appropriate sensory pathways (Ellis 89–91).

Interestingly enough, the cortex can be a source for stimulation, which activates the RAS, which in turn stimulates the cerebral cortex. This cycle of *cortex, RAS, cortex* stimulation may help explain why sometimes at night, when trying to get to sleep you just can't seem to shut your thoughts off. You experience something similar to this in classes when there is very little external stimulation. The instructor who speaks in monotonous tones and who presents his material in a complex manner sets the stage for RAS-cortex cycle, which is often manifest in daydreaming.

Just as the parasympathetic nervous system tends to be an antagonist system to the sympathetic nervous system, there appears to be neural function in the brain stem which serves as an antagonist to the RAS (Glietman 67). Thus, during situations of under stimulation, the antagonistic portion of the brain stem may be activated which leads to drowsiness or sleep. Similarly, sleep may occur under less than ideal situations, if the subject has been deprived of sleep for any great length of time. Once, during my younger years, while on a personal adventure hopping freight trains, I fell exhausted onto the hard metal floor of a slow moving box car. The clatter of metal wheels and the uneven movement of the train was soon forgotten as my need for sleep diminished the activity of the RAS. Twelve hours later, I awakened, along with my partner, to find that our car had been detached from the train and was sitting alone on a siding. We had slept through the entire event. Students have been known to do the same thing through an entire class, again demonstrating the RAS inhibiting effect of other portions of the brain stem. This inhibiting effect is probably related in some way to the cerebral cortex. Ellis argues that the cortex "acts back on the RAS to inhibit arousal if the stimulus input is repetitious, expected, innocuous, irrelevant, redundant, etc." (91). Such may be the case; however, Glietman argues for an RAS antagonist, which is activated under those circumstances or follows sleep deprivation (67).

Within recent years, attention has been paid to the relationship of a family of neurotransmitters called *catecholamines*[4] to arousal (67). Chief among these are norepinephrine, epinephrine, and dopamine. Zuckerman suggests that individuals with a high need for arousal may be manifesting unusually high amounts of these neurotransmitters. Evidence for this notion is found in the behavior of individuals who have been given chemicals to inhibit monoamine oxidase (MAO), a chemical that is believed to regulate the supply of neurotransmitters. People given MAO inhibitors demonstrate dramatic elevations in mood, thus suggesting the relationship of catecholamines to arousal. His hypothesis is that high sensation seekers have low MAO levels and low sensations seekers have high MAO levels (Zuckerman 96).

That there exists a relationship between certain subsystems within the brain and arousal, and that basically a person attempts to direct his or her behavior in a way that enhances the probability of optimal levels of arousal is clearly apparent. But, what of the variation among individuals? Research on the dual nature of the brain may give us some insight.

The Dual Brain and Leisure

For well over a century medical science has known that the brain was divided into two hemispheres. There was even some thought that each hemisphere was a duplicate of the other; sort of an ultimate redundancy. A. L. Wiggan, a 19th century physician performed autopsies on people with only half a brain, but who had lived normal lives. He reasoned that if one hemisphere "were capable of all the emotions, sentiments and faculties, which we call the aggregate mind—then it necessarily follows that Man must have two minds with two

4. These are biologically active amines which have a marked effect on the nervous and cardiovascular systems. An amine is any of a class of compounds derived from ammonia by replacement of one or more hydrogen atoms with alkyl groups.

brains" (Fincher 32). Nearly a century later, in the 1930's surgeons found that by cutting the tissue that connects the hemispheres of the brain, patients suffering from epileptic seizures showed astonishing improvement. Furthermore, just as Wiggins had theorized, the patients showed no apparent negative effects (Fincher 32).

The principal tissue connecting the two hemispheres is called the **corpus collosum**. Prior to the surgeries in which the corpus collosum was severed, it was believed that the purpose of the corpus collosum was to permit communication between hemispheres. Indeed, because of its location and its size it was assumed to possess important neural functions. However, the surgeries in which the corpus collosum was severed revealed no significant clues as to its purpose. Since patients who had undergone the surgery showed no adverse effects, it seemed to have no purpose at all (Fincher 33). Later research confirmed the earlier notion, the corpus collosum was responsible for interhemispheric communication.

In the 1960's psychobiologist Robert Sperry, set forth on a series of experiments designed to unravel the mystery of the "split brain." These experiments, which ultimately led to Sperry and his associates winning a Nobel Prize, revealed that each hemisphere has subtle and important differences. Sight and touch experiments revealed that the left hemisphere is designed to deal with analytical and verbal skills, while the right is more oriented to spacial skills and pattern perception. Sperry's research suggested that the left hemisphere is better at logical, linear thinking—taking fragments and processing solutions. As Fincher puts it, the "left hemisphere sorts out the parts (32). The right hemisphere on the other hand tends to see things as a whole." It is equipped to generate mental images of sight, sound, taste, touch and smell. The right hemisphere is important in creativity and intuition. Restak summarizes the difference between hemispheres by referring to the left hemisphere as the **symbolic-conceptual** hemisphere, and the right as the **nonsymbolic directly perceived** (252). Sperry's research also refuted that idea that the corpus collosum served no purpose. He demonstrated conclusively that the corpus collosum serves as a communication channel between the two hemispheres. He found that it is the corpus collosum that allows the brain to integrate the information held in the separate hemispheres. It is through the functioning of the corpus collosum that an individual is able to effectively utilize the capabilities of each hemisphere.

At first glance, it would appear that the right hemisphere is more associated with leisure than the left hemisphere. It is the left hemisphere that we use on the job, in the classroom and solving important quantitative problems. Whereas it is the right hemisphere that we use in our creative endeavors, our play, and sensual pleasures. But, as Restak (73) points out, "The human brain doesn't break down into neat categories." The brain must be thought of as a functional whole. Although different parts of the brain have special functions, these functional areas are in contact with and interact with other functional units. For example, it is the left hemisphere that enables a person to understand a joke, but it is the right hemisphere that enables him/her to get it. It is the left hemisphere that enables a person to understand the concept of leisure, but it is the right hemisphere that is equipped to facilitate the leisure experience. It is the right hemisphere that enables one to engage in flights of fancy, but it is the left hemisphere that enables one to appreciate happiness. And, oddly enough, it is the right hemisphere that allows one to feel the emotions of sorrow and empathy (Carlson 518). To achieve a leisure lifestyle it is important that a person develop his or her ability to use both hemispheres. Unfortunately, it is not always easy to access the right hemisphere in a world structured along left hemispheric lines.

We grow up in a world that emphasizes left-hemisphere thinking. Our schools place great emphasis on language and quantitative reasoning. As a consequence, as we mature, the shift from symbolic thinking to nonsymbolic may become more difficult. Consequently, by young adulthood many of us have difficulty with tasks that require creativity, spatial awareness, artistic expression and other skills often associated with recreation and leisure. Unable to access our right hemisphere potentials, we are limited in our choice of recreational activities. Rather than composing our own music, we listen to the compositions of others; unable to appreciate graphic art, we overlook it as a source of leisure; unable to tap our potential for fantasy, we turn to television and movies; with limited right brain access, we find our ability to be playful and humorous lacking.

Learning to access the right hemisphere is a skill that can lead to important leisure outcomes. By becoming more right brain oriented, we can begin to appreciate the novelty and beauty in our surroundings;

we can learn to be more creative in our daily activities; we can learn to look for the novel and incongruous in otherwise normal affairs; we can bring more play and humor into our lives; we can bring more joy into our lives through the appreciation of art and music; and, we can enjoy the pleasure of increased self expression.

In considering the relationship of the brain to leisure, it is probably best to think of the hemispheres as two sides of a balanced scale. The left hemisphere enables us to do many things that are essential to leisure. For example it is the left hemisphere that facilitates reading a novel or solving a brain twister. Even though the right hemisphere is associated with deep emotion, it is the left hemisphere that is associated with deep thought. As Restak states:

> There is little doubt, however, that we need both sides of our brain. In fact, one can state with equal validity that we are not just the right and left sides of our brain, but simply we are our brain, and wouldn't want to lose any part of it if we had a choice (265).

It is quite clear from the foregoing discussion that leisure behavior is, at least in part, a function of the interaction and interrelationship between subsystems within the brain; a relationship that seems to be directed toward allowing the brain to achieve an optimal level of stimulation. Nevertheless, regardless of the elegance, the neurophysiologic explanation of leisure motivation offers us only a partial explanation. The motivational basis for leisure is far too complex to be limited to the unique demands of one's neurophysiology. Indeed, as will be seen in the next section, there is evidence that one's biological response to astral and temporal rhythms may also play a role in shaping leisure behavior.

Circadian Rhythms and Leisure Behavior

That heavenly bodies influence human behavior is not a new idea. Astrology, which traces its beginnings back to the ancient Assyrians and Chaldeans, is based precisely on this belief. Astrologers believe that the configuration of the stars and planets at the time of one's birth predestines one to certain fortunes, liabilities and temperaments. Horoscopes, heavenly maps showing the position of celestial bodies at the time of one's birth, appear regularly in modern newspapers, along with brief explanations of their meaning. Unfortunately, astrology appears to have little more than entertainment value. The notion that a person's life is influenced by stars *one-hundred trillion* miles away is, as Carl Sagan says, "demonstrably erroneous (Sagan 247)." But, on the other hand, there is evidence to support the idea that human behavior is influenced, to some degree, by certain astral relationships much closer to home.

The movement of the moon about the earth in conjunction with the movement of the earth around the sun has a strong influence on human and animal behavior. This is not astrology! Here we are talking about the gravitational influence of our nearest astral neighbor, the moon, and the relationship of the earth to the only star close enough to influence life on earth, the sun.

The influence that the sun and moon exert on earth life is far different from that taught by astrology. The greatest effect seems to be associated more with the temporal rhythms produced by the earth's revolution about the sun, producing seasons and the rotation of the earth on its own axis giving rise to the daily shift from light to dark and back to light. This cycle of alternating light and dark has a powerful affect on human, animal and plant behavior. These rhythms seem to govern such natural phenomena as the opening and closing of flower petals, and in animals and humans, changes in body temperature, blood pressure, urine production, and metabolic rates. Even mood appears synchronized with circadian rhythms.

Some animals tend to be activated by daylight (such as roosters), whereas other animals are activated by night (such as bats). Animals that are active during the daytime are referred to as *diurnal*; night animals are called *nocturnal*. That the consequences of circadian rhythms can be far reaching is suggested by one of the theories developed to explain the disappearance of the great dinosaurs. This theory is based on the fact that dinosaurs, being reptiles were, out of necessity, diurnal. This was due to their cold-blooded biology which rendered them essentially immobile by night-time temperatures. To avoid falling prey to these diurnal reptiles, mammals found it essential to remain concealed during daylight hours, and hence, this became their resting time. At night, they became the hunters, and their favorite prey—the eggs of sleeping giants. Controlled by circadian rhythms that rendered them helpless at night, the great reptiles of the past fell victim to their much smaller nocturnal cousins (Sagan 142).

Another, more popular explanation for the demise of the dinosaurs also illustrates the powerful role of circadian rhythms. In this theory, the extinction of the dinosaurs is viewed as the result of the earth colliding with a great comet or meteorite. The collision resulted in the release of vast amounts of steam and smoke into the atmosphere creating a primitive "nuclear winter." Light, the principal cue for circadian rhythms was blocked by dense clouds, thus disrupting the normal rhythm of all living things. The net result was the extinction of all but the most adaptable life forms on the planet.

If circadian rhythms have had such a profound effect on the history of life on earth, just imagine how your life is influenced by these same rhythms. When we arise in the morning and when we go to bed at night is largely a function of our personal circadian rhythms regarding sleep. Restak reports that early risers tend to manifest more introverted behavior than late risers; that they tend to increase their body temperatures and alertness much earlier than late risers, and they tend to decrease in alertness as evening approaches (Restak 112). Night persons take longer to warm up, but they can function effectively much later into the night than their early-rising counterparts. Furthermore, it has been demonstrated that sleeping patterns can have a powerful affect on mood. Depressed people, for example, often show an elevation in mood when their sleeping patterns are altered to make adjustment for unusual circadian rhythms (Restak 114). Work efficiency and effectiveness also appear to be influenced by circadian rhythms. For example, most people tend to show a decrease in alertness around 1:00 p.m. regardless of whether they have had lunch or not. It is for this reason that I never get a haircut in the early afternoon. It has also been demonstrated that most people, regardless of their sleeping patterns don't function very effectively in the early morning hours (Restak 112). A tragic example is the Three Mile Island accident. The events that led to the near meltdown of this nuclear power reactor began with a series of mistakes that started around 4:00 a.m.

Researchers believe that deep within the brain, located in the hypothalamus, is an organ responsible for tracking time and reminding the automatic nervous system of certain biological functions, and the cerebral cortex of certain temporal behaviors. Referred to as the *suprachiasmatic nucleus* (SCN), this tiny mass of neurons may be the long sought after biological clock (Restak 215). It is theorized that the SCN may modulate not only circadian, but also ultradian (more frequently occurring than every 24 hours) behaviors. These rhythms may account for behaviors that tend to follow cycles ranging from 20 minutes (the amount of time I can study without a break) to cycles of up to several hours. These ultradian cycles are often biological in nature, but may also be related to mood and alertness.

In addition to circadian and ultradian rhythms are monthly and circa-annual rhythms. Men show a rhythmic monthly weight gain and loss, women experience a monthly menstrual cycle often characterized by dramatic shifts in mood. On a circa-annual basis, it has been demonstrated that people tend to the changes in the amount of available daylight. During late fall, winter and early spring, people experience more depression than during seasons marked by more daylight (Restack 216).

When a circadian or ultradian rhythm is disrupted, it usually produces stress. Given enough time, however, the body's internal rhythm can adjust to new conditions, but usually during the interim—mood, alertness and physical health suffer. Jet lag is a good example of this as is the effect that shift work has on workers.

Although not the ultimate "force" in the universe, it is one that you will definitely feel. The rhythms of nature have a powerful influence on our behavior and the quality of our lives. By understanding our own circadian and ultradian rhythms, we can better organize our activities to conform to our unique rhythmic needs. This implies an important condition for optimal functioning—synchronicity of behavior and natural rhythms. For want of a better word, call it *circadian congruity.* To depart from one's optimal circadian pattern is to invite stress and a reduction of perceived freedom and intrinsic satisfaction. In our pursuit of the leisure lifestyle we would be wise to follow the admonition of the Hopi medicine man who, one winter evening, over a dinner consisting of beans and pike bread, gently reminded me of the Hopi's secret for successful living—"Walk with nature."

As we have demonstrated, leisure behavior, indeed all behavior, has a physiological basis. But the form that leisure activities take, vary so greatly from person to person, it is readily apparent that more must be at work than physiological responses to external and internal stimuli. What produces optimal arousal for one, may bore someone else. How can this be explained?

Cultural Values

When something is important to us, when it is viewed as worthwhile, desirable, or consequential, such thing is said to have ***value***. Values permeate society and influence all aspects of social life. They can be viewed from a ***societal, group, or individual perspective***. Values have a profound influence on what we view as leisure, and the types of leisure activities in which we choose to participate.

In American society there are some values that all citizens hold in common. For example, Americans generally value freedom of expression, self-direction, independence, and participatory government. These values trickle down through all layers of the society. But as you get more specific and away from the general population, you find that different subgroups in the society, although sharing some of the more common cultural values, have some very specific values that are quite different from those held by most people. For example, people who share a certain religious belief will share certain religious values in common (Mormons don't drink or smoke, but at one time practiced polygamy). People in the same political party will have similar political values (some people take Ross Perot seriously). People of the same generation will hold some values in common (few of my age group have pierced tongues). People from different racial groups will have some common values (few white people hip-hop). Yet, in spite of differences, trickling down throughout all of these groups will be values common to all members of the society.

You can see the "trickle down" phenomenon when you travel. Traveling allows you to look at visitors against the social background of a different cultural value system. In so doing, it helps you see the differences in values and how some values seem to be held in common. Not long ago, I was in China. While shopping in a public market in Shanghai, I heard a clearly American voice proclaiming the superiority of American fruit. The loud American was a member of a tour group from Arizona. I learned that they were ending their first week of a two week tour that had taken them from Hong Kong to Shanghai and would end in Beijing. The loud American took delight in pointing out that American fruit was bigger. "Why the grapefruit we raise in Arizona makes these grapefruit look like lemons." He said nothing about the color, the texture, the display, the fragrance—only the size. His statement suggested that in America, "bigger is better."

It is easy to see how one's culture influences leisure choices. Since we make our leisure choices within a social context, the dominant values of the society will determine to a large extent what activity choices are available. A year ago I visited The Netherlands. While still in the airport terminal, I was surprised to smell marijuana smoke. I soon found that marijuana was viewed as socially acceptable in The Netherlands. You could even buy marijuana confections at coffee shops, and while I was there I learned that a conference for marijuana growers was in session. This contrasts with the United States where the federal government is currently waging a war against any type of marijuana use, including medical applications. A similar contrast can be drawn between the United States and The Netherlands on the value of gun ownership. Private ownership of guns is prohibited in Holland, in the United States gun ownership is a cherished right. Social values evolve and in the process new values emerge. What was viewed important to society a few years ago may now seem outdated and possessing little value. This is clearly demonstrated in our leisure choices. At one time, Sundays were reserved for religion not recreation, sex was reserved for the bedroom not the television screen, and leisure was viewed merely as a reward for work. Obviously these values have changed, and just as they have changed so will are our contemporary values. For example, Kelly suggests that in the next few decades cultural values will change to influence American leisure in the following ways:

1. The value of religion in the United States is diminishing. Consequently, religious values such as sacrifice, worship, and adherence to the Puritan Work Ethic, are also lessening. There are those who are concerned that decline of religion will mark a decline in moral values, and that society will engage in leisure that will be characterized by excess and degradation. Kelly doesn't see it this way. Rather he views a decline in religious values as having important implications for leisure. A reduction in the importance of religion may lead to an increase in the value of the leisure ethic. The value of intrinsic motivation (satisfaction), freedom, and personal expression in leisure may increase (179).
2. Decisions regarding the environment may be influenced by an increasing appreciation for the role that leisure has in enhancing the quality of life. Today such decisions are based on economics. In the near future, Kelly believes that decisions regarding outdoor recourses will be based more and more on their leisure value.
3. Kelly believes that in the future, there will be a general value shift from extrinsic motivations to the intrinsic. In today's value orientation, we often have to legitimize our leisure behavior in terms of social benefits, economic gain, or personal development. Kelly believes that our value-orientation is moving toward greater emphasis on intrinsic values. He believes that we will come to a time when a leisure activity ". . . need not be good for the community, family, employment status, or social prestige it if yields a full measure of personal satisfaction" (179).

The society in which we live influences the kinds of leisure activities we value. Cultural values create common threads among a society, and although they evolve and change, they persist as a powerful force in determining the kinds of recreation and leisure people choose. But, among the members of any society there will be variation in leisure choices. That difference is reflective of the variation one finds in personal values.

Personal Values

Personal values, and this is true of cultural values as well, can be thought of as being of two types: **instrumental** and **terminal**. Terminal values are those that reflect a person's belief about ends to be achieved, and instrumental values reflect beliefs about how one might achieve desired ends. In other words, instrumental values are the means to achieving terminal values.

- Terminal values include such abstract goals as a comfortable life, sense of accomplishment, family security, self-respect, peace, freedom, and harmony.
- Instrumental values include good health, ambition, knowledge, creativity, independence, and wealth.

You may have seen the bumper "snicker" that said, "He who dies with the most toys—wins!" Implicit in this aphorism is the idea that material possessions (toys) are instrumental to the terminal value of winning (happiness or sense of accomplishment). This is illustrative of how personal values influence our leisure choices. It also introduces the concept of **beliefs**.

Beliefs are related to values in that beliefs refer to what we know about the world, and values relate more to what we find desirable in the world. Beliefs play an important role in determining leisure choices. We only select activities that we believe will produce positive outcomes. What is considered a positive outcome is determined by our values. If there is a low congruence between what one believes about a recreational activity and what one values, the probability is low that such an activity will be included in one's recreation. Conversely, where there is high congruence between values and the degree to which we believe an activity produces valued outcomes, the probability of participation is increased.

That values are an important influence on leisure motivation can be seen through the work of psychographic researchers. This is a relatively new field which attempts to use psychology to identify market segments. By identifying the predominant values in the buying public, businesses can better design marketing strategies to reach those market segments in which they have an interest.

Typical of the type of work done by psychographic research is the work of Yankelovich Clancy Shulman. The *Yankelovic Monitor* tracks trends in population among two major value groups, or as they are called in marketing, **value segments**:

Old-Values Segments

1. Traditionalist—middle aged people who have accepted the traditional values of hard work and material success.
2. Retreaters—older, poorer people who have given up on achieving success.

New-Values Segments

1. New Conformists—younger people who have largely substituted self-fulfillment for traditional work oriented values.
2. Forerunners—young, upscale people who place a high value on intellectual and creative achievement.
3. Autonomous—upscale consumers who have achieved success and turned their attention to self-improvement and personal fulfillment (In Pope, 246–249).

Personal values can be further categorized into aesthetic values, social values, political values, religious and moral values, and economic values. When values relate specifically to leisure or leisure activities, they can be referred to as **leisure values**. As you can imagine, all of these clusters or groups of values overlap.

Leisure Values and Needs

Triandis (1972) views values as "relationships among abstract categories with strong affective components, implying a preference for a certain kind of action or a state of affairs" (16). Rokeach (1980) points out that there is a close relationship of values to attitudes. He states, ". . . humans have thousands of attitudes, but only dozens of values, that attitudes are biases and values are metabiases. . . ." (272) Jeffres and Dobos (1993, 205) define leisure values as personal "assessments of the worth or utility" of leisure. When considering leisure values, we are considering those abstract categories associated with leisure for which we have strong feelings. In selecting leisure activities, some people place value on feelings of excitement, some place value on perceptual freedom, some value self-expression, others place value on personal growth and so on. These in turn are a reflection of attitudes that support these values. Since values are a reflection of an array of attitudes, a person will always have fewer leisure values than leisure attitudes.

An example of the kinds of values that people hold for leisure is suggested by the pioneering work in leisure motivation by Beard and Ragheb (1980). In developing a scale to measure leisure motivations, Beard and Ragheb identified six categories of leisure motivations (26):

1. **Psychological:** sense of freedom, enjoyment, intellectual challenge
2. **Educational:** intellectual stimulation
3. **Social:** rewarding relationships with other people
4. **Relaxation:** relief from stress
5. **Physiological:** staying fit, healthy, weight-control
6. **Aesthetic:** appreciation of beauty

In a subsequent study these six categories were reduced to four:

1. **Intellectual:** expand interests, satisfy curiosity, expand knowledge.
2. **Social:** be with others, interact with others, belonging.

3. **Competence Mastery:** challenge, achievement, competition.
4. **Stimulus Avoidance:** relax physically, relax mentally, relieve stress, escape.

There are other values that can be associated with leisure. For many people, one of the principal values of leisure is the opportunity to experience freedom, to be in control of one's choices. This is sometimes referred to as *self-determination*. Another important value associated with leisure is the opportunity for *intrinsic satisfaction*. Underlying many of the values of leisure is a desire for intrinsic reward. In fact, it is fair to say that one's need for intrinsic satisfaction explains many of the values that we associate with leisure. A person chooses a trip to a scenic area for aesthetic and relaxation values, but underlying these two values is the intrinsic satisfaction one derives from such an experience. An individual chooses to play racquetball for physical exercise, but again, underlying the physical value is an intrinsic reward.

Although, not the only precursor to a leisure choice, it is fair to say that our leisure values play a role in deciding how we view leisure and the types of activities in which we choose to participate. How values influence our leisure choice can be illustrated in the following thought-experiment:

You have an opportunity to participate in one of three leisure activities.

1. One-hour of basketball with good friends.
2. Two-hours of socializing at your local bar.
3. A quiet evening at home by yourself.

Which activity did you choose?

Which one "feels" the most attractive to you? Why?

The *why* might involve a number of factors, but ultimately you will conclude that there was some element in the activity that you chose that had significant value to you.

In doing this exercise, you no doubt found yourself asking several questions: What is the context of the activity? What is my situation prior to making the decision? Are there other competing activities from which to choose? Change the context of the activity, and see if it affects your decision. For example, if you had worked all day moving heavy boxes at your work, would you be as interested in a vigorous racquetball game as you would be had you spent the day working on your computer? If you have been fasting and are hungry how would this affect your decision? If you have pressing demands at your work or school would you be similarly affected? Your answers to these questions illustrate a point: although leisure values are important, **other factors influence our leisure choices as well**. In making any decision, there will be fundamental needs at work which will call for attention. These needs will be modulated by the social and physical context in which they occur, and naturally depending upon the situation, some of these may not support a decision to engage in a leisure activity.

Needs and *values* are obviously closely related. For example, we place great value on those items that we need to survive. Go without sleep for 24 hours and see how much value you place on sleep! Deprived of water for any length of time, you become preoccupied with obtaining water. Relating more to leisure, Iso-Ahola cites several studies which indicate that most human beings have a strong need for affiliation with other people (Iso-Ahola 242). When a person's circumstances isolate her from others, it is likely that leisure activities that meet the need for social interaction will take dominance over other needs.

That some needs are more essential than others is suggested by Maslow's theory of human motivation. In this theory, needs are organized by priority or importance to survival. Only when lower order needs are met can one attend to the higher order needs. In fact, it is only when lower order needs are met that higher order needs emerge and press for attention. The needs in order of survival importance are:

1. Physiological Needs: hunger and thirst
2. Safety Needs: protection from the elements and other dangers
3. Social Needs: love and belonging

4. Ego Needs: approval and recognition
5. Self-Actualization: acquisition of knowledge and appreciation of beauty

Although Maslow's hierarchy of needs has been criticized as being too facile or simplistic, it does suggest that people tend to identify a personal hierarchy of needs and to some extent base their personal goals on this hierarchy. As Iso-Ahola states, "Apart from homeostatically motivated behavior, human actions are motivated by subjectively defined goals and reward" (Iso-Ahola 230).

Philosophers and social scientists are not completely in agreement as to what constitutes leisure needs. Different authors offer different opinions. For example, Driver, Tinsley, and Manfredo (1991) identify nineteen specific needs that could be met by leisure experiences. These are summarized as follows:

1. Enjoy nature
2. Physical fitness
3. Reduce tension
4. Escape stress
5. Outdoor learning
6. Sharing similar values with friends
7. Independence, autonomy
8. Family relations
9. Introspection, spiritual reflection
10. Be considerate with people
11. Achievement/stimulation
12. Physical rest
13. Teaching/leading
14. Risk-taking
15. Meet new people
16. Risk reduction
17. Creativity
18. Nostalgia
19. Agreeable temperatures

When specific needs, such as those listed above are organized into related groups, smaller and more general needs are identified. For example, it is reasonable to say that leisure activities can meet a person's need for personal freedom, or self-expression, or intrinsic motivation. Following is a list of some of the general needs that people try to meet through leisure involvement.

1. Self-Determination: the need to make choices.
2. Optimal Arousal: the need to experience the most appropriate level of physiological stimulation.
3. Perceived Freedom: the need for being free to make choices.
4. Competence-Affectance: the need to demonstrate a skill.
5. Affiliation/social interaction: the need to interact with other people.
6. Stimulus Avoidance: the need to relax, to be away from stress or stimulation.
7. Intrinsic Satisfaction: the need to experience the intrinsic reward that comes from doing an activity.

This is not a complete list, nor is it rank ordered in any way. The potency or importance of a leisure need is unique to the individual and it is subject to various influences. It is related to other needs, and consequently it is affected by other pressing needs. It is also affected by the individual's situation, and the context in which the activity occurs.

Leisure Attitudes

A leisure attitude can be described as "the expressed amount of affect toward a given leisure-related object" (Iso-Ahola, 251). More simply put, a leisure attitude is a positive or negative feeling one has about some aspect of leisure—a program, an event, a block of time, a policy, outcome, or an activity. Leisure attitudes have an impact on our leisure choices, but attitudes alone don't predict behavior very well. Because of the weak causal relationship between leisure behavior and leisure attitudes, current research has emphasized the role of situations and context on leisure choices. Rokeach points out that psychologists and researchers tend to concur that:

1. Behavior is determined by more than single attitudes.
2. Selected social situational factors must be included (i.e. perceived social influence, normative beliefs, peer pressures) as influences.
3. Attitudes tend to be embedded in more general values.

Further, a person's intent to participate should be considered. **Intention is viewed as more important in predicting leisure involvement than attitude.** As Iso-Ahola states, "If the purpose . . . is to predict participation in a specific leisure activity, the prediction should be made from intentions to engage in it rather than from an attitude toward that leisure activity" (252). Clearly intentions are the product of needs and values. When one feels the need to experience a certain leisure value, an intent is formed. The closer in time to the activity and the formation of the intent, the greater the probability that participation will occur. Of course intention to participate is modulated by other important factors such as the value one holds for competing opportunities, the intensity of the intention, and the presence of interfering constraints.

Intrinsic Motivation vs. Extrinsic Motivation

Goals and rewards can be either intrinsic or extrinsic. Extrinsic goals are those that yield some reward which is separate and apart from an activity. You rake a lawn, not because you like raking lawns, but someone has offered you $10.00. You like the offer well enough to rake the lawn. The reward comes not in the doing, but from the doing. All of us are familiar with the power to motivate that external rewards possess. We all know of people who have made tremendous sacrifices in order to achieve wealth, status, notoriety, or power. I had a friend who was heavily extrinsically motivated. He worked very hard to acquire as much wealth as he could. He placed very little value on intrinsic motivation, he placed very little value on leisure. The stress and strain of working so hard to acquire wealth and status took a terrible toll. He died of a heart attack at age 42. The tragedy of this man's life was that he never took time to enjoy the fruits of his labors. Had he actually enjoyed his work, it could be said that he obtained some leisure value on the job. But, the fact was that he really didn't like what he was doing, but he was highly motivated to become wealthy. This is not to say that all extrinsically motivated activity is without leisure value. Indeed, there are some careers that provide both intrinsic satisfaction and extrinsic rewards. Unfortunately in my friend's situation, this was not the case.

When no apparent external value is found in an activity, it is said to be intrinsically rewarded. You like raking lawns, it gives you a feeling of satisfaction. It is so pleasant you wouldn't think of taking money for it. The reward comes in the doing not from it. We talk a great deal about intrinsic satisfaction in leisure studies. I suppose this is because, underlying most leisure values is this important construct. I interact with others because it gives me an internal feeling of satisfaction. I play sports because the feelings that are generated from physical activity are intrinsically satisfying. I enjoy self-expression through art because the artistic process causes me to feel pleasantly rewarded. *Perhaps no other construct explains our desire to engage in leisure pursuits better than the human desire to experience intrinsic satisfaction.*

Perceived Freedom and Locus of Control

As we have pointed out in previous discussions, intrinsic motivation is one of the criteria used to define leisure. The other major criterion is perceived freedom. These two elements are closely related and help explain the variance among leisure choices within a given population. When a person feels free to select leisure activities, these activities normally reflect his/her intrinsic desires. When such freedom is lacking, conformity results as a function of reduction in the number of alternatives. Unfortunately, freedom of choice, is not limited to one's perception. It appears that freedom to choose is also hampered by a number of social, situational

and personality variables. On a daily basis behavioral expectations are communicated to us. These messages began with our births and will continue to our deaths. It always seems that someone is either directly or indirectly influencing us to behave in a certain manner. For some people, it is easy to acquiesce and give up a certain measure of self-control to these external influences. To others, these forces seem to have little influence. The extent to which one feels free to pursue leisure is, in part, a function of the extent to which one is in control of his/her behavior.

Externally directed people are individuals who fundamentally feel that most important things in their lives are controlled by forces outside of themselves. On the other hand, **internally directed** people feel that most important things in their lives are under their personal control. Naturally, this construct is appropriately viewed on a continuum with extreme cases of locus of control falling on either end. Most people fall somewhere in the middle. Those who tend toward the external side are people who frequently feel helpless and tend to conform to the expectations of others, regardless of personal values. Internals on the other hand tend to be happier and more positive, and are likely to find greater expression in their personal leisure. Consequently it appears that locus of control is an important factor in explaining leisure behavior.

Another factor, related to locus of control, which helps explain leisure motivation is **perceived competence**. People tend to participate in activities in which they perceive themselves as competent and tend to avoid activities in which they perform poorly. When people feel that they are in control of their leisure choices, they choose activities that enable them to demonstrate their skills and abilities. Well learned responses tend to be facilitated by social settings. In other words, people like to be in the presence of others when they feel that they are reasonably skilled. And, generally, the presence of others facilitates their performance (*social facilitation*), thus, increasing their satisfaction with the activity. Conversely, when a person is poorly skilled and attempts the skill in the presence of others an inhibiting effect occurs (*social inhibition*). This leads to a poorer performance of the skill and a reduction in satisfaction. You see this occasionally illustrated at country dance venues. Experienced dancers thrive in the presence of other dancers, whereas the novice, after trying one line-dance often retreats in discouragement to the bar.

Self-Concept and Leisure

How a person perceives him or herself will have considerable bearing on how he or she relates to leisure experiences. Psychologists tend to agree that "one's self-picture" tends to correlate with behavior. People who see themselves as athletic usually participate in athletic activities; whereas, individuals who view themselves as unathletic tend to seek alternative diversions. In psychology, this tendency to conform to one's self expectations is referred to as the "self-fulfilling prophecy." The power of the self-fulfilling prophecy is illustrated by the behavior of a West African tribe, the Ashanti. These people believe that the day of the week on which a child is born will influence the behavior of the child in adult life. Children born on Monday are expected to grow up to be peaceful and quiet. Wednesday's children are expected to become troublesome. Police records tend to support this belief system. Monday's children have an unusually low crime rate; whereas those born on Wednesday tend to have an unusually high rate (Glietman 544). Clearly, how one views himself is going to influence leisure choices.

Flow as an Explanation for Leisure Behavior

That people gravitate to activities that seem to possess neither utility nor material rewards has been long recognized. Workers congregate around the water cooler, students doodle, housewives watch the soaps, children play tag, and executives daydream. On a deeper level, there are those who pursue the arts, create inventions, restore cars, climb mountains, and explore the seas. Although diverse in form, each of these behaviors has one commonality—they are all **autotelic** in nature. That is, they are activities (1) possessing an intrinsic reward potential, and (2) requiring a certain degree of self-directed concentration. These are to be compared with those activities (**exotelic**) which are characterized primarily by extrinsic potential and external locus of control or externally directed concentration. The former class of activities are generally associated with leisure, whereas the latter are related to work. Similarly we frequently view autotelic activities as yielding enjoyment whereas the motivation for exotelic activities is materialistic. We play for fun, we work for substance.

Recognizing that autotelic activities are universal and as such may possess hidden utilities, Mihalyi Csikszentmihalyi undertook a series of studies to examine the dynamics of enjoyment and the nature of activities that "appear to contain rewards within themselves, that do not rely on scarce material incentives . . ." (5). In his studies he looked at people who were deeply involved in activities which required time, effort and skill, yet produced little or no financial reward, social status or other recognizable forms of extrinsic reward. In general his findings indicated that the fundamental motivation for involvement in such activities was the enjoyment inherent in doing the activity. Furthermore his research suggested that enjoyment is a state of being characterized by a "feeling of discovery, a challenge overcome, a difficulty resolved. . ." (181), and that such a condition occurs when an individual experiences a matching of personal skills with "physical or symbolic opportunities for action that represent meaningful challenges" (181). He referred to this state of being as **flow**.

Flow activities are described by Csikszentmihalyi as activities providing opportunities for action which match a person's abilities with clearly defined **goals**, which possess sufficient arousal potential to captivate a person's **interest**, and which provides the individual with regular and relevant **feedback**. These activities tend to be associated with, but not limited to autotelic activities. For example, it was demonstrated that for some individuals their employment provided them with substantial flow experiences. Furthermore, a distinction was made between relatively simple and superficial autotelic activities producing relatively small amounts of flow, which he referred to as microflow, and more complex and substantive activities yielding what he coined **deep flow**. Regardless of intensity, flow activities tend to be viewed as enjoyable and produce a state of being as characterized by varying degrees of the following features: (1) concentration on a limited stimulus field, (2) loss of awareness of personal problems, (3) a loss of time awareness, (4) a sense of harmony and union with the immediate surroundings and (5) a feeling of competence.

That flow is a desirable condition was demonstrated through a series of experiments where individuals were asked to eliminate microflow from their behaviors for a 48-hour period. The activities prohibited were such seemingly incidental activities as chewing gum, passing time in idle conversation, playing simple games, telling jokes, watching television, etc. The results of this experiment suggest that when people eliminate seemingly nonessential autotelic behavior they feel more tired, less healthy, and less relaxed. They report more headaches and backaches, they feel less creative, and more inclined to irrational behavior. Normal tasks become a source of irritation, they report feeling depressed and incapable of effective concentration (Csikszentmihalyi 177). Although not directly examined in this study, these findings suggest a relationship between autotelic activities and optimal functioning. Csikszentmihalyi suggests this relationship in the following statement.

> By reversing these symptoms, one may infer that the function of microflow experiences is to keep a person alert, relaxed, with a positive feeling about himself, a feeling of being spontaneously

> creative. . . . To be able to do things that may not appear necessary to one's survival gives one a feeling of effectance. . . . (177)

According to flow theory, when a person believes that his action opportunities are too demanding for his capabilities, the result is anxiety. When the ratio of capabilities is higher, but the challenges are still too demanding for his abilities, the net result is worry. In situations where the individual's skills outweigh his opportunities for action, boredom results; anxiety again results when a significant disparity exists between perceived opportunity and skill (Csikszentmihalyi 49). Flow can only occur when the opportunities or challenges are in balance with the individual's abilities. Hence, activities are only enjoyable to the extent to which an individual's capacity to influence a given situation are in balance with the challenges presented by such a situation.

Maria Allison and Margaret Duncan (1987) undertook a study to determine the role of flow in the lives of working women. They also looked at factors that contributed to what they referred to as **antiflow**. Essentially their study revealed, as flow theory would suggest, antiflow tended to be associated with repetitive household tasks, repetitive tasks at work, unchallenging tasks, and meaningless tasks.

In examining the nature of enjoyment, Csikszentmihalyi did not limit his research to autotelic activities, rather he also looked at jobs that were viewed by the workers as enjoyable. In so doing, he found significant similarities between play and satisfying work experiences. So great was this similarity that he drew the following conclusion:

> The concept of flow makes it possible to see work and cultural definitions of lifestyle in general, as much more flexible than they are usually thought to be. It allows us to question the necessity of drudgery and anxiety, and it suggests ways in which everyday life can be made more free. There is no reason to believe any longer that only irrelevant play can be enjoyed, while the serious business of life must be borne as a burdensome cross. Once we realize that the boundaries between work and play are artificial, we can take matters in hand and begin the difficult task of making life more livable (191).

Csikszentmihalyi argues that there is no logical justification for the idea that work must be devoid of pleasure. Rather, he points out that were the rule of logic to be the guide, employers would attempt to structure work situations so that employees would be matched with tasks appropriate to their skills, provided with timely feedback and meaningful challenges, and that by so doing, otherwise extrinsic tasks would develop intrinsic justification.

Closing Note...

Motivation essentially means "to move," and in this chapter we have looked at what moves people to engage in leisure activity. Early in the chapter, we looked at some of the physiological aspects of motivation. It was pointed out that many of our basic behaviors are a function of biological needs. Eating, drinking, sleeping, and eliminating are all behaviors that are governed by biology. One theory (Ellis) argues that people engage in play, recreation, and other leisure behaviors because of a fundamental need to achieve optimal arousal. In this theory, when faced with too much arousal, an individual engages in behaviors designed to dampen arousal; when faced with boredom, an individual engages in behaviors designed to elevate arousal.

One of the fundamental lessons of this chapter is that when you are faced with boredom, engage in an activity which is novel or complex, arousal will be elevated. When anxious, reduce complexity or novelty.

REFERENCES

Allison, M.T. and M.C. Duncan. "Women, Work, and Flow." *Leisure Sciences* 9.3 (1987): 143–161.

Beard, J.G. and Ragheb, M. "Measuring Leisure Satisfaction." *Journal of Leisure Research* 12 (1980): 20–33.

Bexlon, W.H., U. Herone and T.H. Scott. "Effects of Decreased Variation in the Sensory Environment" *Canadian Journal of Psychology* 8 (1954): 70–76.

Csikszentmihalyi, M. *Beyond Boredom and Anxiety.* San Francisco: Jossey Bass, 1975.

Ellis, M. *Why People Play.* New York: Prentice-Hall, 1973.

Gleitman, H. *Psychology.* New York: W.W. Norton Co., 1981.

Harris, W.H. and J.S. Levey, (Eds.) *The New Columbia Encyclopedia.* New York: Columbia University Press, 1975.

Iso-Ahola, S.E. *The Psychology of Leisure and Recreation.* Dubuque: Wm. C. Brown, 1980.

Lilly, J.C. "Mental Effects of Reduction of Ordinary Levels of Physical Stimuli on Intact Healthy Persons." *Psychiatric Research Reports* 5 (1956): 1–28.

Maslow, A.H. *Motivation and Personality.* New York: Harper and Row, Publishers, 1954.

Morris, D. *The Human Zoo*, New York: Dell Publishing, 1976.

Munn, N.L. *Introduction to Psychology.* Boston: Houghton Mifflin, 1962.

Restack, R., M.D. *The Brain.* New York: Bantam Books, 1984.

Rombold, P. Unpublished manuscript. Department of Recreation and Leisure. California State University, Sacramento, 1986.

Sagan, C. *The Dragons of Eden.* New York: Ballantine, 1977.

Sapora, A. and E.D. Mitchell. *The Theory of Play and Recreation.* 3rd Ed., New York: Ronald, 1961.

Schierman, M. and G. Rowland. "Sensation Seeking and Selection of Entertainment." *Personality and Individual Differences* 6.5 (1989): 599–603.

Vander, A.J., S.H. James and D.S. Luciano. *Human Physiology: The Mechanisms of Body Function.* New York: McGraw-Hill Book Company, 1985.

Zuckerman, M. (Editor). *Biological Bases of Sensation Seeking, Impulsivity and Anxiety.* New Jersey: Lawrence Eflbaum Associations, Inc. Publishers, 1979.

Triandis, A.K. "A Comparative Analysis of Subjectivity Culture." In H. Triandis (ed.) *The Analysis of Subjective Culture.* New York: Wiley, 1972, (3–22).

Rokeach. M. "Some Unresolved Issues in Theories of Beliefs, Attitudes, and Values." Nebraska Symposium on Values, 1980.

CHAPTER 7

Human Development and Leisure

Just because something occurs, "on the average," at a certain time in a person's life does not guarantee that it will occur at that time in everyone's life. That's the problem with averages, they are not an accurate reflection of reality, they don't speak for the extremes. Oddly enough, this idea is well illustrated by my brother's account of a day spent hunting the vicious, ferocious, Utah jack rabbit.

> *I went hunting the other day. I saw this rabbit hightailing it across the countryside. I fired. My first shot went six inches in front of the rabbit. I fired again. My second shot passed six inches behind the rabbit. On the average, I guess you can say I shot a rabbit.*

And, that is how it is with the studies and theories presented in this chapter. Many of them are based on probabilities and averages and as such they only have meaning in general terms. They cannot be applied to specific (individual) cases, only to the populations as a whole from which they were extracted. Just because, on the average something occurs to people at a certain age, does not mean that it will happen to everyone at that time. For some it will occur earlier than the average, for others it will occur later, and for some it might not occur at all!

Stage Theories of Development

We begin with a discussion on three major stage theories. *Stage theories view development as occurring in a series of steps or stages.* Freud viewed development as passing through oral, anal, phallic latency, and genital periods. Erik Erikson theorized eight major stages in the life cycle.Piaget believed child development occupied four different stages.

Freud

This theory (Bavelas 18–28) is based on the premise that all human beings pass through a series of psychosexual developmental stages. Each must be successfully completed before an individual can move on to the next phase. If an individual fails to move on to the next stage, it is said that the individual experiences *fixation*.

The individual then tends to manifest personality traits related to the developmental stage of the fixation. The following is a simplified summary of Freud's psychosexual stages of development:

Age	Name	Physical Zone	Characteristics	Outcome
0 - 18 Mos.	Oral	Mouth	Demanding, need for mothering, interest in oral behaviors.	Passive, sarcastic, talkative, obsessive eating, smoking.
8 Mos. to 3 Yrs.	Anal Explusion Retention	Rectum Bladder	Hostile, super conformist, stingy, miserly.	Destructive, cruel, sting, miserly.
3 to 7 Yrs.	Phallic	Genitals	Oedipal Complex, Electra Complex, so-called "penis envy."	Emotional disorders, homosexuality behavior.
7 to 12 Yrs.	Latency	Suppression	Interest in nonsexual activity.	Unable to form sexual relations.
Puberty	Genitals	Genitals	Romantic infatuation and emotional upheaval.	Unable to make commitments, infatuation.

Erikson

Whereas Freud tended to focus on the relationship of sexual development to psychological development, Erikson focused on the relationship of social influences to psychological development (1963). Erikson theorized that human development follows the *epigenetic principle*, i.e., everything that grows has a life plan, and if a capacity fails to develop on schedule, the rest of the development is hampered.

Erikson's Eight Stages of Development the Epigenetic Principle

Stage	Function	Outcome
1. Infancy	Basic Trust vs. mistrust	Trust in self-others
2. Early Childhood	Autonomy vs. shame, guilt	Self-control
3. 4th–5th year	Initiative vs. guilt	Self-direction
4. 6th–12th year	Industry vs. inferiority	Mastery
5. Adolescence	Identity vs. role confusion	Sense of self
6. Young adult	Intimacy vs. isolation	Extended intimate relationship; capacity to work toward career
7. Adulthood	Generativity vs. stagnation	Concerned beyond family
8. Old age	Integrity vs. despair	Sense of satisfaction

Piaget

According to Piaget, development is basically a process of adaptation. Children, on the basis of their interaction with their environment, develop cognitive structures or *schemas*. Piaget viewed adaptation as involving *assimilation* and *accommodation*. Assimilation involves taking in new information and interpreting it by current schemas. Accommodation refers to changing schemas to fit new information. The balance of accommodation and assimilation is *equilibrium*, and is the basis for new assimilations. This process leads to constant change in the organization of one's thinking. As new information is accommodated, the ability of the child to perceive new information more accurately is enhanced. Consequently, accommodation influences assimilation which in turn affects accommodation and so on. This concept is suggested in the term *constructivism* which is used to describe this process of constructing knowledge, and which has come to be associated with Piaget's ideas regarding cognitive development.

The stages through which a child passes, according to Piaget, are summarized in the following table:

Age	Name	Characteristics
0 to 2 years	Sensorimotor stage	Preoccupation with the relationship between sensations and motor behaviors
2 to 7 years	Preoperational stage	Development of the ability to use symbols; egocentric
7 to 11 years	Concrete Operations	Rational thinking
11 years on	Formal Operations	Ability to deal with abstract concepts and constructs

The extent to which any of these models is an accurate portrayal of child development is subject to debate. However, as suggested by all three theories, it is generally agreed that early development consists of several critical periods, which if missed have long-term consequences. Also, it seems generally agreed upon that childhood, and to less extent, the experiences of infancy, correlate with adult behavior. In short, the years of infancy and childhood are very important. And inasmuch as play is the preoccupation of infancy and childhood, it can be inferred that it serves an important role in the development process.

Notes on Freud

Sigmund Freud (1856-1939) was a Viennese physician. Trained In neurology and with a keen interest in the psyche, Freud received his medical degree In 1881. After studying with Jean Martin Charcot in Paris, who was investigating the usefulness of hypnosis as a treatment for hysteria, Freud returned to Vienna. The work being done by Charcot inspired Freud to look further into solving problems associated with the mind. This led to a collaboration with Josef Breuer, a Viennese physician, who had received notoriety through his use of hypnosis in treating hysteria. Later Freud rejected hypnosis in lieu of **free association**, a process he believed permitted unrecognized ideas to emerge from the subconscious. By this time, Freud had theorized that the symptoms of neurosis were directly traceable to a traumatic experience earlier in one's life, experiences that led to unresolved conflicts which were being struggled with on an unconscious level. Because of Freud's belief that such conflicts were largely a function of an individual's sexuality, he fell in to disrepute with such prominent men as Jung and Adler. Even though criticized for basing his conclusions from observations of his patients, a rather biased sample, Freud Is considered the Father of Psychotherapy. He died in England In 1939.

Freud's concept of the unconscious mind helps us understand why people often make what seems inexplicable decisions regarding their choice of leisure activities. According to Freud the unconscious mind has a powerful influence on all aspects of our behavior.

Notes on Erik Erikson

Erik H. Erikson was born In Frankfurt, Germany in 1902. After studying psychoanalysis at the Vienna psychoanalytic Institute, he moved to the United States In 1933. He taught at Yale, Berkeley and Harvard. He retired In 1968. He rejected Freud's psychological determinism and advocated a much broader approach to psychoanalysis. His model of human development places greater emphasis on social Influences than did Freud.

Notes on Piaget

Considered the most Influential student of cognitive development of this century (Carlson 132), Jean Piaget was born in 1896 and died In 1980. Although trained in biology, he is principally known for his contributions to child psychology. He argued that development follows a genetically determined sequence of events. His conclusions were based on his observations of his own children at home and then later children at his Center for Epistemology in Geneva.

The Epigenetic Brain

The stage theorists, following their observations of human behavior, concluded that people pass through a series of developmental steps. It appeared that development followed a kind of schedule, and that certain developmental tasks best occurred at certain times. They also observed that if certain developmental outcomes were not achieved on schedule, the probability of those outcomes ever being achieved were minimized. Why does this occur? A partial answer may be found in recent research. Physiologists have concluded that there are specific times in one's life when the body is most effective in producing certain developmental outcomes, and this seems to be particularly true of the developing human brain.

A child is born with as many neurons (brain cells) that he or she will ever have. We enter the world with literally billions of neurons, but from the time of birth on this number slowly diminishes. While the rest of the body produces new cells to replace worn out cells, the brain does not. The brain comes equipped with all of the cells necessary to form the neural patterns that allow an individual to develop the concepts, constructs, skills, and attitudes necessary for growth and development. At the time of birth these cells are generally not connected to one another. Rather they stand relatively isolated waiting to be linked together to form neural patterns. These patterns may be thought of as the circuitry of the brain and are essentially the physical analogues to Piaget's concept of informational units. During early childhood, through daily sensory input, these free-standing neurons are linked to one another. This is accomplished through the production of synaptic connections in which the axons of nerve cells connect with other nerve cells. These neural connections form structural units reflecting the child's unique perception of his or her environment. Restak describes this process:

> Increases in the number of synapses are associated with corresponding increases in the complexity and number of dendritic spines. This process is dependent on environmental stimuli.If the brain is deprived of environmental stimulation, the number of spines and, by implication, the complexity of synaptic connections is reduced. For instance, raising an animal in darkness reduces the number

of synapses in the animal's visual area. Even more dramatic are the differences in brain organization that can be found between animals raised in deprived versus enriched environments. Merely adding a few toys to play with, or mazes to run through, leads to an increase in the number of synaptic contacts as well as a thickening of the animals' cerebral cortex (47).

Physiologists tell us that early in development there are certain "critical periods" during which certain organizational neural patterns may occur, but which resist later modification. These periods of maximal structural and functional growth depend upon the availability of proper internal and external environmental stimuli (Restak 47). Restak, as mentioned above, noted that animals raised in darkened environments experience retarded synaptic development in the visual area of the brain. What is more important is to note that if the light deprivation occurs during the first few weeks of life, the visual system is permanently retarded. This is also true for other systems in the brain; if a developmental window is missed, developmental retardation is likely to occur. Vander Shennan and Luciano stress the importance of critical periods:

> . . . in the case of either limited or lengthy periods of modifiability, it can occur only within the constraints imposed by the neuron's genetic code and its experiential history. The genes specific the capacity, whereas the environmental stimuli determine the specific expression and content of the neuronal output (709).

The implications should be clear. If a child is to achieve his or her intellectual potential, attention must be given to stimulating neural connections early in life and at a rate consistent with child's developmental needs and capabilities. Many of the developmental tasks of childhood are dependent upon the ability of a parent to produce an intellectually enriched environment. Where a parent fails to do so, a child misses out on an opportunity for enriched cognitive, emotional, and intellectual growth and development. Placing a child in front of a television, for example, is perhaps the worst thing a parent can do. The images that are presented to the child on a television screen have the potential for forming neural patterns which in the long term can have an adverse impact on the child's ability to think intellectually and creatively as well as relate to others socially. A parent is wise to provide a child with a rich array of stimulating experiences. Particularly good are play activities that involve music, rhythm, movement, creativity, visual expression, and fun problem solving.

Although, it is in early development that most neural connections are formed and brain organization occurs, there is research that suggests some circuits in the brain can change even though the critical period may have passed. The ability of the brain to reorganize itself is referred to as "brain plasticity." Recent research by Karni and Berntini on brain plasticity in adults suggests that some degree of "behaviorally relevant degree of plasticity is retrained in the adult cortex" (1997). For example, research indicates that when parts of the brain are damaged by disease, new message routes can be produced which compensate for the loss of the damaged areas (Golden and Tsiaras, 1994). Thompson (1993) cites several studies which support the notion that reorganization can occur in adult rats and primates. One particular study showed that when rats that were denied stimulation were placed in a stimulus rich environment, some brain growth occurred (323–325). Thompson concludes that even though experiences early in life have a profound effect on brain development, "Organization and reorganization of the cerebral cortex is not limited to development, it appears to occur throughout the lifetime of each individual" (329). What this essentially means is that even in adulthood, it may be possible to stimulate the production of new neural connections, and continue to create new neural patterns.

The implications of this discussion should be clear: (1) It is important to provide children with appropriate developmental experiences during critical periods, and (2) it is also important for adults to continue to stimulate and challenge their own adult brains. In respect to stimulating the adult brain, Golden and Tsiaras suggest that people benefit most when they select activities that are "diverting, and more important, unfamiliar" (62). This offers another excellent reason for making discovery events an important part of your life. When you are discovering, you may be helping keep your brain circuitry healthy.

The Components of Human Development

In spite of the apparent simplicity and the elegant explanations of human development provided by the stage theories, human development remains, in reality, a very complex process. Development is the result of the unique unfolding of human potential arising from a complex of factors too numerous to fully comprehend. In an attempt to gain insight into this complex and dynamic process, scientists have arbitrarily divided the development process into logical and reasonably manageable categories. These categories have been created for the convenience of researchers and educators to provide a structure or framework to facilitate scientific investigation. By using a classification system based on different aspects of human development, science can examine relationships between some of the major constituents in the development process. Perhaps the most common way of examining human development is to examine it from the perspective of the following four subdivisions: (1) physical development. (2) cognitive development, (3) personality development, and (4) social development. One of the problems associated with looking at human development from this perspective is that it fails to account for the mutual interdependence of each of these areas. It must always be kept in mind that none of the areas included can be considered independent of the others.

1. **Physical Development.** Here, the emphasis is on quantitative measures that indicate physical change. Physical development is essential to cognitive and personality development because it is through the physical senses that we acquire the information necessary to function within the various contexts that our bodies carry us. Much of one's early knowledge is a result of early exploratory behavior. This type of behavior may appear of insignificant value but in reality be the source of large amounts of information critical to the child's successful deve lopment. In later life, the aging process affects the body adversely by imposing physical limitations foreign to younger years. This in turn, is reflected in one's feelings about self and in the type of leisure activities one chooses. Furthermore, the physical body is the repository of one's genetic potential which has a profound effect on all aspects of one's growth and development.
2. **Cognitive Development.** Here, we are concerned about the various mental abilities that a person brings to bear in his/her attempts to solve problems. In the formulation presented here, cognitive development specifically refers to learning, memory, reasoning, and creativity. In other words, cognitive development refers to the process of acquiring and applying information. It is believed that leisure experiences make an important contribution to one's understanding of self, knowledge about other people, and of course, about the nature of leisure and its concomitants. This suggests a kind of synergism where leisure influences cognitive deve lopment, which, in turn influences leisure choices and involvement, which, in turn contributes to additional learning, memories, reasoning ability and creative growth.
3. **Personality Development.** Most people have a fairly good "intuitive" idea as to the meaning of the word "personality," but among social scientists there seems to be a lack of agreement as to its definition. As a consequence, the literature regarding personality is filled with discussions on its definition and meaning. Trait theory takes a position different from phenomenological theory, both of which disagree with the psychodynamic theories, etc. One definition frequently found in psychology texts is typified by the definition found in the *Dictionary of Psychology* (Stutt 94), which basically states that personality is the sum total of one's beliefs, attributes, behaviors, and values. *Webster's Unabridged Dictionary* defines personality as "an individual's emotional and behavioral tendencies."
4. **Social Development.** Much of what we call personality is a reflection of the quality of one's interactions with significant others. The formal and informal learning that accrues as one interacts with such important others as parents, siblings, peers, and others is believed to be a major factor in personality and cognitive development. The **socialization** values of leisure experiences can have positive or negative consequences depending upon the nature of the event.

Types of Play Behavior and Development

During the first few months of childhood, amazing developmental changes occur. Born with little motor capabilities, the infant is soon capable of sitting erect, grasping, holding, crawling, and often within the first year, walking. Similarly during the first few months, important strides are taken in cognitive, personality, and social development. There is a certain irony in that among the various factors facilitating these important developments is a behavior often looked upon as trivial and unessential—this behavior is play.

In examining the relationship between play and development, it is important to recognize that just as there are different types of human development there are also different types of play, some of which are more suited for development in one area of human growth than in others. Naturally, play during early infancy is rooted in the child's exploration of his sensory and motor abilities. As these are mastered, they then provide the basis for subsequent exploration in the cognitive and social areas. In examining and classifying these different play forms, there are several alternatives available to us. One, we could categorize them by developmental stages and discuss them in sequential order. Another approach would be to classify and analyze them by developmental functions (cognitive, physical, personality, social). A third approach would be to categorize them by interaction patterns.

An example of this third approach is found in the now classic study of Mildred B. Parten (1932) who observed the play of school children in nursery school settings. She identified six types of play. Each of these types of play behavior have developmental implications, and provide us with a sort of taxonomy for examining the relationship of play to development. Parten's six types of play are summarized below:

1. **Unoccupied play**. Children spend their time watching others, idly glancing about, or engaging in aimless activities (standing around, tugging clothing, etc.)
2. **Solitary play**. Children play with toys by themselves and make no effort to get close to or speak with other children.
3. **Onlooker behavior**. Children watch other children at play, occasionally talking to themselves or asking questions. However, they do not themselves join in the play.
4. **Parallel play**. Children play independently beside other children but not with them. Although they play close together and with similar toys, they do not interact
5. **Associative play**. Children interact with one another, borrowing or lending play material, following one another with carts, cars or trains and attempting to influence each other's behavior. Each child does as he or she sees fit; no division of labor or integration of activities take place.
6. **Cooperative play**. Children integrate their play activities. In this kind of play, the members usually take on different role responsibilities, and they often think of themselves as belonging to a group from which other children are excluded.

In 1968, building upon the theoretical work of Piaget, Smilansky suggested that play falls into four stages of development: (1) functional play (corresponds to Piaget's Sensorimotor stage), (2) constructive play (refers to play which involves the manipulation of the environment and objects within the environment to produce something new), (3) dramatic play (based on a child's ability to use language and symbols in the thought process), and (4) play involving rules and set procedures (related to Piaget's formal operations stage).

Gunn and Peterson, in their text, *Therapeutic Recreation Program Design: Practices and Principles* (1978), argue that leisure activities (including play) can be examined from three developmental perspectives: (1) psychomotor, (2) cognitive, and (3) affective. They suggest that each of these dimensions can further be analyzed by the interaction patterns in the activity. Borrowing from Avedon, they identify eight interaction patterns: (1) intraindividual (action taking place within the individual), (2) extraindividual (action directed toward an object, not a person), (3) aggregate (action done in the presence of others directed at some object), (4) interindividual (action of a competitive nature), (5) unilateral (action of one against many), (6) multilateral (every player is against every other player), (7) intragroup (action of a cooperative nature), and (8) intergroup (team against team) (157–172).

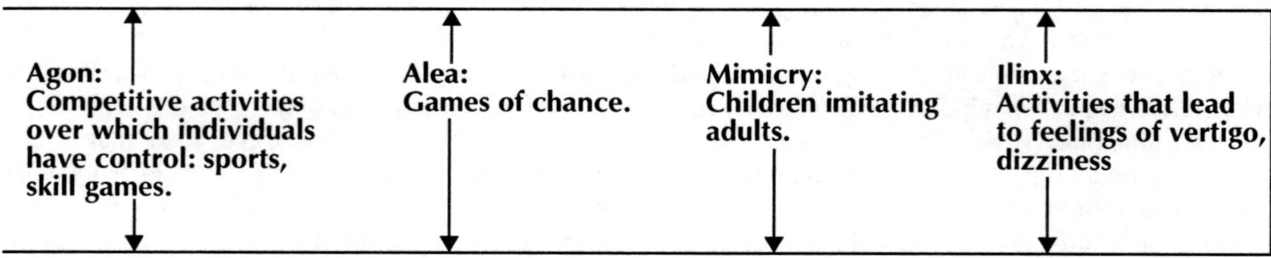

Although there are several other models applicable to a discussion on play behavior as it relates to human development, we will review only one additional model. This model was originally established as a model or system of classification of games (Callois, 1961). Nevertheless, it provides a useful framework for examining play and leisure behavior. In its simplest form this model consists of four behavior categories viewed on a bipolar continuum. They are summarized below:

Categories:

1. Agon—competition is the dominant theme of the behavior.
2. Alea—chance or luck is the dominant theme.
3. Mimicry—focus on stimulation.
4. Ilinx—pursuit of vertigo (disequilibrium) is the dominant theme.

Continuum:

Plaidia—one side of the continuum representing freedom from structure, internal locus of control and internal motivation.

Ludus—opposite to paidia represented by structure, discipline, control, rules and regulations.

This classification system grew out of an analysis of play activities found in different cultures. These categories of play emerged as common patterns between cultures were discovered. My own experience with Native American children (Hopi and Zuni) and then later with my own children demonstrated to me the fact that children engage in similar play patterns regardless of culture. Callois' research reinforces the idea that play is universal, that children, regardless of culture, experience similar types of activity in their play.

Inasmuch as behaviors vary by age, it might be well to view leisure behavior from the theoretical framework most appropriate to a given developmental phase. For example, Smilansky's model is particularly applicable to the play of childhood and early adolescence, but is relatively limited in application for adult years. Gunn and Peterson present a model particularly attractive for use in therapeutic settings and perhaps for adults, but place too much emphasis on social interaction to effectively accommodate early sensorimotor play. Callois fails to place adequate emphasis on cognitive play to be useful in a broad application. The point should be clear. No one model of play is equally effective across all age groups and in all situations. In discussions of play, one may have to refer to a number of models to describe the behavior under discussion.

Zanden's Summary of Play Contributions to Human Development

After a review of studies dealing with play and human development, Vander Zanden identified five major contributions that play makes to the development process:

1. Through play, children make motor and sensory discoveries; they learn about the properties of things.
2. Play prepares children for life, but on their own terms. Children at play can experience themselves as active agents in their environment, not merely as resting ones.
3. Play provides opportunities for rehearsing adult roles, a process called **anticipatory socialization**.
4. Play helps children build their own individual sense of identity. It allows them to get outside themselves and view themselves from other perspectives.
5. Play allows for both reality and fantasy. It is a pliable medium that enables children to come to terms with their fears—of villains, witches, ghosts, lions, dogs, etc. Through imaginary episodes, children can harmlessly confront these creatures and perhaps even triumph over them (Zanden 363–364).

The following discussion expands on Zanden's observations with particular emphasis on the relationship of leisure and its concomitants, play and recreation, on physical, cognitive, personality, and social development.

Leisure Activity and Physical Development

When parents talk about newborn infants, the discussion often flows around physical attributes such as height, weight, and mobility. A frequent statement made by new parents goes something like this, "I can't believe how fast she is growing!" This reflects the fact that rapid growth is one of the most notable features of the first few years. Physical development occurs more rapidly during the first three years than at any other time in a person's life. By the first year, a person's brain will reach two-thirds of its adult size. Infants generally learn to sit alone around six months. It is around this same time that they master rolling from stomach to back. Most babies are able to crawl by nine to ten months. Babies can usually stand unsupported by 13-14 months; walking comes about a month later. By age two, most toddlers are able to run, climb and manipulate objects rather well. The combination of these three physical skills coupled with what parents see as unbounded energy, produces a developmental phase both dreaded and enjoyed by most parents. The phrase, "The Terrible Two's," suggests the essence of this delightful but challenging period. During this period of rapid development, play is the principal means by which new skills are learned and practiced, and through which coordination and muscle strength is promoted. As someone once keenly observed, "Play is the work of the child."

A Personal Note: I recall very clearly when my son was two-years old. He wasn't really '"terrible" but he was very active. He was also particularly fond of chocolate chip cookies. Consequently, the chocolate chip cookies were generally placed beyond his reach. They usually could be found in the cookie jar perched on top of the refrigerator. You can imagine my surprise one day when I walked into the kitchen to find him sitting on top of the refrigerator stuffing cookies into his mouth. He had cleverly pulled open the cupboard drawers to form a stairway, and then used a bread box to get to the top of the refrigerator. Needless to say, after this display of ingenuity and dexterity, I had no worries about his cognitive and physical development. I also relocated the cookies.

Before adolescence, boys are slightly stronger than girls, but the differences are only slight After the adolescent growth spurt (usually in girls around age ten and in boys around 12-14), the male's larger muscles, larger heart and lungs, and greater capacity for carrying oxygen in the blood provide the male with the strength and endurance for highly competitive and physical activities. This does not mean, however, that women are necessarily inferior to men in strength and endurance. A cursory look in any gymnasium will reveal some very powerful women.

That physique influences one's leisure is not a particularly new notion. The idea that an individual's inherited physique helps determine an individual's inherited physique helps determine an individual's character has its roots in folklore and mythology. Some of these early myths suggest that the depth, color or shape of a person's eyes can reveal personality traits. Strength and beauty have long been associated with valor and virtue. People with slight builds have often been judged as artistic or effeminate. In the 1800's the idea that physical features were related to behavior became formalized by Franz Joseph Gall in his theory of "*phrenology*." This theory, which assumed a relationship between the shape of the skull and behavior, was later refuted by anthropologists and psychologists.

Of more recent origin is William H. Sheldon's theory that one's inherited physique predisposes one to certain emotional, cognitive and behavioral traits. Initially, Sheldon set out to classify human body types. After an intensive study of photographs, Sheldon and his colleagues concluded that all body types fall within three classifications: *endomorphic* (fat), *mesomorphic* (muscular), and *ectomorphic* (frail). These three classifications are not to be taken as mutually exclusive, but rather as often being present in varying degrees in the same person. For example, a person may be ectomorphic above the waist, mesomorphic through the legs and endomorphic in the middle—an all too common complaint.

Sheldon proposes that each component is associated with different temperaments, and as such, by knowing an individual's *somatotype*, an individual's temperament can be predicted. He proposes three universal dimensions: *viscerotonia* (a love of food and comfort), *somatonia* (a craving for physical action), and *cerebrotonia* (an inclination for restraint, inhibition and apprehensiveness). According to Sheldon, body type is a stimulus for certain responses from one's social environment, which then shapes an individual's temperament according to cultural expectations. Hence, in a society where leisure activities include football, basketball, and baseball, forces are put into action early in one's life that direct the mesomorphic toward such activities and those of less athletic somatotypes into less athletic endeavors. The extent to which Sheldon's theory adequately explains the relationship between physical characteristics and leisure remains to be seen; nevertheless, it does provide a theoretical basis for arguing that leisure behavior may be influenced by anatomical and physiological factors.

Activity Deprivation and Development

The relationship of leisure to development can be viewed.from a direction opposite to that provided in Sheldon's formulation. Here, we are interested in the influence leisure activities have on physical development. There is good evidence that physical deve1opment is strongly influenced by the play patterns of early childhood. In a now famous study involving Iranian orphanages during the 1960's, it was demonstrated that when children are deprived of physical play, their physical development is adversely affected. In this study, children in two orphanages were studied. Due to understaffing, overworked attendants seldom handled the children. The children had no toys and were never put in a sitting position or placed on their stomachs. Once a child was able to sit on the floor, there were no toys, no play furniture, and no play apparatus. *The net result of this type of child rearing was severe motor retardation.* The results clearly demonstrated the developmental role of physical play in child development. As a control, a third orphanage was studied which employed acceptable child rearing practices. In this orphanage, the children were frequently handled, were placed in playpens at four months, had many toys, and were given considerably more play opportunities than their less fortunate counterparts. The children in this orphanage showed normal motor development (Papalia and Olds 100).

In a study of 288 infants from Yucatan, Mexico, it was found that in the first three months Yucatan children developed manipulative skills faster than a sample of U.S. chi1dren.However by 11 months they were far behind the American sample on all motor skills. The explanation of this turnabout can be in part attributed to the differences in play behavior between the two groups. American children were encouraged to play in a much more unrestricted manner than Yucatan children, given more objects and afforded greater freedom of movement. Papalia and Olds summarize the restrictive child rearing pattern of the Yucatan parents thusly:

> . . . the more advanced manipulative abilities of Yucatan babies may arise from their not having toys to play with. As a result, they discovered play with their fingers at earlier ages. Their delayed skills in moving about are probably related to several conditions in their lives: as infants, that are swaddled, which restricts their freedom of movement, as older children, they continue to be restrained by being held more in the arms or on the hips of their parents and older brothers and

sisters, by sleeping in hammocks (which become net cages compared to the open space of a firm-mattressed crib), and by not being put on the ground to play . . (101).

Gender Differences

There is a plethora of studies that demonstrate a difference in the play behavior of boys and girls (Lehman and Witty, 1927; Britt and Janus, 1941; Smity and Conolly, 1972; Rubin, 1977; Barnett and Chick, 1986). Fundamentally, these, and similar studies, suggest that certain aspects of play behavior may be predicted solely on the basis of gender. Macoby (1980) nicely summarizes the differences generally observed in the play of young boys and girls.

1. Boys tend to be more boisterous and aggressive.
2. Boys play involves struggles for dominance.
3. Boys tend to be more competitive than girls.
4. Girls tend to avoid conflict by establishing rules, etc.
5. Girls tend to be more empathetic in their play.
6. Girls are less likely to avoid "tomboyish behavior" than boys are to avoid "sissy behavior."

There is evidence to support the notion that some of the differences in play behavior between the sexes is the result of the basic biological differences between boys and girls. At about the sixth week of gestation, embryos destined to become males are exposed to relatively large quantities of androgens (substances producing or stimulating the development of male characteristics). These hormones stimulate the formation of the male body structures, destining the developing male to greater physical strength and greater tendency toward aggressive and physical play behavior.

Testosterone has been shown to be related to aggressive behavior in neophilic animals, including humans. Prolactin (a hormone secreted by the pituitary gland, which, in association with estrogen stimulates breast development and formation of milk during pregnancy) has been demonstrated to produce motherly behavior in virgin male animals (Papalia and Olds 213). Papalia and Olds cite a study by Crowley (1962) which showed the relationship between *idiopathic hypogonatropic hypogonadism* (a disorder resulting in abnormally low amounts of male hormone being produced at puberty) and spatial skills. When the subjects suffering from this disorder were compared to a sample of normal males on their ability to identify certain geometric designs camouflaged by distracting lines, the normal group did far better than those with low hormone levels (213).

Further evidence showing the relationship of gender related constitutional predispositions is cited in Glietman (516). In a longitudinal study, 70 men and women were first observed as infants and then again as adults. A strong correlation was observed between aggressive behavior as infants and aggressive behavior as adults among the men in the subject pool. No such correlation was found among females. The researchers argue that this difference resulted not from a biological predisposition, but rather from socialization practices which legitimize aggressive behavior in males and limits aggressive behavior among females. The greater predisposition for aggression among males, may interact with socialization practices which sanction aggression among males and prohibit it among females. This bias in socialization practices is illustrated clearly by a cursory analysis of gender specific games and recreation activities, as well as a review of the content of much of our television and movie productions.

It is suggested by Iso-Ahola that under situations of extreme stimulus deprivation, anatomical and biochemical changes can occur which can have far reaching effects. He points out that rearing animals in conditions of complete stimulus deprivation affects the production of ribonucleic acid. A decrease in this acid minimizes the body's ability to synthesize protein, which, of course, is essential for physical growth and repair. On the other hand, he presents evidence to suggest that opportunities for optimal stimulation contributes to the development of the cerebral cortex (Iso-Ahola 83).

Play and Cognitive Development

Cognitive development refers to the growth of human properties essential to the process of acquiring knowledge. As Zanden states, "It encompasses such phenomena as sensation, perception, imagery, retention, recall, problem solving, and thinking" (Zanden 247). That play contributes to cognitive development can be evidenced through several studies.

According to Zelazo and Kearley, at some point early in infancy, children begin to generate ideas. They refer to this stage as *cognitive metamorphosis*: This is believed to usually occur between nine and 16 months. It is not clear as to the extent that cognitive metamorphosis can be encouraged through play, but this study does demonstrate that there is a high correlation between play complexity and age. So certain of this relationship are Zelazo and Kearley that they concluded that play can be used as an indicator of the cognitive level of babies (95–117).

Not only can play be used as an indicator of intellectual ability, but some studies indicate that it makes a major contribution to its development. As a child explores and manipulates his/her environment, a sense of competence occurs. This provides the basis for subsequent exploration. New situations are arousing and challenge the developing cognitive and motor stills of the developing child. Redundant situations loose their arousal potential, and thus, the child is motivated to seek out new and stimulating activities. Conversely, situations that tend to be too arousing compel the child to withdraw and look for other less arousing opportunities. By providing a child with play items appropriate to his arousal needs, a parent supports the natural learning process found in play and recreation. When a child is prevented from experiencing optimal arousal, or when a child is subjected to too much arousal, the net result is a reduction in learning.

Adaptation and Organization

Piaget postulates that children's play is dependent upon cognitive structures that are presumed to be inherent to the process of maturation and development. These structures are referred to as *schemas* and are the *basic cognitive units*. Cognitive schemas are primarily the function of the child's interaction with the environment. As time passes, the child accumulates knowledge which gives rise to new schemas. Two general principles govern this process: (1) adaptation and (2) organization. Adaptation is the process children use to produce new cognitive structures. Organization involves the integration of all schemas into one overall system. *Adaptation* is dependent upon *assimilation* and *accommodation*. Assimilation involves incorporating new information derived from experience to a child's existing cognitive structures; accommodation is the process by which children change their cognitive structures to better fit their perceptions of their environment. These two processes operate together to produce changes in the child's conceptualization of the world and appropriate reactions to it.

As pointed out earlier, Piaget identified four major phases in the development of the child: sensorimotor (birth to two years), pre-operational (two to seven years), concrete operations (seven to 11 years), and finally, a stage of formal operations. Each of these stages is characterized by specific cognitive capabilities. During the first stage, the child is limited to thinking about sensory input and the manipulation of objects. Thinking during this phase does not involve symbols. The use of symbolic thinking follows, where a child is able to think about objects without the object being present. Their use of mental representation of things and events allows them to become proficient at classifying, dealing with numbers, and understanding the principles of conservation. Eventually, the child learns how to think in abstract, as opposed to concrete terms.

The form that children's play takes can be viewed as a function of the stage of development in which the child is currently operating. Sensorimotor play tends to involve the exploration of the environment through motor activity and the senses. During the preoperational phase, children are able to imitate actions or objects and can play games where one object stands for another (symbolic play). During the concrete operational phase, children are able to use representational symbols in logical patterns, thus, permitting word plays and jokes that depend upon reversal. and transformations. In the formal reasoning stage, play reflects the ability of the individual to go beyond a concrete situation and think in abstract terms and hypothetical situations.

Play is not only a function of development, but also a factor contributing to it. It is chiefly through play that children learn about and understand their relationship to their environment. Starting with the most fundamental concepts, a child begins to acquire information which enables him to think in an increasingly sophisticated fashion. Simple explorations, through play, often provide children with essential insights and understanding. Piaget was a champion of this view even to the point of advocating the use of play in the otherwise formal environment of the modern school:

> Children should be allowed to do their own experimenting and their own research. Teachers, of course, can guide them by providing appropriate materials, but the essential thing is that in order for a child to understand something, he must construct it himself; he must re-invent it. Every time we teach a child something, we keep him from inventing it himself. On the other hand, that which we allow him to discover himself will remain with him visibly. . . for all the rest of his life (Piaget 27).

The balance between accommodation and assimilaton is seen as the basis for intelligence. The counter balance between these two cognitive functions is referred to by Piaget as *equilibrium*. As new responses are added to cognitive structures, the perceived constraints of the environment are carefully evaluated against previous experience. This produces a dynamic which permits increasingly complex thinking. This becomes the basis for new accommodations. As Ellis states:

> Change in assimilatory processes produce new accommodations and the accommodatory changes alter the cognitive schemata and the assimilatory constraints p1aced on immediate experience. The individual's complexity spirals upward over time as assimilation and accommodation interact (66).

As the child learns about his/her environment, he/she tests these learnings by manipulating objects in the environment to determine if they respond in ways predicted by recently assimilated information. When results are as predicted, the child develops a sense of competence which serves to validate both assimilated information and the child's perception of self. This process of *affectance-competence* plays an important role in helping an individual learn about the environment and her/his relationship to it

Central to stage theories, such as Piaget's, is the notion that people are somehow inherently motivated to pursue activities that contribute to the developmental tasks of each of the phases. There is little doubt that the play of children and young adults contributes to the tasks of each of these phases, but just what motivates people to engage in play behavior in the first place? Particularly useful to this discussion is the work of anthropologist, Desmond Morris, who argues that all mammals are fundamentally stimulus or novelty liking. This observation suggests that the more intelligent an animal, the greater its probability of participating in "non-utilitarianism" or playful behavior (Morris 23). This observation gives rise to the idea that neophylic (stimulus seeking) animals possess some kind of stimulus seeking drive.

Ellis explored this area in 1973. His work led to a book entitled *Why People Play*. In his formulation, he argues that sensation seeking behavior is rooted in the reticular arousal system, a structure in the brain which modulates incoming sensory data allowing only stimulation to the cerebral cortex which has a high probability of producing a level of arousal optimal for the context in which the stimuli is perceived.

In this theory, it is argued that in order for a stimulus to be viewed as possessing arousal potential, it must be viewed as novel, complex or possess significant uncertainty. When a stimulus possesses too much arousal potential, the individual receives too much stimulation and will engage in behaviors designed to reduce the stimulation. The state of too much arousal is referred to as *supraoptimal arousal*. The inverse situation is where too little arousal is present. This state is referred to as *suboptimal arousal*, and usually triggers strategies to increase the level of stimulation reaching the cerebral cortex. Suboptimal arousal (frequently referred to as boredom) comes as the result of the absence of new information to assimilate or new situations requiring the accommodation of old information. In a situation such as this, there is high congruity between existing information and context. Situations of this sort lack the novelty, complexity, or uncertainty required to produce elevated levels of arousal, and thus, leads to arousal seeking behavior. It is through this type of exploratory or sensation seeking behavior that many play behaviors are invented. Through searching for novel, complexity or uncertainty, the developing individual acquires new information which provides the basis for subsequent learning.

Unfortunately, not all attempts to minimize suboptimal arousal lead to productive behavior. Too frequently, arousal seeking leads to watching television, which in turn, may result in exposure to incorrect ideas about society and even physical reality. Stimulus seeking most not be confused with what may be called *epistemic behavior* or knowledge seeking behavior. Knowledge seeking has the same characteristics as stimulus seeking, but it involves more formal operations and abstract thinking. Not normally classified as play, these explorations may take the form of reading, studying, philosophizing, etc. That this type of arousal seeking is not as frequent an occurrence as stimulation seeking is manifest in a study by Kohlberg and Gilligan (1971) in which they reported that almost half of American adults never reach the formal operations stage. In their study, a sample of adults was asked to perform certain tasks requiring cognitive development typical of the formal operations stage. On average, only about 50% were able to successfully complete the tasks.

In part, these relatively discouraging statistics might be due to the tendency of people in this society to engage in leisure activities which are principally stimulating to the limbic system, but don't tax the cerebral cortex. In many respects, we are a society of spectators, far less a society of critical and creative thinkers. It is doubtful that contemporary American culture encourages play that contributes to high levels of cognitive development. As Papalia and Olds point out:

> Even if young people have the necessary neurological development to reach the stage of formal reasoning, if they have not been encouraged in this direction culturally and educationally, they may never attain this highest level and final qualitative leap of cognitive development (325).

Creativity and Leisure Behavior

One of the most important cognitive skills is the ability to think in creative terms. Essentially, creativity is the ability to see things from an unusual perspective, to solve problems in a unique and novel fashion. That creative thinking is related to leisure is relatively easy to see. Creative thinking occurs when an individual is free to examine alternative solutions to some problem. The extent to which this occurs is in part dependent upon the individual's ability to function without constraint from external forces. That is to say, a creative person must possess what psychologists refer to as *internal locus of control*. Internal locus of control is related to the two principal components of the leisure state of being—perceived freedom and intrinsic motivation. Consequently, creativity and leisure are closely related.

That leisure and creativity are closely linked can be illustrated by a review of studies showing the relationship of play to creativity. (It can be presumed that play is representative of leisure activity in that it is characterized by perceived freedom, intrinsic motivation, and optimal arousal.) Of the many studies dealing with this problem (Leiberman, 1965; Feitelson and Ross, 1973; Simonton, 1975; and Hirshfeld and Hirshfeld, 1977) a study done by Bruner and reported in Iso-Ahola (97) is most revealing. In this study, Bruner tested the assumption that learning through play produces optimal arousal, which leads to creative problem solving. To test this notion, he divided his subject pool into four groups.The first group was shown how to do part of the assigned task. The second group was shown how to do the entire task. The third group played with the tools used in the solution but was given no further information. The fourth group received no input at all. The results were as predicted: The children who received no training but played with the tools solved the task as well as the students who had seen the entire solution. Iso-Ahola concludes his discussion of this study by stating, "It is clear that an appropriately stimulating play environment enhances problem solving ability in children" (96).

Papalia and Olds (1984) summarized 61 studies dealing with creativity. Following is a review of their findings:

1. Social class is positively related to creativity.
2. Family size appears unrelated to creativity.
3. Highly creative children often have a young sibling close in age.
4. Girls are more likely to be verbally gifted, boys tend to show creativity in figural tasks.
5. Creative children usually have parents who are secure, uninhibited and unconventional.

6. Creative children usually have parents who are enthusiastic about their personal leisure pursuits.
7. Creative children are granted both freedom and responsibility.
8. Creative children often come from homes possessing little cohesion.
9. Creative children usually have parents who are not rejecting, hostile or detached.
10. Perceived freedom is essential to creative growth. As Papalia and Olds state, "The most consistent and best supported finding to emerge from this review. . . is that parental vigilance, authoritarianism, dominance and restrictiveness inhibit the development of creativity" (263).

The evidence seems clear. Play and leisure are closely related to creativity. What applies to children may, to a lesser extent, apply to creativity in adults. People need a sense of freedom and intrinsic motivation in order to be creative. People who are constantly directed and molded are not likely to possess the confidence and spontaneity essential for the creative process.

Play and Cognitive Development: A Summary

That play is a contributing factor in cognitive development seems relatively well established. To apply this knowledge in a way that will give a youngster an opportunity to achieve his cognitive potential is a serious challenge to parents and schools alike. By recognizing the powerful influence of play in cognitive development, parents and educators can tailor their respective responsibilities in a way that will provide youngsters with a rich opportunity for intellectual and creative growth.

Early Brain Development—Lifetime Consequences

Within recent years, science has come to understand the mechanism that helps to explain stage theories and epigenesis. At birth the infant's brain possesses most of the neurons (brain cells) that s/he will ever have. These neurons are relatively independent of one another. They are essentially waiting to connect with other neurons to form neural patterns that are analogous to Piaget's notion of schemata. These connections are made when axons and dendrites extend from a neuron to connect with other neurons.

The weight of the human brain at birth is about 350 grams, by one month it has increased to 450 grams, and by one year it is about one-half the size of an adult brain (Restak 47). Though, bear in mind, the number of neurons (roughly 100 billion) don't increase much after birth. And in fact, generally speaking, it appears that brain cells diminish in number as we get older.[5] What accounts for the growth of the brain is an increase in connective tissues and neural connections that make up the complex web of connections between brain cells. Intelligence isn't so much a function of the number of brain cells, but more likely a reflection of the complexity of the neural connections.

What stimulates these neural connections? Current theories suggest that neural patterns arise from external stimulation (including vigorous physical activity). Consequently, it is very important that a child receive stimulation that will produce a variation of neural patterns ranging from arts to science. The types of stimulation a child experiences is remarkably important due to the fact that once these connections are made, they are relatively permanent. In a sense then, learning is a physical phenomenon measured by the number and placement of dendrites and axons. Once they have been established they are part of one's anatomy, and as such a relatively permanent part of a person's personality.

5. Research dating back as far as the 1960's suggests that mammalian brains have the capacity to produce neurons throughout life; however, the number of cells actually produced and the degree to which they compensate for cells that are lost through normal attrition remains to be seen. There is some belief that hippocampus actively produces cells throughout life, but the purpose for such cells may be to facilitate short-term memory, not replace cells that are lost during the aging process. For more see *Gould, E., et.al. "Neurogenesis in the Neocortex of Adult Primates." Science. October 15, 1999.*

The time frame during which children have the capacity to produce neural connections may not be particularly long. It is now commonly held that this process is limited to between the first 15 to 20 years of a person's life, and with the most activity taking place in the first few years. Learning that occurs following this period, appears to involve using existing neural patterns. An example of this can be seen in language acquisition.

A child who learns a second language in the early years usually does so flawlessly and without an accent. A person who tries to learn a second language late in this period, or after this period has essentially ended, must use existing patterns. For example, the word "hau" in Chinese will invariably pronounced "how" in the older language student. A child will automatically pronounce it correctly, and a neural pattern will be formed representing the correction pronunciation and meaning of the word. The older student is stuck with "how." What is true of language is also likely true of recreational skill acquisition, and social behaviors. Thus, behaviors, values, and skills learned early in life will be relatively stable throughout the whole of life. Certainly changes will occur, but they tend to be founded on the framework produced during the formative years. This helps to explain why children who are exposed to violence and dysfunction during the formative years may have difficulties in later life coping with negative childhood experiences. Once something has been learned it cannot be unlearned.

This phenomenon (the brain's ability to produce neural connections) has ramifications for all aspects of development. It influences physical growth and development, social development, personality development, and spiritual development. As a parent, guiding a child during these first few years of life is the most important thing s/he will ever do. There is no success in life that can compensate for failing a child during the time when he or she needs you most. Invest in a child during the first five years of life and they will reward you many times over. That's one investment worth making.

Personality Development and Leisure

As pointed out earlier, one of the major problems associated with a discussion on personality as it relates to leisure is the difficulty we have in finding a universally accepted definition of the word "personality." From one perspective, personality attempts to deal with the whole person. Indeed, in its literal sense, the word "personality" means the state or quality of being a person. In a sense then, personality theories encompass the other three divisions of human development presented in this chapter. It can be argued that if otherwise disparate theories of personality have something in common, it is the tendency to integrate a great many aspects of human behavior into a single theoretical framework. To attempt to integrate the sum total of human attributes into a section within a chapter of a handbook on leisure is beyond the scope of human capability. Consequently, in addressing the question of personality and leisure, personality will be defined in accordance to Webster's Dictionary, "... an individual's emotional and behavioral tendencies." Inasmuch as one's perception of the conscious and unconscious self is at the heart of emotional and behavioral tendencies, this discussion will focus on the relationship of leisure to such variables as *self-esteem, self-image*, and *psychological adjustment*.

In explaining emotional and behavioral tendencies, social scientists have devised a number of theories. Freud makes four basic assumptions about personality: (1) the unconscious portion of the mind has a great deal to do with behavior; (2) sexual and destructive instincts comprise a large portion of the unconscious mind; (3) these impulses are protected from the scrutiny of society by the conscious mind; and (4) in disguised form, subconscious motivations break through the conscious barrier to influence behavior (Freud, 1943). As pointed out earlier, Freud identified five separate stages of development. These stages each had a specific role to play in the development of an individual's personality. If something went wrong during these stages, he theorized that the effect would continue into adult life by way of a behavioral characteristic. To Freud, pleasure gratification was viewed as a strong motivator, and the pivot point upon which the direction of personality development was determined. For example, during the oral stage, a child takes pleasure in eating, nursing and exploring objects orally. For the most part, this form of pleasure is dependent upon other people. If a child is deprived of oral pleasure or is over-indulged, a dependent and passive personality may emerge in adulthood. Similarly, Freud argues that during the anal stage severe or over gratification during toilet training can produce a person who is either disorderly, destructive and messy, or one who is orderly, stingy and obstinate. During the next phase, children resolve issues surrounding their sexual identity and how they relate to members of the same and opposite sex. Again, unresolved issues are believed to carry on into adulthood. Freud feels that all of this usually occurs before a child's sixth birthday.

In considering psychoanalytic theory as an explanation of personality development, one must remember that Freud's psychoanalytic theorizing was based on his work with neurotic patients. Consequently, reflected in this formulation is the skewed experiences and viewpoints of the mentally and emotionally disturbed. Had Freud based his theory on a random sample of a normal population, his theorizing may have taken a different turn. As it stands, however, it is reminiscent of the old saying, "As the twig is bent, so grows the tree." As such, it leaves little room for self-determination, free will, or rational thought as causal factors in personality development.

Raymond B. Cattell proposes that human behavior is a function of structural units which make up the personality. These structural units are the relatively stable traits which allow us to describe and predict an individual's nature. To Cattell, the source from which traits spring is less important than that they exist. Like many psychologists, Cattell believes that most traits are acquired through early socialization, but he does view some as being of physiological in origin. Like Freud, he believes that traits are established early in life and that once traits are established, social forces have little effect on them. Cattell is the author of a widely used personality test, which is frequently used to create personality profiles. If traits are relatively stable, as theorized by Cattell, and if they provide the structural units of personality, it is logical to assume that research could show a relationship between Cattell's personality traits and leisure behavior. Unfortunately, at this point there is little evidence to support this assumption (Iso-Ahola 208–109).

Within recent decades, psychologists have become increasingly convinced that genetics play an important role in personality development. Studies of twins separated at birth have produced some remarkable findings. For example, traits such as anxiety, extroversion, values, sexuality, sociability, and vocational interest have been linked to genetic influences; whereas the need for achievement and intimacy seem to be influenced little by genetics (Thorton, 1990). I suppose most parents, upon reflection, will tell you that they had a pretty good idea as to a child's personality as early as infancy. In looking back at my own children, I can't help but believe that a significant portion of their personalities came with them into this world. It seemed, and history has borne this out, that one daughter was born to be more reflective and social in her recreation while the other is more competitive and physical in her recreation. One plays the piano and is a creative writer, the other holds a black belt in TaeKwondo and competes nationally. I couldn't predict the form that their adult leisure activities would take from observing their behavior as children, but as I watched their interests emerge, I was never surprised by their choices. Their fundamental personalities seemed established by birth. Most researchers would agree that the basis for one's personality is genetics, but also that social learning plays an important role.

Unlike trait psychologists, those who accept social learning as the basis for personality development view traits as less than stable. They view behavior as a function of situation interacting with previous experience. They disagree with trait theorists regarding the power of socialization in adolescent and adult life. Albert Bandura and Richard Walters are the foremost proponents of this approach (Bandura and Walters, 1963). According to their formulation, human beings, as a result of their superior cognitive abilities, have the ability to think with insight and foresight, and consequently consciously influence their behavior. Following this notion, this theory emphasizes: (1) learning from models as opposed to learning through personal and direct experience; (2) the symbolic and cognitive aspects of learning as opposed to stimulus followed by response and; (3) self-regulation modulated by external behavior reinforcement. Like many theories, the results are not yet in. For example, the role of modeling in personality development is not clear; similarly, the extent to which personality formation is influenced by rewards remains a question yet to be fully examined (Bevalas 208–209).

The Myers-Briggs Type Indicator

Within recent years, it has become popular, particularly in educational settings, to measure personality types through the use of the Myers-Briggs Type Indicator (MBTI). This instrument was developed by psychologist

Isabel Briggs Myers. She based her instrument on the theoretical work of her mother Katherine C. Briggs, who in turn was an adherent to Carl Jung's theory of personality. Essentially she theorized that the human personality could be measured along four bipolar dimensions. These are:

1. extroversion-introversion
2. sensing-intuition
3. thinking-feeling
4. judging-perceptive

You have heard people talk about being an ESFP or an INTJ etc. These letters represent the initial letter of the bipolar dimensions on which they scored the highest. To break the Myers-Briggs code you need to know the abbreviations for each of the traits. Here they are (after Drummond 256):

E = extrovert:	one who relates more easily to other people.
I = introvert:	one who relates more easily to ideas.
S = sensing:	one who prefers to work with concrete, known facts.
N = intuition:	one who prefers to look for intuitive, conceptual relationships.
T= thinking:	one who bases judgments on objective analysis and logic.
F = feeling:	one who bases judgment on more personal, subjective values.
J = judging:	one who prefers a planned, organized way of life.
P = perceptive:	one who prefers a flexible, spontaneous way of life.

There are essentially 16 different personality types according to this instrument.

Keirsey and Bates published *Please Understand Me*, a book for the popular press with their own version of the Myers-Briggs. Their instrument is called the "Kiersey Temperament Sorter" (KTS), and is often used in classes and is readily available on the Internet. One difference between the MBTI and the KTS is that the KTS assumes that the 16 types can be lumped together into four temperaments. The KTS and the MBTI are similar but not the same. (Layne 1)

The MBTI and KTS are frequently used in personal counseling, career guidance, increasing the effectiveness of educational programs, team building, in human resource management, and self-enrichment. The MBTI is viewed by many as well researched and of significant practical value. (Psychiatry on Line, 1/2/97)

If you haven't taken either the KTS or MBTI, you can get an estimate of your personality type by estimating where you would fall on the following continuum. (Modeled after Porthouse)

<<<WHICH SIDE OF THE CONTINUUM DO YOU MOST IDENTIFY WITH?>>>

Extrovert - Introvert

Typically: social, external, gregarious, talkative, interactive, broad in scope, outgoing	Typically: territorial, internal, intensive energetic, reflective, few relationships, low energy, narrow

Sensor- -Intuitive

Typically: sequential, present, realistic, down to earth, factual practical, specific, convergent	Typically: random, conceptual, inspired, head in the clouds, theoretical, general, divergent

Thinkers - Feelers

Typically: objective, firm-minded, legal minded, just, impersonal, analytical, logical, detached	Typically: subjective, fair-minded, personal, humane, involved

Judgers -Perceivers

Typically: decided, fixed, in control, closed, structured, definite, scheduled, organized, closed-ended	Typically: flexible, tentative, adaptable, open, spontaneous, unplanned, unstructured

To take the KTS as well as receive a personal analysis of your scores, I suggest you visit the Internet. There are a number of sites that will be of interest to you, but the one I recommend is **http://sunsite.unc.edu/personality/keirsey/html** or you could access **http://sunsite.unc.edu** and find personality tests through the SunSITE Directory. In addition to the test, there is a wealth of information on personality theory with special reference to the Myers-Briggs.[6]

What value might come from taking the KST? Assuming that the KST, or any other personality inventory, models the human personality with some degree of accuracy, I can see two values coming from taking such a test: (1) it provides the individual with a better sense of self, and thus may contribute to increased self-awareness and perhaps self-esteem; (2) it might help an individual understand how he or she relates to others, and thus contribute to better interpersonal relationships.

It is important to recognize that these instruments are not perfect, nor are they measures of mental health. They simply give an indication as to the extent to which a person's approach to life can be related to selected variables. In the KST and MBTI, it is assumed that most people will fall into one of 16 different combinations of four sets of opposing variables. It is important to recognize that no attempt is made to value one personality type over another. All have equal validity, all are equally good. In each personality type you will find examples of people who are famous, successful, and who have made outstanding contributions to society. For an extensive list of famous (including fictional) people by personality type I suggest, once again, that you visit SunSITE at **http://sunsite.unc.edu/pub/academic/psychology.personality/type.info/famous.types**.

6. SunSITE is one of the best sites on the Internet. It is operated by the University of North Carolina, Chapel Hill in cooperation with Sun Microsystems. It is an eclectic collection of art, educational, political, and recreation information. It is worth a visit, if for no other reason than the potential it holds for discovery. Be prepared to spend some time if you pay it a visit, it is full of interesting things to do, to see, and to learn from.

Leisure and Personality Research

To date, there appears to be little research where the above and other personality theories have been related to questions of leisure. This is not surprising when one considers the complexity of this type of research undertaking. In spite of the claims of leisure practitioners regarding the relationship of leisure to personality variables, few credible studies have been produced. Turning to Iso-Ahola, we read:

> But what is known about the effects of leisure experiences on personality? The answer is very simple: very little is known because systematic research is conspicuously lacking. Merely to correlate participation in various recreation activities with selected personality traits does not reveal when, why, and how leisure creates the effects it does in various persons (Iso-Ahola 210).

Studies dealing with the relationship of personality to leisure are faced with a variety of problems. Initially, one must determine a theoretical basis for his or her research. A responsible researcher will do this for two reasons: (1) social science can only progress if research projects are designed to test the validity of theories, and (2) a theory is essential for it provides the logical framework from which a hypothesis can be drawn. In respect to personality studies, attention has to be paid to the dynamic nature of the human condition; and as they relate to leisure, attention must be paid to the variety of interpretations explaining and identifying the leisure condition. To deal with these concerns, Iso-Ahola provides the following guidelines:

> . . . the following four parameters have to be considered as part of a continuous process of change: (1) dimensions of personality, (2) situational social influences, (3) type and degree of leisure involvement, and (4) an individual's developmental stage. The effects in turn may be one of three: (1) they may improve, (2) they may deteriorate, or (3) a person may maintain his present level at a given personality dimension. The resultant change in personality may be measured in absolute or relative terms; the former refers to change within a person, and the latter to a person's change in relation to other individuals on a particular personality dimension. . . it is important to realize that leisure involvement itself does not lead to any changes in personality. Rather, what an individual is able to derive psychologically from leisure participation is critical (210–211).

Self-Esteem and Leisure

In a study done in 1971 by Koocher (reported in Iso-Ahola 211), boys ages 15-17 who were participants in a YMCA program were divided into three groups. One group consisted of boys who knew how to swim and who had passed the swimming test at the beginning of camp. The second group consisted of boys who refused to take the swimming test or failed, and the third group consisted of boys who learned to swim during the 12-day camping period. All participants were given a self-concept test at the beginning of the program and at the end. The results showed the learners improved in self-concept, whereas the other two groups showed no change. This type of study is typical of studies done in recreation and leisure and exemplifies studies showing relative change on a personality dimension. This type of study is important because it does lend credibility to the claims made by recreation practitioners that leisure has a positive effect on self-image. More specifically, this study illustrates the role that learning new recreation activities has on how one views himself. If in fact learning new leisure skills brings about a desirable change in personality, then it makes sense that individuals whose background includes a history of successful leisure skill acquisition will have a stronger self-concept than those who don't.

Psychological Adjustment and Leisure

Another area related to personality and leisure is that of psychological adjustment. Studies dealing with this area suggest that a rich variety in recreational experiences is inversely correlated with neurotic tendencies (Cavanaugh, 1942; Hendry and Douglass, 1975). That early leisure socialization may have a relationship to adult psychological adjustment was demonstrated by Brooks and Elliott (1971). In their study it was shown that children who experienced leisure satisfaction were better adjusted 20 years later than children who were not as fortunate.

It is important to recognize that active leisure involvement doesn't always correlate with psychological adjustment. Under some circumstances, passive recreation seems to show a higher correlation with adjustment than active leisure. For people whose work may be highly active or physically tiring, leisure patterns may take the form of relaxation and stimulus avoidance behavior. In situations where a passive pattern is an appropriate response to leisure, physical activity may be correlated with poor psychological adjustment (Bishop, 1973).

Leisure and Social Development

When we speak of social development, we are basically referring to the acquisition of skills and knowledge associated with successful interpersonal involvement. It is assumed that as one matures, he or she interacts with others in such a manner as to reinforce earlier interaction, and sets the stage for future social patterns. The extent to which these interactions involve leisure activity is the extent to which one's development is influenced by leisure, and conversely, leisure involvement is a function of one's past experience. Again, we see human development and leisure as a two way street—each influencing the other. The process wherein social factors influence development is referred to as "socialization." The process whereby social factors affect leisure involvement is referred to as "leisure socialization."

In more specific terms, socialization can be thought of as the process whereby an individual acquires self-concept, an understanding of who he/she is in relationship to his/her society. Modern social psychologists attempt to explain this process through *social learning theory*. In this theory, the effect of modeling is emphasized. It is argued that the acquisition of new responses is dependent upon exposure to a model for the new response. This notion may have important implications for parents who are concerned about the effect of television on the behavior of their children; for that matter, it has important implications for all of us regarding the possible socializing influence of television and theater.

In a now classic study testing the social learning theory, children were shown a film in which a large plastic "bobo doll" was treated in an abusive manner by an adult. The adult walked over to the doll and ordered it out of the way. Obviously, the doll could not comply, so the adult punched it out of the way. This was followed by kicking, additional punching and even hitting it with a mallet. In addition to striking the doll, the adult also abused the doll verbally by repeating phrases such as, "Sockeroo, stay down," or "Right on the nose, boom, boom." One experimental group saw the film up to this point, while another group saw a final segment wherein the malicious adult was disciplined. After the film viewing, all of the children were placed in a room containing toys including the Bobo doll. The children who did not see the concluding segment of the film imitated the behavior of the adult model. The children who were witness to the entire film were less inclined to aggressive behavior (Glietman 500).

Television

Research on the effects of TV have been accumulating since the 1950's (Zandon 86–89). With few exceptions, the results of these studies have produced results similar to the Bobo doll studies—watching violence on TV tends children to aggressive behavior. A report issued by the National Institute of Mental Health concludes that television encourages aggressive behavior in at least two ways: (1) children (and possibly adults) come to accept aggression as acceptable behavior and (2) children (and possibly adults) imitate what they see on television. Next time you go to a movie, pay attention to the behavior of the patrons as they leave. You should not be surprised to see imitative behavior even on the part of adults.

That viewing television violence has a serious impact on the viewer is clearly illustrated by Eron's study of the viewing habits of 427 young adults. This longitudinal study (a longitudinal study is one that is done over a long period of time) revealed that the best single predictor of a young man's aggressiveness at age 19 was the programs he liked to watch at age eight. In a follow-up study, it was found that the parents of aggressive children were less inclined to monitor the shows watched by their children (In Papalia and Olds 224).

Russell (1996) points out that viewers of television violence are more likely than nonviewers to display aggressive and violent behavior. In addition, she points out that some individuals develop a "victim" mentality from watching television violence. These people tend to exhibit paranoid behavior; they tend to carry guns, be distrustful of others, and demonstrate self-protective behavior. She also talks about the "bystander effect." This refers to the notion that television violence can desensitize an individual to violence and its effects. These individuals are more likely than others to be callous toward victims, and apathetic toward people who carry out violent acts.(181)

Watching television may have other developmental consequences. Russell asks, "When too much time is spent watching television, is the development of social interaction and communications skills impeded? Are growth, experimentation, creativity, and the development of physical and mental skills stifled?" (181) Kelly points out another problem with television, and that is it portrays an unrealistic image of life. It presents a caricature, a distorted view of how things really are, thus giving viewers an unrealistic benchmark against which they can measure their lives and define and evaluate their behaviors. (261)

Children absorb a tremendous amount of information from an afternoon of watching television. And given the fact that if the set has cable or satellite capabilities, the child will have his/her selection from as many as 100 channels. The larger the number of channels the more difficult it will be for the child to seek other recreation. There will always be something to catch the viewers interest. And, of course, this is not just a problem for children. Adults have been know to be captivated by television. But, the developmental implications make television particularly detrimental to children. Nancy Paula (1997) summarizes the concerns of many educators, counselors, and psychologists regarding the harm that too much television can do to children:

- It can expose children to too much sex and violence.
- Children can be unduly influenced by the junk food and toys advertised in commercials.
- It can give children a poor model for good behavior before they have developed a clear idea of what is right and wrong.
- Young children do not have the experience and wisdom to understand complicated plots or scary scenes.
- Sitting passively in front of the set for extended periods of time can slow young children's social and intellectual development.

Television isn't in and of itself evil. There are some wonderfully uplifting and educational programs. However, the unfortunate truth is that most of the programming possesses little positive developmental value. Kaufman citing a UCLA study points out the following:

- In television, perpetrators of violent acts go unpunished 73 percent of the time.
- About 25 percent of violent acts involve handguns.

- About 47 percent of violent situations present no harm to the victims and 58 percent depict no pain.
- Only 4 percent of violent programs show nonviolent alternatives.
- About 85 percent of programming on premium movie channels is violent compared to 44 percent on the broadcast networks. (2)

The government has been slow to take action, even though it has been recognized for a long time that television is not a benign form of recreation. It was in 1990 that Congress passed the Children's Television Act which required the FCC, when reviewing TV broadcast license renewals, to consider the extent to which television programs met children's educational needs. In July, 1996, the White House, the four major networks, and the National Association of Broadcasters agreed to broadcast at least three hours of educational programming. And, the Telecommunications Act of 1996, now requires the manufacturers of television sets to install the new "V-chip" into all new sets. This chip will allow parents to block out programs they don't want their children to see. These actions taken by the government are important, but the ultimate solution to the problem of children and television rests with the parents. What can parents do? Obviously one solution is to turn off the set. A more realistic approach would be for parents to help children develop good television viewing habits. Nancy Paula makes the following suggestions for bringing this about:

- Limit televiewing to two hours a day. Keep a diary of what children watch.
- Learn about current TV programs and videos; select good ones.
- Plan with your children what they will watch and schedule these programs. Turn the set off when programs end.
- Watch television with your children, interact with them regarding what they watch.
- Follow-up TV with activities or games. There may be benefit in selecting games that relate to the program.
- Make certain that TV isn't used as a baby-sitter.

A Personal Note: My son wanted to watch television, he was about eight-years old. I agreed, but only if he watched "educational television." He wanted to watch an action adventure program—"The A-Team." I compromised, "You watch five minutes of "The Life of the Honey Bee," and then you can watch whatever you want. He wasn't very interested at first, but as the program unfolded, he became increasingly captivated. The five minutes passed, and when I asked him if he wanted to change the station he said, "No, this is good." Later, I was impressed to hear him tell a neighbor why honey bees were attracted to flowers. I haven't asked him about this, but I imagine he can still recall information from that program these many years later.

The Internet and Computer Games

With the development of the computer and the advent of the Internet, computer technology may pose just as big a threat to normal development in children as television. It is quite likely, that in spite of denials by the computer industry, violent video and computer games contribute to aggression and violence among young players. Dr. David Walsh of the National Institute on Media and the Family cites a meta-analysis by Dr. Craig Anderson and Dr. Brad Bushman in which 35 studies were statistically analyzed to determine the extent to which contemporary research supported the assumption that children were adversely affected through playing violent video or computer games. The results clearly supported the assumption. (For more on this research visit http://www.uua.org/re/reach/fall01/parenting/media_violence_research_update.html.) Just as with computer and video games, the Internet poses numerous risks to children. Through the Internet, children can be exposed to sexually explicit materials, gambling, violence, gore, frightening images, and predators stalking chat rooms. Certainly, the Internet, and this is true of some computer games as well, can afford one marvelous opportunities for learning and development, but, it must also be recognized that unsupervised, the Internet can have a profound and negative affect on a developing mind.

What kind of influence can viewing adult material on the Internet or playing violent games have on the developing child? As pointed out earlier, the "wiring" of the human brain primarily occurs during childhood and is essentially the product of sensory stimulation. The arrangement of the synaptic connections of the developing brain, the hard wiring, is both a reflection and result of the type of stimulation the brain receives. If, for example, the sensory input is largely of a violent nature, the synaptic patterns will reflect that content. Furthermore, it is generally considered common knowledge, in scientific circles, that the frontal lobe of the brain continues to develop until early adulthood. This is an important consideration since the frontal lobe plays a critical role in controlling antisocial behavior. If the type of sensory-stimulation a child receives includes an inordinate amount of violence while the frontal lobe is still developing, it may fail to develop the capabilities to control anti-social behaviors in adulthood.

It may be too early to know what kind of long term effect playing violent video games or surfing websites containing graphic violent or sexual material will have on today's children, but it is quite likely that it will result in both a dumbing down intellectually of those most exposed to this form of stimuli, as well as a diminishing of the ethical values essential to a healthy society.

What can one do? If you want your child to learn about a tree, rather than finding one on the Internet, go outside with your child and climb one. If you want your child to get along well with others, encourage him or her to interact with other children. If you want your child to be an effective thinker, encourage reading, writing, and creative activities. To help your child develop an appreciation for creative expression, encourage your child to draw, paint, and play a musical instrument. Of course, there are resources on the Internet and there are computer programs that can have a positive impact on the developing child, but if in doubt, unplug the computer for awhile. Active play is a probably one of the most important things parents can encourage if they want their children to develop in a healthy and socially productive manner.

Parenting Practices

It has often been theorized that parental behavior provides a model for the developing child. Lynn Barrett and Garry E. Chick of the Leisure Behavior Research Laboratory at the University of Illinois, examined this notion. They hypothesized that a parent's leisure attitudes, participation in leisure activities, and their personal leisure satisfaction would be indicative of the role structure of the parents and be reflected in their children's orientation toward play. In this study, 97 preschool children enrolled in several local day-care centers were rated by their teachers on five playfulness factors: physical spontaneity, social spontaneity, cognitive spontaneity, manifest joy, and sense of humor. Both parents were then asked to respond to the Leisure Satisfaction Scale, the Leisure Attitude Scale and identify their participation in leisure activities.

The results of this study indicate that playfulness in children is only moderately related to the leisure of their parents. The strongest relationships were cross-sex typed, i.e. the leisure behavior of mothers tended to correlate more closely with their sons than daughters, while fathers showed a stronger correlation with daughters than sons. The most playful boys tended to have mothers who were "very satisfied" with their leisure. These mothers reported that their leisure provided them with social, aesthetic educational, and physical benefits. Boys were more influenced by their mother's activity preferences than by their father's choices.

This study is illustrative of the kinds of problems one has in examining a hypothesized relationship which is part of an incredibly complex dynamic. The apparent ambiguity in the findings of this study are consistent with the complex nature of human development. One problem Barnett and Chick were faced with, which is typical of any study of this type, was the fact that socialization is not the only factor influencing personality development. Recent studies on infant temperament make it very clear that heredity plays a role in shaping personality. One infant may be passive and relatively happy, whereas another may be aggressive, despondent or assertive. Thomas, Chess and Burch have shown conclusively that such traits persist for at least two years and quite much beyond (Glietman 506). This poses a significant problem for the researcher because it may well be that the child's temperament determines to some extent the manner in which he or she is treated by the parent. In a sense, the infant's temperament serves as a socializing influence on the parent, just the reverse of what social learning theory predicts.

In trying to understand the influence of a parent on a child's playfulness, it might be well to consider the child's stage of development. The leisure behaviors appropriate for pre-schoolers are significantly different from the behavior appropriate for young and middle-aged adults. Preschool children (two-five years) are characterized by physical activity. Just having emerged from the sensorimotor stage, they demonstrate significant progress in coordination and muscular development. The net result is that children during this period focus on activities involving both fine motor skills and gross motor activity. In addition, the child is just learning to use symbols in the thinking process, which permits the child to incorporate language and perceptual images into their play. Parents, particularly fathers, are less likely to exhibit active recreation in the presence of children. Parents tend to engage in more passive recreation at home, and participate in active recreation away from home (at health clubs, jogging, playing tennis, etc.). Consequently, the leisure behavior of the parent may be inconsistent with the developmental needs of the child, and hence, give the appearance that no leisure modeling is occurring or that the child's behavior is more consistent with the behavior of the parent of the opposite sex.

The notion that leisure satisfaction among mothers appears to be the most significant predictor of playfulness in boys, but not girls, may find explanation in the fact that girls are socialized to behave in a "ladylike" manner. Boys are socialized to more aggressive and seemingly more playlike behavior. What may be at work here is more the influence of perceived freedom in the home than any specific modeling.

That playfulness in the home environment is in part a function of a parent's cognitive style was demonstrated by Bishop and Chace (1971). By correlating creativity scores in children with measures of cognitive style in parents, it was demonstrated that "children's creativity improves as the playfulness of the home environment is increased" (Iso-Ahola 100). In a home where a mother expresses a high degree of satisfaction with her leisure, it would not be surprising to find an atmosphere characterized by high degrees of perceived freedom and intrinsic motivation. Such a home naturally would provide a rich environment for a child to develop a strong play orientation. In homes where the mother is the dominant socialization force, it is consistent with social learning theory to show a correlation between a mother's leisure satisfaction and a son's playfulness. Similarly, it is not inconsistent to show a relationship between a father and daughter on this measure. Young fathers may be less satisfied with their leisure simply because of their dedication to their careers. A preoccupation with work is not uncommon for young fathers. A young mother, who has chosen to spend her days with her children may find great satisfaction from her interaction with her children, thus reinforcing her perception of her leisure satisfaction and her capacity to socialize leisure and quite likely gender specific behavior.

One further problem faced in this type of study is found in the difficulty associated with controlling for other socialization factors. As already illustrated, it appears that television has a profound effect on children. Certainly in some families, the principal modeling influence is television, while in other families, television plays a minor role. And to what extent did teachers, peers, siblings, and others play in determining the playfulness of the children in the study? And, of course, the role of genetics needs to be explored as well. Another question that needs to be answered relates to the amount of time parents spent with their children.

The Barnett and Chick study makes an important contribution to the growing body of knowledge related to leisure and human development. It also illustrates the difficulty inherent in trying to validate the various theories advanced to explain the ways in which people acquire leisure behaviors. As pointed out earlier, the socialization process overlaps the other areas of human development and consists of a wide array of interlocking factors, including physical characteristics, temperament traits, and social factors such as economic forces, sociocultural values, and patterns of child rearing.

> The secret of being a good parent is to always strive to give children good memories.
>
> —Sara Louise

Competition vs. Cooperation

In a capitalistic society, the value of competition largely goes without question. Basically, in this society, there seems to be an implicit faith in the value of competitive behavior. So it is not surprising to learn that American children are more competitive than children from other countries. Similarly, children from parents of high socioeconomic status are more effective competitors than children from lower socioeconomic strata. Prior to age two there appears little urge on the part of children to compete; however, once in the preoperational stage, children begin to recognize the nature of competitive behavior. This corresponds with the child's increasing ability to recognize concepts such as value and possession. Once a child has begun to exhibit competitive behavior it tends to increase until about age 11 (Iso-Ahola 115). Following an extensive review of studies dealing with competitive play behavior (particularly Little League baseball), Iso-Ahola summarized his findings thusly:

- Competitive tasks lower the quality of interpersonal relationships, whereas cooperative tasks tend to enhance social relationships.
- In competitive rather than cooperative situations, children tend to be more anxious, tense and less secure.
- Cooperative tasks enhance social perspectives, which in turn is related to social adjustment, effectiveness of communication, personal identify and self-awareness, moral judgment, open-mindedness and acceptance of individual differences (116).

In reference to Little League Baseball he draws the following conclusions:

1. Other things being equal, cooperation is superior to competition because of the positive effects of the former on interpersonal and intrapersonal behavior. . . . With major emphasis on ingroup cooperation and minor emphasis on intergroup competition, Little League is psychologically healthy, assuming that competition between teams does not become too serious.
2. Self-serving causal attributes for team outcomes suggest that players are capable of coping with winning and losing. However, there are reasons to believe that repeated and uncontrollable failures give rise to feelings and inferences of helplessness.
3. Intensive involvement by coaches and parents in Little League has turned children's recreation into work. The use of external rewards and sanctions has reached a point where players have to infer extrinsic reasons for their participation. This clearly reduces the player's intrinsic interest in Little League Baseball and makes it seem more like work. . . .
4. Before and after the baseball season, players rate higher than nonplayers on self-concept and certain socially desirable characteristics (e.g., leadership and emotional adjustment). . . .
5. ... due to its highly structured nature, Little League does not provide players with skills and characteristics (e.g., creativity, innovation) needed for change and improving the prevalent society; if anything, it will only reinforce those traits that tend to maintain the status quo.

From this point of view, Little League programs are contributing very little to child development (126–127). It is not that youth sports don't contribute to a person's development, it is rather that the elements of the youth sport's experience may have contradictory effects. In addition, because of the progressive exclusion that occurs in youth sports, there is a possibility that as youngsters are eliminated from the more prestigious sports groups, deleterious effects on both the favored and the unfavored may occur. Speaking to this point, John Kelly has this to say:

> More than those who lose a particular contest, there are those who lose out in the progressive exclusion model of school sport. As more and more are left out of participation and asked to take secondary supporting roles for the few who still play, most young men and women become losers. They are left and judged unqualified to compete. The consequences of this filtering that begins in elementary school and sport programs for the very young have yet to be measured. (205)

It is interesting to note that children are less likely to emphasize winning in youth sports than parents and coaches. Clark (1996) states that there is a significant difference on the emphasis adults and children place on winning. Clark cites a national survey of young people between ages 10-18 who were asked to rate the importance of winning in relationship to why they chose to participate in youth sports; winning was not even in the top ten reasons for girls, and only number seven for boys. When asked what they would change about sports, both genders indicated they would prefer less emphasis on winning. Clark also points out that attitudes change with age. The older the child, the more emphasis he or she places on winning.

I think many, if not most, people have a belief that youth sports are good, that they build character and promote fitness. Those claims may have some validity, but on the other hand, the indications are that too much emphasis on winning may have negative consequences. Too much emphasis on winning makes sports an extrinsically motivated experience, and where this occurs the joy inherent in activity may be supplanted by anxiety. Where winning is emphasized, the relative distance between victory and defeat is exaggerated, and victory may be viewed as success and defeat as failure. Parents and coaches can do a great deal to assure that children benefit from sports. By emphasizing the value of participation and activity and diminishing the importance of winning, by focusing on the individual growth and development of each player, and recognizing the validity of fun in youth sports, coaches and parents can help youth achieve their physical, social, and emotional potential.

Closing Note...

In our discussion of leisure socialization, we have only scratched the surface. So broad is this topic that it could easily fill an entire textbook. The purpose of this discussion has not been to conduct an extensive review of related literature and studies, but rather to point out some of the salient issues surrounding the process whereby one learns basic knowledge about leisure, develops attitudes and values associated with play, and learns various leisure skills.

In this chapter, we have examined the relationship of human growth and development to leisure. Specifically, we have looked at the following areas: (1) physical development, (2) cognitive development, (3) personality development, and (4) social development.

Throughout this chapter, three points have been stressed. First, play and recreation activities influence a person's growth and development. Second, one's stage of development is related to recreational patterns. And, third, human growth and development is a dynamic so complex that establishing clear relationships between development and leisure is very difficult; however, the evidence generally supports the idea that play and recreation are essential to healthy growth and development.

As presented earlier, much of this learning occurs in childhood (about 50% of one's adult activities can be traced to childhood) (Iso-Ahola, 1980), and is the result of modeling, imitation, and identification with behavior of significant others.

In this cursory look at social development and leisure, several important, interesting areas have been neglected. This is due to the limiting effect of time and space, not the result of a lack of interest in the topic or lack of attention to detail. Although the limiting influence of time and space can justify omitting certain related areas, it would be remiss to ignore one final concept. It is important that the student of leisure recognize that leisure socialization does not end with childhood. It is an ongoing process that causes us to continually grow and develop. This process can be facilitated by seeking leisure activities that promote feelings of self-confidence, by engaging in activities that are intrinsically rewarding, that contribute to feelings of perceived freedom, and activities that are optimally stimulating.

Just as social development goes well beyond childhood and continues to influence behavior and emotions throughout life, so do all other aspects of human development. In the next chapter, we will look at human development as it relates to leisure throughout the rest of the life cycle.

REFERENCES

Bach, R. *Jonathan Livingston Seagull*. New York: Avon Books, 1970.

Bandura, A. and R.H. Walters. *Social Learning and Personality Development*. New York: Holt, Rinehart and Winston, 1963.

Barnett. L and G. Chick. "Chips off the Ol' Blocks: Parent's Leisure and Their Children's Play." *Journal of Leisure Research* 18.4, (1968): 266–283.

Bishop, D.W. "Psychological Adjustment and Leisure-Time Activities." *Final Report for Grant MH 17913*, Department of Recreation and Park Administration, University of Illinois, Urbana-Champaign, 1973.

Britt, S.H. and S.Q. Janus. "Toward a Social Psychology of Human Play." *The Journal of Social Psychology.* 13, (1941): 351–384.

Callois, R. *Man, Play and Games*. New York: Free Press, 1961.

Carlson, N.R. *Psychology.* New York: Allyn Bacon, Inc., 1987.

Cattell, R.B. *Personality and Motivation.* New York: World Book Co., 1957.

Cavanaugh, J.O. "The Relation of Recreation to Personality Adjustment." *Journal of Social Psychology.* 15, (1942): 63–74.

Clark, M.A. "Winning, How Important Is It in Youth Sports?" http://www.educ.mus.edu/units/Dept/PEES/ysi/spotlightf94/winning.html (Jan. 3, 1997)

Csikszentmihalyi, M. *Beyond Boredom and Anxiety.* San Francisco: Jossey-Bass, 1975.

Drummond, R.J. *Appraisal Procedures for Counselors and Helping Professionals.* Englewood Cliffs, New Jersey: Prentice-Hall, 1996.

Dyer, W. *The Sky Is the Limit.* New York: Avon, 1978.

Ellis, M.J. *Why People Play.* Englewood Cliffs, New Jersey: Prentice-Hall, 1973.

Erikson, E.H. *Childhood and Society.* (2nd ed.). New York: Norton, 1963.

Feitelson, D. and G.S. Ross. "The Neglected Factor." *Play and Human Development* 16 (1973): 202–223.

Freud, S. *A General Introduction to Psychology.* Garden City, New York: Doubleday, 1943.

Gleitman, H. *Psychology.* New York: W.W. Norton and Company, 1986.

Golden, D. and A. Tsiaras. "Building a Better Brain." *Life Magazine.* July (1994) 62.

Gunn, S.L and C. Peterson. *Therapeutic Recreation Program Design. Principles and Procedures.* Englewood Cliffs, New Jersey: Prentice-Hall, 1978.

Hendry, L.G. and Douglass, L. "University Students: Attainment and Sport," *British Journal of Educational Psychology.* 45, (1975): 549–560.

Hirshfield, S.F. and S.L. Hirshfield, "The Use of Games in Developing Analytical and Combinatorial Reasoning." *Journal of Creative Behavior* 11 (1977): 101–104.

Iso-Ahola, S.E. *The Social Psychology of Leisure and Recreation.* Dubuque, Iowa: Wm. C. Brown Company Publishers, 1980.

Kaufman, R. *Kill Your Television: Children and TV.* http://www.netreach.net/people/kaufman/children.html. (Jan. 2, 1997)

Karni, A. and G. Bertini. "Learning Perceptual Skills: Behavioral Probes into Adult Cortical Plasticity." *Current Opinion in Neurobiology* 7.4 (1997): 530–535.

Layne, V. "Myers-Briggs Psychotypology: A Brief Primer" http://web.mit.edu/dagoura/www/Working-Drafts/psychotypology.html.

Lieberman, J.N. "Playfulness: An Attempt to Conceptualize the Quality of Play and of the Player." *Psychological Reports.* 19, 1278.

Morris, D. *The Human Zoo.* New York: Dell Publishing, 1974.

Papaha, D.R. and S.W. Olds. *Human Development.* New York: McGraw-Hill, 1986.

Paula, N. In *The Parents' Resource Almanac.* http://family.starwave.com/resource/pra/BONUS82.html (Jan. 3, 1997).

Parten. M. "Social Play among Preschool Children." *Journal of Abnormal and Social Psychology* (1932): 243–269.

Piaget, J. *Play, Dreams and Imitation in Childhood* (Trans. G. Gattegno and F.M. Hodgson). New York: Norton, 1962.

Porthouse, W. *Summary of the Myers-Briggs Type Indicator MBTI* http://1ongwood.cs.ucf.edu/porthous/mb-score.shtml (Summer, 1997).

Psychiatry On-Line. "Using Myers-Briggs in the Workplace—an extract" http://www.gold.net/users/ad88/mbwp.htm (1998).

Restak, R. *The Brain*. New York: Bantam Books, 1984.

Rubin, K.H.J. "Play Behaviors of Young Children." *Young Children* 32 (1977): 16–24.

Russell, R. *Pastimes: The Context of Contemporary Leisure*. Chicago: Brown and Benchmark, 1996.

Sheldon, W. (with S.S. Stevens). *The Varieties of Temperament: A Psychology of Constitutional Differences*. New York: Harper, 1942.

Simonton, D.K. "Sociocultural Context of Individual Creativity: A Trans-historical Time-Series Analysis." *Journal of Personality and Social Psychology* 32 (1975): 1119–1123.

Smilansky, S. *The Effects of Sociodramatic Play on Disadvantaged Preschool Children*. New York: Harper John Wiley and Sons, 1968.

Smith, P.K. and K. Connolly. "Patterns of Play and Social Interaction in Preschool Children." *Ethological Studies of Child Behavior*. Cambridge: The Cambridge University Press, 1972, 62–65.

Statt, D. *Dictionary of Psychology*. New York: Barnes and Noble Books, 1981.

Thompson, R.F. *The Brain: A Neuroscience Primer*. New York: W.H. Freeman and Company, 1993.

Thornton, J. "Personality Puzzle: What Researchers Studying Twins Can Tell Us About Ourselves." *Self* 12.2 1990): 198, 199, 227, 229.

Vander, A.J, J.H. Sherman, and D.S. Luciano. *Human Physiology: The Mechanisms of Body Function*. New York: McGraw Hill Book Company, 1985.

Zanden, J.W.V. *Human Development*. New York: Alfred Knopf, 1978.

CHAPTER 8

Leisure and Successful Aging

The saddest words of tongue or pen are just four words—it might have been.

—Anonymous

I recently saw an eight-frame cartoon. The same person was featured in every frame, starting with infancy and ending in old age. Finally in the last frame, you see this very old person looking directly at you. Above her head is the caption, "Well that sucked!" I suppose for some people that succinctly summarizes how they feel about the aging process. But, it doesn't have to be that way. Aging doesn't have to be traumatic or frightening. It doesn't have to lead to dissatisfaction or disengagement. There are some things that you can do to make the aging process a positive experience. In this chapter we look at some of some of the things you can do to ensure that when you reach that last frame, you will be inclined to say, "That was great!"

Does Leisure Socialization Continue?

Although the leisure socialization that occurs early in one's life has a tremendous impact on one's leisure values, attitudes, and behaviors, don't think that social learning is only limited to these "formative" years. Social learning occurs throughout all of one's life. The relative impact of later-life socialization on leisure (and the socializing role of leisure) may be less than during earlier years, but to assume that "you can't teach an old dog new tricks" is an overstatement of the facts.[6] It is generally true that older people learn more slowly and because of deteriorating health may be less physically capable than in earlier years. And it is true that some skills must be learned during one's youth; nevertheless, many people successfully adapt to the aging process and continue to live productive and enjoyable lives right up until their departure. Some even learn new skills. For example, the great cartoonist Al Hirschfield learned to draw on the computer after he was well into his 90's. Iso-Ahola identifies three limitations that serve to render socialization less effective in later life. These limitations of later-life socialization are summarized as follows:

1. As one gets older, one's physical abilities diminish, predisposing an individual to certain activities.
2. Some physical skills are best acquired in childhood, otherwise their development in adult life is doubtful.
3. The acquisition of favorable attitudes toward leisure during formative years lays the foundations for satisfactory socialization in later life (Iso-Ahola 175–182).

Even though socialization limits may be very real and pose a challenge for leisure socialization in later life, it is reasonable to believe that people can change and continue to grow even as older adults. People may not learn as quickly during adulthood and later years, but change is always possible. Perhaps the most important thing a person can do to ensure a continuation of new experiences during adulthood is to develop a positive attitude about leisure during one's youth. If such an attitude fails to develop, the adult interested in maintaining a rich repertoire of leisure activities is faced with a double burden. Not only will he or she have to deal with the limitations inherent in the aging process, but also the limitations associated with the social learning that occurred during youthful years.

Overview of the Adult Life Cycle

One of the factors that influence the aging process is ***age norms***. Society expects people to act, dress, think and behave in certain ways at certain stages of their lives. These norms are linked to certain assumptions about different age groups. For example, people are expected to be less active in their senior years than when they are younger, they are supposed to dress more conservatively than when they are younger, they are supposed to be more responsible than when they are younger and so on. Robert Atchley tells us that age norms have a profound effect on a person's personal expectations about the aging process. This is because "Age norms tells us what people in a given stage are allowed to do and to be, and what they are required to do and to be" (34). When a person "violates" an age norm, she is often ridiculed and ostracized by those who adhere to such expectations. Tony Randall, actor, became the object of national ridicule when he announced that he was about to become a father in spite of being in his late 70's. When school teacher Mary LeTourneau had sex with her 13 year old student, society labeled him a victim and sentenced her to prison.

The different stages of life that people pass through are largely defined by society's understanding of what people are capable of at different ages, and what is appropriate behavior at life's different stages. Consequently, underlying much of the socialization that one experiences in early life is designed to prepare an individual to conform later in life with the expectations society holds for older people. When an older person demonstrates a variance from these expectations it is viewed by many members of society as disruptive and pressure is brought to bear on the "rebellious" senior citizen.

6. For a discussion on the ability of the adult brain to reorganize itself and possibly even produce new neural connections see Chapter 5.

When my father turned eighty, he and one of his "old buddies" decided to rent a motorhome, drive to Alaska and spend the summer fishing. This act of rebellion was treated with grave concern by all who heard of his plans. After all, this was the recreation of a young man. Certainly, if he wanted to fish, he didn't have to drive from Central Utah up the Alaskan Highway to Fairbanks, Alaska. Neither he nor his traveling buddy had ever been to Alaska, they had no family or friends in Alaska, there were Grizzly bears in Alaska, felons fled to Alaska, it was cold in Alaska, the mosquitoes in Alaska were the size of hummingbirds. He went anyway. Fifteen thousand miles and three months later he returned with wonderful stories, great photographs, and in very good health. So much for age norms.

Most people conform, it is easier for them, and much of the socialization they experience in later life is designed to promote behaviors that conform to society's expectations for older people. In a way this is good, because it permits people to anticipate their future and enter into transitional activities that enable them to move smoothly through life. On the other hand, there is a problem when people age slower than the norm. They are encouraged to age more quickly, to keep up with others in their age group. This was illustrated recently in my mother's life. She was out for her morning jog when she heard an elderly woman callout, "Morning neighbor, I want you to meet my homecare worker. You know, I can't go anywhere without her. When you get my age you will understand." My mother asked, "How old are you?" The neighbor replied, "I'm eighty." After a few minutes of conversation the neighbor asked, "And, how old are you?" My mother said she felt embarrassed to tell her neighbor that she too was eighty. After all you shouldn't be out jogging at eighty. That's an activity for a much younger woman. Or is it?

Perhaps, we age more quickly than we need to or should. I once attended a lecture in which a biochemist argued that biologically humans are designed to live about 150 years! Due to diet, environmental factors, and social learning, he concluded that people inevitably hasten the aging process. Perhaps our expectation regarding appropriate behaviors for different age groups needs to be reevaluated. Perhaps we need to be engaging in behaviors that fit a model of greater longevity. Perhaps if society viewed aging in different terms, and organized itself to promote longevity, people would continue to engage in such physical activities as jogging well past their eighties.

The way that society looks at aging can be illustrated by looking at different life-cycle models. These models are the efforts of authors and writers to relate behaviors to chronological age. By looking at these models, we can get a good idea as to the expectations society has for different stages of life. Society has a way of making these expectations very real in a person's life in three ways: (1) occupational patterns, (2) specific age norms, and (3) specific decisions one is expected to make at different ages (Atchley 34). We are excepted to have a job by age 25 and retire by age 65; we are permitted to drive at 16 and vote at 18; and we are expected to choose a mate and begin a family in our twenties. An awareness of these expectations will help us understand the role of age in the socialization process, and help us better understand the underlying cause of the pressures to conform to certain behaviors as we age. This is particularly important for people who because of attitude, genetics, and healthy behaviors maintain their youth well beyond the average. As someone once said, "To be forewarned is to be forearmed."

In 1976, Gail Sheehy's book, *Passages*, was released with critical acclaim. Many years later, it retains its popularity and is frequently cited in college classes, talk shows and in articles, and books dealing with the topic of aging. Based on her interviews with 115 men and women at different stages in the life cycle, Sheehy has identified several stages through which she believes all people must pass. The continual optimist and a born cheerleader, Sheehy argues that by successfully engaging the challenges of each stage, one can achieve an "authentic identity." It is through the acquisition of identity that Sheehy feels people achieve happiness. Another perspective, somewhat similar to Sheehy's model, is that of Roger Gould (1975). Both Gould and Sheehy view life as a series of crises, and like Sheehy, Gould feels that in learning to handle crises one is likely to have a happier and healthier life. Gould's "Seven Stages of Adult Life" provides a useful overview of the life cycle (Gould 74–75).

Gould's Seven Stages of Adult Life

Stage	Approximate Age	Development
1	16–18	Desire to escape parental control.
2	18–22	Leaving the family: Peer group orientation.
3	22–28	Developing independence: Committing to a career and to children.
4	28–34	Questioning self: Role confusion, and career vulnerable to dissatisfaction.
5	34–43	Period of urgency to attain life's goals: Awareness of time limitation. Realignment of life's goals.
6	43–53	Settling-down: Acceptance of one's life.
7	53–60	More tolerance: Acceptance of the past; less negativisim; general mellowing

In his well known book, *The Seasons of a Man's Life* (1978), Daniel Levinson uses biographical material to illustrate the stages and transitions that he sees as characterizing the aging process. Levinson views specific developmental tasks as central to each of the major stages of development. For example, according to Levinson, the first phase of adulthood is a period of transition where an individual passes from dependence to independence. This is marked by a clarification of one's expectations for family and career and an assertion of one's individuality. From about the ages of 28–30, the emphasis is on becoming successful in one's chosen career. This thrust continues into the 40's where the focus shifts to concerns about middle age. The period from 40–45 is referred to as the mid-life transition. Levinson views middle adulthood as culminating at age 60 with the late adult transition occurring between ages 60–65. Levinson's life cycle model is presented in the following diagram:

Levinson's Developmental Periods in Adult Life

Late Adulthood	65
Culmination of Middle Adulthood	60
Age Fifty Transition	55
Entering Middle Adulthood	50
Mid-life Transition	45
Settling Down	40
Age Thirty Transition	33
Entering Adult World	22
Entering Adult Transition	17

Using the work of Sheehy, Levinson and Gould as a basis, the following outline of the human-life cycle has been prepared. Although all three models are based on empirical data, it is important to remember that one cannot predict from this general overview to specific cases. In principle, it appears that people pass through essentially the same patterns of experience as they get older, but this does not make such patterns either desirable or inevitable.

A Summary of Life Cycle Study Findings

Twenties

1. During this period, the emerging adult is concerned with questions of personal identity.
2. During the early 20's, concern with acquisition of job skills is important.
3. Related to one's identity are concerns relating to becoming less dependent upon parents and others, and strengthening one's independence.
4. Issues associated with developing intimacy with members of the opposite sex becomes increasingly important.
5. During this period people begin to make important decisions about career and family concerns.

Thirties

1. Usually by the 30's, a person has embarked on a career, and as such, becomes increasingly preoccupied with career issues.
2. During this period, intimate relationships which in the 20's and that evolved into marriage, begin to lose their appeal.
3. During the mid-30's, people take stock of their lives, which sometimes leads to abrupt lifestyle changes.
4. Usually there is a marked interest in acquisition of "things" and an emphasis on gratification.
5. Usually people begin to show a decline in physical well being.

Forties

1. Often during the 40's, people feel discouraged about the direction their lives have taken.
2. Guilt for past mistakes is sometimes a problem at this age.
3. People begin to notice how rapidly time is passing.
4. During the early forties, satisfaction with marriage ebbs to an all-time low but by the late 40's shows a dramatic rise.
5. Faced with a recognition that time is finite and that we are not immortal, people begin to evaluate and rearrange their priorities.
6. Usually there is an increase in social activity as well as an increase in physical fitness activities.

Fifties

1. The early fifties are marked by acceptance of how one's life has gone and a philosophical attitude about the future.
2. People tend to "mellow out" and become more tolerant.
3. During the middle and late fifties, the family and friends become more important, but the social interest of the 40's diminishes.
4. People become more concerned with the quality of an experience than the quantity.
5. Health problems become of increasing concern.
6. People begin to think and plan for retirement.

Sixties

1. The 60's usually are considered the beginning of late adulthood, but most people report that they don't feel they have changed a great deal since their youth.
2. Most people report relatively high satisfaction with their work.
3. For most people, the 60's is a time of retirement, which necessitates an acceptance of a new role and a realignment of priorities.
4. During this time, the spouse becomes the principal recreation partner.
5. Health becomes a critical concern for many people during this period.
6. Some people, during the last years of their life, experience a feeling of isolation and fear which leads to their withdrawal from society. Other people actively resist disengagement from society.

Seventies and Beyond

1. People during 70's usually begin their personal preparation for death.
2. Many people during their 80's and 90's disengage from society, their range of opportunities diminish to the time of their departure.

The Life Cycle and Leisure Activities

As one's physical characteristics are altered by the genetic and environmental clocks, and as cognitive, personality and social changes occur, it follows that one's leisure activities should also change. Bammel and Bammel (1982) in their book, *Leisure and Human Behavior*, examined this question using essentially the same life cycle divisions as presented in this unit. As one might hypothesize, active participation in physical recreation decreases with age. Spectator, television and recreational reading tends to increase with age. As one gets older, family recreation tends to become more important. One thing seems certain, retirement doesn't generally lead to a dramatic increase in new activities. In fact, one study (Vinick and Ekerdt, 1991) found that following retirement, over 50% of men surveyed reported no increase in activity; whereas 40 of the wives reported a decrease in personal leisure activity. On the plus side, Vinick and Ekerdt found that couples engaged in more activities together following retirement.

The following chart summarizes recreational activity by age as outlined by Bammel and Bammel.

Changes In Recreation Activities by Age

Stage	Activity
Teens	Socializing seems to be a central-life interest, peer recreation is very important. Movies and music characterize this period. Physical activity, team and individual sports is high.
Twenties	Socializing becomes more important as the search for that right person picks up speed. Dancing, socializing, night-clubbing, dinners out, etc., are all important. Once married, this pattern changes and spectating becomes more the order of the day (or night). Outdoor recreation and fitness activities are important.
Thirties	Social involvement centers around home and friends. Family get-togethers provide recreation and family contact. Outdoor recreation and physical recreation give way to cultural arts. Women show particular interest in competence and mastery.
Forties	Social recreation tends to revolve around the family, until the nest empties; then travel and social involvement increases. Camping and outdoor activities continue to show a decrease; for a minority there may be a renewed interest in physical conditioning.
Fifties	Social recreation tends to become more home oriented with an emphasis being placed on family get-togethers and visits with old friends. Travel interests may diminish. Television may be major source of entertainment. Involvement in sports is usually limited to spectating.
Sixties	Grandchildren provide a source of pleasure for many people during this period. For some, retirement provides an opportunity to start new hobbles and participate in civic affairs. Television provides much of the entertainment. Gardening and home based activities fill a large portion of time.
Seventies	Social involvement may revolve around newly retired friends. Card playing and social activities are popular. For some, interest in church activities increases. Other people move to retirement communities where a wide array of planned recreation is available.

In this overview, it is important to recognize that this portrait of recreation patterns is a generic picture. It may not be applicable to all people or to all cultures. It does, however, illustrate the affect aging has on leisure behavior. In most cases, people slow down and become less physically active. Their recreation becomes less physical and more cerebral. That this is true for most people doesn't mean that it has to be true for an "age norm breaker" like Australian actor, Paul Hogan, who at 45 mastered the skateboard! It certainly wasn't true of my student who went bungee jumping at age 83!

Paul Hogan and my student probably represent the minority. As people get older, they tend to have an increasingly difficult time mastering new activities. Think of the number of older people you know who don't know how to access the Internet, or don't know how to operate a computer, or don't know how to set the timer on their VCR. This is due to the fact that as we get older our mental capacities diminish slightly, and our ability to learn new skills minimizes. This also helps to explain the concept of **continuity** in leisure activities.

Continuity refers to the tendency of a person to act out his/her life against ". . . a backdrop of familiar and relatively persistent attributes and processes for both the self and the environment" (Atchley 149). Atchley goes on to say that "One of the most frequent findings in gerontology is that continuity overshadows change for most people in midlife and after" (249). In other words, as people get older they tend to engage less in novel activities and engage in behaviors with which they have familiarity. Generally these are the activities of one's youth. The activities of senior years are often a reflection of those that were important to you in earlier years. When physical limitations make such activities difficult a recreational vacuum is left that is difficult to fill. This observation speaks volumes to the importance of acquiring a rich background in leisure activities while in your more formative years. Even if you have a positive attitude toward leisure you will largely be limited to participating in leisure activities for which you have the prerequisite skills. To think that you will learn new skills after retirement may be too optimistic. I often hear young men say that when they get older they will take up social dancing. This may be difficult if the appropriate coordination and sense of rhythm hasn't been earlier developed. The earlier you start preparing for retirement the better!

Studies show that as people get older they tend to engage in less active recreation than when younger. This is particularly true for men (Stanley and Freysinger, 1995). A surprising finding is that there is one area in which men tend to show a significant increase in activity—housework, including cooking and decorating (Vinick and Ekerdt 1991; Verbrugge. Gruber-Raidini, and Fozard 1996). It is interesting to note also that up to a point as women get older they experience a decrease in housework and an increase in paid work.

Successful Aging

My concept of successful aging is simply not dying. Although a terrific idea, it is an entirely different definition from that used by social scientists. To Iso-Ahola it means aging "without suffering a loss of high-level intellectual functions and the maintenance of mental, physical and social health" (175). It essentially means to age with a minimum of inconvenience.

What role can leisure play in helping people age successfully? Common sense and scientific research suggest that physical recreation can play a vital role in helping people maintain physical health. Unfortunately this realization often comes too late for many people. Once you reach middle or late adulthood, it is very difficult to "get back in shape." If you are interested in aging successfully, you would be well advised to make exercise an important part of your lifestyle during adolescence and young adulthood. Young adults are in their prime as far as physical performance and health are concerned, but they still need to be careful not to "overdo it." Because they can handle stress much easier than older people, young adults often ignore stress and the impact short-term and long-term stress can have on their bodies. Often the negative effects do not surface until much later in life when it is too late to prevent or change them. I often counsel young people who express an interest in being active in later life to be conservative when it comes to activity while young. It is no coincidence that many of the senior runners you see are runners who didn't start until later in life. Stress injuries are often a problem for the individual who was athletic in his or her youth. For these people vigorous athletic activities in their senior years may be difficult.

A study done in 1975 showed a strong relationship between successful aging as measured by scores on physical and mental health, intellectual performance, and recreational pursuits throughout the life cycle (DeCarlo, 1975). The findings showed that as recreation participation increased, so did the quality of life in later years. It is important to note that DeCarlo differentiated between recreation activities by classifying them as sensory-motor, cognitive, and affective. Of these three activity categories, it is interesting that the strongest predictor of physical health was involvement in cognitive activities. In a more recent study Swan and Carmelli found that intellectual curiosity was related to longevity in both men and women, once again demonstrating the importance of cognitive recreation for golden agers.

In the DeCarlo study, mental health was related to involvement in all three activities. What this tells us is that physical activity alone is not sufficient to maintain sound health. It is likely that cognitive recreation contributes to longevity by stimulating the central nervous system. It is also likely that a healthy intellect contributes to longevity in another way. Undoubtedly, people who regularly enjoy intellectually stimulating activities have learned to think and reason effectively. A logically thinking person recognizes that in addition to fitness training one needs to use good sense in selecting a diet, dealing with stress, and getting ample rest. As for the findings regarding leisure and mental health, it stands to reason that involvement in a wide array of activities would be characteristic of a person who is interested in life and curious about its possibilities. Such a person would most likely be enthusiastic about learning, interacting, and doing. And, as discussed in Chapter 5, recent brain research indicates that an enriched intellectual environment helps generate neural connections which in effect helps keep the brain young.

Although not explored by DeCarlo, the explanation for his findings may be found in reviewing what we have already discussed regarding the relationship of leisure to optimal arousal. Human beings have an inherent need to seek stimulation. Ellis has shown that when arousal seeking yields optimal physiological arousal, there is a direct correlation to task performance and feelings of satisfaction. In other words, optimal arousal produces relatively satisfying and stress free responses. Stress, on the other hand, is a function of too little or too much arousal. Stress has a negative impact on the body. It also has often been linked to adverse physiological reactions and disease. Leisure involvement, on the other hand, tends to be associated with increased optimal arousal. This produces optimal physiological functioning which in turn contributes to successful aging.

Beck, (1993) following a 30 years longitudinal study found a correlation between retirement and a diminution of happiness. In this study, he found that it was not retirement per se that reduced one's happiness, but rather a decline in health, widowhood, and a reduction in income. This study supports the notion that when conditions persist that lead to supraoptimal or suboptimal arousal, feelings of satisfaction and happiness may be diminished. When an individual is able to function in an optimal manner, it is likely that feelings of happiness will be enhanced.

As people get older, they tend to see themselves as increasingly unable to defend themselves from life's dangers. Atchley identifies the following areas in which older people often feel unprotected: physical, mental, financial, social and environmental. In addition, he points out that many older people feel increased vulnerability to crime, exploitation, and abuse (107–118). **If one is to truly age successfully, vulnerability must be minimized**. Consequently, it is important that people develop strategies early in life to ensure that they will have adequate financial resources when they are old; that they will have a safe and comfortable living environment; that they will have satisfying social contacts, and that they are protected from crime and exploitation. Older women may have special concerns regarding vulnerability. As Sharon Harold (1992) points out, women are more vulnerable in old age because of the gender related limitations they have faced their whole lives. This coupled with the fact that women often outlive their partners makes old age more challenging for women than men.

Recommendations for Successful Aging

Aging doesn't start when you turn 60. It begins the moment you are conceived and continues, nonstop, right up until the moment you die. The quality of the process is largely up to you and the earlier you start paying attention to your personal aging process, the better off you will be. Here are some simple guidelines that, if practiced, will help you forestall the inevitable and make the trip a little more enjoyable.

1. Pay attention to and develop sound health practices. This includes making exercise an important part of your life. It also means becoming well-versed in nutrition and diet, and then developing the attitudes necessary to implement what you know.
2. Learn how to control stress. The old adage, "Stress kills," should be emblazoned across your mind. It not only contributes to one's death, but it also kills the fun of living.
3. Foster cognitive development through formal education and play. Learning can be one of the most pleasurable of pursuits. As a child, your quest for learning proved to be a strong motivation leading

you into one challenging situation after another. As an adult, you can derive the same satisfaction and benefits that you received from cognitive playas a child.

4. Remember that socialization continues throughout life, and will occur with or without your input. Choose your situations and your social contacts wisely. By involving yourself with other dynamic and interesting people, the possibility of experiencing continued social development is increased.
5. Make play and recreational experience a continuous part of your life. As the DeCarlo study showed, the more you make recreation a consistent part of your lifestyle, the more successfully you will age.
6. Include a variety of activities in your recreation. Again, referring to the DeCarlo study, mental health in old age was related to a recreation pattern that contained continuous involvement in physical, cognitive and emotional activities.
7. Recognize that optimal arousal is associated with successful aging, and that in highly aroused situations, it is essential to reduce arousal; whereas, in suboptimal situations, arousal needs to be increased. Generally, in supraoptimal situations, one must withdraw physically or attitudinally to affect a decrease in arousal. In low arousal situations, an increase may be produced by increasing the complexity of an activity or by introducing novelty into it. Learning to monitor and control one's arousal level is an important skill.
8. Begin your financial portfolio early. Although money can't buy happiness, it can go a long way toward ensuring peace of mind. With adequate income you can minimize the feelings of vulnerability that older people often experience. You can live in a safe neighborhood, afford good medical care, remain independent, and maintain an interesting and pleasurable lifestyle.
9. Make leisure learning a lifelong process, and begin early. It has been known for a long time that if leisure skills are not learned prior to the midlife, they may never be. It is also generally recognized that as one gets older, acquisition of new skills is dependent upon the presence of prerequisite skills. For example, a person who developed good rhythm and balance as a younger person will be able to apply these skills to new activities in later life. But, a person who never developed these prerequisites may find it impossible to learn new recreational skills which require rhythm and balance. Our schools are excellent at teaching us the skills to do our jobs, but miserably inadequate at teaching the prerequisites for lifelong leisure. Wise parents will make every effort to see that their children acquire competence in as many recreational areas as possible. Similarly a young adult will be wise to immerse him or herself in a wide array of enrichment learning as early as possible.

Norman Cousins, the prominent writer and thinker who laughed himself well (see Chapter 10) was a critic of education's emphasis on career learning. As he put it, "I contend that science tends to lengthen life, and education tends to shorten it; that science has the effect of freeing man for leisure, and that education has the effect of deflecting him from the enjoyment of living" (20). I couldn't agree more. Education has a responsibility to train and educate people for the creative and pleasurable utilization of their free time. It appalls me to see school districts cutting back their arts programs, music and theater programs, and sports programs. It is as though they see their only obligation to educate for leisure is to make certain that children can read the television schedule.

Closing Note...

I was listening to a country song on the radio, and although I didn't catch all of the lyrics one stuck with me. It went something like this, "I don't mind growing old as long as I depart feeling young." As I mentioned, for me that's not good enough. But unfortunately, my preferences in this matter hold no weight. Ultimately, we must all face old age, and its eternal consequence. For some of us, aging is such an unpleasant thought that we ignore its inevitability and live only for the moment. But eventually, moments add up, and the sum total of those moments are where we are right now! By recognizing that we have a great deal to say about our old age, right now, right at this moment, and by structuring every moment in such a manner as to produce an optimal yield, we can do a lot to ensure that our lives are richly lived, and our longevity extended. As Henri Frederic Amiel said over 100 years ago, "To know how to grow old is the master work of wisdom, and one of the most difficult chapters in the great art of living."

REFERENCES

Administration on Aging. http://www.aoa.dhhs.gov/aoa/pages/profil95.html (October, 16, 1998).

Atchley, R.C. *Aging: Continuity and Change.* Belmont, CA: Wadsworth Publishing Company, 1983.

Bammel, G. and L.L. Burrus-Bammel. *Leisure and Human Behavior.* Dubuque, Iowa: Wm. C. Brown, Publishers, 1982.

Beck, S.H. *Journal of Gerontology* 37.5 (1994): 616–24.

Cousins, N. "Art, Adrenalin, and the Enjoyment of Living." *Saturday Review* 20 April, 1968: 20–24.

Ellis, M. *Why People Play.* New York: Prentice Hall, 1973.

Gleitman, H. *Psychology.* New York: W.W. Norton and Company, 1981.

Gould, R. "Adult Life Stages: Growth toward Self-Tolerance." *Psychology Today* 8 February 1975: 74–78.

Guyet, R.S. "A New Theory about the Ages of Man." *International Journal of Aging and Human Development* 36.2 (1992-93): 91–98.

Harold, S. "Education in Later Life: The Case of Older Women." *Educational Gerontology* 18.5 (1992): 511–527.

Iso-Ahola, S.E. *The Social Psychology of Leisure and Recreation.* Dubuque, Iowa: Wm. C. Brown, Publishers, 1980.

Levinson, D.J. (with C.N. Darrow, E.B. Klein, M.H. Levinson and B. McKee), *The Seasons of a Man's Life.* New York: Alfred A. Knopf, 1978.

Sheehy, G. *Passages.* New York: Dell Books, 1976.

Swan, G. E. "Curiosity and Mortality in Aging Adults: A 5-year follow-up of the Western Collaborative Group Study." *Psychology and Aging* 11:3 (1996): 449–453.

Verbrugge, L.M., Gruber-Baldini, A.L; and J.L. Fozard. "Age Differences and Age Changes in Activities: Baltimore Longitudinal Study of Aging." *Journals of Gerontology Series B Psychological Sciences and Social Sciences* 51B.1 (1996): 30–41.

Vinick, B.H. and D.J. Ekerdt. "Retirement: What Happens to Husband-Wife Relationships?" *Journal of Geriatric Psychiatry* 24.1 (1991): 23–40.

CHAPTER 9

Wellness and Leisure

To enjoy one's leisure, recreation, and play to the fullest, one must be free from external and internal constraints. In the discussion of potential constraints, health emerges as one of the most important factors influencing one's ability to fully enjoy a leisure lifestyle. To many people, health means being free from illness. While this is a logical assumption, being free from illness is only a small part of total health. The World Health Organization explains, "Health is a state of complete physical, mental, and social well-being, and not merely the absence of disease or infirmity" (1946).Health, viewed as overall well-being, introduces the concept of **wellness**. Jesse Williams redefined health from the wellness perspective as:

> . . . that condition of the individual that makes possible the highest enjoyment of life, the greatest constructive work, and shows itself in the best service to the world. . . Health as freedom from disease is a standard of mediocrity; health as a quality of life is a standard of inspiration and increasing achievements (Hafen 2).

The differences between "health" and "wellness" are apparent. The concept of health is rather simple. Health is a **state of being**, either you are sick or you are not. Wellness is more complex and multifaceted. Wellness can be thought of as an **active, lifelong process** of first becoming aware of the way you are affected by your nutrition, fitness, stress, interpersonal relationships, and environment; and, second, using this knowledge to make choices that will lead you toward a higher state of well-being (Hafen 2). To simplify this notion we can examine the relationship of wellness to three dimensions: physical, mental, and social health.

Physical Health

This dimension includes: nutrition, exercise, and self-care. A person who follows good nutritional practices, exercises regularly, gets plenty of rest, and restricts intake of harmful substances is usually energetic, trim and fit. Optimal physical health is one of the foremost characteristics of a healthy person.

Mental Health

Included in this dimension is emotion, spirituality, stress management, and coping. Like physical health, mental health is more than merely the absence of disease. Mental health greatly determines one's overall health. Negative emotions can prolong and even provoke illness. On the other hand positive thoughts, emotion and attitudes have a strong relationship to good health.

Spiritual health can be thought of as the ability to discover one's inner-self and how to experience love, joy, peace, and harmony. This helps people to reach their full potential and feel fulfilled. A spiritually healthy person feels that life is meaningful with a sense of purpose and direction (Hafen 5).

Stress (distress), an unavoidable aspect of life, is associated with a variety of health problems including muscular aches and pains, high blood pressure, and headaches. Stress can be managed in a healthy manner through techniques such as relaxation, identifying and avoiding stressors, exercise, and time management. When stress is dealt with effectively, a positive mental attitude is maintained, life is considered meaningful, and overall health approaches optimum.

Social Health

Relating, belonging, and communicating are included in this dimension. A socially healthy person has the ability to be friendly, polite, outgoing, and affectionate towards others. This stems from a good self-image and confidence in one's abilities. Such a person respects other people ideals and beliefs while remaining true to his or her own personal beliefs and ideals. A socially healthy person has the ability to respond to another person's needs without sacrificing his or her own.

These dimensions are interrelated to one another. In other words, they are influenced by each other. Therefore, it is important that each dimension is developed and all three exist in harmony and balance. Look at the diagrams below. The one on the left shows all dimensions in balance with one another. Contrast this with the diagram on the right. This diagram is unbalanced with one dimension over-emphasized leaving the other dimensions under-developed. This is what happens when one focuses on only one aspect of health.

The following scenario illustrates the interrelation of these dimensions. You have just taken an English exam and feel certain that you did not do well. You go home feeling stress and frustration. To get your mind off "things" you sit down to watch television and proceed to consume a bag of chips and whatever else is handy. Hours later, full and lethargic, you feel guilty about wasting so much time watching television and pigging out. Each dimension has been affected. Your physical health has been affected by forgoing exercise and a healthy meal for chips and television. By staying home alone, you have not improved your ability to interact and communicate with others. This in turn can lower your self-image and confidence. On the other hand, having gone on a bike ride or jog with a friend would have affected all dimensions as well, but in a manner that leads to optimal well-being.

Based upon what you now know about the dimensions involved in the wellness model, draw your own model based on your development in each dimension. Are these elements balanced in your life?

A wellness lifestyle involves a change in attitudes and beliefs as well as active involvement and commitment to improving personal health practices. Traditionally one's health becomes an issue only after it is lost and illness occurs. Medical practice or the "treatment" model seeks to bring an ill person back to the point where he/she can function normally. Wellness efforts seek to go a step further by promoting a lifestyle in which one can eliminate risk factors, prevent disability and disease, and improve the quality of one's life. This approach has been termed the "prevention" model.

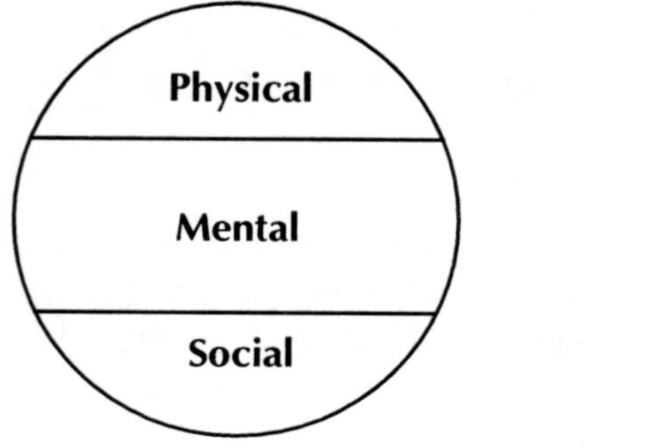

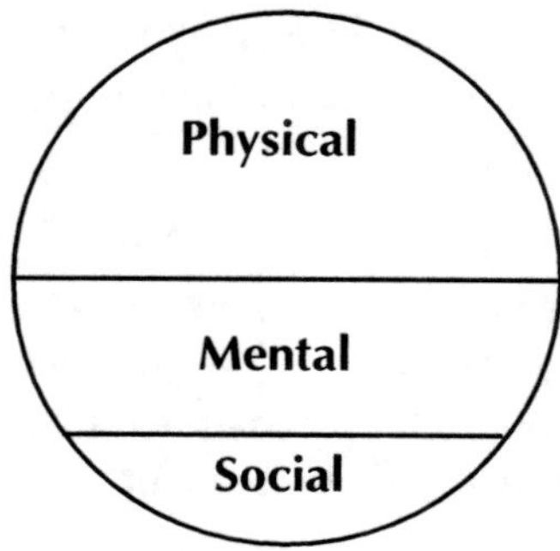

Leading Causes of Death[7]

	Top 10 of 1900		Top 10 of 1996
1.	Tuberculosis	1.	Heart disease
2.	Pneumonia and influenza	2.	Cancer
3.	Enteritis, colitis and gastritis	3.	Stroke or apoplexy
4.	Heart diseases	4.	Chronic Pulmonary Disease
5.	Stroke or apoplexy	5.	Accidents
6.	Kidney diseases	6.	Pneumonia/Influenza
7.	Accidents	7.	Diabetes
8.	Cancer	8.	HIV/AIDS
9.	Diseases of early infancy	9.	Suicide
10.	Diphtheria	10.	Chronic Liver Disease

Although wellness has been defined, the question may still remain: Why wellness? Why not continue my lifestyle as is and gamble that I will not get sick or if I do a doctor can take care of it? Looking at recent statistics, the adage that, "an ounce of prevention is worth a pound of cure" still looks to be true.

Look back to the beginning of the 20th century at the top ten killers of that time and compare them to the top ten killers of today. We see that the killers of today are largely lifestyle related and hence preventable.

The top killers of 1900 were for the most part communicable. Through medical and sanitary improvements, the incidence of these diseases dropped dramatically. The treatment model worked well in combating diseases in the early part of the 20th century, but today, treatment of disease in an after-the-fact manner is not as successful as preventing it. Not only does living a lifestyle that seeks to prevent illness enhance the quality of life, but it keeps the billfold healthy as well. According to the United States Department of Health and Human Services, Americans spend more that $1,500 per person in health care per year, which makes us the highest health spenders in the world. With so much money spent on health care, it is logical to assume that Americans rank highest in the quality of health. Sadly this is not the case. We have the highest rate of heart disease among nations in the developed world and some of the highest rates of colon, rectum, breast, and lung cancer (Hafen et al 3).

Not only do visits to the doctor add to health care costs, but annually billions of dollars are spent by Americans on prescription and over-the-counter drugs and remedies—pills to eliminate headaches, prevent sleep, cause sleep, calm an upset stomach, lose weight, you name it. By adopting a wellness lifestyle, and eliminating risk factors associated with many of the top killers, much of the expense related to health care can be avoided.

What are risk factors then? A risk factor is defined as something associated with an increased likelihood that a disease will develop. Specific risk factors that have been linked to the major killers today include:

- Eating foods high in fats.
- Smoking.
- Lack of regular exercise.
- Excessive intake of alcohol.
- Failing to take hypertension medications.

(Hafen 6)

What these risk factors have in common is that *they are all lifestyle related*. For example, smoking is one of the most hazardous behaviors being linked to 4 of the 5 top killers today. Estimates are that smoking is

7. Center for Disease Control. *Monthly Vital Statistics Report* 46.1 (1996). For more current statistics see: http://www.cdc.gov/ nchswww/fastats/lcod.htm. It is interesting to look at the statistics for different groups. For example, the leading cause of death for Californians between 1–19 years of age is firearms, followed closely by vehicular accidents. Suicides and homicides accounted for more deaths than all deaths caused by disease.

responsible for "30 percent of all cancer deaths, 30 percent of heart disease fatalities, 85 percent of all chronic bronchitis and emphysema deaths, and it is an unquantifiable risk factor in cerebrovascular disease." (Hafen 6) According to the World Health Organization, "The control of cigarette smoking could do more to improve health and prolong life in developed countries more than any other single action in the whole field of preventive medicine."

Along with the elimination of the risk factors listed above, researchers have found that the inclusion of the following lifestyle habits leads to both the quality and quantity of life:

- Sleeping for seven to eight hours each night.
- Eating breakfast every day.
- Not eating between meals.
- Maintaining an ideal weight.
- Exercising regularly.
- No drinking or in moderation only.
- No smoking.

(Hafen 6)

As you can see, personal health is something that you do have a certain amount of control over. The key to a wellness lifestyle is self-responsibility. To start, you must accept responsibility for your health knowledge and lifestyle.

Through a conscious effort to improve health you begin to move toward your optimal health, and hence towards a leisure lifestyle. First, you must identify what areas you need to improve and start to incorporate changes into your daily routine. In the following spaces provided, using the wellness concept as a guide, identify some of the areas in which you need to improve.

1.______________________________
2.______________________________
3.______________________________

Overall, the guiding principle behind the wellness lifestyle is that a "state of high level wellness is within the reach of every person. In order for you to achieve a high level of wellness, you must accept full responsibility for your own sense of well-being" (Hafen 11).

The following section of this chapter focuses on the dimension of physical health. More specifically nutrition and exercise will be addressed.

Physical Fitness

The word "fit" usually conjures up different images for different people. For some people, Michael Jordon, basketball player, is the image; for others, Lance Armstrong, cyclist; or Tyra Banks, model. What does it mean to be fit? Fitness has been defined by the President's Council on Physical Fitness as the "ability to carry out daily tasks with vigor and alertness without undue fatigue and with ample energy to enjoy leisure-time pursuits and to meet unforeseen emergencies" (*The Wellness Encyclopedia* 213). In short, fitness can be defined as having the ability to do one's work with energy remaining for recreational activities. Clearly there is no set criteria for fitness, for fitness is highly individualized. As the *University of California, Berkeley Wellness Encyclopedia* states, "you may be fitter than you were last year, or than your neighbor, but there is no clear cut point at which you are fit" (213).

Physical fitness is a vital part of the wellness lifestyle and exercise is the pathway to achieve the goal of fitness. By engaging in regular vigorous activity, one can enjoy the benefits related to exercise such as: less fatigue, healthier more alert appearance, increased physical and mental efficiency, a sense of well being with more vitality and zest for life, better sleeping patterns, better body composition and weight control, improved ability to handle stress and crisis situations, minimized risk of osteoporosis, the lowering of blood pressure, and possible protection against coronary heart disease. Lack of exercise contributes to the probability of physical weakness, adult onset diabetes, osteoporosis, and heart disease (Hafen 202).

Clearly it is obvious that engaging in exercise is worth the investment of time, effort, and commitment. Physical fitness consists of four basic components:

1. Cardiovascular endurance
2. Muscular endurance
3. Muscular strength
4. Flexibility

An exercise program should include and develop each component. The first and perhaps the most important component is cardiovascular endurance. This means the heart can withstand greater loads during exertion. Physiologically, cardiovascular endurance means that the heart, blood vessels, and cells are able to efficiently carry oxygen to the tissues and carry wastes away. Every cell requires oxygen to function and during physical exertion such as running or swimming, the cells require more oxygen and faster waste removal. Basically, physical fitness increases the ability of the heart, lungs and circulatory system to function properly.

Cardiovascular endurance is developed by doing exercises which require oxygen be delivered to working muscles for a sustained period of time, 15–60 minutes. This type of activity is called "aerobic." Types of activities considered aerobic include not only aerobic dancing, but jogging, swimming, hiking, racquetballing, bicycling, cross-country skiing, rowing, and even walking. Aerobic fitness will develop a stronger heart which can pump blood more efficiently, deliver oxygen to the muscles, and the muscles in turn will develop a greater ability to use oxygen. As a result, your heart rate will decrease following exercise and you will recover more quickly.

If an activity is engaged in which requires short bursts of energy, this activity is termed "anaerobic" or literally "without air." In activities such as weightlifting, basketball, or football, the muscles do not require oxygen. This is because the energy required for the muscles can be derived from the quick energy source, glucose, which is found within the muscles themselves.

To develop and maintain cardiovascular fitness, aerobic activities must be engaged in for the proper **intensity, duration, and frequency**.

Intensity

This refers to the rate at which your heart beats. During aerobic activity, the heart rate should increase to a level where it is operating between 60% and 90% of its maximum. This range is called the "training zone." To compute your training heart rate and maximum heart rate use the following formula:

> Find your resting heart rate by taking your pulse at the wrist (thumb side) and count for 30 seconds and multiply this number by 2. This is your resting heart rate (RHR). Subtract your age from 220. This is your maximum heart rate (MHR).
>
> The low end of your training zone (LTZ) is calculated this way: MHR x .6 = LTZ.
>
> The high end of your training zone (HTZ) is calculated this way: MHR x .9 = HTZ.
>
> Take a few minutes and do these calculations.

During exercise you should check approximately every ten minutes to see if you are exercising within your training zone. A convenient counting method is to take a six second count. In this case, divide the training zone numbers by ten and use those numbers to determine if you are exercising within your training zone. The *University of California, Berkeley Wellness Encyclopedia* recommends not to exceed 80% of your MHR unless you are in peak physical condition (214).

Duration

This refers to the length of time spent in aerobic activity. For cardiovascular fitness to become a reality, the heart needs to regularly work within its training zone for a period of time ranging from 15–60 minutes. For example, when riding a bicycle or engaging in any aerobic activity, allow approximately 5 minutes for the heart to reach your training zone and remain exercising at the training zone for 20 minutes. It is important to monitor your heart rate during the exercise by taking your pulse. If the intensity is too high, slow down. If the intensity is too low, increase activity.

Frequency

Here we are referring to how often you engage in aerobic activity. The American College of Sports Medicine suggests aerobic activities be engaged in for 15–60 minutes, within your training zone, three to five times a week. Exercising less than three times a week produces minimal results, while exercising more than five times produces little additional cardiovascular improvement.

If one of these factors is low, compensate by increasing the others. If you exercise for only short periods of time (20 minutes or so), compensate by increasing the frequency of the activity or gradually increase the intensity (*The Wellness Encyclopedia* 227).

Finally, the key to cardiovascular fitness is consistency and commitment. To maintain fitness you must exercise regularly. As Hafen states, "After only two weeks without training, your fitness level will decrease significantly. After ten weeks to eight months, you may be no fitter than you were before you started training" (207).

Muscular Endurance

Muscular endurance is the "ability of a muscle group to apply repeated force over a period of time (isotonic), or to sustain a contraction over time (isometric)" (Hafen 205). Weights and weight machines, as well as floor calisthenics such as sit-ups and push-ups are effective tools for developing muscular endurance. The key is to use a workload of 55% to 75% of the maximum amount you can lift and perform 15 or more repetitions.

Muscular Strength

Muscular strength is generally thought of as the maximum force a muscle can produce in a single effort. Examples of muscular strength are seen in kicks, throws, jumps, lifts, and the like. The most effective way to increase strength is by working out with weights. Building strength is the opposite of building endurance. Use heavier weights and fewer repetitions on free weights or weight machines. An important concept in building strength is called "overloading." Overloading increases strength by using heavier than normal resistance. Heavier resistance "compels muscle tissue to contract with all or almost all of its fibers. . . over an extended period of time [overloading] encourages biochemical adaptation in the muscle that increases strength" (Greenberg 188).

Flexibility

We generally think of flexibility as the ability to use muscles and joints through their full range of motion. Flexibility helps avoid injury in any type of activity. To obtain and maintain flexibility, stretching before and after a workout is a good idea.

Stretching should be static and controlled. This means that the stretch is gradual, and should encompass the full range of movement and be sustained for 10 to 30 seconds. Contrast this type of stretching to ballistic or bouncing stretching. Stretching in short quick movements is potentially harmful to muscles by causing them to shorten, which increases the risk of tearing, soreness and injury.

The University of California, Berkeley Wellness Encyclopedia lists several tips for stretching. These are summarized as follows:

1. Warm-up before stretching.
2. Stretch 3 to 4 times a week.
3. Stretch for about 10–20 minutes, using static stretches.
4. Begin stretching by focusing on major muscle groups and make certain to stretch muscles involved in your sport exercise.
5. Do not compare your flexibility with others; flexibility varies from person to person.

Strong, flexible muscles are important for everyone to develop; hence, exercises to develop muscular strength, endurance, and flexibility are important components of an exercise program. The benefits that result from well-conditioned muscles and flexible joints are: improvement in exercise performance, decreased risk of injury, good posture, and improved efficiency in everyday tasks (*The Wellness Encyclopedia* 267).

Starting an Exercise Program

To start an exercise program it is important to design one specific to you. According to personal trainer, Thomas K. Kahn,

> An exercise program can be incorporated into everyone's life. Exercise is highly individualized; people are at different levels of fitness and excel at different activities. It is because of these differences that no predetermined routine works for everyone. By designing a personal exercise program that considers an individual's goals and abilities, exercise can be enjoyed rather than tolerated and is more likely to be engaged in consistently.

Designing a personal program involves examining several factors which affect your choice of exercise. These factors include time constraints, location, access to equipment, physical limitations, exercise preferences, and abilities. You can illustrate the difficulty inherent in designing a personal fitness program by doing the following exercise. In the space below, list aerobic activities in which you would like to engage.

1. ____________________
2. ____________________
3. ____________________
4. ____________________

Take a look at what you have written. Is it realistic? Are you likely to engage in one or more of these activities on a consistent basis? If you have never exercised in a routine manner or have taken a lengthy leave of absence from exercise, start with a lower intensity activity. Low impact aerobics, water aerobics, swimming, walking, and moderate cycling are good starter exercises. If you have been exercising for some time, try increasing intensity, duration or try **cross-training**. Cross-training incorporates several different activities into your program. Running, swimming, biking, and aerobics classes are examples of a good combination of aerobic exercises which increase your fitness level by working different parts of your body. A typical exercise program should include all four components of exercise and include the following five phases.

1. **Warm-up.** 5–10 minutes. Before stretching cold muscles it is important to warm them up, "get the blood pumping." This can be accomplished by a general all over body exercise such as walking, jogging and cycling lightly or specific warm-ups which are moderate rehearsals of the specific sport or activity you are going to engage in. After warm-up, include stretching exercises.

2. **Aerobic Activity.** 15–60 minutes. This includes your chosen aerobic activity. During this phase remember to keep your heart rate in your training zone by frequent monitoring.
3. **Cool-down.** 5–10 minutes. This is similar to the warm-up. The purpose of the cool-down phase is to gradually bring your heart rate back to the resting level. This should include performing your aerobic activity at slower rates and continued movement.
4. **Muscle Strength and Endurance.** 10 minutes minimum. Endurance exercises include exercises which require repeated movement such as stomach crunches, leg lifts, and push-ups. Strengthening exercises include working out with weights such as dumbbells and machines. For strength and endurance exercises to be beneficial and injury free, it is important that attention be paid to proper form and body alignment.
5. **Flexibility.** 5–10 minutes. This phase should include gradual stretching of muscle groups and specific muscles used in your exercises. Stretching helps to decrease the chance of injury and muscle soreness.

An exercise program that includes these five phases should be engaged in three days a week. As you advance, increase frequency to five days a week. Regardless of your fitness level, it is important to give your body time to rest and recuperate. Ideally you should allow 24 hours rest between vigorous activities, but no more than 72 hours. In short, this usually works out to working out every other day.

Remember to be flexible and work exercise into your schedule when it is convenient for you. Whenever and whatever you do for exercise, remember the principles of frequency, duration, intensity, and consistency.

Exercise should be enjoyable and the benefits of exercising make life even more enjoyable. However, there are risks to exercise and it is important to be aware of them and your body while exercising, so you can avoid injury. First, before starting a vigorous program, check with a physician for medical clearance, especially if you have a history of medical problems.

The *University of California, Berkeley Wellness Encyclopedia* identifies several basic tips to exercising safely which are summarized below.

- **Whatever Activity You Pursue, Do Not Overdo It.** Start any new exercise at a lower intensity avoiding the "too much, too soon" syndrome. Listen to your body and if a particular activity or weight is too difficult, do not feel constrained to perform it. Set goals and record your progress. Find others to exercise with.
- **"No Pain, No Gain" Is a Myth.** Exercise requires effort but not discomfort. Feeling the "burn" or pains is a warning signal. Aches and pains during exercise may indicate that you are not warming up sufficiently or are exercising too long or hard. Also, keep yourself well hydrated. Drink plenty of water before, during, and after exercise.
- **Use Adequate Shoes and Clothing.** Of all sports injuries, 90% occur in the feet, knees and hip areas. This often is due to old or poorly fitting shoes. Clothing should be appropriate for the activity. For example: layer clothing for easy removal as your body warms.
- **Control Your Movements.** Rapid, jerky movements can cause injury to muscles and joints. Be sure to learn the proper form and techniques for whatever activity you engage in. When stretching, do not bounce. "Ballistic" stretching greatly increases the chance of muscle tears and soreness. Opt for "static" stretches, which gradually stretch the muscle.
- **Add Variety.** Not only can engaging in the same exercises become boring, but the chances of injury from overuse and repetition increases. Variety adds some "spice" and motivation to your workout.

By applying the principles presented in this section, you should be able to design a safe and fun program that will lead you toward optimal health.

What about Those Extra Pounds?

Many of us are overweight. **Or at least we think we are.** Unfortunately, the weight you see on the scale is not necessarily a good indicator of whether or not you are carrying too much fat. Muscle weighs about 75% more than fat, so consequently, if you are building muscle, you might weigh more than you think you should. In fact, it is possible to gain weight and while at the same time, become leaner. A flight attendant who was also a body builder often had a difficult time meeting her weight requirement. Even though she always looked lean and trim, the scale constantly put her career in jeopardy. She had to eventually get a doctor's note explaining that the reason that she weighed so much was not that she was fat, but rather, just the opposite—she was carrying only about 12% fat. A better indicator than your actual weight, of whether or not you are "overfat," is to look at yourself naked in a mirror, or pay close attention to how your clothes are fitting. A more scientific method is to have your body composition tested by a professional physical educator.

The American College of Sports Medicine **recommends** the following body fat levels in men and women:

	Male		Female
Low:	6–10% fat	Low:	14–18% fat
Moderate:	18–20% fat	Optimal:	19–22% fat
Optimal:	11–17% fat	Moderate:	23–30% fat
Obese:	Greater than 25% fat	Obese:	Greater than 30% fat

Obesity can be a serious health problem. It increases a persons chance of becoming seriously ill. "Hypertension and stroke are twice as likely to occur in obese people than lean people. Coronary heart disease is more common. . . adult onset diabetes mellitus is five times more common among obese people. . . osteoarthritis may be aggravated by obesity." (AMA, 738) Also related to obesity is increased chances of cancer of the colon, rectum, prostate, breasts, uterus and cervix. It should go without saying that if you are carrying more than the optimal percentage of body fat, appropriate steps should be taken to lower that percentage.

The extent to which you exercise will have a profound impact on your body composition. It takes about 3,500 calories to burn up one pound of fat. If you are not currently involved in an exercise program, it is conceivable you can lose fat by simply increasing your activity level. By regular aerobic activity, you will increase your metabolism which essentially means you will burn fat. If you couple aerobic activity with weight and strength training, you will increase your muscular strength, increase muscle mass, enhance bone density, and develop a leaner body. By exercising at least three times a week, and then by following a diet low in fat, the chances are very good you can favorably modify your muscle to fat ratio. The next section of this chapter focuses on nutrition and diet.

CALORIES BURNED DURING EXERCISE. Want to burn calories? Well, then grab a snow shovel and move to Alaska. That's right, heavy snow shoveling can burn a lot of calories, in fact, up to twenty-calories in one minute. That is roughly five times more efficient than going for a walk. In addition, don't forget that even after you have stopped your vigorous snow shoveling or whatever physical activity you choose, your basal metabolic rate will remain elevated and continue to burn calories at a higher rate than were you a sedentary sort. The key to successful weight loss is movement. Climbing, walking, jumping, carrying or swimming will all help you burn calories. Even mowing your lawn with your power mower will enable you to burn up to as many as 5 calories per minute. The following chart will give you an idea as to the number of calories various activities burn. Note that one's weight must be taken into account when reading this chart.

Calorie Burned per Minute for Various Activities

	105–115 lbs	127–137 lbs	160–170 lbs	182–192 lbs
Aerobic Dancing	5.8	6.6	7.8	8.6
Biking 10 mph	5.4	6.2	7.4	7.5
Dancing (Rock)	3.3	3.8	4.4	4.9
Hiking 20 lb pack	5.3	6.7	7.9	8.8
Jogging 5 mph	8.6	9.8	11.5	12.7
Power mower	3.5	4.0	4.8	5.2
Running 8 mph	10.4	11.3	14.1	15.6
Active Sex	3.9	4.5	5.3	5.8
Skiing (downhill)	7.8	10.4	12.3	13.3
Skiing (x-country)	13.1	14.0	17.6	19.3
Snow shoveling (light)	7.9	8.1	10.6	11.8
Snow shoveling (hard)	13.8	15.7	18.5	20.4
Swimming 55 yd/min	11.0	12.5	14.8	16.3
Tennis (singles)	7.8	8.9	10.5	11.6
Volleyball	7.8	8.9	10.5	11.6
Strolling 2 mph	2.4	2.8	3.3	3.6
Walking 4 mph	4.5	5.2	6.1	6.8

But, I Don't Have Time to Exercise

When someone says he or she doesn't have time to exercise, what this generally means is that he or she doesn't have time to go to the gym. Granted, in this very busy world, it may be true that finding time for formal exercise is difficult. However, it is not impossible, it is a matter of choice, and for many people the decision is to do something other than go to the gym. But, that doesn't mean that you can't exercise. Refer back to the above calorie chart. Note that the activity which consumes the most calories is shoveling snow! Rapid walking burns between 4.5 and 6.8 calories per minute. Stair climbing—5.9 to 8.8 calories per minute, and even sex can burn up to 5.8 calories per minute. If you walk briskly for about 20 minutes during the course of a day, you will consume about 100 calories. Do this five times a week and you will consume about 500 calories. If you consume approximately 500 calories more per week than you have been, and providing you don't alter your diet, you will lose about one pound per month. This amounts to 12 pounds in one year. In a hurry to lose weight, then walk briskly for about one hour and twenty minutes per day, and you will lose one pound in one week! And, all this without going to the gym or altering your diet.

In addition to aerobic exercises such as walking or climbing stairs, you can include throughout your daily activities exercises which will strengthen your muscles, improve muscle tone, and add to your flexibility . . . and again, you can experience gains in these areas without going to the gym.

Stretching. You can do various stretches while at work, while getting ready for work, while closing out your day. The basic rule in stretching is to stretch slowly and smoothly. Never bounce when stretching. Hold your stretch for from five to ten seconds then alternate to another stretch. Repeat for several times. You can easily stretch your quads, hamstring, calf and achilles, shoulder and arms, triceps and shoulders, neck and shoulders while doing other activities. For example, while working at your computer, you can periodically take a break and for a few moments to stretch your shoulders, arms and neck. To develop your own stretching routine, consult a fitness consultant or visit your local library and check out a good book on exercise.

Muscle Toning and Development

The best approach to muscle training and development is to seek the guidance of a fitness trainer. But, there are some exercises that you can do on your own, and as part of your regular day. The primary rule in muscle training is to progressively add greater levels of resistance to increase the size and strength of the muscles affected. Weight lifting machines, such as the Nautilus, are typical of the kinds of machines devised to provide body builders with progressive resistance. But, you don't have to use such a machine to get similar results. For example, you can do pushups, or crunchies, or leg lifts, or isometrics, or pull-ups to get similar results. These activities use the body's own weight as the source of the resistance. And, many of these activities can be done while at work or while studying. For example, while sitting at your desk, you can strengthen your biceps by placing your hands under the desk and simulating the curling motion you have seen weight-lifters do. Don't try to lift the table, merely apply resistance to your biceps for 10–15 seconds. Do a few repetitions of this exercise and then return to work. You can do crunchies while sitting at your desk. You can even drop to the floor and do a few pushups. If that doesn't appeal to you then stand in a doorway and do the same motion against the door frame. While standing in line at the grocery store, you can strengthen your buttocks by turning your toe outward and doing slight leg lifts. As with the stretching exercises, consult a good exercise book and then use your creative capabilities to adapt these exercises to the workplace or home. Along these lines, Robert Spackman has some suggestions that I think are worth noting (62–65):

1. As you brush your teeth, pull your stomach muscles in tight and pinch your buttocks together.
2 Stand on one leg when you put on your underwear or sox instead of sitting.
3. If you are driving a car, pull in you stomach muscles every time you come to a red light, hold to green.
4. Don't ride elevators, walk as many stairs as you can.
5. If you are making your bed, do part of it while still under the covers—stretch your covers as you stretch your arms and legs.
6. If you are picking up a baby, slowly lift her above your head at least five times.
7. Pause now and then and rise up on your toes for six seconds.
8. Every time you go to the refrigerator, place both hands on the sides of it and compress for six seconds before opening the door.
9. When standing in a doorway, place your hands on the door frame and try to push it apart.
10. As you do your dishes, do slight knee bends.
11. While watching television, do arm curls; use a can of soup for weight.
12. While sitting at your desk, squeeze the buttocks so that you rise an inch off the chair, hold for 5 seconds.

You get the idea.

As with the stretching exercises, consult a good exercise book and then use your creative capabilities to adapt these exercises to the workplace or home.

Strains and Sprains

It is ironic but true, many of our attempts at fitness leave us feeling stiff and sore, and in some cases actually cause injury. Whenever you injure yourself, it is important that you seek professional care. In the meantime, you can apply first aid to the injured body part. Use the RICE treatment for most soft tissue injuries. RICE stands for "rest," "ice," "compress," and "elevate."

Rest involves taking some time away from activity that affects the injured area. You may have to take a day off from work, use crutches, or a cane. Ice refers to the application of a cold compress to the injured area. Experts tell us that applying a cold compress to a musculoskeletal injury is one of the best first aid measures you can take. A cold compress will help reduce swelling, reduce pain, and decrease muscle spasm.

Consequently, it can help you recover more quickly from your injury. Experts advise that you can apply ice packs for up to twenty minutes at a time, but no more than two such treatments per hour.

(http:www.worldguide.com/Fitness/med/html) And, remember, the sooner you get the ice on the injury, the more good it will do! Compression usually involves wrapping an injured area with a compression bandage. Elevation, refers to using gravity to minimize swelling. See a doctor, regardless of how insignificant you want to believe the injury is. Complications from seemingly simple injuries can often be long lasting, particularly if gone untreated.

A Word about Your Ears and Eyes

A Personal Note: A few years ago I was exposed to a loud sound, it resulted in a loss of hearing in one ear and the onset of what became chronic tinnitus. Tinnitus generally appears as a high pitched ringing. It is similar to the sound you hear following a loud concert. Unfortunately, in chronic tinnitus, the sound never lessens, it never goes away. In a small percentage of cases, it gradually worsens. This condition has made me keenly aware of the danger loud sounds pose to one's hearing. It seems that we live in an increasingly loud environment, one for which our evolutionary history has not prepared us, at least when it comes to our hearing. Our ancestors were rarely exposed to loud sounds—no jack hammers, jet planes or rock bands disturbed their environments. Consequently, we are not at all capable of adapting to loud sounds. This explains why most Americans have lost some degree of hearing by the time they reach adulthood. The hearing loss that occurs from exposure to loud sounds is cumulative and irreversible. Every time you are exposed to sounds over 60 decibels, you are damaging your delicate hearing mechanism. To put this in perspective, recognize that a kitchen blender produces about 90 decibels, a vacuum cleaner about 80 decibels, power motors about 100 decibels, and a loud human scream over 100 decibels. A rule of thumb is that if you have to speak loudly to be heard, you are in an environment that is harming your hearing. (Guiness, 208-217)

Although disease and injury account for a small percentage of hearing loss, most of it is the result of exposure to loud sounds. To protect your hearing and to avoid the inconvenience of hearing loss and the discomfort of tinnitus, you must protect your ears from noise. This can be done by avoiding loud environments, or protecting your ears through the use of ear plugs. Some people are embarrassed to be seen in a bar or at a concert wearing ear plugs. Such vanity can be extremely costly in the long run. If vanity has prevented you from using ear plugs, you might want to try the silicone variety which can be shaped and pressed into the ear canal. They aren't as noticeable as the other styles, and can serve as an effective sound barrier. Oddly enough, when you are in a loud environment, and you are wearing ear plugs, you will be able to hear the people around you better than without them. . . an added bonus. Remember, it is difficult to have a leisure lifestyle if you cannot hear well, or if every sound you do hear is heard through a screen of high pitched ringing.

Mom was right, do not put sharp objects into your eyes, but there is more to protecting the eyes than that. Evolution didn't prepare our eyes for the jobs they are called upon to perform today. One of the biggest problems facing our eyes today is the up close work most of our jobs require. Sitting in front of a computer screen is a good example of the kind of work our eyes are called upon to perform for which there is no analogous task found in nature. This kind of work can lead to eye stress, and this in turn can manifest itself in a variety of symptoms. Experts suggest that to protect your eyes from stress you should avoid over working them, take frequent vision breaks, give them a chance to focus on something in the distance, close them for several seconds at a time.

Diseases such as conjunctivitis, can be uncomfortable, and ocular herpes can lead to severe vision impairment. Be careful about touching your eyes. A sharp blow to the eye can definitely contribute to the premature development of a cataract. There is some indication that over exposure to sunlight can hasten the onset of cataracts as well. Good ultraviolet blocking sunglasses may be a wise preventive measure, and safety glasses are a must for many sports and home repair projects. Glaucoma, which can easily be detected by your optometrist, can lead to blindness unless treated. (Guiness, 204–205)

Mental Health

Good physical health can optimize mental health but what about a healthy state of mind optimizing physical health? In the West, the concept of the mind/body connection is taking hold. This idea makes intuitive sense in that the body's physiological systems: nervous, endocrine and immune systems, act as feedback systems for one another. Researchers have found that hormones (products of the endocrine system) and neurotransmitters (nervous system messengers) can influence the immune system and vice versa (Moyers, 1993). So, one's thoughts (e.g. "Oh man, I have a ten page paper due in two hours and have not even started!") can elicit a stress response in the body which has a cascade effect that can manifest in a myriad of physical symptoms (not necessarily desirable ones).

A healthy state of mind encompasses many facets (emotion, spirituality, coping, etc.). If these are developed in a positive way they can ultimately result in a healthier physical body as well as a more balanced perspective of oneself and life. In a major study, patients *optimistic* about their health (even if their physicians reported them in poor health) survived at a higher rate than those who were pessimistic (Ornstein, R. and Sobel, D., 1989).

A "good" attitude can also enhance aspects of the self such as self esteem, confidence, sense of purpose, etc. Leisure and recreational activities can be instrumental in developing these. For example, trying new activities that peak your interest and foster learning, such as cooking a new dish or learning to play a sport can increase one's sense of confidence (Ornstein, R. and Sobel, D., 1989). **What I am trying to say is that ATTITUDE counts!**

During the 1960s and 70s there was a lot of talk about Type A and B personalities. It appeared that the more aggressive, ambitious, and impatient Type A's were subject to more stress related problems like heart attacks and strokes. Subsequent research has suggested that hostility, cynicism, and self involvement are more critical risk factors than ambition. Some studies have shown that people who demonstrate Type A behaviors can lessen their chance of disease by learning to react more calmly to pressure and criticism (160). Ilona Jerabek has developed an instrument to measure the degree to which a person engages in Type A behaviors, with her permission, I have modified the instrument slightly and present it to you here. For an analysis of your score, again based on Jerabek's work, refer to the scoring guide following the test.

Read every statement carefully. Indicate the extent to which you agree or disagree. In order for the test to be valid, please answer every question. Use this format to answer:

a=STRONGL Y AGREE b=agree c=undecided d=disagree e=STRONGL Y DISAGREE

______ 1. I never seem to have enough time to accomplish my goals.

______ 2. It is easy for me to understand people who get so impatient in traffic that they start honking.

______ 3. It is important to me to make it to the top of my field or chosen career.

______ 4. I find it difficult and useless to confide in someone.

______ 5. It should be more difficult to obtain a driver's license in order to keep idiots off the highways.

______ 6. It bothers me when I can't accomplish what I planned for a day.

______ 7. Important tasks often keep me from spending time with my family or friends.

______ 8. I am rarely satisfied with my achievements.

______ 9. It is important for me to own nice things.

______ 10. It is difficult for me to express my feelings.

______ 11. People who don't know what they want get on my nerves.

______ 12. I think hobbies such as fishing or bowling are just a waste of time.

______ 13. When I finish a task I feel good about myself.

______ 14. I function best under stress.

______ 15. Talking about emotions is a sign of weakness and can be used by others to get to you.

______ 16. Financial security is the basis for a successful family.

______ 17. If everybody did their job properly, my life would be much easier.

______ 18. I find it difficult to relax when faced with free time.

______ 19. I find that I often get angry at people who show incompetence or who are poorly organized.

______ 20. I think there is more wrong with the world than there is right.

This test is easy to score. Every statement with which you STRONGLY AGREE give yourself 5 points. For every "agree" answer, give yourself 4 points. "Undecided" is worth 3 points. "Disagree" is worth 2 points and STRONGLY DISAGREE is worth 1 point. There are 100 points possible. The higher the score the more inclined you are to Type A Behavior.

If you scored between 20 and 40, your behavior is likely to fall on the Type B, the leisure side of the continuum. Your attitude is more of a "smell the roses" approach to life. You value relaxation and know how to relax. You are easy to be around. You might appear to lack ambition, but generally this is considered a healthy approach to life.

If you scored between 40 and 60, you fall near the middle. Being in the middle in this case is good. You know when to relax, and yet you have the ability to be aggressive when necessary.

If you scored between 60 and 100 you fall on the Type A side of life. This behavior pattern is characterized by an exaggerated sense of urgency. Relaxation is difficult, people get tense around you, and may even feel threatened by your presence. Continuous stress and piled up unexpressed feelings are not good for your health. (1–3)

Regardless of your personality type or the behavior patterns that characterize your lifestyle, regular exercise and eating wisely will keep you well and healthy.

Nutrition

With an abundance of advice coming in from a myriad of sources, the average person may be left confused, overwhelmed, and questioning. What is a nutritious diet? Where do I start? Sanford A. Miller, Ph.D., Director of the FDA's Center for Food Safety and Applied Nutrition states:

> Consumers are bombarded constantly from many sources with an overload of information and misinformation about nutrition and health. Realistic, reliable guidance is critically needed to help the public sift and weigh this barrage of information, to make intelligent nutrition choices among the thousands of attractive foods in supermarkets and to select food in many places where it is consumed away from the home (Hafen 115).

However complex as it seems, eating right can be simplified into understanding and applying a few key principles. It is important to know what nutrients are essential to a healthy diet. The nutrients fall into six classes. Our bodies are composed of all six as well as most foods we eat. These nutrients are:

Carbohydrates	Fats
Proteins	Water
Vitamins	Minerals

Carbohydrates, fats, and proteins are further classified into the "energy" nutrients. These are the nutrients which supply calories or energy to the body. The body in turn uses these calories in several ways: to produce heat, build, repair and store energy (Hamilton 40).

Carbohydrates

These have in the past been considered fattening and avoided in order to lose weight. This is because excess carbohydrates are converted and stored as fat within the cells. In fact, carbohydrates are the largest supplier of energy for the body. Carbohydrates include a wide variety of foods, from refined sugar to apples, broccoli, muffins, pretzels, and rice. Although carbohydrates come in a variety of shapes, textures, tastes, and colors, they are all transformed in the body to glucose. Glucose is the body's usable form of carbohydrates. There are two classes of carbohydrates.

Simple These carbohydrates contain sugars such as fructose (fruit sugar), glucose, galactose, sucrose (table sugar), lactose (milk sugar), and dextrose

Complex These carbohydrates contain starches, cellulose, and fiber. Complex carbohydrates are found in foods such as pasta, bread, potatoes, and grains.

Although the body converts all carbohydrates into glucose, one type has more nutritional value than the other. Simple carbohydrates provide a quick source of energy, but not much else. These are often called "empty calorie foods." Candy, soda pop, popsicles, and sugar concentrated foods are simple carbohydrates. Naturally occurring sugars found in fruits are simple carbohydrates, but not necessarily "empty calories" because they contain many of the essential vitamins, minerals, and even fiber.

Complex carbohydrates are, as the name implies, complex. They are not only a good supplier of energy, but also contain many vitamins and minerals, and fiber. Fiber is an important component of carbohydrates. Insoluble fiber such as wheat bran helps regulate elimination as well as protect against colon cancer. Soluble fiber may help lower blood cholesterol and reduce heart disease (*The Wellness Encyclopedia* 87).

Protein

Originating from the Greek root meaning" of first importance," protein is responsible for growth and many bodily processes. Protein makes up muscles, organs, bones, tissues, cartilage, skin, antibodies, some hormones, and all enzymes. Proteins are made of different combinations of amino acids. These amino acids are most often reused in the body, however, we must continually replace some of those that are lost.

Scientists have identified 22 amino acids, of these the human body can manufacture 13; these are called non-essential amino acids. The other nine amino acids are called essential. These are essential because we must supply these amino acids via our diets so our bodies can make proteins.

Dietary proteins have been divided into two categories; complete and incomplete proteins. Complete proteins contain all nine essential amino acids. These are usually found in animal derived foods such as meat and dairy products. Incomplete proteins are found in food which supplies some, but not all, essential amino acids such as fruits, vegetables, and grains. Complete proteins can be made by combining incomplete proteins. This is how vegetarians meet their requirements. Examples of combinations are: beans and rice, bread and peanut butter, beans and tortillas, cereal and milk, cheese and pasta.

Fat

Probably considered the biggest culprit of nutrition, fat is an essential nutrient. One main function of fat is to serve as a source of stored energy. Fats are the most concentrated source of energy. A gram of fat contains nine calories whereas one gram of protein and one gram of carbohydrate each contains only four calories. Also fat promotes satiety, carries the fat soluble vitamins A, D, E, and K and supplies fatty acids. They are important for several hormone-like compounds which help control body functions. Furthermore, fat serves to protect vital body organs.

Saturated Fats

These are made of fatty acids which are loaded or "saturated" with all the hydrogen atoms they can carry. These are usually solids at room temperature. The main source of saturated fats come from animal sources such as lard and butter. Since saturated fats are stiffer in structure, they have a greater tendency to adhere to the walls of arteries and vessels rather than be excreted from the body. Saturated fats are considered more harmful than unsaturated because they elevate blood cholesterol and increase the risk of heart disease.

Unsaturated Fats

These are made of fatty acids which are not loaded with all the hydrogens they can carry. These are called polyunsaturated and monounsaturated depending on the number of missing hydrogen atoms. These are usually liquid at room temperature and are derived from vegetables and some fish. These are considered better than saturated fats because they decrease levels of LDL or "bad" cholesterol and make the blood less likely to clot. Structurally, unsaturated fats still have room to bond to other fatty acids. As they flow through the bloodstream, these fats can bind to the saturated fats (which are also in the bloodstream and along the vessel walls) and eventually both can be excreted from the body.

Vitamins

A vitamin is an organic substance needed by the body in small amounts to regulate metabolic functions within cells. Although they do not provide the body with energy, they are essential to life. There are 13 vitamins identified as essential to humans. Vitamins A, D, E, and K, are grouped as fat soluble, meaning they are stored in the body and the "B" complex vitamins, thiamine, niacin, riboflavin, B6, pantothenic acid, biotin, folacin, B12, and vitamin C are considered water soluble and are not stored within the body. They need to be replenished frequently. Each of these vitamins carry out specific and important functions and many diseases are linked with deficiencies or excess of these vitamins.

Minerals

Inorganic substances needed by the body in small amounts to help build strong bones and teeth, make hemoglobin in red blood cells and other important uses. Twenty-two of the more than 60 minerals have been identified as essential. These are further classified into the macrominerals and microminerals. Calcium, chloride, magnesium, phosphorous, potassium, sodium, and sulfur are considered the major or macrominerals. The other 15, such as iron, zinc, iodine, manganese, and copper are called the trace microminerals. Problems arise with excessive intakes, such as with sodium, and inadequate intakes such as with iron or calcium.

Nutrient Recommendations (Adapted from Hamilton 19)

Nutrient	Recommended	Comments
Carbohydrate	58–60% of diet	Increase to 60-70% for endurance athletes. No more than 15% of total calories should come from simple carbohydrates.
Fats	30% or less	Less than 10% should come from saturated fats.
Protein	12–15% of diet	The average American gets more than enough. Excess protein does not build muscles, it is stored as fat instead. Supplements are costly and unnecessary.
Vitamins	See RDA chart	Vitamins do not provide energy or build muscles. Supplements and high dosages are usually unnecessary and can be harmful.
Mineral	See RDA chart	As with vitamins, a varied diet provides the minerals needed. Supplements should be doctor directed.

Water

Referred to as the "forgotten nutrient," water is essential to life. The human body is 65–80% water. Water aids in the transport of nutrients, removal of wastes and regulates body temperature (Hafen 123). Water is needed daily (8 to 12 eight oz glasses a day) to replace the water that is lost.

With nutrients defined and discussed, the question remains, how do I incorporate these into a healthy balanced diet? How much of each nutrient do I need?

The key to meeting the recommended daily amounts of these nutrients is to eat a balanced and varied diet. The following food groups recommended daily servings, provides a good general guideline to a balanced diet.

Recently the four food groups have been modified to include a fifth food group called "others." Included in this group are sweets such as jam, jelly, sodas, candy and fats like salad dressings, mayonnaise, syrup, but-

Food Groups (Adapted From Hamilton 19)

Food Groups	Daily serving	Foods/Serving Sizes
Milk/Milk Products	2	1 C (8 oz) milk, 1 C yogurt, 1 oz cheese; opt for low or nonfat.
Fruits/Vegetables	5	1/2 C fruit, vegetable, juice, apple, banana, peach, or carrot. Choose dark green and leafy vegetables and deep colored fruits. These contain several vitamins.
Grains/Whole Grains	4	1 slice of bread, 1/2 C cooked cereal, 1/2 C cooked rice or pasta, 1/2 English muffin. 1–6 in. tortilla. Choose whole grain products such as whole rice, wheat, barley millet and oats.
Meat and Fish	2	2–3 oz cooked meat, 1/4 C tuna, 2 eggs. Options: 4 tb. peanut butter, 1 C cooked legumes; avoid fried food.

ter, and creamy sauces. Also included are the alcoholic drinks. The foods in this group should be avoided or seldom used due to the fact that these foods are primarily of little or no nutritional value. They are empty calorie foods.

A visual guide to food has recently been developed by the U.S. Department of Agriculture in cooperation with the Department of Health and Human Services. This model is called the "Food Guide Pyramid." The pyramid emphasizes foods from the food groups discussed previously, with the base consisting of foods from which most of your daily calories should be derived. It is emphasized that all food groups are necessary to a healthy diet. It is the portions that differ.

The *University of California, Berkeley Wellness Encyclopedia* lists twelve steps to a healthy diet:

1. Keep your total fat intake at or below 30 percent of your daily intake. Limit your intake of fat by choosing lean meats, skinless poultry and cut back on mayonnaise, fried foods, and whole dairy products.
2. Limit your intake of saturated fat to less than 10% of your fat calories. Saturated fats contribute to high blood cholesterol. A void animal derived fats and choose vegetable oils.
3. Keep your cholesterol intake to less than 300 milligrams a day. Cholesterol is found only in animal products. Limit intake of meat and egg yolks.
4. Eat a diet high in complex carbohydrates. Eat 5–6 servings of a variety of vegetables and fruits. Choose green, yellow and orange fruits and vegetables such as broccoli, spinach, cantaloupe, oranges, and carrots.
5. Maintain a moderate protein intake. Choose low fat sources of protein.
6. Eat a variety of foods. By eating from a wide assortment of foods, nutritional needs are easily met and in addition avoids the possibility of toxic amounts of pesticides or certain nutrients that may come from eating the same food daily.
7. Avoid too much sugar. Foods high in sugar are often empty calorie foods and are often high in fat.
8. Limit sodium intake to no more than 2,400 milligrams a day. This is approximately equal to one teaspoon of salt. Cut back on adding salt to foods. Try not to buy processed, dry, or canned foods.
9. Maintain an adequate calcium intake. Calcium is important for strong bones and teeth. Get calcium from skim milk and nonfat yogurt.
10. Get your vitamins from foods, not supplements. Especially avoid supplements that provide more than RDA. Toxic effects can result from megadoses and self-supplementation.
11. Maintain a desirable weight. Balance your energy (calorie) intake with energy output. Eating a low fat diet in combination with exercise will help maintain a lower weight. Maintain an adequate calcium intake. Calcium is important for strong bones, teeth, and proper functioning of nerves and muscles.
12. If you drink alcohol, do so in moderation. Drink no more than one serving of alcohol per day. This translates into one 12 oz. beer, a glass of wine or an ounce of liquor.

Remember, pregnant women should avoid alcohol due to the damage alcohol can cause to a developing fetus.

Eating right begins with shopping right. Become a label reader. Keep in mind the principles listed above when you shop. Try to avoid the highly processed packaged, snack foods. An occasional ice cream cone or candy bar will not kill you. Go ahead and enjoy one from time to time. Just be sure to load your shopping cart with staple foods such as fresh fruits and vegetables, whole grain breads and cereals, low fat and nonfat milk products and lean meats. Leave very little room for foods from the "other" food group.

Closing Notes. . .

A leisure lifestyle is complemented by a wellness lifestyle, and indeed, a wellness lifestyle is complemented by a leisure lifestyle. Engage in leisure and recreational pursuits with wellness in mind. In fact, wellness and leisure pursuits can be one and the same. For example, riding a bike, skiing, and hiking can be engaged in as leisure activities and at the same time enhance your health. A leisure/wellness lifestyle is a win/win proposition. For more information on wellness and health related topics, see the following references.

REFERENCES

Arden, D.B. *High Level Wellness: An Alternative to Doctors, Drugs and Disease.* Ten Speed Press, Berkeley, CA. 1986.

Bailey, C. *Fit or Fat?* Houghton Mifflin Co., Boston, MA. 1978.

Greenberg, J.S. and D. Pargman. *Physical Fitness: A Wellness Approach.* 2nd Ed. Prentice-Hall, Englewood Cliffs, NJ. 1989.

Guiness, A. (ed.) *ABC's of the Human Body.* Pleasantville, NY: Readers Digest Association, Inc 1997.

Guiness, A. (ed.) *ABC's of the Human Mind.* Pleasantville, NY: Readers Digest Association, Inc 1997.

Hafen, B.Q. and A.L. Thygerson and K.J. Frandsen. *Behavioral Guidelines for Health and Wellness.* Morton Publishing Co., Englewood, CO. 1988.

Hamilton, E.V.N. and E.N. Whitney and F.S. Sizer. *Nutrition: Concepts and Controversies.* West Publishing Co. St. Paul, Minn. 1985.

Jerabek, I. *Type A Personality Test.* http://www.deltaworld.com/cgi-bin/type-a.pl. (November 17, 1996).

Moyers, B. *Healing and The Mind.* Doubleday, New York, NY. 1993.

Ornstein, R. and D. Sobel. *Healthy Pleasures.* Addison-Wesley Publishing Co, Inc. Reading, MA.

Spackman, R. In *Keeping Fit: How to Live a Longer and Healthier Life.* New York: Berkeley Books.

University of California, Berkeley. *The Wellness Encyclopedia: The Comprehensive Family Resource for Safeguarding Health and Preventing Illness.* Houghton Mifflin Co. Boston, MA. 1991.

Your Health, Prentice Hall, (adaptation) 1996. http://wwwl.mhv.net/-donn/calorie.html (October 20,1996).

CHAPTER 10

Work and a Leisure Lifestyle

This chapter is designed to demonstrate how work may serve as a foil to leisure, or be considered a valuable component to the leisure lifestyle. Work is defined, extrinsic and intrinsic aspects of work are examined, and alternatives to traditional work models are reviewed.

The Meaning of Work

In primitive times, people had to be self-sufficient. Survival depended upon their ability to protect, feed, clothe and shelter. The work of primitive people was not rewarded by financial gain, but rather survival. Civilization altered this model. Organized communities produced specialization and soon economic systems were devised. One's specialization allowed one to generate income that provided the means to procure the products or services of other specialists. Thus, work became associated with income, but the net result was, as it had been in earlier times, the acquisition of food and clothing and shelter. *When viewed from this perspective, one can argue that work is the energy utilized in acquiring food, clothing, and shelter* (Bammel and Bammel 3).

From an economist's point of view, work is usually an activity for which there is remuneration (Wolfbein 3). This point of view is of practical value to a social scientist because money provides an efficient way to measure value in society. Unfortunately, it fails to account for work done which is not directly paid for. Examples of this are the housewife who works daily in the house, or the unemployed individual who exerts energy in seeking a job, or the self-sufficient individual who directs his/her energies to producing food, clothing and shelter.

In physics and mechanics, work refers to the energy of a force acting against some resistance resulting in the displacement of the source of the resistance. Work is equal to the product of the force and the distance of the movement. Unlike social definitions, the time factor doesn't enter into the physical science of work. The ability to work for any period of time is associated with the concept of power (Harris and Levey 3007). *To the physical scientists, work is energy to create movement.*

Borrowing from physical science, one can argue that work is any activity in which one uses energy to bring about a change in something. From this standpoint, work is associated with any human activity that is directed toward any goal or objective. Work can range from mowing a lawn to playing a vigorous game. From this viewpoint, work is nothing more than the application of force or energy.

Ann Harriman, following her study of work patterns among managers and professionals, concluded that work is the set of meaningful activities by which an individual defines him or herself. Work provides intrinsic rewards; it may or may not be undertaken for its own sake and not because it is prescribed by one's role as job-holder or by any other social or family role. It is akin to the notion of a "calling or vocation" (12).

To Harriman, a job is how one "earns a livelihood," work is something else (12). Although a logical perspective, and one that corresponds to Neulinger's Model, it is important to note that in common parlance, work and job often are used synonymously. This is manifest in how people use the word "work" in their daily conversations. When one is at his place of employment, *he is at work.* Or, when she is going to her job, *she is going to work.* As summer approaches, students are heard to say, "*What will you do for work*?" When a person receives employment, *she has found work.* When one loses a job, *he is out of work.*

I owe, I owe, It's off to work I go . . .

—Linda Lucky

The Purposes and Importance of Work

Clearly, one's job is important from the standpoint of financial reasons. Few of us are born with discretionary wealth, most of us have to "work" in order to survive. But in addition to the monetary value of work, there are other important outcomes.

Extrinsic Rewards Other Than Money

Normally, when one thinks of extrinsic rewards, money is the first thing to come to mind. But, for many people, one's employment may provide them with a number of non-monetary yet extrinsic values. *Status* is an important reward for work. *Recreational opportunity* afforded under the heading, "employment recreation," may be thought of as an extrinsic reward. *Schedule flexibility* is an extrinsic value that attracts many people to jobs such as teaching. In fact, for many people, time is viewed as being as important as money. In one survey, workers, when offered the choice between more time off or money, opted for the time off (Harriman 8). These are but a few of the non-monetary extrinsic rewards offered by one's employment.

Work provides people a social group with whom to associate and identify. Such a group is important for at least two reasons: (1) it provides a group against which one can mirror his or her social, emotional, and economic characteristics and (2) it provides a community within which one may socialize, contribute, and seek support.

Importance to Society

A society unwilling to work is ultimately doomed. The progress of the Western World is certainly, in part, related to the work upon which much of Western Culture is based. It would also appear that freedom is an essential component to successful economies, suggesting that successful work in contemporary society may be more similar to current thinking about leisure than early thinking about work.

Alternatives to Traditional Work Models

Labor does not, by its very nature, fall into units of eight-hour days, five-day weeks, and 50-week years. . . Jobs have been designed to fit into this pre-determined workweek, rather than the reverse. . . There is no moral or ethical value to a five day, 40-hour workweek except that which society conferred upon it. The length of the standard. . . is a phenomenon dating back only to the 1930's and determined not by nature but by the United States Congress (Harriman 163).

Within recent years, several alternatives to traditional work models have emerged. These appear to take three forms: (1) schedule alternatives, (2) management style and (3) combinations of time and style.

Schedule Alternatives

FOUR-DAY WORKWEEK (THE 4/40). Bammel and Bammel indicate that even though management consultant, Riva Poor, has been advocating a four-day workweek since the early 1970's, it was estimated that only 1.4% of the labor force worked a 4/40; whereas 15% worked more than five and one-half days per week (276).

Advantages associated with 4/40 are summarized by the following chart (276):

Advantages of 4/40 Work Schedule

Efficiency	Effectiveness
Less expense	More production
Less travel time	Less fatigue
Less turnover	Recruitment appeal
less absenteeism	Improved morale
Less scheduling conflict	

THREE-DAY WORKWEEK. Some jobs commonly employ such a schedule. Firemen, doctors, pilots, university professors, some attorneys, and other professions operate on such a basis (Bammel and Bammel 279). The benefits from this model have not adequately been tested to argue from an empirical perspective, but it is likely that a three-day workweek would be a mixed blessing. Some might find the extra discretionary time more of a burden than blessing.

FLEXITIME OR GLIDE TIME. One of the schemes to vary the workday is flexitime, which allows workers to select starting and stopping times. Usually a core time, determined by management, is required of everyone (Harriman 10). Flexitime is likely to promote increased morale, worker responsibility, and overall efficiency and productivity.

JOB-SHARING. This scheme involves two comparable workers, each working half-time doing the same or complementary components of the same job.

Management Styles

Flexibility in work scheduling has two effects on one's leisure lifestyle: (1) more time for leisure and (2) as time scheduling falls within the control of the employee, the greater the workers' perceptions of freedom; hence, a greater sense of leisure during work. Management styles have a similar impact.

AUTOCRATIC STYLES. Management styles based on the machine model approach tend to minimize perceived freedom by removing decision making capacity from the rank and file. Under some circumstances, this approach may be the most appropriate choice. In situations where critical decisions must be made quickly, and where great risks are involved, an autocratic style may be the best choice. However, in most contemporary business and industrial organizations, a more democratic approach may be warranted.

PARTICIPATORY MANAGEMENT. Within recent years, management theorists have recognized the value of involving workers in the decision process. As indicated earlier, this has implications that go beyond the workplace. When workers are given a voice in the management of an organization or business, the probability of workers' perception of freedom is increased. In addition, improved worker satisfaction is likely to result. Thus, participating in management is likely to contribute to a leisure-job attitude among employees.

The Importance of Work in Your Life

Those of us who study leisure have often suggested that work-time will eventually give way to leisure-time, that people will be required to work less, and hence, will be given the opportunity to enjoy more free-time. In fact, it wasn't more than a decade or two ago that we were very much concerned about what people were going to do when faced with the unprecedented leisure the near future guaranteed. We were afraid that unprecedented leisure would pose more problems than benefits, largely because people were so accustomed to being externally directed. The big fear was that the majority of people would not know how to use leisure to their advantage. But, as of the present, the indicators are that as a society, we are spending more hours at work than we did at the end of World War II. We have not become a society of leisure. The 1991 Harris Poll revealed that the average American worker "works about forty-seven hours per week spent at and getting to one's job". . . this is up from 40 hours per week in 1973. Our worries about unprecedented leisure seem to have been unfounded, at least for present and the near future.

Why? Paul Wallich tells that we have developed a "workaholic economy." He states, "Provisional and managerial employees supply the most obvious lesson. . . once people are on salary, their cost to the firm is the same whether they spend 35 hours a week in the office or 70." This is apparent even in such diverse fields as medicine and education. To encourage extra production more universities are offering performance pay, while in HMO's the physician who keeps costs down and sees the most patients can receive a handsome bonus (*The Sacramento Bee*, November 11, 1996). In regard to factory workers, ". . . it is more profitable to ask 40 employees to labor an extra-hour each than to hire one more worker to do the same 40 hour job. Given the expense of benefit packages, it is often more profitable for a company to pay overtime, than to hire new employees. The net result is that employees, regardless of their job, are working more hours."

Even two-career households don't generally generate enough money for a family to acquire all of the "things" that "money can buy." In spite of our workaholic economy, there are always new things to buy, and things we must have. Our high technology society makes products almost obsolete at the time of the creation. The cost of education is constantly increasing, medical costs are increasing, the cost of living always seems a step ahead of most Americans. For people living on a minimum wage "it now takes between sixty and eighty hours of work per week to feed a family." (Hughes, 2) As a consequence, in many households both spouses work, many teens are forced to work, and many individuals have more than one job. The great irony is that many of the things we buy are for leisure purposes, but unfortunately many of us simply don't have time to enjoy them. So much for the leisure society.

> Forty-years ago people worked 12 hours a day,
> and it was called economic slavery. Now they work 14 hours a day,
> and it's called moonlighting.
>
> —Robert Orben

Faced with what appears to be a decline of leisure-time, it becomes increasingly important that people find employment that offers them more than just a salary. Unfortunately, many people find dissatisfaction with their jobs. Hughes cites a study (3) that shows that even though highly career oriented, only one in four workers between ages 18–50 are satisfied with their jobs. Some simple mathematics make it clear how damaging an unsatisfying career can be to one's lifestyle. Even if an individual only works eight hours a day, that is 1/3 of available time. Add to that eight hours travel time, and incidental but related activities, and it is not unreasonable to argue that one's work accounts for as much as ten hours per day. Factor six to eight hours for sleep, and you have six to eight hours remaining in which to attend all other activities: take the kids to school, bathe and groom, eat, do domestic chores, shop, household maintenance, yard work, television, family activity, paying bills, and the list goes on. For many people, time for discretionary activities is generally nonexistent.

Consequently, it becomes extremely important that one selects a job that offers some of the opportunities and benefits associated with leisure. In seeking a career one should be mindful of the extent to which the job offers the principal elements of leisure: (1) perceived and perceptual freedom, and (2) intrinsic satisfaction. When a job is rich in intrinsic satisfaction, when people feel that they have a significant say as to how they are going to complete their tasks, when there is a genuine sense of pleasure associated with their work, and when pleasant interactions are associated with the work-place, it can be said that one's work offers some of the benefits of leisure (see Mihalyi Csikszcentmihalyi and John Neulinger).

I often tell people, "If your work makes you sick, you should call in well." It has been clearly established that jobs that are primarily extrinsically motivated, that offer little intrinsic satisfaction, or that are essentially devoid of perceived or perceptual freedom erode self-identify, stifle initiative, and impair mental health, leading to injuries, absenteeism, and staff turnover. Many health problems can be traced back to an unhealthy or unhappy work environment.

> Behold the little turtle. He only makes progress when he sticks his neck out.
>
> —James Bryant Conant

Calling in well is often an act of courage. Many of us remain in unsatisfying situations because we are afraid of an uncertain future. Many people stay in bad marriages for the same reason. William Shakespeare said, "Doubt is the thief that makes us fear to tread where we might have won." Many of us dream of a different life, a better career, but day in and day out continue to plug along, inwardly knowing that we will never make a change. It is just too frightening. However, there are those who take the chance. I know several people who have called in well. Stephan Duncan called in well. He was studying accounting, his future was defined for him. He was going to be an accountant. Stephan was one of my students. After the lecture on "calling in well," he approached me and asked what I thought about calling in well if your major was making you ill. We chatted for awhile. In the course of our discussion it became clear that Stephan's greatest desire was to become a jet pilot. Although competent in accounting, he felt he was best qualified to fly jets. It was the thing he wanted most to do. I suggested he had two alternatives (1) become a very successful accountant and buy his own jet, or (2) since at that time there was a need for air force pilots, enlist in the air force. Two weeks later Stephan stopped by my office to tell me that he had called in well, he had enlisted in the Air Force. A year passed and I received a note in my mail box saying that Lt. "Been Through the Sound Barrier" Duncan had called. Stephan was on a training mission, and was just checking in. Later we had lunch, and Stephan regaled me with his stories about flying a jet fighter. Stephan took charge of his future by calling in well, and working for a future that he could enjoy.

Happiness is essentially a state of going somewhere, wholeheartedly, one-directionally, without regret or reservation.

—William Sheldon

Choosing the Right Job

As of 2003, the Bureau of Labor Statistics predicts that over the next several years (to 2010) professional and related occupations will grow the fastest and add more jobs than any other occupational group. It is expected that in this category, there will be a 26 percent increase and a gain of about 6.9 million job opportunities. It is predicted that nearly 75% of these jobs will come from three areas: computer and mathematical occupations, healthcare, and education. The second category of growth will be in the service occupations. It is estimated that about 19.5% of the growth to 2010 will be in food preparation and hospitality service, with a near equal growth in health care support occupations. Little growth is expected in such areas as farming, forestry, and production work (manufacturing).

In considering a career or a career change it is a good idea to look at such projections. Making a reasonable career choice, in part, will rest on the projected opportunities available to you. A good resource for you, and this is available at almost any library, is the *Bureau of Labor Statistics Monthly Labor Review.* Another source is the *Occupational Outlook Quarterly*, or the *Occupational Projections and Training Data*. Both are produced by the Bureau of Labor Statistics. Much of this information is available on the Internet at **http://stats.bls.gov/oco/coc/2003.htm** or **http://stats.bls.gov/news.release/eco.toc.htm**.

Faith Popcorn, yes, that is her name, is the head of an organization that does market projections for business.

In her book, *The Popcorn Report*, she identifies ten trends that her organization believes will have an impact on business in the United States up to the year 2010. Her analysis goes beyond that of the Bureau of Labor Statistics and considers the social and psychological factors at play as well as the implications of such factors. A summary of her "report" is presented in the table at the end of this chapter. It might be particularly helpful for those of you who have an entrepreneurial spirit.

The haves and the have-nots can often be traced back to the dids and the did-nots.

—D.O. Flynn

One of the obstacles to a career of your choice is failure to prepare properly. Everyone would like a well paying, satisfying career. But, when faced with the preparation required for such jobs, many people feel they just don't have the time. I frequently hear students say that they feel life is passing them by, that they need to get out and start making a living. Consequently, many students decide not to go on to graduate school, or take a major that might require an extra year or two. In effect, it is a career that passes them by, not life.

One student told me that what he would really like to do is become a physician, but felt that it would take him too long to get where he wanted to be. I pointed out that if he didn't take the steps necessary to become a physician, then he would never end up where he wanted. With a bachelor's degree in biology, he felt he might be happy in pharmaceutical sales. I gently warned him that with every call, every visit to a hospital or clinic, he would be reminded that he was not doing what he really wanted. His choice almost seemed a form of punishment for not taking the steps to achieve his goal. My talk with this young man reminded me of the words written by some anonymous writer: "The saddest words of tongue or pen are just four words—it might have been." I once talked to a working mother who said she wanted to be a teacher, but going to school part-time would take her almost eight years to get her credential. I pointed out to her that those eight years would pass regardless of whether or not she went to school, and wouldn't it be better to have her teaching credential at the end of that time. A friend of mine told me that he really wished he had studied law. "What's stopping you?" I asked. He said that it was his age. . . he'd almost be sixty when he graduated. My response was, "Well, wouldn't it be better to be sixty and be a lawyer, than sixty and still wishing you had gone to law school?"

The point is obvious. To become what one desires requires preparation and perseverance. As Henry Ford said, "Getting ready is the secret to success."

Some Practical Tips

1. **To paraphrase Shakespeare, "To your own self be true."** So many people choose careers for the wrong reasons. They are told by their parents what to study, or because they believe that to be considered a success they must be either an accountant, doctor, engineer, or lawyer. Some select a career strictly for the money that it offers. Regardless of your motivation, once you start a career path it is difficult to leave it. Consequently, it is important that you find a career track that you will enjoy. One way to enhance the possibility of a "successful" career is choose a career for which you are well suited. A person who is spatially gifted and highly creative will probably be very unhappy in a career that denies her the opportunity to exercise her unique talents. If you are a right hemisphered person, look for a career in advertising, art, music, creative writing, or graphic art. If you are left hemisphered, then choose accounting, engineering, or research. The frustration that comes from not finding your niche may make it difficult for you to enjoy your work, and for that matter achieve your career goals. You simply cannot have a leisure lifestyle, if you are unhappy in your work.
2. **Decide what is more important to you: The geographical area in which you live and work, the industry in which you work, or the discipline itself.** If you like living in a rural setting, and this is the most important factor for you in choosing a career, then you will have to be very flexible. I know of one young man who was so committed to living in a rural setting that he accepted work as a correctional officer at a remote prison rather than work in an urban setting as a business manager. The greatest employment opportunities are found in urban areas, so you will have to decide what is most important—where you live or what you do. Chances are you will have to compromise. As for the industry you work in, some industries are growing, expanding and employment opportunities are good for qualified individuals. Other industries are cutting back, dwindling. In making a career choice, you need to evaluate the extent to which you value the industry, and the extent to which opportunities exist in that industry. Some people really don't care about the industry, they just want to work in their discipline—be chemists, work in public relations, do social work, etc. Where they work and with whom is secondary. Generally speaking, all of these factors will have to be taken into consideration. For example, some people may find a conflict between the job and where it is located, or find employment out of their discipline. You see, finding a job is more than just finding employment.
3. **Don't overlook the possibility of finding employment in related disciplines.** You may find that you really don't want to work as an accountant, but what other careers are available? Well, for an accountant, law enforcement might be an attractive alternative. One discipline the FBI recruits from is accountancy. You studied psychology, but you really don't want to be a psychologist or counselor. If you possess people skills, and are suitably creative you might find a career in public relations or advertising interesting. Don't lock yourself in a box. You are more than your degree, and if your personality and talents compel you in a direction different from your discipline, look for those fields which can accommodate both your training and talent. My tax preparer is such a person, although trained in the academic side of physical education, her propensity toward quantitative analysis coupled with her entrepreneurial interests led her into the field of tax preparation. Today she has her own tax service and does very well.

4. **If you have a good idea, are creative, and independent—you just might want to try your hand at being your own boss.** One of my students, when I taught at San Diego State University, was such a person. Although, she graduated in recreation and leisure studies, she had talents and skills that tended her toward public relations. In fact, during her short tenure in the recreation field, much of her work was of a public relations nature. Eventually, she set out on her own and established herself in the field of public relations. Today she holds the controlling interest in one of the most prestigious public relations firms in Northern California.
5. **Do your research.** Good decisions cannot be made without good information. Today there is no reason for not having good information about the geographical areas in which you might reside, or about the industries in which you might work, or about the opportunities different disciplines afford. The Internet is filled with information, as is your library (*Ward's Business Director, Moody's Industrial Manual, Standard and Poors Register of Corporation*s to name but three library resources.) A quick call to a prospective employer will often produce an annual report. Before taking a job, make certain you do your homework. For example, find out if a company is privately owned or public. A publicly owned company is controlled by a board of directors responsible to shareholders, important jobs in such a company are more objectively awarded than in "family businesses." Find out exactly what you would be doing on the job—if you wouldn't like the routine, you probably wouldn't like the job. Find out about the opportunities the job offers. Of course, eventually you will get down to pay and benefits. Benefits can add a lot to your base pay, and investment programs can be quite beneficial in the long run. But remember, don't put all your eggs in the salary basket, no amount of financial success will compensate if your job makes you sick, or disrupts your life, or prevents you from enjoying a leisure lifestyle.
6. **Learn from the "Peter Principle."** *The Peter Principle* was first introduced, in a book of the same title, by J. Laurence Peter, educator, philosopher and humorist. Dr. Peter's book describes the pitfalls of bureaucratic organizations. He argues that in a hierarchically structured organization, people tend to rise up through the administrative ranks to a "level of incompetence." In other words, people continue to get promoted as long as they are demonstrating competence. Once they reach their level of incompetence, they cease to function effectively, become unhappy, and tend to compromise the efficiency and effectiveness of the organization. According to Dr. Peter, when a manager stops getting promoted, its because he or she has exceeded his or her potential. No wonder, so many organizations are in trouble! Shortly following the publication of *Peter Principle*, Dr. Peter published the *Peter Prescription.* In this book he suggests a solution to the Peter Principle—don't allow yourself to be promoted to a position for which you aren't qualified or prepared. In other words, stay at your level of competence.

Closing Note. . .

Work is more than a foil against which one measures the value of leisure. It provides us with financial resources and rewards. It contributes directly to leisure by providing us with the means to recreate, and under some management schemes, it becomes a source of pleasure and personal satisfaction. You spend a lot of your life in the workplace and at work. It is important that you consider carefully what it is that you want to do for a job. Look at financial reward, intrinsic reward, locale, advancement opportunities, company philosophy, and how career will mesh with your interests, attitudes, and values. It is a good idea to look at trends as well. Technology and culture often combine to eliminate certain jobs that just a few years ago were popular and viable.

A Summary of Trends to the Year 2010 Identified by Brain Reserve Marketing Consultancy[1]

Trend	Characteristics	Indications	Implications
I. Cocooning	Withdrawal from society, doing more things at home, more urban hermits, more concern with home and car security and safety, only allowing select individuals into the home.	Home shopping network, VCR's. Internet, home computers, computer games, home offices, home delivery, home and car security systems, home exercise equipment, increases in household pets.	More recreation will be home based. Increase in home entertainment systems. Increase in home offices and communication systems. Cabin fever may increase leading to more novel in-home activities and design.
2. Fantasy Adventure	Emotional escape through fantasy, vicarious escape through consumption, lessened risk-high adventure.	Increase in action-adventure video rentals/movies, theme parks, exotic foods, novel safe, clothing, adventure tours/travel chatrooms and Internet surfing.	More recreation will offer vicarious adventures, adventure tours will be popular, erotica will increase in popularity, fashion will often follow an adventure/fantasy themes.
3. Small Indulgences	Limited self-indulgence. small luxuries. rewarding yourself with the best you can afford.	Increase in massage therapists and salons, increase in sales of quality toiletries, rise in sales of speciality coffee drinks, etc.	Value will replace image, intrinsic worth will replace name. Possession will be more important than the experience of acquiring.
4. Egonomics	Experiences and objects which convey the uniqueness of the individual: individualizing, customizing, and differentiating.	Specialization in media, identification through trademark (DKNY, NIKE etc.), increase in custom-made products.	More services and products will be sufficiently flexible to allow for custom modifications: custom cruises, tours, athletic equipment, automobiles etc.
5. Cashing Out	Changing career to one that is satisfying, slowing down one's pace or moving to rural states. Simplifying one's life, quality over quantity.	More people are working from out of the home. Increased regional travel. Increasing popularity of camping, growth in popularity of country music.	More emphasis on outdoor recreation, increasing popularity in activities, that put us in touch with the folk/country-side America: summer camps, arts and crafts, folk dancing, historic tours etc.
6. Down-Aging	An increasing refusal to be bound by traditional age limitation.	Adult attendance at theme parks, special interest classes. adult camps; adults engaging in behaviors associated with younger people.	Recreation programs will offer more youth oriented programs for older people, programs designed to get in touch with the youth within.
7. Staying Alive	Increased attention to preventing illness and maintaining health and wellness.	Increased concern over threats to one's health, increased attention to exercise and "healthy" diets.	Increasingly, travel and recreation will be designed with health benefits as an important goal.
8. Vigilante Consumer	Increased concern over the quality of products and services and a willingness to take punitive/ corrective action.	Increased frequency of boycotts, lawsuits, and consumer advocates. Increase in consumer oriented service, demystification of the corporate structure (e.g. Southwest Airlines Pres. Herb).	Accountability if recreation agencies will increase, consumers will be consulted more frequently, quality will be measured in terms which include social and environmental responsibility.
9. 99 Lives	Life is becoming more complex, options are increasing, and hence. people seem to have increasingly less time in which to pursue their interests.	More people must have multiple jobs to make ends meet, modern technology makes more work possible, fast food is increasingly popular, day planners and organizers are increasingly important, businesses are becoming multifunctioned.	More recreational services will be offered in conjunction with other services-recreation in the workplace, doctor's office, schools, etc. Recreation agencies will offer programs that help consumers streamline and simplify their lives.
10. Save Our Society	Increased ethical concerns relative to education, environment and ethics.	Volunteerism is up, charitable giving is up. social and political action groups have increased.	More recreation programs will focus on environmentally positive activities, more activities will be designed to have positive social outcomes.

[1]Adapted from *The Popcorn Report*, 1991.

REFERENCES

Bammel, G. and L.L. Burrus-Bammel, *Leisure and Human Behavior.* Dubuque, Iowa: Wm. C. Brown, 1986.

Harriman, A. *The Work/Leisure Trade Off.* New York: Praeger Scientific, 1982.

Hughes, J.(ed). *EcoSocialist Review.* 5.2 http://www.dsausa.org/ESR/Work.html (Summer, 1991).

Peter, J.L. *The Peter Prescription.* New York: William Morrow and Company, 1972.

Peter, J.L. and R. Hull. *The Peter Principle.* New York: William Morrow and Company, 1970.

Popcorn, F. *The Popcorn Report.* New York: Double Day, 1994.

Wallich H. www.uakron.edu/eduecone/201/hw/wallich.html (October 17, 1996).

CHAPTER 11

Leisure and Humor

The old man laughed out loud and joyously, shook up the details of his anatomy from head to foot, and ended by saying that such a laugh was money in a man's pocket, because it cut down the doctor's bills like everything.

—Mark Twain in Moody

In my opinion a book on recreation and leisure would be incomplete without an examination of humor. Humor in its various forms plays an important role in the leisure lifestyle. You see humor demonstrated in many ways in leisure. For example, you see it in the witty repartee in a conversation between friends, explosive laughter in the heat of play, and the good-natured chuckle in an athletic contest. You need not look far to see that humor is a frequent contributor to the quality of one's leisure.

The Meaning of Humor

Humor has not always been a funny topic. At one time it had a very different and serious definition. During ancient times it was believed that the body was composed of four basic elements called **humors**. Hippocrates (460–370 B.C.) believed that an imbalance among these humors (blood, phlegm, black bile and yellow bile) resulted in pain and disease, and that a cure could only be accomplished by bringing the humors back into balance. For centuries this idea was one of the fundamental foundations of medicine. Galen (130–200 A.D.), the personal physician of Marcus Aurelius, theorized that in addition to being related to physical health, these humors were also related to personality or temperament. Eventually, any personality trait came to be referred to as a humor. To this day you occasionally hear people refer to humor in this way. A person in a disagreeable mood may be described as being in a "black humor." By the 19th century and particularly following the discovery of cellular pathology, the idea that health and temperament were the function of bodily humors fell into disrepute. To understand today's meaning, you need to know that to the ancient Greeks the principal manifestation of an imbalance of an individual's humors was ludicrous behavior accompanied by laughter. Aristotle viewed laughter as a means of controlling inappropriate or excessive behavior. In fact, people who demonstrated silly or absurd behavior, or who laughed excessively came to be known as **humorists**. Once humor lost its credibility as a medical theory, all that remained was its connection to ludicrous behavior, and that is how it came to have its current meaning.

Modern Definitions of Humor

Defining and analyzing humor is a pastime of humorless people.

—Robert Benchley

I do not agree with Robert Benchley. Personally, I think he was just being humorous. But, while we are looking at clever definitions, let us look at some other **one liners** about humor:

Humor is emotional chaos remembered in tranquillity.

—James Thurber

Humor is the sense of the absurd which is despair refusing to take itself seriously.

—Arland Ussher

Humor is what happens when creativity takes time out for play; laughter is a piece of happiness that escapes.

—Sara Louise Williams

Humor may be defined as the kindly contemplation of the incongruities of life and the artistic expression thereof.

—Stephen Leacock

Humor is what you have left, when you have nothing left.

—Ernest Jones

The dictionary defines humor as a noun meaning' 'the capacity for perceiving the amusing or ludicrous" or "anything, as speech, writing, or action which stimulates laughter." Thus, in common parlance it has two distinct meanings: (1) a state of mind and (2) an attribute capable of producing laughter. Paul McGhee, developmental psychologist and humor researcher, amplifies this idea. He states:

> We may have difficulty in defining humor, but we know it when we see it, and we know that we are more likely to see it in some moods than in others. Most dictionary definitions emphasize two distinct meanings of the more specific usage of the term. The basic one is the mental experience of discovering and appreciating ludicrous or absurdly incongruous events or situations. Humor is also defined as those attributes of an event that make us laugh; namely attributes that lead us to perceive the event as ludicrous or humorous. The problem is that this is a very circular definition. We must conclude then that humor is something that exists only in our minds and not in the real world (4).

McGhee's point is that ultimately in order for something to be considered as possessing humor, it must first be perceived as humorous. Ultimately the decision as to whether something is funny rests with the perceiver. Therefore, argues McGhee, humor is ultimately a function of perception. He argues that it is not an emotion, an event, a situation, or a behavior (4–5). Rather, humor is described as a state of mind that follows exposure to something viewed as humorous. This condition is characterized by certain behavioral manifestations such as smiling and laughter, certain biological manifestations such as increased arousal, and certain psychological manifestations such as feelings of well-being. Thus, to McGhee, it is not the cartoon that is humor, but the state of mind invoked by the stimulus of the cartoon interacting with the perceptual set of the receiver. Humor is not the situation or event, but the perceiver's cognitive and emotional response to it; not the behavior but the perceiver's reaction to it.

From a philosophical point of view, McGhee's idea that humor is a state of mind is logical and laudable; however, from a practical standpoint, it may be too limiting. In practical everyday usage, it is not uncommon for people to use the word humor in reference to the object of perception as opposed to a cognitive/emotional product. For example, you may have heard people say, "I don't understand *that type of humor*," or "I don't see the *humor in that*." Implicit in these examples is the idea that people view humor as an attribute, something to be perceived and evaluated. In day-to-day conversation, this may be a more popular usage than the state of mind definition.

These two notions do not have to be viewed as mutually exclusive. Indeed, just the opposite is true. You cannot have one without the other. Something is only potentially humorous until it is perceived by someone who has the capacity to understand and appreciate the humorous attributes of the perceived object or phenomenon. For example, when a person is in a had mood, it may be impossible for him or her to perceive the humor in something, even though that something is rife with potential humor. Try to make a depressed person laugh and the response might be something similar to this, "That's not funny; I'm not in the mood!" Later on, following a change in mood, the same stimulus might be perceived as very humorous. The object of perception has not changed, but the perception of it has. The person, no longer influenced by a negative mood, is able to perceive the humorous elements and experience the pleasant sensation of humor.

It is this capacity to selectively perceive humorous elements that we refer to as a **sense of humor**, and it is the sense of humor that brings together the two definitions of humor. The extent to which one possesses a sense of humor is the extent to which he or she is capable of perceiving the humorous elements in some object or phenomenon. The extent to which this is possible is also the extent that one is capable of experiencing the "mental experience of discovering and appreciating ludicrous or absurdly incongruous ideas, events or situations" (McGhee 6). Thus, it can be said that humor is both object and outcome, bound together by one's perceptual abilities. In the next section we will focus on humor as an object or phenomenon of one's perception—something holding the potential to produce laughter in a perceiver.

Types of Humor

The fact that humor is diverse and extensive can be presumed from the numerous types of humor found in daily life. In researching this unit, I found reference to 40 different types of humor. I have ordered these different types into what I perceive as the most logical categories: jokes, witticisms, wordplay, pranks, comedy, and visual humor. Although, these are not mutually exclusive categories, they do provide some basis for organization and comparison. These six categories are summarized below:

Joke. A joke is a short story that leads the listener to an unanticipated humorous outcome. Jokes are typically classified by content. Jokes involving racial elements are called ethnic jokes; jokes dealing with sex are referred to as "blue" or dirty jokes; jokes devoid of ethnic slurs or prurient matters are often called "good" jokes; a "shaggy dog" joke is one which has an atypically long "setup" or "lead in" to the punchline. Jokes generally consist of three elements: the setting, the setup, and the punchline. Following is an example of a typical joke:

A wealthy man was about to die. He called three of his friends to his bedside: a priest, a doctor, and a lawyer. He told them that he intended to take all his wealth with him, and that he wanted them to help. He then gave each of them a large envelope filled with very large bills. "During the viewing, I want each of you to drop your envelope into my casket. These envelopes contain all my money," he told them. Shortly thereafter he passed away. Just as they promised, each of the friends dropped the envelope into the open casket. Later, over drinks the three men talked about their departed friend. The priest said, "I have a confession. I took some of the money from the envelope and donated it to the orphanage." The doctor said, "I'm glad you told us that because I too took some money from the envelope and donated it to the free clinic." With that the lawyer slammed his hand down on the table, "I am surprised at you two, how could you deny our friend his last wish! As for me, I want you to know that my envelope contained my personal check for the entire amount!"

Jest. A jest is usually an informal, playful or amusing statement made in the course of conversation. A jest can be thought of as a spontaneous joke. "He's a light eater. As soon as it gets light, he starts eating."

Gag. A gag is a rehearsed joke used by comedians and entertainers.

Witticism. A witticism is an unusually clever or intelligent statement which tends to express surprising, incongruous, subtle or ludicrous relations between ideas, people or things.

Quip. A form of witticism presented as a sarcastic observation or comment.

Bon Mot. From the French for "good word," this is a clever comment or observation made as a witty repartee.

Here are some samples of witticisms, quips and bon mots.

One of my friends told me she was in labor for 36 hours. I don't even want to do anything that feels GOOD for 36 hours.—Rita Rudner

My husband and I are either going to have children or get a dog. We can't decided whether to ruin our carpet or our lives.—Rita Rudner

This guy says, "I'm perfect for you, 'cause I'm a cross between a macho and a sensitive man." I said, "Oh, a gay trucker?" —Judy Tenuta

Never lend your car to anyone to whom you have given birth to—Erma Bombeck

I would love to speak a foreign language, but I can't. So I grew hair under my arms instead—Sue Kolinsky

I think—therefore I'm single—Lizz Winstead

"When women are depressed they either eat or go shopping. Men invade another country."—Elayne Boosler

Repartee. A conversation consisting basically of witty responses.

Aphorism. A precept or principle cleverly presented in a few words. "Great principles do not need men and women as much as men and women need great principles."

Epigram. A short poem, brief and witty, the last line of which contains an unexpected change of thought or biting comment.

Double Entendre. A word or phrase with two meanings, one usually ludicrous or provocative. Mae West was known for her double entendres.

Apothegm. A clever, short instructive saying. "People are like boats, they toot the loudest when they are in a fog."

Gibe. A witty, sarcastic taunt.

Wordplay. As the name implies, this type of humor involves playing with words. Homonyms, synonyms, antonyms and unusual syntax, are employed in clever and amusing ways.

Uncommon Medical Dictionary

Artery—The study of fine painting

Barium—What you do when the patient dies

Benign—What you are after you are eight

Colic—A sheep dog

Congenital—Friendly

Dilate—To live long

Medical Staff—A doctor's cane

Minor Operation—Coal digging

Morbid—A higher offer

Nitrate—Lower than day rate

Organic—Church musician

Out Operation—A person who has fainted

Post-Operative—A letter carrier

Protein—In favor of young people

Secretion—Hiding anything

Tablet—A small table

Tumor—An extra pair

Urine—Opposite of you're out

Varicose Veins—Veins very close together

Pun. Here the play is upon words alike or nearly alike in sound, but that have different meanings. "How do you like the socks I mended?" "Pretty darned good!"

Anagram. This is the rewriting of a word or sentence in a different order for humorous effect. A word spelled backwards for example. "Stressed" spelled backwards is "desserts."

Acrostic. A poem or puzzle in which the first, the middle or the last letters of each line, when taken in order spell a word or sentence.

Amphibole. An ambiguous statement, something which clearly has no single clear meaning. "According to the Institute of Incomplete Statements, nine out of ten."

Palindrome. A word or sentence that when reversed has the same meaning. Example—radar.

Spoonerism. Named after the Reverend W. A. Spooner, this involves a sentence or phrase where the first sound of key words are transposed. "In the happy days where then was no harcity of scam, and when por nicks were a chopple a piece, there lived an old puther mig (in other surds a sow) and her sea thruns."

Malapropism. Originally from Richard Sheridan's play, *The Rival's*, malapropisms were popularized by TV's Archie Bunker. A malapropism refers to the ludicrous misuse of words through the selection of an incorrect word that sounds like the correct one. "After the wedding we all went up to the conception."

Riddles. A riddle is a clever question for which there is usually a humorous answer.

Conundrum. A riddle turning on a play of words.

Prank. This refers to a category of humor which involves tricking another person. The motivation is usually to provoke humor; however, some pranks may be motivated by mischief. Pranks tend to rely on action rather than words.

Practical Joke. A practical joke is a form of prank where the punchline comes at the expense of the individual designated as the victim of the prank.

Antic. An antic involves some sort of ludicrous or silly behavior. Synonymous with "caper," or "shenanigans."

Comedy. This type of humor is associated with the theater. Standup comics develop routines that evoke laughter from an audience. A comedian generally comes to be associated with a particular comedic style. Jerry Lewis, for example, is internationally respected for his particular type of physical comedy. Some comics are known for their intellectual humor while others specialize in sight gags or the clever use of props. Still other comedians use music or mime.

I don't know whom to credit for this comedic story. It came to me in the form of a ditto some years ago. It reads like the work of a standup comic from the 1950's. I have tried to identify the author, but have had no success. So many people have asked for copies that I am including it in this chapter. If anyone knows who the author is, please let me know.

Everybody who has a dog calls him "Rover or Spot" but I made the mistake of naming my dog, "SEX." Now Sex has been very embarrassing to me. When I went to city hall to renew his dog license I told the clerk I would like a license for Sex. He said "I'd like to have one too!" Then I said, "But this is for a dog." He said, "I don't care what she looks like." Then I said, "You don't understand, I've had Sex since I was nine years old. He said, "You must have had a very happy childhood."

When I got married and went on my honeymoon I took the dog with me. Not wanting the dog to bother us I told the clerk that I wanted a room for my wife and I needed a special room for Sex. He said that every room in the place was adequate for sex. I said, "You don't understand, Sex keeps me awake at night." He said, "Me too."

One day I entered Sex in a dog show, before the competition began, another contestant asked me what I was doing. I told him that I planned to have Sex in the show. He said that I should have sold tickets!
I left my dog at the veterinarian. When I went to pick him up I said, "I've come for my dog." She said, "Which one Spot or Rover?" I said, "I came for Sex." She slapped me. After I thought I had things straightened out, "I asked her if Sex was good for her." She slapped me again.

Then my wife and I separated. We went to court to fight for custody of the dog. I said "Your honor I had Sex before I was married." He said, "What's your point, so did I." I said, "But, my wife wants to take Sex away from me." He said, "That's what happens in a divorce." Last night Sex ran off. I spent hours looking for him all over town. A cop came over to me and asked, "What are you doing in this alley at 4 a.m.?" I said I was looking for Sex. My trial is on Monday.

Burlesque. This is a form of comedy which tends to employ exaggerated behaviors and ludicrous images in bawdy or debasing caricature. It was particularly popular during the late 1800's and in the mid 1900's. It is often associated with provocative skits and strip tease.

Slapstick. A type of comedy where the humor is based on rough, knockdown, play behavior. The term finds its origin in the comedy of harlequins and mimes who used a stick for striking other performers.

Mime. From the word "mimic," mime has come to refer to a type of comedy when the actor, through bodily movement, imitates some person, event, or thing.

Farce. A play which depends for its humor on low comic devices such as slapstick and ridiculous situations.

Camp. A viewpoint which holds that something can be enjoyed aesthetically even though it may be banal, crude, distastefully extravagant or pretentious. Improvisation. A form of comedy where the content of the presentation is extemporaneous, i.e., created spontaneously using materials at hand or ideas contributed by the audience.

Impersonation. Comedy derived by mimicking the voice and mannerisms of all known personalities.

Visual Humor. Visual humor as the name implies involves the presentation of all or part of a humorous situation or concept through the use of visual cues usually in the form of pictures.

Logogram. Here a visual symbol is created to represent a word or sentence.

Cartoon. Usually consisting of a one-frame, or three-frame format, a cartoon illustrates through comical characters some humorous idea.

Cartoon Laws of Physics

Bradley Gong of San Francisco based ThinkSolutions sent me these via email.

Cartoon Law I—Any body suspended in space will remain in space until made aware of its situation.

Cartoon Law II—Any body in motion will tend to remain in motion until solid matter intervenes suddenly.

Cartoon Law III—Any body passing through solid matter will leave a perforation conforming to its perimeter.

Cartoon Law IV—All principles of gravity are negated by fear.

Cartoon Law V—The time required for an object to fall twenty stories is greater than or equal to the time it takes for whomever knocked it off the ledge to spiral down twenty flights to attempt to capture it unbroken.

Cartoon Law VI—As speed increases, objects can be in several places at once.

Cartoon Law VII—Certain bodies can pass through solid walls painted to resemble tunnel entrances, others cannot.

Cartoon Law VIII—Any violent rearrangement of feline matter is impermanent.

Cartoon Law IX—Nothing falls faster than an anvil.

Cartoon Law X—For every vengeful act, there is an equal and opposite vengeful act.

Cartoon Law Amendment A—A sharp object will always propel and individual upward.

Cartoon Law Amendment B— The laws of object permanence are nullified for" cool" characters.

Comics. A collection of cartoons, usually the three-frame variety, filling a page in a newspaper.

Caricature. A special kind of cartoon illustration where the intent is to portray an individual in a humorous way; a funny portrait.

Animated. A movie where comics have been photo-mechanically (more recently by computer) made to appear to move.

Classification by Purpose

Wit. The primary characteristic of wit is intelligence. A person who is witty has the capacity to perceive clearly, comprehend fully, and express his/her observations in an amusing manner.

Parody. A parody is a form of imitation, usually a literary composition, where the subject is charged to be incongruous or the treatment is done in a humorous way.

Satire. Satire is humor with a social cause. In satire, comedic techniques are used to point out vice, foibles, inefficiency, etc. Sarcasm. This is a bitter, cutting expression (it comes from the Greek for "a bitter laugh") designed to evoke humor through disparagement.

Irony. Irony is a condition where one seems mocked by fate such as when a speaker says something of significance without being aware of it.

Travesty. A travesty is when a literary work, historical fact, or artistic work is characterized in a brutal or ludicrous way; it's an absurd imitation.

Laughter is the sensation of feeling good all over and showing it principally in one place.

—Josh Billings

If you are not allowed to laugh in heaven, then I don't want to go there.

—Martin Luther

Theories of Humor

Lefcourt and Martin contend that all humor theories can be categorized into three main types: arousal theories, incongruity theories, and superiority theories (4). In addition to these, McGhee and Goldstein would have us add linguistic and brain psychophysiological theories (29).

Arousal Theories

Central to the theories under this heading is the notion that humor is a function of an individual's need to experience satisfying arousal or stimulation. This notion may have grown out of early theorists' attempt to explain the physical manifestation of humor—laughter. Arousal theory, as you know, is also useful in explaining play and leisure activity. The degree to which a joke or other humor stimulus is likely to produce laughter is dependent in large measure to its arousal potential. This in turn is dependent upon the degree to which it is perceived as novel or complex. Humor that is redundant or predictable may have little potential to induce laughter. Representative of arousal theories are Spencer (1860), Freud (1928), Berlyne (1969), Apter (1977).

Incongruity Theories

Whereas arousal theories try to explain humor in terms of biological arousal, incongruity theories explain humor as a cognitive process which occurs when two or more unequal or incomparable ideas, concepts or situations are brought together in an unexpected manner. As Paul McGhee states, ". . . the perception of an incongruous relationship (absurd, unexpected, inappropriate, and otherwise out of context) forms the basic foundation for all humor. . ." (42). The notion is not particularly new. As early as 1560, in his "Treatise on Laughter," Laurent Jobert explained laughter thusly:

> Now in all laughable matters there must be something new and unexpected, beyond what is hoped for very intensely. For the mind, suspended and in doubt, reflects imaginatively on what will be coming, and in facetious things, the end is usually quite the opposite of what is expected, which causes us to laugh (McGhee 26).

The concept of incongruity can be illustrated by the following observation by Virginia Ostman (Peter 496):

If lawyers are disbarred and clergymen defrocked, doesn't it follow that electricians can be delighted; musicians denoted; cowboys deranged; tree surgeons debarked and dry cleaners depressed?

Here's an excellent example of incongruity:

Mother to daughter: "What kind of person is your new boyfriend? Is he respectable?"
Daughter to mother: "Of course he is, Mom. He's thrifty, doesn't drink or smoke, has a very nice wife and three well-behaved children."

One more:

A patient walked into the doctor's office with a banana up his nose, a carrot sticking out of one ear, and stalk of celery sticking out of the other ear. "Doctor, what's wrong with me?" "Simple," the doctor replied. "You aren't eating right."

Theories viewed as representing this category include: Koestler (1964), Narhardt (1970, 1975, 1976), Suls (1972, 1983) and Leventhals (1977).

Superiority Theories

In Paris they simply stared when I spoke to them in French: I never did succeed in making those idiots understand their own language.

—Mark Twain

Superiority theories argue that humor results when one perceives another as inferior. Humor that attacks others is referred to as **tendentious** humor. Through disparaging another, it is argued that one enhances his or her feelings of self-worth. This idea traces back to the observations of Plato and Aristotle who concluded that laughter occurs in response to "weakness and ugliness" (Lefcourt and Martin 10). Representing this point of view are the following: Hobbes (1651), Wolff, Smith and Murray (1934), LaFave, Haddad and Maesen (1976), Sillman and Canlor (1976) and Zillman (1983).

Three recreation professors were walking in an open field when they came across a set of tracks. The first professor kneeled down to take a closer look and said, "Look at those bear tracks." The second one kneeled down for a closer look and said, "No, those are moose tracks." The third was about to speak when a train hit them.

Linguistic Theory

In the study of humor, linguists have been concerned with one specific type of humor—humor resulting from manipulating words, i.e., arranging words in such a manner as to create a humorous effect. Studies of this sort focus on the mechanical and structural aspects of humor, and "describe how phonological, morphological, and syntactic categories can be manipulated to produce ambiguities. . ." (Pepicello and Weisberg in McGhee and Goldstein 60). Following is an example of linguistic humor:

Q. Why isn't a person's nose 12 inches long?
A. Because then it would be a foot.

Q. Why is the center of a tree like a dog's tail?
A. It is farthest from the bark.

Q. Why did the mushroom go out with the toadstool?
A. She heard he was a FUNGI.

Q. Why did the melons get married?
A. Because they cantalope.

Q. Why did the raisin go out with the grape?
A. Because he couldn't get a date.

Brain Lateralization Theory

Although this theory is consistent with the explanation afforded by incongruity theory, it explains humor by examining the functional disparity between the two hemispheres of the brain. This theory argues that the left hemisphere processes information up to the point of incongruity, at which time the right hemisphere takes over to produce the effect of humor. As McGhee states:

> In the case of straightforward communications, the left hemisphere is fully competent to understand statements and information and respond appropriately. When the unexpected and incongruous information in a joke is delivered (in the punchline), however, the left hemisphere appears unable to go beyond registering surprise. It is the right hemisphere that comes into play at this point and produces the simultaneous awareness of two meanings (as in a pun) or of diverse elements that must be brought together in order to appreciate the humor potentially present (30).

Even though a relatively new approach, this line of research is extremely important and promises to lead to a greater understanding of the cognitive functions of the brain. As we learn more about the brain and the differences between the right and left hemispheres, our understanding of humor is certain to increase.

Presumed Benefits of Humor

Physical Benefits of Humor

We have all heard it said that "laughter is the best medicine." This is certainly not a new idea. It is a subject that has occupied writers and thinkers throughout recorded history. For example, the *Book of Proverbs* in the **Old Testament** addressed the topic thusly, "A merry heart doeth good like a medicine" (17:22). Plato and Aristotle addressed the subject. Galen, physician to gladiators and prominent philosopher, pondered the relationship of laughter to health. Joubert, a Renaissance philosopher, wrote extensively on the subject. Within recent years it has been the subject of formal scientific research (McGhee and Goldstein, 1983).

The current interest in the healing power of humor can be traced back to Norman Cousins' book, *Anatomy of an Illness*. In it he recounts his amazing story of his recovery from **ankylosing spondylitis.** His doctors only gave him one chance in 500 to recover. Rather than giving in to the prognosis he undertook a radical form of self-treatment. He immersed himself in humorous films and books. He put to test the old axiom about laughter being the best medicine, and soon he was experiencing some pretty amazing results.

> I made the joyous discovery that 10 minutes of genuine belly laughter had an anesthetic effect that gave me at least two hours of painfree sleep. . . . When the painkilling effect of the laughter wore off, we would switch on the motion picture projector again, and not infrequently it would lead to another painfree sleep interval. (Cousins 39)

Dr. Laurence J. Peter believes that humor contributes to pain control in four ways: (1) it can cause a person to focus his attention away from the sources of pain; (2) laughter reduces muscle tension around the affected part of the body, thus decreasing pain; (3) it can contribute to a positive attitude which is associated

Theories of Humor

Theory	Cause	Comment	Criticism
Spencer (1860)	Humor is the result of an individual's need to release pent-up energy or tension.	Laughter, the physical manifestation of humor, results in a release of tension followed by relaxation and/or catharsis.	There is no evidence to support the biological functions premised by the theory.
Freud (1905-1928)	Humor is the result of an individual's need to release certain types of tension (energy). (1) Inhibitory energy (2) Ideational energy (3) Emotional energy Laughter occurs when excess energy (in any of the above forms) needs to be physically consumed.	Inhibitory energy is released when sexual or aggressive impulses are expressed (the *tendentious* element in humor. Ideational energy is the result of anticipating an outcome in a nonverbal (slapstick, etc.) situation which does not occur, rather an unanticipated outcome renders the anticipated "idea" redundant. Emotional energy occurs when a negative situation is rendered less threatening by a shift in mood.	Does not account for situations where libidinal behaviors are expressed which do not produce a mirthful response. Similarly ideational situations don't all produce laughter. Emotional situations may be viewed from alternative perspectives which do not produce a humorous response.
Berlyne (1969)	Humor occurs when artificially created tension boosts arousal beyond the optimal level thus creating a situation highly amenable to the humor "punchline" which yields a sudden reduction of tension and a rapid increase in pleasure. This "arousal jag" is accompanied by a physiological release of tension in the form of laughter.	Berlyne believed that humor provided a form of catharsis resulting from a decrease in activity in the sympathetic nervous system.	Subsequent research has failed to support the notion of the "arousal jag."
Apter (1971) Reversal Theory	Humor involves both an increase in arousal and a reversal from *telic* (work) to a *paratelic* (leisure) state of mind; laughter is viewed as "increased" arousal as opposed to "reducing" it.	Arousal in a telic state is distressing; while in a paratelic state it is pleasurable. Humor is viewed as therapeutic in that it allows one to experience arousal from a positive viewpoint.	Fails to account for distressing responses in *paratelic* states and humor in *telic* moods.
Koestler (1964) Biosciation Theory	Humor occurs when an individual perceives a situation in two self-contained but mutually incompatible frames of reference or associative contexts. The jump from one associate context yields a pleasurable response often accompanied by laughter.	The biosciation process occurs in art and science, but only in humor does it evoke laughter. This is believed due to the difference between the emotional states of these endeavors. Humor is associated with an aggressive or anxious emotional state.	Does not account for situations where the disparity between frames of reference is so great that humor potential is lost, or situations where no resolution seems necessary (Nerhardt, 1970).
Nerhardt (1970, 1975,1976) Incongruity without Resolution	Humor is caused by discrepancies between expectations and actual outcomes; the resolution of the discrepancy is not essential for humor to occur.	Nerhardt views humor as being contingent upon the perception of the incongruity falling within the boundaries of a non-threatening environment.	Most humor has resolution structure. (Schultz 1977) i.e., "I get it."

(continued)

Theory	Cause	Comment	Criticism
Suls (1972, 1983) Incongruity Resolution	Humor results when an incongruity is resolved i.e., the biosciation is satisfactorily comprehended. Humor occurs when the perceiver cognitively "gets it."	Allows one to cognitively distance self from stressful associations (O'Connell, 1976).	Nerhardt created an experiment to demonstrate that humor could be produced in non-resolution format. Some jokes lead to another incongruity. "Why did the elephant sit on the marshmallow?" Answer—"To get out of the hot chocolate!"
Leventhals (1977) Dual Process Model	Humor is a function of both cognitive analysis and social or external influence i.e., contextual factors such as other people laughing.	Females are more likely to be influenced in their appraisal of humor by social influences than males (Leventhal & Upchich, 1976).	Fails to account for humor which occurs in context devoid of social stimuli or where humor results strictly from contextual influences—"I can't stop laughing."
Hobbes (1651) Superiority Theory	Popularized the notion that the infirmities of others constitute the principal sources of humor.	"By the apprehension of some deformed thing in another, by comparison suddenly upstand themselves (1651/ 1968,125)."	Fails to account for humor in which no disparagement is found.
Wolf, Smith & Murray (1934) LaFave, Haddad & Maesen (1976) Disparagement of the Unaffiliated	Humor occurs when the object of disparagement is *something* of an unaffiliated object, i.e., something to which an individual is not bound by or finds repulsive. Affection humor also occurs when a situation enhances some object about which a positive attitude exists.	We like to see the good guys stick it to the bad guys.	Fails to account for the lack of humor in situations where an affiliated object is enhanced.
Zillman & Canlor (1976) Disparagement Dispositional Theory of Humor	Humor results when someone for whom the perceiver holds a negative disposition is disparaged.	Mirth is viewed as varying proportionally to the degree of negativity held for the disparaged and the degree of positiveness held for the disparager.	Fails to account for linguistic humor, or humor induced by situational humor stimuli.
Zillman (1983) Misattribution Theory	Humor occurs when one is able to attribute the cause of his or her pleasurable response resulting from the perception of someone's misfortune to some innocuous humor clues; thus eliminating cognitive dissonance.	Humor yields enhanced feelings of self-worth, without feeling guilty.	Fails to account for humor devoid of disparagement.
Pepiccello & Weisberg (1983) Linguistic Humor	Humor occurs when a word or phrase that has one or more possible meanings is used in such a manner that one implied meaning is incongruous with the perceiver's expectations.	Linguists look at the nature and meaning of words, they examine the phonological, morphological and syntactic elements of humor. Language is viewed as a system of rules, the manipulation of which a playful manner can produce a humorous or witty response.	Fails to consider the psychodynamics of humor, or contextual influences.
McGhee (1986) Balanced Hemisphere Involvement Theory	The left hemisphere processes verbal information in an analytical and sequential function, but it is the right hemisphere that identifies the humor potential (through integration or insight) in uninterrupted or incongruous information.	A prolonged buildup of highly complex information may weaken humor potential by over-stimulation of the left hemisphere.	Fails to account for the elements stimulating right hemisphere integration and insight.

with pain tolerance; and (4) humor may stimulate the brain to produce catecholamines, which in turn stimulates the production of endorphins—the body's natural pain killers (6-9).

There is some evidence that not only does humor contribute to the healing process, but that it also is important to health maintenance. Allen Klein cites several medical authorities that believe humor stimulates the immune system, thus helping an individual stave off the ravages of common viral infections. Furthermore, he cites physicians that view humor as having a positive effect on blood pressure and heart rate. This phenomenon is similar to the bodily changes that take place during aerobic exercise.

Psychological Benefits of Humor

> A person without a sense of humor is like a wagon without springs—jolted by every pebble in the road.
>
> —Henry Ward Beecher

Although many claims are made regarding the psychological value of humor (Peter 1979 and Moody 1978) a careful review of the literature reveals that most empirical studies have focused on two categories: (1) anxiety or stress reduction, and (2) overcoming depression.

There is considerable evidence to support the value of humor in controlling distress and anxiety. Following an extensive study on the relationship of humor in regards to stress and anxiety, Lefcourt and Martin report the following:

> . . . we have found that humor, measured in various ways serves to moderate stressful experiences, whether they are stressors peculiar to the plight of the physically handicapped or to university students encountering hardships during their studies. Similarly, we have found evidence that marriage partners with a good sense of humor seem to be more active and constructive in the resolution of potential conflicts. Further we found that crippled victims of accidents and birth defects, who revealed a greater sense of humor in our investigations, were characterized by greater activity and engagement in life pursuits than were those with lesser sense of humor (124).

People who have healthy self-images are likely to have a good sense of humor and are likely to do better during times of stress. Such people seem to maintain their sense of humor even in the most uncomfortable of circumstances. Some people cry or get angry, some people laugh. People with healthy self-esteem are more likely to find humor in stressful circumstances. The connection between self-esteem, humor and stress was demonstrated in a 1993 study by Kuiper and Martin. They surveyed 227 university students. The students completed questionnaires designed to measure self-esteem and various aspects of humor. The results of the study demonstrated a linkage between humor and positive, healthy self-esteem. In addition the study demonstrated that individuals with high self-esteem were more resilient to stress.

Depressive disorder, or as it is more commonly called **depression**, is a relatively common problem (Weiten 457). It is estimated that each year about 15 million Americans suffer depression, and this does not include the minor lows that most of us experience from time to time (Peter 70). Depression can be viewed as a form of psychological distress marked by feelings of sadness, dejection, and despair. Weiten describes the symptoms of depressive disorder as follows:

> Depressed people tend to lose interest in activities from which they used to derive pleasure. . . . Appetite and sleep disturbances are common. Usually they experience reduced appetite and suffer from insomnia, although a minority shift the other way, toward excessive eating and sleeping. People with depression often seem to lack energy; they frequently move slowly and talk slowly. Indecisiveness, anxiety, irritability, and brooding are commonly observed. Self-esteem typically

sinks like a rock; an unrealistic sense of worthlessness comes to dominate one's self-concept (457).

Serious depression is a disorder of such significant proportions as to justify professional treatment. Severe and persistent depression may have a physiological basis. Peter states:

> Research with antidepressant medicines has shown how body chemistry affects the ability of the brain and nervous system to respond. If the body is low in chemical neurotransmitters, the whole system becomes sluggish, resulting in depression. . . . It is important therefore that the person suffering from a long-term severe depression be diagnosed and receive medical or psychiatric treatment (75).

In the treatment of serious depression some therapists have had success with various applications of play and humor therapy (Moody, 1978); however, it is important to point out that humor is not universally used or advised in the treatment of the emotionally disturbed. McGhee cautions that in some cases humor therapy may be inappropriate and potentially dangerous to the patient who is unable to accurately interpret the object of the humor (240). Naturally there is much that could be said regarding the therapeutic application of humor; however such a discussion goes beyond the purview of this text. On the other hand, the application of humor in helping cope with the normal dips in mood that most of us experience requires no special training and can easily be applied on a self-help basis. In reference to this, Dr. Peter suggests that we use humor to do the following:

1. Use humor to reduce tensions and to create a relaxed atmosphere.
2. Use humor as an outlet for unacceptable feelings, behaviors or impulses.
3. Use humor to improve your frame of mind.
4. Use humor to facilitate conversation regarding sensitive matters.
5. Look for humor in seemingly serious situations.
6. Laugh at least 20 times a day (76–77).

Even if you are unhappy, laughing 20 times a day will certainly give others the impression that you are doing just fine. Indeed, one of the surest ways for an outside observer to judge the mood of an individual is to look at his or her face. One's facial anatomy is closely connected to one's emotions. It is difficult to smile when you are unhappy, and even should you succeed odds are that it will be viewed as a sad smile. On the other hand, an individual who is happy is given to pleasant expressions, often punctuated by broad smiles and laughter. As Joubert said:

> . . . the face of man is most excellent in that it is not covered with hair, scales of feathers. . . and for this reason the face of man is appropriate for all its changes, like a chameleon to make manifest and put into evidence the passions and internal movements, a condition truly human and praiseworthy (6).

The connection between one's internal state and facial expressions raises a provocative question. Does it work both ways? Can one influence his or her internal state by intentionally assuming the posture and expression of humor. Perhaps that is asking too much; future research will have to make that determination. What does seem probable, however, is the idea that exposure to appropriate amounts of humor can contribute to one's feeling of well being, help minimize stress, and counter depression.

Leisure And Humor

> The most fundamental, most important function of humor is its power to release us from the many inhibitions and restrictions under which we live our daily lives.
>
> —Harvey Mindness

All of us live within social environments consisting of social mores and values that combine into powerful social expectations possessing the potential for minimizing one's sense of individuality and freedom. When one's sense of freedom is diminished by social influences, one's capacity to experience leisure is greatly compromised. It is in situations where one feels least free, that humor demonstrates its strongest connection to leisure. In humor one is able to momentarily free himself or herself from the social (and even the physical) bonds that stifle perceived freedom and its concomitant emotion, intrinsic satisfaction. Indeed, during such times, humor may be the only representation of leisure to which one can aspire, or into which one can escape.

Leisure oriented individuals, i.e., people possessing a high degree of internal locus of control and intrinsic motivation, tend to possess both a sense of appreciation of, and capacity for finding humor in diverse situations. Indeed, research has demonstrated a significant relationship between humor and healthy psychological adjustment (McGhee 236). Those individuals whose lives are largely directed by external factors often show little response to humor (McGhee 234). These people, lacking in internal control, are as McGhee puts it, ". . . chained to the social expectations for reasonable behavior and thinking" (234). People whose lifestyles are marked by little freedom, and thus little leisure, tend to have limited capacities for humor. McGhee believes that such people could develop a greater feeling of freedom through learning to appreciate and demonstrate humor (234). To the extent to which humor contributes to such feelings, is the extent to which humor is connected to leisure. Although, there is little research examining this connection, it is quite likely that subsequent research will eventually demonstrate that when one is at humor, one is also at leisure.

The Dark Side of Humor

I do not like to focus attention on negative behaviors. My preference is to look at the positive, but to neglect the fact that not all humor is good would be an error in objectivity. Unfortunately, humor is not always a manifestation of a well-adjusted individual. Even though, for most of us, play and laughter are associated with healthy personalities, there are times (and people) for whom laughter marks maladjustment. The laugh of a disturbed patient in a mental hospital is easy to discern from the laugh of a healthy person. The distorted smile of an emotionally disturbed individual is often a caricature of the pleasant smile of a normal person. Not only do we see a difference in the physical manifestations of humor among certain patients, but we also see such patients often laughing at inappropriate times or at inappropriate circumstances, situations or events.

There is yet another side to humor that must be discussed, and that is the use of disparaging or *tendentious* humor. This is humor that comes at the expense of another. We have all heard the cruel laughter of people who find humor in the misfortune of others. Disparaging humor may take the form of sarcastic comments or jokes which focus on another's misfortune or immutable characteristics. People who make such jokes often do so from a personality foundation affected by instability, low self-esteem and weak interpersonal skills. There is some evidence to suggest that the type of humor an individual uses or is sensitive to may be related to areas in which he or she is having emotional difficulty (McGhee 238–239).

> A person reveals his character by nothing so clearly as the joke he reveals.
>
> —G.C. Lichtenberg

Developing Your Humor Potential

Most of us could benefit from learning to take life a little more leisurely, and as pointed out above, in part that might mean taking life a little more humorously. Some of the benefits that one can expect from an expanded sense of humor are summarized by Dr. Peter:

> A sense of humor gives you the ability to (1) relax so that your objectivity can help you see the inconsistencies in your own behavior and the incongruities in the human condition, (2) resolve problems, (3) laugh at illness and trouble, (4) create your own mirth, and (5) communicate effectively (186).

These are all very attractive outcomes, but if one wants to increase his or her sense of humor, where does one start? Following are two steps that I think are important, if you want to expand your appreciation and capacity for humor.

Step I. Develop a Playful Attitude

An attitude is fundamentally a construct that refers to the extent to which you feel positive toward something. To alter an attitude toward greater appreciation of play may not be an easy task, particularly in cases where there are underlying unresolved psychological issues that confound one's interest in learning to be more playful. In such cases, self-help may be an unrealistic solution; rather, professional counseling may be in order. For the majority of us however, a shift in attitude is not an unreasonable goal.

It is theorized that an attitude can be changed by altering the basic beliefs about an object or by changing one's evaluation of the attributes or characteristics of the object of the attitude (Iso-Ahola 270). What this implies is that if you want to change your attitude about playfulness, or humor or anything else, you need to alter the appropriate values. Inasmuch as most adult values are rooted in childhood socialization, a concerted effort may be required to not only learn about the object of the attitude but to also unlearn the concepts of early childhood.

To accomplish this, two strategies are suggested: (1) become thoroughly familiar with the literature regarding the value of play and humor; and (2) practice using humor in your daily life. By familiarizing yourself with the literature regarding the values of leisure, you begin to establish a cognitive basis for modifying your attitudes regarding humor. By actively trying to look at life a little less seriously, and by trying to find humor in events that are neither inherently funny nor serious, you can begin to experience some of the intrinsic value of the humor experience. This will reinforce the cognitive shift that is promoted by the information you are acquiring through your study. Practice makes perfect and changes attitudes.

Practice what? Dr. J. Laurence Peter has some suggestions worth noting:

- Adopt an attitude of playfulness. This does not mean that you will do outrageous things, but that your mind is open to uncensored, iconoclastic, silly or outrageous thoughts.
- Think funny. See the funny side or flip side of every situation. Select and refine your outrageous thoughts that best expose our conceits, pomposities and incongruities.
- Laugh at the incongruities in situations involving yourself and others.
- Laugh only with others for what they do rather than for what they are.
- Laugh at yourself. . . with acceptance of self.
- Take yourself lightly. Take your responsibility to yourself and others seriously.
- Make others laugh.
- Realize that a sense of humor is deeper than laughter and more satisfactory than comedy. . . a sense of humor sees the fun in everyday experience. It is more important to have fun than to be funny (Peter 193).

Step 2. Acquire Some Humor Skills

In addition to Dr. Peter's list, I have a few suggestions for you:

1. **Read the Comics**. The humorous perspective can't be better illustrated than in the daily comics. Succinct and to the point, they present the world from a humorous perspective.
2. **Collect Humorous Material**. There is a wealth of jokes, songs, poems, stories, novels, illustrations and videos that are of a humorous nature. By using your free time to enjoy the creative efforts of others, your own creative juices will be stimulated.
3. **Try Your Hand at Creating Humor**. Try cartooning for example. You don't have to be an artist to be a cartoonist (James Thurber proved that). Try poetry, short stories, or even wacky inventions. Let your mind play with some ideas, and then try your hand at creating something humorous from them.
4. **Create a "Humor Stimuli" Kit**. This is something I have been doing for years. When I find a toy or other humorous object that I like, I buy it and put it in a utility kit. Just opening the kit makes me smile. Lately I have been collecting magic tricks to include in it.
5. **Having a Sense of Humor Doesn't Mean You Have to Be an Entertainer**. It means that you have a sensitivity to humor; that you can recognize humor in the incongruities of life, and that you don't take things too seriously. But, I do believe that it is a good idea to have a few good stories, jokes, gimmicks or gags that you can use now and then. It's not always enough to be someone else's appreciative audience. When you find something worth sharing—practice it a few times so that you will deliver it with good timing and you won't forget the punch line.
6. **Take Every Appropriate Opportunity to Be Creative, Playful and Fun**. Sometimes that can take the form of a playful note to someone you care about; dressing in a creative and playful way; interjecting humor at a meeting; sharing a smile with a stranger.

> Humor has an enormous half-life; once you start the reaction it goes on forever.
>
> —Mildred Williams

Closing Notes...

When you make someone laugh, an amazing thing happens. You feel terrific. A smile is disarming, a laugh denotes acceptance. In humor, a kind of sharing occurs that bonds people together. Someone once said, "Humor is the shortest distance between two people." That is part of the message of this chapter, by enriching your sense of humor you enrich your life because of the quality of interpersonal relations which emerge. A second message of this chapter is that emotional and psychological health is associated with a healthy sense of humor. As Evan Esar put it, "It is the uncensored sense of humor. . . which is the ultimate therapy for man in society." This is another way of saying, as did Dr. Laurence J. Peter, "He who laughs. . . lasts." And finally, humor is an essential ingredient to the successful leisure lifestyle.

REFERENCES

Apter, M.J. "Humor and the Theory of Psychological Reversals."

Barlyne, D.E. "Laughter, Humor and Play." In G. Lindzey and E. Aronson (Eds.) *Handbook of Social Psychology*, 2nd Ed., Vol. 3, pp. 795–852. Reading, Mass: Addison-Wesley, 1969.

Freud, S. *Jokes and Their Relation to the Unconscious*. Leipzig: Deutiche, 1905. "Humor." *International Journal of Psychoanalysis*, 1928, 9, pp. 1–6.

Hobbes, T. *Leviathan*. 1968 (originally published 1650). Hammondsworth: Penguin.

"Incongruity and Funniness and Dissimilarity of Figures: Divergency from Expediency." *Scandinavian Journal of Psychology*, 11, (1976): 185–195.

Koestler, A. *The Act of Creation*. London: Hutchinson, 1964.

Kuiper, N.A and R.A. Martin. "Humor and Self-concept" *International Journal of Humor Research*. 6.3 (1993): 251–270.

LaFave, L., H., and N. Marshal. "Superiorly, Enhanced Self-Esteem, and Perceived Incongruity Humor Theory." In A.J. Chapman & H.C. Foot (Eds.) *Humor and Laughter—Theory, Research and Applications*. London: Wiley, 1976.

Leventhal, H. & Safer, M.A. "Individual Differences, Personality and Humor Appreciation." In A.J. Chapman and H.C. Foot (Eds.) *It's a Funny Thing, Humor*. 1977. London: Pergamon Press.

McGhee, P.E. "The Role of Arousal and Hemispheric Lateralization in Humor." In P.E. McGhee and J.H. Goldstein (Eds.) *Handbook of Humor Research: Basic Issues*. Vol. I, New York: Springer Verlag, 1983.

Pepicello, W.J. and Weisberg, P.W. "Linguistics and Humor." In P.E. McGhee and J. H. Goldstein (Eds.) *Handbook of Humor Research: Basic Issues*. Vol. I, New York: Springer Verlag, Inc. 1983.

Spencer, H. "The Physiology of Laughter." *MacMillan's Magazine*, 860, 1, pp. 395–402.

Suls, J.M. "Cognitive Processes in Humor Appreciation." In P.E. McGhee and J.H. Holdstein (Eds.) *Handbook of Humor Research*, Vol. I, pp. 39–58. New York: Springer Verlag.

Weiten, W. *Psychology Applied to Modern Life*. Monterey, California: Brooks/Cole Publishing Co., 1986.

Wolff, H.A., Smith, C.E., and Murray, H.A. "The Psychology of Humor: A Study of Responses to Race-Disparagement of Jokes." *Journal of Abnormal and Social Psychology*, 28, (1934): 341–365.

Zillman, D. "Disparagement Humor." In P.E. McGhee & J.H. Goldstein (Eds.) *Handbook of Humor Research*, (Vol. I, pp. 85–108). New York: Springer Verlag.

Zillman, D. & Canlor, J.R. "Affective Responses to the Emotions of a Protagonist." *Journal of Experimental and Social Psychology*. 13, (1977): 155–165.

CHAPTER 12

Creativity and Leisure

- How many uses can you find for a toothpick?
- How many uses can you find for the cap from a ball point pen?
- How many uses can you find for a paper clip?
- How many uses can you find for these questions?

A problem in creative thinking. . . A MINUTE MYSTERY

It was a windy night, the curtains in the children's bedroom were waving wildly in response to the strong wind coursing through the mesh screens covering the window. The temperature was chilling, as the first signs of winter made their presence felt in the unheated house. Garrett walked into the master bedroom irritated that Gayle had not closed the windows before leaving for work. He had left home early, and now was home several hours before his wife and favorite whipping girl. As he reached for the window lever, his peripheral vision caught the reflection of the ceiling light in the form of twinkling diamonds leaping from off shards of glass. He turned his head abruptly and cast his gaze at the floor. He uttered a gasp at the sight. He reached for the body nearest him, it was cold and clammy to the touch. He recognized them immediately, the two of them, their small bodies lying amidst wrecked glass. He looked closer. There was a stain on the carpet. . . it looked like water, just plain water.

What Happened?

Clue: In order to make discoveries you must free yourself of rules, restrictions and restraints. We'll get back to this, but first let's discuss ***creativity.***

Introducing Creativity

The word *creativity* simply means "the act or process of being creative." The root word, "create," essentially means to "produce something new." In this usage, it is similar to the word invent. *Creative thinking* refers to the ability to see things from an unusual perspective, to solve problems in a unique or novel fashion. That creative thinking is related to leisure is relatively easy to see. Creative thinking occurs when an individual is free to examine alternative solutions to some problem. The extent to which this occurs is in part dependent upon the individual's ability to function without constraint from external forces. That is to say, a creative person must possess what psychologists refer to as *internal locus of control*. Internal locus of control is related to the two principal components of the leisure state of being—*perceived freedom* and *intrinsic motivation*. Consequently, creativity and leisure are closely related.

Creative thinking can be thought of as a cognitive style. It is a style that is characterized by the ability to look at a situation from various perspectives. This quality is often referred to as divergent thinking. A divergent thinker does not allow himself to be limited in his attempt to solve a problem. He is willing to entertain ideas that fail to conform with the expectations of common wisdom. For example, when my oldest daughter was just learning to walk, she stepped into an uncovered sidewalk drain hole. My wife, unable to free Tamara's foot, and unable to reach me by phone, called the fire department. When I arrived home, I was horrified to see my daughter surrounded by burly fireman, who were just beginning to break up the cement in an attempt to free the tiny, fragile foot. Common wisdom held that the only way to free her foot was to break the cement which held her as firmly as a bear trap. As a young father, I was not about to let the firemen unloose their sledge hammers and chisels near my daughter. They claimed that they had examined all alternatives, and the only thing that could be done was what they were about to do. The words "all alternatives" rang through my mind and rankled my creative instincts. I knew there were other alternatives—safer alternatives, but I just didn't know what they were.

I considered a few facts. A child's foot consists of 26 bones, and the younger the child the softer those bones and the more flexible the foot. Secondly my daughter was terrified by the action of the firemen, and quite likely this was causing her to flex her foot causing further resistance to the efforts to pull her foot free. In addition, the attempts to pull her foot free no doubt had produced some swelling, a natural phenomenon that no doubt contributed to the difficulty the firemen had encountered when they tried to manually pull her foot free. One further fact was noted, the surface of the hole was somewhat rough creating a certain amount of friction.

To calm Tamara, I asked the firemen to step around the corner. Once the strangers had removed themselves from Tamara's vision, she quickly calmed down. With both her mother and father reassuring her, she noticeably relaxed. To minimize her discomfort and to quell the swelling, cold water was gently poured around the foot. After a few seconds it seeped into the hole and a gentle tug of her relaxed foot was all it took to set her free—unharmed.

I share this example with you for two reasons: (1) it illustrates the concept of divergent thinking and (2) it points out that creative thinking is not limited to recreational activities such as art, drama or music. Indeed, when you learn to be a divergent thinker, every act, every behavior, virtually every thing you do can be an exercise in creativity.

> When you refuse to accept the obvious, you've taken
> your first giant step toward creativity.
>
> —Eugene Raudsepp

Why Be More Creative?

In a word, you want to be more creative because it makes life more fun! As you become more creative you not only become better at solving life's little problems, but you also begin to look at life from a more novel perspective. You become more humorous as you learn to see incongruities in situations. You develop greater self-confidence as you begin to see yourself as a person capable of ferreting out alternative solutions to tasks that stump less creative people. You become less externally directed as you learn to rely on your ability to solve problems. And, because the creative process is intrinsically rewarding, you will find increasing satisfaction in the process of creative thinking, irrespective of its outcomes.

Principles of Creative Thinking

Over the years I have explored creativity from both a scholarly and heuristic point of view. I have studied creativity from the standpoint of a professor and leisure adviser, and I have explored my own creative potential and systematically tried to achieve it. The more I explored my own creative potential, the more I come to understand that regardless of the activity, the creative process was essentially the same. In exploring the dynamics of creativity, I have identified the following principles:

1. **Creativity Is Directly Related to Locus of Control.** Once, a long time ago, I worked in an art studio. The art director was a tyrant (I hope he reads this). He was constantly criticizing my work, and the work of my colleagues. He regularly imposed strict limitations on our creativity, exacting humiliating sanctions on those who deviated from his expectations. This might not have been so bad had he been a more creative individual, but unfortunately he was not inclined to creative thinking. His cognitive mode tended toward convergent thinking. To this day, the quality of my work under this art director remains an embarrassment. Later, I had the privilege of working with a much more supportive and creative director. Given artistic license, my work improved greatly. In addition, I had a lot more fun.

   In order to be creative, you must feel free to select your own alternatives, from a field of many, and then explore and develop your choice. If you are continually afraid of what others expect from you, your ability to be creative will be compromised. Unless you feel in control of your creative efforts, it will be difficult to rise above the expectations of others.
2. **Creativity Is a Function of Knowledge Interacting with Intuition**. Since the 1950's, behavioral scientists have examined the functions of the hemispheres of the human brain. The evidence compels one to acknowledge that each hemisphere has a different mode of processing information. Creativity appears to occur as an interaction between these two different modes. Neither approach is sufficient by itself. Over-emphasis of one can minimize the creative value of the other. By ignoring the intuitive function of the right hemisphere, one is limited to the logical functions of the left hemisphere, which tends to specialize in convergent patterns of analysis and deduction. By focusing on the right hemisphere, one may not have adequate information to create a viable idea. Both modes are essential, and both should be developed.
3. **Creativity May Be Willful or Spontaneous**. Some of my most delightful experiences have involved highly creative conversations with friends. Often these creative interludes have taken the form of humorous stories and/or ideas. During Haley's Comet's 1986–87 visit, a friend entertained me for several minutes with spontaneously produced slogans for hypothetical Haley's Comet memorabilia. Later, I saw commercially produced Haley's Comet memorabilia and recognized similar ideas. No doubt, the process was similar, but the purposes were different. My personal experience in advertising and entertainment tells me that in order to produce creative thoughts for extrinsically motivated reasons you must create conditions similar to those that produce spontaneous creativity.
4. **Creativity Is Fundamentally a Form of Play**. The conditions that produce creativity appear to be essentially the same that are associated with play. When you are being creative, you tend to be optimally aroused, conceptually free, and intrinsically rewarded.
5. **The Creative Process Begins with Play and Usually Evolves to Work**. Creativity occurs when you put old concepts together in a new way, generate novel or new ideas or combine old information with new in a unique way. This normally represents the early stages of the creative process, because the new idea usually requires considerable energy in order to take it from inception to perfection. Once you embark on the perfection process, you, by definition, give up a certain amount of freedom, tend to experience supra and sub-optimal arousal, and experience varying degrees of intrinsic reward. Song writers experience this evolution. The initial idea is usually born in play, but the refining often takes a great deal of work. The primary motivation in pursuing the perfection process

comes in knowing that once the idea is refined, a new song will have been born, and with it usually come feelings of relief, satisfaction and self-esteem.

6. **The Creative Process Often Involves a Period of Incubation.** Many times I have set out to solve a problem, only to find my attempts frustrated. Unable to see a solution, the problem is usually set it aside. But on many occasions, when I least expected it, a creative solution presented itself. It appears that oftentimes, conscious efforts are incapable of modifying inappropriate sets which restrict the ability to solve a problem. Although one may consciously give up, the unconscious mind continues to work on the problem until a solution is reached.
7. **Creativity Can Be Learned.** Just as some folks are more adept at aerobic exercise, just as some are better suited for football, some people seem destined to be more creative than others. Nevertheless, it is my firm conviction, and it is based on both scientific data and personal experiences, that people can learn to be more creative, that training in creative thinking can help people be more divergent and innovative thinkers. For example, Baer (1994) demonstrated that training in divergent thinking can increase creativity in children. Kasof (1995) presents ways in which attributional principles can be used to enhance creativity. Feldhusen and Goh (1995) describe elements that should be included in programs designed to stimulate creativity.

And now another opportunity to test your *creativity* on a . . . MINUTE MYSTERY

He was a strange man; some would say eccentric. But regardless of how you viewed him, one fact remained, he was regular as clockwork. Every morning at precisely 7:45 he would board the elevator, and leave his 20th floor penthouse for the ride to the ground floor. He would then walk to this office three blocks away. At 5:00 p.m. he would return to his apartment building and ride the elevator to the 14th floor and then climb the stairs to his apartment. This he would do without deviation, except on rainy days when he would ride to the 20th floor.

Why?

Clue: Sometimes familiar paths lead you only further away from the creative solution. It is often best to ignore the tried and true when seeking a creative solution to a problem.

Steps To Creativity

Step 1. Be Free

To start the creative process, you have to convince yourself that you are free to be creative. This may require some cognitive restructuring, but the effort will be worth it. Convince yourself that you aren't afraid of criticism, that you do not need the approval of others, are not afraid to fail and are willing to see others reject your creative efforts. In addition, there are times when you need to suspend the rules, to put yourself in a boundless state of mind. By stripping a problem of expectations or limitations you are then free to consider even the wackiest alternatives in seeking a solution.

Some of Our Best Ideas Come from Arranging Old Ideas in Unconventional Ways. . . .

EXERCISE. Learning to break boundaries is often difficult. The following puzzle is a good indicator of how you are influenced by perceived boundaries. Try your hand at this problem.

DRAW FOUR STRAIGHT LINES THROUGH THESE NINE DOTS **WITHOUT RETRACING AND WITHOUT LIFTING YOUR PEN FROM THE PAPER**.

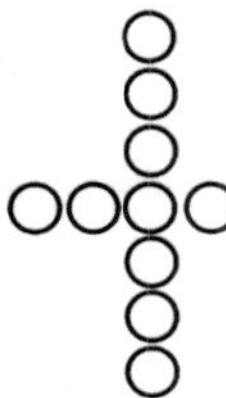

EXERCISE. The following problem is similar to the previous one in that both require divergent thinking. **ARRANGE 10 COINS LIKE THIS.**

Now, move just two coins to another position so that two rows, containing six coins each when added up either horizontally or vertically, will be formed.

THE KEY TO SUCCESS IN THESE TWO PROBLEMS IS FREEING YOURSELF FROM THE EXPECTATIONS INFERRED FROM THE DIRECTIONS YOU WERE GIVEN.

To solve these problems you must suspend your preconceptions about these tasks. The most formidable barrier to their solution will be found in your expectations.

An example of how our expectations can close our minds to creativity is suggested in your answer to a riddle posed by the following nursery rhyme:

> As I was going to St. Ives,
> I met a man with seven wives,
> Every wife had seven sacks.
> Every sack had seven cats.
> Every cat had seven kits.
> Kits, cats, sacks, wives
> How many were going to St. Ives?

Most people will fall victim to their tendencies for convergent thinking and multiply seven times seven times seven. Only one is going to St. Ives.

To test your ability for flexible and divergent thinking, I invite you to answer the following questions.

1. How many three cent stamps are there in a dozen?
2. A doctor is about to operate on a little boy. "This child is my son," exclaims the doctor. The doctor is correct, but the doctor is not the boy's father. What's going on here?
3. A farmer had seventeen sheep. All but nine died. How many were left?
4. How many times can you subtract 5 from 25?
5. In Canada is it legal for a man to marry his widow's sister?
6. If you have in your hand two coins that total thirty cents and one is not a nickel, what are the coins?
7. Read the following sentence once, slowly. How many F's are there in this sentence?

   FINISHED FILES ARE THE RESULT
   OF YEARS OF SCIENTIFIC STUDY

8. The number of people in a classroom doubles every five minutes. After an hour, the classroom is full. When was the classroom only one-half full?
9. If a bus leaves from Boston for New York an hour before another bus leaves from New York City for Boston, which bus will be closer to Boston when they are passing each other?
10. Mary and Jane were born on the same day of the same year of the same father and mother. They look almost exactly alike, yet they are not twins. How can this be? [8]

Now, I suppose you want the answers. Okay, see below.

Roger von Oech, Ph.D. is the author of a *Whack on the Side of the Head: How to Unlock Your Mind for Innovation*. This wonderful book on creativity offers many useful suggestions for the person interested in becoming more creative. To help people be more divergent thinkers, he suggests that in the early phases of the creative process, it is a good practice to engage in "soft thinking." In later stages, "hard thinking" may be more appropriate. Soft thinking is more playful, less structured, and more flexible than hard thinking. He describes it as ". . . metaphorical, approximate, diffuse, humorous, playful, and capable of dealing with contradiction" (30). Hard thinking is "more logical, precise, exact, specific, and consistent" (30). He cleverly illustrates the difference between these two styles of thinking in the following passage.

> Soft thinking tries to find similarities and connections among things, while hard thinking focuses on their differences. For example, a soft thinker might say that a cat and a refrigerator have a lot in common, and then proceed to point out their similarities ('they both have a place to put fish, they both have tails, they both come in a variety of colors, etc.'). The hard thinker would establish the cat and the refrigerator as being members of two different sets. A person using soft thinking might ask a question such as 'What would furniture look like if our knees bent the other way?' The hard thinker would say, "What materials should be used in manufacturing to optimize the rate of return on this new line of chairs?" (31)

Soft thinking allows you to explore a concept, hard thinking allows you to implement your solution. In trying to find a creative solution to some problem, it is a good idea to engage in some playful, imaginative, unstructured soft thinking. Once you have identified a creative solution, hard thinking becomes more appropriate. Where we get into trouble is when we employ hard thinking early in the creative process. In the exercises you just completed, you may have found that hard thinking got in the way of a creative solution. In soft thinking you suspend the rules and explore freely.

> Every rule can be broken except for this one.
>
> —Roger von Oech

Step 2. Be Fun

Have fun with your creative endeavors. Don't look beyond the immediate moment. Lose yourself in the process. Play with ideas. Reverse them, minimize them, magnify them, substitute them, rearrange them, reverse them, combine them. Quite often in the disorder of this kind of play you will hear yourself say, "Ah hah!"

EXERCISE. An epigram is a short, witty saying often paradoxical or satirical. Have some fun creating your own epigrams relating to your work. For example:

---

8. Answers: (1) 12. (2) The doctor is the boy's mother, (3) The ones that didn't die—9, (4) once, (5) the man is dead, (6) one is a nickel, (7) most people see 3 or 4, but there are 5, (8) at 55 minutes, (9) If they are passing one another they are the same distance from Boston, (10) How about triplets?

> A person's work gains in status the farther away he is from it.
> Work is the refuge of people who have nothing better to do.
>
> —Oscar Wilde

Your Turn.

> Creativeness often consists of merely turning up what is already there. Did you know that right and left shoes were thought up only a little more than a century ago?
>
> —Bernice Fitz-Gibbon

> No matter how old you get, if you can keep the desire to be creative, you are keeping the man-child alive.
>
> —John Cassavetes

Step 3. Separate Yourself from Your Creative Ideas and Products

In order to allow yourself to be perceptually free and intrinsically motivated, you must be able to see the difference between you, the person, and your creative products. Your creative efforts might not be perfect, but they should not be viewed as a negative reflection on you. You are not your creative products. Be able to look at your work objectively, recognize that it probably won't be perfect, but parts of it will be excellent.

> Laugh at the imperfections, glory in the excellence.
>
> —Phyllis Donovan

EXERCISE. Think of captions for the following cartoon. Let yourself go. Don't restrict yourself.

Step 4. A Good Idea Isn't too Sacred to Change or Discard

When I worked as a graphic artist, art director Stuart Heimdahl once suggested that I modify an illustration. In response to my hesitation, he asked, "What is it, too sacred to change?" That thought has influenced a lot of my work. Quite often the good is the worst enemy of the best. Don't get stuck on an idea just because you are afraid that you won't have a better one. Roger von Oechs tells the story about the two frogs that fell into the milk pail. One frog was a hard thinker who immediately recognized his predicament and realized there was no way to get any footing so he accepted his fate and drowned. The other frog, a soft thinker, kept churning around looking for alternative solutions. After awhile, all of his churning turned the cream into butter and he hopped out. Moral: Sometimes you shouldn't stick with the first or most obvious solution (123).

EXERCISE. People are always telling me, "I wish I could draw." Well in this exercise I am going to ask you try your hand at cartooning. And, I am going to ask you to keep modifying your illustration in a prescribed way. A simple cartoon face can be made from an oval with two dots for eyes, a half-circle for a nose and a larger half-circle for a mouth. IN THIS EXERCISE YOU ARE TO DUPLICATE, TO THE BEST OF YOUR ABILITY, THE CARTOON FACE BELOW. THEN YOU ARE TO CHANGE IT SO THAT IT SHOWS DIFFERENT EMOTIONS. FOR EXAMPLE ADD EYEBROWS THAT ARE POINTED DOWN TOWARD THE CENTER OF THE HEAD AND THE CHARACTER BECOMES MEAN OR ANGRY. GO AHEAD, GIVE IT A TRY. USE A PENCIL SO YOU CAN ERASE.

Step 5. Be Informed

There is no substitute for knowledge. In fact, it may be the raw material upon which creativity does its magic. Fuel your creative abilities by learning as much about everything that you can. Load your left brain with data and let your right brain play with it. Rumor has it that this was Einstein's secret. Carl Ally, founder of a well respected advertising firm is reported to have said, "The creative person wants to be a know-it-all. He wants to know all kinds of things. . . . he never knows when these ideas might come together to form a new idea." (Oechs 6).

EXERCISE. In the previous exercise, did you have difficulty visualizing the facial expressions that would best illustrate the emotion your were trying to capture? Part of the problem in conveying emotion in cartooning is simply a lack of information. We simply aren't certain how a person really looks when he or she is angry, lustful or sad. GO BACK TO THE PREVIOUS EXERCISE AND TRY IT WITH THE AID OF A MIRROR. THAT'S RIGHT, BE YOUR OWN MODEL; OR IF YOU HAVE ACCESS TO A WILLING MODEL, USE A MODEL FOR THIS EXERCISE. NOTICE THE DIFFERENCE WHEN YOU DRAW FROM THE VANTAGE POINT OF INCREASED INFORMATION.

Creativity Stretcher

*Now that you are more **creative**, imagine this. . .*

> *The DC3 had held together for nearly 50 years and a million air miles. Now it was showing signs of fatigue. But, you don't have too much to worry about, this will be your only trip in it. As a pilot specializing in ferrying aircraft from sellers to buyers, your responsibility will end once you land*

in Amazonia. Suddenly smoke begins to issue from the control panel, flames begin to lick around the panel setting your flying suit on fire. You think quickly and rip your suit off while you reach for a fire extinguisher. Unfortunately the fire extinguisher hasn't been charged and meets the fire with a dribble of foam. You have no alternative but to abandon the dying plane. Unfortunately your flying suit is burning, and you don't have time to get a change of clothes. With no time remaining to get equipment or supplies, you slip out of the burning flying suit and into your parachute and jump from the plane. You watch the aging DC3, rapidly disintegrating, descend into the jungle below. Wearing only your parachute, knowing that the nearest settlement is still 200 miles away, you gently fall toward the verdant green jungle below. ***Finish this story***. *Illustrate, diagram, cartoon, write . . . be creative. (I'd love to see your solution to this scenario, send me a copy.)*

I was going to visit the Brazilian Rain Forest once, but when I learned I would need more than an umbrella, I stayed home and watched National Geographic.

—Thelma Wilson

Creativity Stretcher

Now that you are more ***creative*** *imagine this. . .*

You have just rented an apartment. It is raining heavily, and unfortunately the drain pipe for the entire building empties near your bedroom window. The irregular sound of the water hitting the pavement is driving you batty. The manager is not home and you need your sleep. List at least ten creative solutions for this problem.

1. ______________________________
2. ______________________________
3. ______________________________
4. ______________________________
5. ______________________________
6. ______________________________
7. ______________________________
8. ______________________________
9. ______________________________
10. ______________________________

Select your most creative answer. Points to ponder: What makes it unique? Would you actually do it? What do you suppose others would think of your idea?

Examples of Creativity from Real Life

HE DOESN'T PAY ATTENTION TO ME ANYMORE: A CREATIVE SOLUTION

One of my students told me that after having been relatively ignored by her boyfriend for several days she decided to do something about it. After considering several alternatives she decided to send herself a dozen roses with a card from an anonymous admirer. She said the roses got his attention and so did she.

A friend of mine wanted a Christmas decoration for his door, but was turned off by the expense of the wreaths and other items he looked at. While browsing at a gift shop, he noticed some decorative candleholders set on a base of artificial boughs. The boughs could easily pass as a wreath. But, what to do with the candleholders? After a little creative thinking, he decided that the candleholders could be used to hold batteries, which then could power a short strand of small Christmas lights. By entwining the candle display in lights and hanging it from the door, he had created an attractive and creative door display.

After having just seen the movie *Star Wars*, one enterprising young man got the idea of taking plastic piping and inserting a flashlight in one end to simulate the light swords used by the characters in the film. This idea turned out to be worth millions of dollars. Of course the Pet Rock was pretty creative, and what about the fellow who invented a toilet bowl light. It turns on when you raise the lid.

Where Can You Be Creative?

I CAN'T THINK OF A SINGLE AREA OF HUMAN ENDEAVOR WHERE CREATIVITY IS INAPPROPRIATE

You can practice being creative in all aspects of your life, for example:

1. Dress in a creative manner.
2. Communicate with others in a creative manner (letters, answering machines etc.)
3. Design your living quarters in a creative fashion.
4. Organize your daily schedule in a creative way.
5. Deal with interpersonal problems in a creative manner.
6. Be more creative in how you have fun.
7. Be creative in making new friends.
8. Show appreciation in creative ways.
9. Be more creative in feeding yourself.
10. Explore creative ways of self-expression.
11. Be creative in how you clean your house or apartment.
12. Be more creative in how you make money.

Without creativity life will completely pass you by; with creativity
you will pass through life complete.

—one of my epigrams E.O.

EXERCISE. In order to become a more creative person, you need to actively apply the ideas presented in this chapter. Consequently the final exercise is designed to help you get started. Here you are asked to write yourself an activity prescription. Identify four tasks that you intend to do today, tasks that could benefit from creative thinking. Apply what you have learned about creativity to come up with several good creative alternative solutions to the problems presented by each task.

MY PERSONAL CREATIVITY PRESCRIPTION

Today I will be seek creative solutions to the following:

1. ______________________________
2. ______________________________
3. ______________________________
4. ______________________________

Now identify four different activities that you think you can do this week that will promote creative thinking.

1. ______________________________
2. ______________________________
3. ______________________________
4. ______________________________

Closing Notes...

What? You want the answer to the Minute Mysteries! The bodies were fish. The man was too short to reach the buttons except on days when he had his umbrella. As for the four lines: you must leave the boundaries.

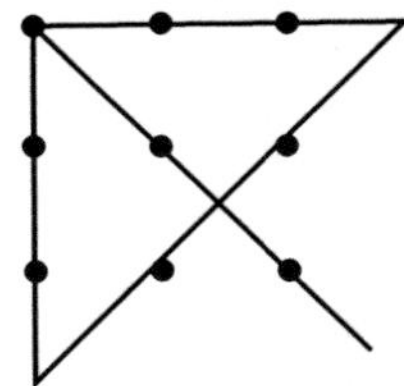

Regarding the coins, pick one up and place it on the coin in the center.

REFERENCES

Adams, J. *The Care and Feeding of Ideas: A Guide to Encouraging Creativity.* Reading, Mass: Addison-Wesley, 1986.

Baer, J. *Creativity and Divergent Thinking: A Task-specific Approach.* Hinsdale, New Jersey: L. Erlbaum Associates, 1993.

Baer, J. "Divergent Thinking Is Not a General Trait: A Multidomain Training Experiement." *Creativity Research Journal* 7.1 (1994): 35–46.

Bransford, J. *The Ideal Problem Solver: A Guide for Improving Thinking, Learning, and Creativity.* New York: W.H. Freeman, 1993.

Carr, C. *The Competitive Power of Constant Creativity.* New York; American Management Association, 1994.

Cropley, A.J. *More Ways Than One: Fostering Creativity.* Norwood, NJ: Ablex Publishing, 1992.

Edwards, B. *Drawing on the Right Side of the Brain: A Course in Enhancing Creativity and Artistic Confidence.* Los Angeles: Tarcher, 1989.

Feldhusen, J.F. and B.E. Goh. "Assessing and Accessing Creativity: An Integrative Review of Theory, Research, and Development." *Creativity Research Journal* 8.3 (1994): 231–247.

Kasof, J. "Explaining Creativity; The Attributional Perspective. Special Issue: Attributional Approach to Creativity." *Creativity Research Journal* 8.4 (1995): 311–366.

Kirst, W. *Creativity Training: Become Creative in 30 Minutes a Day.* New York: P.H. Wyden, 1973.

Miller, W.C. *Quantum Quality: Quality Improvement through Innovation, Learning, and Creativity.* White Plains, New York: Quality Resources, 1993.

Runco, M.H. *Divergent Thinking.* Norwood, NJ: Ablex Publishing Corporation, 1991.

CHAPTER 13

Discovering Freedom from Stress

Stress Sketch

Some days are colder than others, some are wetter, but this day was a cold and wet as I could remember. Not cold enough to freeze, but cold enough to pierce the bone. A few degrees and the torrential rain would have turned into large soft flakes of snow, and instead of drowning the city in its floods, the heaven should have kissed the city with a cleansing blanket of white. I pushed myself closer to the damp building, my trench coat a little tighter around my face and peered out into the neon darkness, wondering how I had managed to come this far. Success meant making contact, delivering the packet and getting back to the embassy. But where was Martin? He should have been here seven minutes ago. Standing in the rain like this was no way to maintain a cover. I stood out like a penguin in Miami and my autonomic nervous system knew it. I could both hear and feel my heart beating. Rapid and strong, pumping blood to my large muscles. Simultaneously the arterioles feeding my skin were constricting like an animal on the hunt or being hunted. I was primed to fight or flee. My eyes dilated to allow the absorption of light, they even changed shape, flattening slightly to increase my distance vision. Martin? He was eight minutes late now! Two more minutes without contact and the mission would be aborted. With each passing second my sympathetic nervous system made further adjustments to cope with what could be certain danger. My energy level rose as the pancreas stimulated glycogen production which in turn lead to an increase in glucose and merged with the already increased levels of epinephrine. My stomach felt like a knot as sphincter contractions inhibited digestive secretions. I was freezing, but I could feel the sweat soaking my shirt. For a moment, I chuckled at the irony—I was sweating in a cold rain.

There was no one on the street that night, and with only one minute left, my natural instinct was to leave as quickly as possible. I felt like a race horse anxiously awaiting the starter's call. It was then that I saw the car. Its lights were off, it was moving slowly down the wet street. I knew it wasn't Martin. He would never come by car, and even if he had, he would have gone directly to the pickup point. They were looking for something, someone. There was no point in waiting. Martin wouldn't be coming tonight, or for that matter, any other night. And, if I didn't get out of there before I was sighted, this cold, wet night would be my last as well. The messages reaching my hypothalamus and surrounding limbic portions of the brain were intense and urgent. The adrenal cortex released another flood of epinephrine, my hair was standing erect now, my heart pumped faster and my bronchial muscles relaxed to allow the intake of a greater volume of oxygen. The car suddenly accelerated. I had been spotted, the starter's call was sounded and I bounced forward, feeling the great power unleashed by my fear. As I sprinted to the alley where my car was parked, a neon lighted snowflake drifted by my face and brushed my lips, and the whine of a bullet cried through the rain turned snow.

Stress Sketch Two

The high country of Utah is a special place. The sky is still blue there, and the wispy stratocumulus clouds that live there are always white. The quaking aspens shimmer against those blue skies and the stately blue spruce stand at attention as though saluting Mother Nature's masterpiece. The streams that flow through those mountains are crystal clear and ice cold and during the summer team with rainbow trout. High country meadows, luxuriantly green from daily afternoon showers, punctuated by a plethora of wildflowers, provide nourishment and shelter for a varied community of wildlife. It is a place where the stress of our smog covered cities and blighted suburbs is simply not allowed.

Fishing for those rainbow trout is a favorite summer recreational activity for a lot of people who have access to Utah high country. And, it is easy to understand why. There are few things more relaxing than casting your line into a crystal clear stream, on a sunny lazy day, in a high valley meadow. The sounds of the stream harmonize with the whisper of the aspens. Birds sing in the forest and the mixed sounds of cicada, crickets, and bees make for a concert that than can never be adequately described, only felt. And, on such a day, in such a place the sympathetic nervous system takes some time off.

It was s such a day that Thelma and her family arrived at the little meadow known as Buttercup Flat. After a delicious picnic, the family spread out along Buttercup Stream for an afternoon of fishing. All was right with the world. The stress of city life was quickly forgotten. Thelma's pancreas was secreting pancreatic enzymes, her heart was beating slowly, her breath came in slow even inhalations, and she was keenly aware of the warmth of the sun on her skin.

Overall, Thelma was experiencing a parasympathetic mountain high—she was relaxed and happy. And, in her blissful state she sought to catch the elusive rainbow trout, and failed to notice the approaching game warden.

The game warden was a kind man, a gentle man, and an intellectual man. He was also a former football player who stood 78 inches tall and weighed nearly 300 pounds. With his western boots on, and with his Smokey the Bear hat, he appeared to stand well over seven feet. On this day he also wore his down filled ranger's jacket. Thelma didn't hear him coming, didn't know that he was there to check her fishing license, didn't know that her parasympathetic leisure was about to take a dramatic turn.

The ranger said, "Excuse me Ma'am, may I see your fishing license?" Thelma didn't hear him; all she heard was the lovely concert that Mother Nature was putting on. Gently the ranger tapped on her shoulder. The ranger must have looked like a giant or perhaps a bear to Thelma that day. The ranger who told me the story doesn't really know what went through Thelma's mind. He didn't stay to ask, for what happened next is a phenomenon that few of us will ever experience, and none of us want to. Most likely what happened was that Thelma's sympathetic nervous system was stimulated by the touch and sight of the ranger, a flood of epinephrine was released, her blood sugar was immediately elevated, her digestive secretions were shutoff, her heart rate increased and blood was shunted from other organs to the large muscles. All of this occurred unnoticed by the ranger, but he noticed one other sympathetic nervous system response: he noticed that Thelma's urinary bladder spontaneously emptied, altering the color of her powder blue slacks. The ranger suddenly at a loss for words heard himself say, "Have a nice day." With that he quickly returned to his truck.

Stress Sketch Three

Jeri felt as though she were going to explode. The children were driving her crazy. Jimmy wouldn't stop crying and Mary kept whining that she didn't want to go to school. The toast was burned again, and the school bus would be there any minute. Some routines don't ever improve with time and this was one of them. No matter how she tried to get Mary to the school bus stop on time, something would go wrong. This morning it was Jimmy. "Probably another earache," Jeri thought as she frantically tried to stuff peanut butter sandwiches into uncooperative plastic sandwich wrappers. The sitter wouldn't be there for another 15 minutes, and she couldn't really attend to Jimmy until Mary was on the bus, and she still had to ready herself for her own school.

Ever since her husband, Eric, had left them, her life and been a whirlwind of despair. Nothing ever seemed to come to completion. Her life was somewhat like Eric's child support checks—missing. She was doing the best she could, working afternoons and evenings, as a waitress, and in the mornings attending accounting courses at the university. Occasionally she would try to go on a date, but the men that were interested in her were rarely interested in her children or her problems. She felt torn in a dozen ways. Too many demands on her time, and resources, left her feeling unable to complete anything to her satisfaction. She felt she was a lousy mother, a poor student, and she hated her work.

Physiologically she was in a constant state of sympathetic arousal. Her autonomic nervous system remained in constant readiness for threatening situations. She was primed for flight or fight, but in reality there was no where to run and no one to fight. Her blood pressure slowly increased, unable to eat she lost weight and energy, she seemed to have constant health problems, as she put it, "If a person with a cold calls me on the phone, I'll catch it."

Through the kitchen window of her two bedroom apartment she could see the school bus approaching. Her head throbbing, she helped a reluctant Mary into her coat, and pushed her through the door. Down the stairs and across the lawn they half-walked, half-ran. As Jeri leaned over to kiss Mary good-bye, Mary quietly asked, "Mommy, where's my lunch box?"

Stress Sketch Four

Trevor's autonomic nervous system switched to the sympathetic every time he thought about the coming weekend. But he liked the feeling. He conjured up a hundred different images. He visualized the drive to the coast, the winding mountain road leading to Stinson Beach, the first sight of the breakers and the little specks that were the surfers he would soon join. He even visualized the cold eyes and jagged smile of the Great White Sharks long believed to breed in the waters off Stinson. It was the thought of the Great White that would push his level of arousal into the discomfort zone, otherwise, his body reacted favorably to the images of the perfect wave and the perfect ride.

What a place to live. Two hours to the beach and two hours to skiing. The best of both worlds within a radius of two hours. Thoughts of either sport would always "turn him on," for he thoroughly enjoyed both. Skiing was even more exciting than surfing. It was probably the speed factor that made the difference for him. On a good run, he could clock up to 60 miles per hour, do several jumps, many up to 30–40 feet, and scare the living daylights out of more timid skiers.

Rarely did he feel bored when skiing. There was always a new approach to a run, a new trick to try, a different jump to take. In fact, to allow yourself to relax when skiing is dangerous. For your own good you had to stay optimally aroused. In skiing your fight is with the hill and if you win you get a good flight. It is much the same with surfing, although while waiting for a wave, it's probably only thoughts of the Great White Shark that keep the sympathetic system functioning, and thus the body ready for the next great wave.

What is Stress?

Stress is what happens when nothing happens.

—Mayor Marie Huff

Stress is the body's response to any demand placed upon it—real or imagined. It is a biological byproduct of millions of years of evolution in a world of uncertainty. In the rest of the animal kingdom and in our not too distant past (say up to as recent as a few thousand years ago) stress was usually the reaction to short-lived emergencies—threats that required immediate action (Robinson et al. 1). Consequently the ability to survive was linked to the extent to which an animal was capable of a rapid response when faced with danger; success was measured in terms of a rapid escape or winning a fight. Thus, we often hear stress referred to as the "flight or fight" response.[9]

It is important to recognize that the danger need only be perceived in order for the body to produce a stress reaction. In the sketch about Trevor, by merely thinking about surfing and skiing, he would become aroused. Of course, in Trevor's case, this was not harmful, nor was it so significant that it provoked a fight or flight response; it instead induced a rather pleasant feeling. And, this makes another important point regarding stress: in and of itself stress is not bad—it is when stress produces negative physiological and psychological outcomes that stress becomes undesirable, and thus should be reduced (Selye 1). In the "Where's Martin" sketch, although intense, our hero's response to his stressful situation may have saved his life. This type of stress is usually short-lived, but accounts for great bursts of energy. Most of us will experience this type of stress when frightened by a strange sound in the middle of the night, or when a police car pulls up behind us, or when engaged in "high risk" recreation.

The "Single Mom" sketch is an example of harmful stress. Jeri was clearly overburdened. Frustrated and angry she was easily annoyed, distracted, and sorrowful. In addition, unable to eat or rest effectively, her physical health was frequently compromised. Jeri was suffering from what is called **chronic stress** (Adams 80), and it is this stress that tends to do the greatest damage to a person. To understand why, we need to look at stress from a physiological point of view.

Hans Selye is a Canadian scientist who has devoted much of his professional career to the study of the body's reaction to stress. (Readers are referred to Selye, Hans (1984). ***The Stress of Life***. New York: McGraw-Hill.) He is known for a theoretical model referred to as the **general adaptation syndrome**. In this model, stress is divided into three phases: (1) The "alarm reaction" phase, (2) the "resistance phase" and (3) the "exhaustion" phase.

Life's Little Ruts

9. Because it is associated with fear and danger, I tend to prefer the "term" distress to describe what most people consider "stress." In reality, not all stress is bad. For example, people subject themselves to stress all the time because of the "rush" that it produces. For example, skiing, sky diving, climbing all can be considered stressful, but they are popular recreational activities.

The Alarm Phase of Stress

When confronted by a perceived threat, the brain (principally the hypothalamus) immediately activates the bodies defense system (Selye 36). The brain sends signals to the endocrine system which releases certain hormones into the bloodstream, which in turn regulate a great number of physiological functions. Activation of the endocrine system occurs along two pathways: (1) the sympathetic division of the autonomic nervous system and (2) the activation of the so-called master gland of the endocrine system, the pituitary.

When the sympathetic nervous system is activated the central part of the andrenal medulla (the middle portion of the adrenal gland, a triangular shaped gland attached to the upper surface of each kidney) is stimulated to produce **dopamine, norepinepherine and epinephrine**. These hormones are transported throughout the body via the bloodstream increasing the body's ability to respond to emergency demands. Among the important changes stimulated by these hormones are: increased heart rate and pressure, increased blood flow, increased respiration rate and oxygen consumption, increased perspiration, inhibition of digestive juices, subtle but important changes in vision, and an increase in blood sugar.

In addition to the above, the hypothalamus activates the pituitary gland, which secretes **adrenocorticotropic hormone** (ACTH), which in turn stimulates the outer portion of the adrenal gland (the adrenal cortex) causing it to release into the bloodstream **cortiocsteriods**. These hormones permit many biochemical reactions to proceed at optimal rates, and therefore make an important contribution in emergency situations (Selye 138–143).

In the "Where's Martin Sketch" the ominous sight of a car without lights, slowly approaching our hero, sounded an alarm. This alarm activated the sympathetic nervous system as well as the pituitary gland. The sympathetic nervous system triggered the release of the catecholamines dopamine, epinephrine, and norepinepherine. These in turn elevated the body's available energy and our hero "felt like a race horse." In addition, the adrenal cortex was stimulated producing adrenal corticosteroids, which further helped bring his body to an optimal state of physical readiness. Thus stimulated, he was able to flee like the wind down rain soaked streets.

On a less dramatic level I recently experienced an alarm reaction while driving home from work at the university. I was tired and anxious to get home. My foot was a little heavier than usual, and it was difficult to keep my high powered, foreign engineered, steel gray 1977 Toyota pickup at the speed limit. Suddenly, as if from out of nowhere, I saw the roof lamps of a California Highway Patrol unit. Panic. My heart leaped into action, perspiration filled my palms, and epinephrine stimulated my musculature. I slowed, took a closer look at the patrol car which was now about to pass me. Inside were several young people, laughing and chatting. The car was filled with skiers headed for the Sierra, and the roof lamps were nothing more than skis. What did I say abut real versus imagined threats...

Resistance Phase

In cases of acute stress, once the immediate perceived danger has passed, the body returns to its normal state. We tend to relax and turn our attention to our daily tasks. But, there are some situations where the perceived threat to our well-being never really abates. Take Jeri for example. Her lifestyle was filled with frustration. Too many demands on her time caused her to feel both helpless and hopeless. It was almost as if her very lifestyle was her enemy. Thus, for Jeri, stress was an ongoing experience. In situations such as this, the body attempts to adapt to the stress through continued autonomic and endocrine responses, but at a slightly lower level than in the initial phase. In addition, one's ability to perform cognitive tasks is usually taxed under stressful conditions. We don't know how Jeri was doing in school, but she obviously had difficulty remembering things such as Mary's lunch box. As the body struggles to resist the effects of stressful conditions, it slowly wears down, slowly deteriorates, ultimately leading to the final phase—exhaustion.

Exhaustion

If stress runs unabated for a long period of time, an individual may simply run out of his supply of certain important hormones (Selye 38). When this occurs, the sympathetic nervous system essentially shuts down, forcing the parasympathetic division of the autonomic nervous system to take over. Such a situation can be described as total exhaustion. During periods of long stress, prior to total collapse, the stress response may do serious harm to certain internal organs and contribute to the onset of disease. For example chronic stress has been linked to coronary heart disease, hypertension, peptic ulcers, headaches, influenza, herpes, skin disorders, chronic back pain, rheumatoid arthritis, stroke, and even cancer.[10] In addition, people under stress may be more inclined toward alcohol, drug usage and cigarette smoking—behaviors which can compound health liabilities produced by chronic stress.

Sources of Stress

You may be familiar with something called the Social Readjustment Rating Scale (SRRS). It is not uncommon for people interested in studying stress to use this instrument to estimate the amount of stress in a person's life. It is frequently seen in articles and books dealing with stress. This scale was developed in the 1960's and essentially consists of a list of life events (n = 43) that are supposed to be correlated with stress. To use the scale you simply check off those events that have occurred to you within a recent time period, add up the values of the events checked and thereby derive a score that purportedly is an estimation of the stress in your life. (The interested reader is referred to Holmes, T.H. and R.H. Rahe, (1967) The Social Readjustment Rating Scale. *Journal of Psychosomatic Research.* 11, 213–218.)

This approach to measuring stress has some serious deficiencies. First, it fails to take into account the difference in perception between people. Not everyone is going to view the 43 events on the SRRS in the same way. For example, an individual whose marriage has been a constant source of stress may find "marital separation" a blessing rather than stressful. Similarly "fired at work" may not be stressful if it leads to a better situation, and a reduction of job related stress. Using average weights (which is what the SRRS does) fails to take into account the fact that people view "stressful situations" differently.

Another problem with SRRS is that it presumes that the 43 events listed are an accurate reflection of the universe of stressful events. It is quite likely that this list is at best incomplete, and at worst, a misrepresentation of the types of stressful events that one is likely to experience. Similarly, the description of the stressful events listed are incomplete and subject to various interpretations, calling into question the reliability of this instrument.

In examining the extent to which you are personally affected by stress, as well as identifying the sources of stress, we think pencil and paper exercises may be useful, but need to be focused more toward the individual and less toward the presumed relationships. Consequently, the following exercise was developed, which, unlike the SRRS and subsequent scales (e.g., The Life Experience Survey), is designed for self-exploratory purposes only, and is not intended for research application.

> I am so accustomed to being stressed, that one day I woke feeling so relaxed that I knew something was wrong. This proved very stressful.
>
> —Dawn Johnson

An Exercise in Self-Understanding: The Oh Oh Scale

Stress can be related to at least four broad areas: environmental ("Oh-oh, it looks like another smoggy day—this smog is going to kill me."), social (Oh no, I've got a zit and my date is tonight.") psychological ("Oh-oh, I am booked on a DC 10; I know that if I fly on a DC 10 I am going to die on a DC 10.") and physical ("...Bennett dashes for the end zone, oh that tackle was brutal, but he breaks free, and oh oh...he just ran into the goal post.") In this scale we will look to see how much of your perceived stress is due to environmental, social, psychological, and physical factors.

10. For more on cancer and stress the reader is referred to: Cooper, CL. "The Social Psychological Precursors to Cancer," *Journal of Human Stress* 10.1 (1984): 4–11.

How's Your Environment?

1.	When I think about my immediate living environment (my house or apartment) my response usually is...	OK	ok	undecided	oh oh	OH OH
2.	The neighborhood in which I live is...	OK	ok	undecided	oh oh	OH OH
3.	When I think of my community, I tend to view it as...	OK	ok	undecided	oh oh	OH OH
4.	The place where I work is...	OK	ok	undecided	oh oh	OH OH

Why the Oh, Oh's?

Briefly analyze what it is about your environment that produce an "oh, oh" response:

____

____

____

____

Social Oh, Oh's

1.	When you think of your needs for affiliation with a special person, how do you feel?	OK	ok	undecided	oh oh	OH OH
2.	How do you get along with your immediate family?	OK	ok	undecided	oh oh	OH OH
3.	Neighbors and friends?	OK	ok	undecided	oh oh	OH OH
4.	Colleagues and work associates?	OK	ok	undecided	oh oh	OH OH

Why the social oh, oh's? In the space below analyze the reason for your oh, oh responses.

____

____

____

____

Psychological Oh, Oh's

1.	How are you when it comes to feelings of guilt?	OK	ok	undecided	oh oh	OH OH
2.	Jealousy?	OK	ok	undecided	oh oh	OH OH
3.	Feelings of inadequacy?	OK	ok	undecided	oh oh	OH OH
4.	Flexibility (when faced with change)?	OK	ok	undecided	oh oh	OH OH

5.	Feelings of "too much to do"?	OK	ok	undecided	oh oh	OH OH
6.	Fear about the future?	OK	ok	undecided	oh oh	OH OH
7.	Worrying about things over which you have no control?	OK	ok	undecided	oh oh	OH OH
8.	Feeling that you are in control of the important things in your life?	OK	ok	undecided	oh oh	OH OH
9.	Is anger a problem for you?	OK	ok	undecided	oh oh	OH OH
10.	How are you when it comes to happiness?	OK	ok	undecided	oh oh	OH OH

In this space identify some of the reasons for OH OH responses.

____

____

____

____

Physical Oh, Oh's

1.	How is your general health?	OK	ok	undecided	oh oh	OH OH
2.	How is your diet? (Low calorie, high fiber diets are best.)	OK	ok	undecided	oh oh	OH OH
3.	Blood pressure?	OK	ok	undecided	oh oh	OH OH
4.	How are you when it comes to alcohol, tobacco and other drugs? (Abstinence is best.)	OK	ok	undecided	oh oh	OH OH
5.	To what extent does your work or lifestyle put stress on your body?	OK	ok	undecided	oh oh	OH OH
6.	How about your weight?	OK	ok	undecided	oh oh	OH OH
7.	How about exercise?	OK	ok	undecided	oh oh	OH OH

Write the reason for your negative response here:

____

____

____

____

If you are a quantitative person, you can total a score by assigning a 4 to OK, 3 to ok, 2 to undecided, 1 to oh, oh and 0 to OH OH. Naturally the higher your score the less likely stress is to be a problem in your life. But, if you are like most of us stress is a problem and its one that you will need to learn to deal with.

Ways of Dealing with Stress

We are not always effective in dealing with stress. Unfortunately many of our responses are negative. One method of rapidly expending stress generated energy is through **aggression**. Striking out at the perceived source of one's stress may temporarily reduce some stress, but it is quite likely, that in the long run it will actually contribute to and compound the original stress. Misplaced aggression may also be a misguided attempt to reduce stress. I spoke to a clerk once who told me that she is often the victim of apparent misdirected aggression. Waiters and waitresses are another group often the recipients of stress related anger. Whether the aggression is physical or verbal (i.e. shame, ridicule, belittlement, etc.) the outcome is usually negative and thus leads to more stress.

Another common response to stress is **withdrawl**. This can take two forms: (1) physical, where you physically stay away from the perceived source of the stress, and (2) mental, where you attempt to escape from the source of the stress by daydreaming, sleeping, denial, or altering your state of mind through the use of alcohol or drugs.

Clearly aggression and withdrawl are undesirable responses to stressful situations, both can detract from the overall quality of one's lifestyle and set the stage for further stress which in chronic conditions can lead to physical and emotional breakdown. Consequently, it is important that positive steps be taken when faced with stressful situations.

Coping with Acute Stress

In situations where stress is a unitary response to a single factor, the emphasis is on discharging the energy produced by the sympathetic nervous system interacting with the endocrine system. This is the kind of stress one might feel immediately before taking a test, going on a date or playing a sport. Usually, once the source of stress is engaged the energy dissipates or is positively directed resulting in a decline in stress and an increase of positive responses. In some situations, it may be essential to redirect your attention, and pursue some activity which can yield a cathartic outcome. For example, when I experience acute stress I get excellent relief from an aerobic workout. The music, movement and increased levels of endorphin resulting from physical exertion usually leave me feeling relaxed and in good spirits.

Coping with Chronic Stress

Essential to successful coping with long term stress is the identification of the sources of stress that are compromising the quality of your life. The OH OH test is one way to do that. Obviously, there are other ways, too. You can accomplish this through introspection, through counseling, and education. This step require honest and objective self-analysis. Until you thoroughly understand why you experience stress, it will be difficult to develop a strategy to eliminate the sources of stress from your life. In terms of chronic stress it is not enough to learn to live with it, rather it is essential that you eliminate it from your life.

Once you have a good idea as to the source of chronic stress in your life, it is essential that you determine whether or not it can be eliminated. There are certain situations and conditions which may be difficult or even impossible to change. If you determine that it is impossible to actually bring about a physical change in the situation, then you have only two options: (1) allow the situation to continue to affect you or (2) adapt to the situation by developing an attitude that allows you to view the situation as less serious or personal. Generally, we can identify things about a stress producing situation that we can change. For example in Jeri's case, she might benefit from working less or taking fewer university classes. Perhaps a low interest loan might help relieve some of her stress. If these alternatives are unavailable then her only alternative is to adapt to her situation by altering her perception regarding the demands on her time, or alter her attitudes about the stress producing events in her life. If she is unsuccessful then the pressures of her life will continue unabated until her own biology forces her to withdraw through a physical collapse.

Bringing about changes in patterns that are producing chronic stress may take time, energy, and assistance. Sometimes, the changes that are required to reduces chronic stress require the assistance of a counselor, psychologist or physician. Sometimes, change can be facilitated through education. But rarely does it happen quickly. Usually it requires time and dedication. During the period of time during which life patterns are being changed, it is particularly important to practice coping skills. I like to call these Stress Skills.

STRESS KILLS, UNLESS YOU POSSESS STRESS SKILLS. . .

Stress Skills

Relaxation Skills

Progressive muscle relaxation and autogenic training are two popular forms of relaxation exercises. Progressive muscle relaxation involves systematically and sequentially relaxing each of the major muscle groups. This is accomplished by flexing each muscle group for a few seconds and then relaxing. This can be done under the direction of a facilitator or through self-direction. A frequently used progression begins with the feet and concludes with the head and facial muscles. Allow yourself at least 15 seconds per anatomical area. Try it.

Autogenic training is somewhat similar to self-hypnosis. It literally means self-generating or self-moving. It is a process whereby you give yourself verbal cues. Cues are presented silently and direct your concentration to a feeling normally associated with relaxation. Such words as warm, gentle, relaxed, quiet, refreshed are good cues are autogenic exercises. Normally in an autogenic exercise you visualize relaxing scenes or pleasant memories. Many people combine the physical relaxation of progressive muscle relaxation with the visualization of autogenics. After about 15 minutes of relaxation you terminate the exercise with an energizer cue. This is a phrase that is associated with strength and energy. You might say, "Now you are about to awaken, and as you do you will feel happy, full of energy and very positive" (see Steinmetz et al. 15–33).

Hypnosis is nothing more than a response to suggestion. The suggestion can come from within or from another person. Some people may be more responsive to suggestion, but generally, given enough suggestions, most people will respond in some way. We hypnotize ourselves everyday through self-talk. A good share of this talk is negative. We are very good about giving ourselves suggestions that talk us out of taking reasonable risks, or challenging our abilities. Even if these suggestions are unreasonable and simply not a reflection of reality, given enough suggestion, they become as though true. I see this at work in interpersonal relationships. For example, "I can't ask her out, she would never go out with me." Of course she won't go out with him, he made the decision for her! Every time he sees her, he is reminded of his perceived inadequacies. It is important that we recognize the influence that self-talk has upon us. By focusing on positive self-talk, we can build ourselves up rather than tear ourselves down. We can reinforce our abilities rather than our deficiencies.

An Exercise in Relaxation and Positive Thinking

Sit comfortably in a chair, your feet flat on the floor. Place your hands on your thighs, palms up. Follow the sequence outlined below. Between each phase, breathe in deeply and exhale slowly.

1. Make a fist of your feet. Curl your toes and apply tension to the muscles of your feet. Hold. Relax.
2. Flex your calve muscles, thighs and buttocks. Hold. Relax.
3. Move up to the lower back and into your shoulders. Hold. Relax.
4. Now, flex the arms and make a fist with your hands. Hold. Relax.
5. Finally, flex the head and neck. Hold. Relax.
6. Now, in sequence beginning with the feet progressively flex all of your muscles until your entire body is rigid. Hold. Relax.

REPEAT

Following this "progressive muscle relaxation" exercise, you should feel very relaxed. Now is a good time to do some positive visualization.

1. Visualize a clear blue sky. See, in your mind's eye, nothing but this gorgeous, clear, clean sky. Hold that image for a moment, and then add a horizon. Make this the horizon line formed by the ocean meeting the sky. Hold the image for a moment.
2. Now, create the image of a beach and a gentle surf. Hold that image.
3. Place yourself in the picture. See yourself standing on the beach looking out at the sea.
4. Now add some sounds. Hear the sound of the water. Add some sea birds to the scene and hear their song. Listen for the sound of the sea breeze passing through the palm trees that line the beach.
5. Feel the warmth of the sun contrasted by the cooling breeze. Smell the aroma of the sea mixing with the scent of flowers and fresh air.

Visualize this as a very special, safe, and quiet place. This is a place you can resort to for solitude, relaxation and privacy. Enjoy this mental vacation for a moment, then, if you feel inclined, give yourself some positive suggestions.

1. See yourself doing some challenging tasks. Tell yourself "I have the capabilities to do this task."
2. See yourself successfully completing the task.
3. Repeat this part of the exercise at least five times.
4. Visualize yourself successfully doing any other activities related to success in the task on which you are working.
5. Return to the beach.
6. When you are ready to end the exercise, simply give yourself the suggestion, "I am ready to return. I will return on the count of five. With each number I will feel more alert, more energized, and more positive." Begin the count.

As with anything, expertise is acquired through practice and study. The bibliography contains some excellent resources to help you learn these techniques. Allow time for practice and application.

Cognitive Structuring

Therapists such as Albert Ellis and Aaron Beck teach that it is not the event that produces stress, but rather it is the interpretation of the event that causes stress. (Girdano, Everley, and Dusek, 203). The interpretation of "stressful events" takes he form of little conversations we have with ourselves as we attempt to solve stress producing problems. This *maladaptive self-talk* is often at the heart of stressful responses. An event occurs, you have a little chat with yourself about it, and the nature of this conversation determines how you feel. It is your own thinking that produces most feelings, not the external event. Unfortunately these little conversations can become habitual and self-reinforcing. They become a cognitive pattern for dealing with distressing issues. Cognitive restructuring is a technique designed to assist you in changing the nature of the conversations that you have with yourself, in order that you become less inclined to talk to yourself into a stressful response (see Steinmetz et al. 37–55).

Self-talk is largely based on what we believe about something. Unfortunately, not all of our beliefs are based on fact. Frequently, we view the world through the expectations of others, through religious belief systems (which call for perfection) and through inaccurate images of ourselves and significant others. These beliefs often fall into the irrational category and frequently contribute to our self-destructive conversations. Girdano, Everly and Dusek illustrate some of the more common maladaptive thoughts in their book *Controlling Stress and Tension: A Holistic Approach* (202–203). For example:

Presenting Problem: The tendency to see things only in extremes, good or bad, all or nothing.

Cognitive Restructuring Solution: Search for gray areas, view things on a continuum.

Presenting Problem: The tendency to blame one's self for problems when there is little reason to do so.

Cognitive Restructuring Solution: Search for reasonable explanations for the problem.

Steinmetz illustrates cognitive restructuring in the following example:

Common Irrational Belief: "If everyone who I feel is important does not like what I'm doing, then I must be a failure."

Restructured Belief: "It would be nice to be respected and loved by everyone, but I am not worthless when I don't achieve this goal" (55).

In talking with students who are attempting to cope with the stress associated with rejection, I often hear something like this: "I feel worthless." To help them start the restructuring process I will often ask, "Would you really want to work for someone who doesn't appreciate your strong points?" Or, "Would you really want to be with someone who can't reciprocate your love?"

> Everyone talks to himself, it's just that some of us have better conversations
>
> —Ernest Jones

Maladaptive as compared to effective thinking can be illustrated by the following diagram:

Activating Event → Maladaptive Thinking: Irrational → Negative Feelings and Behavior
Negative
Self-Defeating

Activating Event → Healthy Thinking: Rational → Positive Feelings and Behavior
Positive
Self-Reinforcing

Learning to look at potentially stressful circumstances in a realistic, reasonable and rational way will take you a long way toward minimizing stress in your life. It is not a quick fix, it will take time and concentrated effort, but in the long term it will be worth it.

> We learn a great deal through our conversations with other. Why then is it that we have such difficulty learning from the conversations with ourselves.
>
> —Jones Williams

Assertiveness

One of the most common sources of stress is not being able to tell someone else what we are thinking or feeling (Steinmetz et al. 75). Some people think that assertiveness is tantamount to being abrasive and egotistical. Not so. Aggressiveness and assertiveness are two entirely different things. One can be assertive without offending. Once can be assertive without being angry.

A key word to remember in being assertive is "I." Take responsibility for your feelings, needs, and desires. State clearly, calmly, and objectively what it is that you desire or require. Be firm, be positive, keep your sentences short, maintain good posture, and eye contact. Avoid "you" statements. (You statements make a judgement about the other person, or demand a certain behavior from the other person.) For the most part you-statements tend to put people on the defensive and often mask the true intent of the message.

"You are such a jerk, you are so rude." This is a you-statement, and may close the other person to discussion.

"I feel rejected and angry." This is an I-statement, and may open the discussion so you can express what you desire or require.

Learn to focus on how you feel and what you need to feel better, and see how less complicated your life can become. As was pointed out in our discussion on interpersonal games, people often go to great circuitous lengths to get what they want. A much better strategy is that of my mother who always advocated the KISS Principle—Keep it Simply Simple. Terry Inagawa would say "There's a short version and a long version. Which one do you want?" Keep it simple, stick with the short version.

Physical Activity

Leisure time physical activity may be viewed as either recreational or conditioning exercise. Each offers benefits related to coping with stress: (1) recreational exercise (walks, bowling, tennis, etc.) provides a diversion and releases tension whereas, (2) the more vigorous, conditioning exercise leads to an increased physical ability to cope with stressful circumstances (Adams 54). In a study at Brigham Young University, Aldana and associates demonstrated that people who regularly participated in "leisure time physical activity" reported about one-half the perceived stress of non-participants (1996). This in part might be due to the fact that when people experience stress, the body prepares itself to fight or flee. When a person is distressed, epinephrine and norepinepherine are released into the body in order that the body might escape or effectively fight off the source of stress. This worked very well in primitive times when the source of stress might be a ferocious beast. Now, the sources of stress are more difficult to deal with. Physical fight or flight is often inappropriate or impossible. Unless these energies are routinely channeled through physical activity they can have serious physical and psychological consequences.

For example, it is generally known that norepinepherine makes a person very volatile. This worked well in primitive times, but it makes for trouble in modern society. When someone "flips out," it may be an inappropriate response to increased secretions of norepinepherine caused by stress. A good strategy to avoid the harmful physical and emotional consequences of stress is to program regular exercise into your life. These exercises should provide a total body workout. Running, cycling, swimming, dancing, vigorous team sports are all excellent. Girdano, Everly, and Dusek suggests the value of this type of physical activity in the following statement:

> "A crystal clear picture that should be forming is that Mother Nature intended that the stress response be nothing more than preparation for physical activity. Thus, a natural release, which is also increasingly socially acceptable for everyone, is no less than body movement. It is a treatment form that everyone can afford (262).

Girdano, Everly and Dusek suggest that in order to get the maximum benefit from exercise, activities should be selected that are not likely to be heavily "ego involved" (264). Competitive activities might actually increase stress, particularly when you don't do very well. Consequently, individual activities (running, swimming, jogging, skiing, etc.) might have greater value in helping you cope with stress than competitive activities. The rule here is that the more an activity requires you to compete against others, the more likely it is to produce stress. Even individual activities can produce stress if you place unrealistic goals on yourself. "Next year I will win a gold medal in the Olympics," may be an unrealistic goal.

Ropes courses are particularly well suited for stress reduction. The risk component of a ropes course simulates the kinds of physical challenges for which our autonomic nervous systems were designed. Yet, the cooperative, noncompetitive nature of the experience meets our needs for affiliation and community. Other risk recreation such as river rafting, spelunking, climbing and so on, have the capacity to allow one to express large amounts of physical energy in noncompetitive physical recreation.

Get Back to Nature

I think one of the reasons that ropes courses and risk recreation work so well in helping people reduce stress is because these activities occur in natural environments. We evolved in natural surroundings, but in our headlong rush to subdue nature we have separated ourselves from our very roots. Nature, in a very real sense, is our Mother. When we are in her presence we feel much more relaxed than when subjected to the rush and hubbub of our cities and factories. This was demonstrated in a study by Hull and Michael (1995). In comparing recreation outdoors to that occurring indoors, they found that the greatest degree of stress reduction occurred within those who participated in outdoor recreation.

Learn to Play

Stress and play are mutually exclusive terms. By learning how to play you can ensure yourself little stress free islands to which you can periodically visit. Make recreation an important part of your life. Include time for jogging, music, art, hobbies, sports, etc. You can't be at stress when you are having fun. The word *recreation* can be thought of as meaning an activity which recreates, which lifts up your spirits and fortifies you against life's daily stresses.

One Reason Why Play Helps Us Cope with Stress

Play has capacity to stimulate the production of very powerful substances which when diffused through the brain have the ability to lessen pain, increase arousal, and produce a generally pleasant sensation. This class of chemicals is known as endorphins (literally inner morphine). Endorphins are sometimes subsumed under the name *euphorigens*.

When under stress, some people feel the need to seek relief through euphorigens. Unfortunately most artificial euphorigens are highly addictive and thus possess the potential of seriously compounding the problems that motivated the euphorigen user to get involved with drugs in the first place. A person addicted to a drug directs his or her life in service to the addiction. The acquisition and ingestion of the drug becomes an obsession affecting all aspects of the user's life. In addition, most drugs have serious side effects. For example, large quantities of alcohol can lead to severe brain damage, the injection of heroin is a leading cause of AIDS, cocaine and amphetamine use can lead to psychotic reactions and hallucinogenic drugs can seriously impair one's judgement. Although providing temporary relief from stress, artificial euphorigens possess too many liabilities to warrant their use. Perhaps the most significant problem associated with euphorigens is that they tend to mask the underlying problems, thus making it that much more difficult to eliminate the underlying source of stress.

Play, unlike "unnatural highs" has no serious side effects, does not impair judgement or produce psychotic reactions. The ability to think clearly is important when it comes to coping with sources of stress. Play stimulates us to effective thinking while simultaneously producing natural euphorigens which tend to produce feelings of well-being, pleasure, and self-confidence.

> The only sure cure for anxiety or boredom is to play...
>
> —Sara Louise Williams

Stay Physically Healthy

Your ability to cope with stressful situations is in part dependent upon your physical health. It is important that during times of stress that you eat a well balanced diet, allow for adequate sleep and get sufficient exercise.

News reporter Beth Duncan was heard to say on a radio talk show that she always carries a few natural food snacks with her when she goes shopping—to keep her energy sufficiently high to cope with the stress of shopping.

John Murphy, a prominent attorney, confides that one hour of exercise is a critical component in his work as a trial attorney. He says knowing that he is toned and cardiovascularly fit contributes to a feeling of self-confidence that enables him to cope with stressful situations in the courtroom.

Five Fitness Questions

1. Do you climb stairs whenever feasible as opposed to riding elevators or escalators?
2. Does your normal routine involve some form of moderate physical activity (walking, gardening, etc.)?
3. Do you participate in some form of aerobic exercise for twenty minutes or more at least three times a week?
4. Do you do some type of resistance training at least three times a week (lifting weights, etc)?
5. Do you do some type of stretching at least three times a week?

Five Nutrition Questions

1. Do I keep my consumption of saturated fats to a minimum?
2. Do I consume about the same number of calories that I "burn off"?
3. Does my diet primarily consist of whole grains, fruits and vegetables?
4. Do I allow time to eat my meals in a leisurely manner?
5. Do I avoid caffeine and alcoholic beverages?

If you answered YES to all of these questions, the chances are good that you are in pretty good shape. If you answered NO to any of them, you might want to consider changing your lifestyle to accommodate better nutrition and fitness practices. The healthier and more fit you are the better you are going to handle stressful moments in your life.

Have a Personal Support Group

During times of stress it is important that you have people to whom you can turn for comfort and support. Family, neighbors, church members or organized support groups can be helpful during difficult times.

> You can always tell a real friend; when you've made a fool of yourself
> he doesn't feel you have done a permanent job.
>
> —J. Laurence Peter

Know When to Turn to Professional Help

In regard to seeking treatment, one of the biggest problems is the tendency of people to delay taking the first step. In cases of chronic stress, or severe occurrences of acute stress, professional counseling or therapy may be the only logical approach to the problem. But for many people the social stigma associated with seeing a "shrink" makes seeking professional help a difficult course to take. If you feel that life is just too stressful, don't hesitate to call for help. When your car breaks down you call a mechanic, don't you?

Stress is a nasty thing, but the unfortunate thing about it is that when we feel like life is giving us a beating, a closer look will generally reveal that we are the ones holding the switch...

—Ed Clark

Closing Note . . .

Most of us call it "stress," but a more accurate description is the term "distress." It generally presents itself in two forms: chronic or acute. Both types can have deleterious consequences. In controlling distress there are a number of strategies that we can employ. Similarly in coping with distress there are strategies that can be useful. But coping and controlling are far less desirable than preventing. One of the very important reasons for developing a leisure lifestyle can be found in leisure's ability to help minimize distress.

REFERENCES

Adarns, J.D. *Understanding and Managing Stress*. San Diego: University Association, Inc., 1980.

Aldana, S.G., L.D. Sutton, B.H. Jacobson. and M.G. Quirk. "Relationships Between Leisure Time Physical Activities and Perceived Stress." *Perceptual and Motor Skills* 82.1 (1996) 315–321.

Cooper, C.L. "The Social Psychological Precursors to Cancer." *Journal of Human Stress* 10.1 (1984) 4–11.

Engstrom, T.W. and R.A. Mackenzie. *Managing Your Time*. Grand Rapids, MI: Zondervan Books, 1975.

Girdano, D.G. Everly, Jr. and D. Dusek. *Controlling Stress and Tension: A Holistic Approach*. Englewood Cliffs: Prentice Hall, 1990.

Holmes, T.H. and R.H. Rahe. "The Social Readjustment Rating Scale." *Journal of Psychometric Research*, 11 (1973) 213–218.

Hull, R.B. and S.E. Michael. "Nature Based Recreation, Mood Change, and Stress Restoration." *Leisure Sciences*. 17.1 (1995): 1–4.

McDowell, C.F. *Leisure Wellness: Coping Strategies and Managing Stress*. Eugene, Oregon: Sun Moon Press, 1983.

Pelletier, K.R. *Mind as Healer, Mind as a Slayer*. New York: Dell Publishing Co., 1977.

Robinson, J.W., R.C. and Joke DeWalle. *Stress in Community Groups*. University of Illinois, Urbana, 1975.

Selye, Hans. *The Stress of Life*. New York: McGraw-Hill, 1984.

Steinmetz, Jenny and Jon Blankenship, Linda Brown, Deborah Hall and Grace Miller. *Managing Stress before It Manages You*. Palo Alto, California: Bull Publishing Co., 1980.

CHAPTER 14

Applying Arousal Theory to the Leisure Lifestyle: The OPZ

Within recent years, I have been exploring the concept of optimal performance, and have become convinced that when people function near their optimal level, they can be said to be in the zone of optimal performance. The concept of being in a zone isn't particularly new. We often hear people who perform at a very high level as being in the zone. A person who dozes off is referred to as "zoned out." In our recently published book, Wayne Bennett and I examine optimal performance, and have coined a term to describe it--the OPZ.[1] When a person is in the OPZ remarkable things happen, and being there should be a goal of everyone. It is also remarkably close to what we refer to as a leisure lifestyle. In reviewing the concepts of sensorstasis and optimal arousal, we do so while introducing the notion of organizing one's life to maximize the probability of living in the OPZ.

There are two conditions that we all experience that are deadly: too much stimulation (anxiety) and too little stimulation (boredom). Both have serious consequences. Too much stimulation produces anxiety and leads to poor decision making, anger, defeatism, and retreat. Too little stimulation produces feelings of lethargy, disinterest, and depression. If one were too look at all of the down-time individuals experience, much of it can be explained in two terms: **suboptimal** stimulation (boredom) and **supraoptimal** stimulation (anxiety/stress). These two factors produce an effect counter to optimal arousal and for that reason we refer to the regions they occupy as the **Zones of Dysfunction** (ZOD). Between "supra-ZOD" and the "sub-ZOD" is the OPZ – the Optimal Performance Zone.

1. Ernest G. Olson and Wayne Bennett, *The OPZ.* Sacramento, CA. Teamworx Publications, 2005.

ZOD	**OPZ**	**ZOD**
Negative Outcomes	Positive Outcomes	Negative Outcomes
Supraoptimal Aroused	**Optimally Aroused**	**Suboptimally Aroused**
Out of Balance	**Balanced**	**Out of Balance**

It is in the OPZ that one experiences optimal performance and feelings of satisfaction and optimism. When one is in the OPZ, it is easy to find the balance point for any situation, the point where the level of arousal matches the demands of the situation. The balance point isn't static. It changes by situation and is largely a function of the autonomic nervous system. The autonomic nervous system has two components: the sympathetic and parasympathetic systems. The sympathetic system uses norephenepherine (NE) to stimulate the body to the "fight or flight mode." The parasympathetic employs acytelcholine (AcH) to stimulate the "relax and digest mode." NE dissipates slowly, Ach dissipates quickly. Hence, it is easier for the body to remain in a fight or flight mode than it is to relax. It is essential that the body experience both types of stimulation. An excess of one at the expense of the other invariably results in serious health consequences. Of the two, sympathetic arousal may have the most detrimental consequences. The term "burnout" is a good descriptor of what happens to a person who is subject to excessive sympathetic arousal. Over stimulation eventually results in a general breakdown of critical hormonal and chemical relationships, which in turn leads to disease, dysfunction, and death.

Where the tasks are demanding and the risks are great, it is essential that the balance point be high on the energy and focus scale. Where the demands are less, the appropriate balance point will be much lower. For example, if you are skiing at 60 miles mph down a steep slope, the optimal arousal point will be fairly high. Skiing at that speed requires attention, focus, coordination, and strength. But, later that night while trying to sleep, the optimal arousal point will be considerably lower.

For some people, it is difficult to make the shift from high arousal to low arousal, and they find themselves constantly operating at a high point on the scale. Since most of the tasks and activities that fill their time require far less energy and focus than they are giving, these individuals often suffer from burn-out and chronic stress. Again, it is about balance. High arousal is meant to be balanced by low arousal and vice-a-versa. A good indicator of whether you are at the balance point or not, is the degree to which you feel either anxious (supraoptimally aroused) or bored (suboptimally aroused). As the chart below indicates. As one moves away from the OPZ into either the supra-ZOD or the sub-ZOD, undesirable consequences follow. For example, supraoptimal arousal produces ineffective thinking and poor decision making. This is coupled with hyper-activity and high motivation results in a person who is frantic, frenetic, and frustrated. Contrast this to the sub-ZOD where lethargy and inactivity result in ineffective and lackadaisical behavior.

The Zone of Dysfunction	Optimal Performance Zone	The Zone of Dysfunction
Supraoptimal Arousal	Optimal Arousal	Suboptimal Arousal
←		→
Out of balance.	In balance.	Out of balance.
Makes mistakes.	Efficient and effective.	Makes mistakes.
Motivation lacks direction.	Appropriately motivated.	Unmotivated.
Unproductive.	Productive.	Unproductive.
Unhealthy.	Healthy.	Unhealthy.
Hyper-activity.	Optimal activity.	Hypo-activity.

We sometimes move artificially into a higher level of arousal than is appropriate. We can do this through exaggerating the importance or risk involved in a task, or we can alter our biology through external means. Drinking caffeine is one example of how we artificially move up the energy scale, and as a consequence use more of our energy than necessary. We sometimes need to be reminded that in many circumstances we can accomplish more by moving slower, and being more thoughtful and deliberate. Supraoptimal arousal confounds careful thinking and distresses the body.

For people looking for a "rule of thumb" to help them assess the degree to which they are in the OPZ, this is a good one: your body will tell you when you are approaching the ZOD. When you begin to feel uncomfortable, begin to make poor decisions, or find your focus moving away from your task, this is your body's way of calling attention to the fact that you are moving toward the ZOD. When your body sends out these signals, it is important that you take steps to change direction

In physiology, the concept of balance between and within organ systems is known as *homeostasis*. Homeostasis is essential to healthy physiological functioning. For example, cellular metabolism requires a constant supply of oxygen. When that supply is interrupted, severe consequences can arise. Denied oxygen for as few as four minutes can result in serious bodily harm, including death. Similarly, we have little tolerance for dramatic temperature change, loud sounds can deafen us, and too much light exposure can result in blindness. We live within narrow parameters, and the fundamental task of the body is to make certain that we stay within those critical boundaries. Too little of this, too much of that, and we cease to be. Balance is critical to health, wellness, and life. This concept is not limited to Western science. It is also found in Eastern philosophies.

Traditional Chinese medicine recognizes the importance of balance as well. Yin Yang Theory is the Eastern equivalent to homeostasis. From this viewpoint, too much or too little of either yin or yang energies can result in disease, dysfunction, distress, and death. For example, an excess of yang energy is the equivalent of supraoptimal arousal. A person with an excess of yang energy will be active but ineffective, will be unable to sleep, will suffer headaches, will be indecisive and often angry. A person with an excess of yin energy will be just the opposite.

A life out of balance is no different than a tightrope walker out of balance. The fall is inevitable, the consequence just as deadly.

When a person is operating within the OPZ, there are certain outcomes that are highly predictable, very desirable, and essential to all of the important goals that people, organizations, and institutions seek to achieve.

These important goals relate to the following categories: Health, Aging, Mood and Attitude, Personal Relationships, Work Environments, Problem Solving, Decision Making, Financial Success, Family Life and Parenting, and Quality of Life. Of course, there are other kinds of goals to which people aspire, but these seem to be the most common.

The OPZ applies to virtually every aspect of your life, and without exception the degree to which they are achieved can in part be measured by the extent to which a person operates within the OPZ. Contrasted with the OPZ is the ZOD—the dreaded Zone of Dysfunction. When a person operates from the ZOD health is compromised, interpersonal effectiveness is damaged, one's professional accomplishments are minimized, and the quality of life generally suffers.[2]

2. Any imbalance produces stress, and stress can result in a myriad of negative consequences.

The Three Steps Leading to the OPZ

1. Your body has a built in OPZ indicator. When you are in balance, when you are in flow, when you are functioning at an optimal level, you can feel it. You function smoothly, you think clearly, you feel positive and in balance, physiologically you feel healthy and sound, at night you rest comfortably.

   When there is too much going on, when you have taken more onto your plate than you can handle, you're body and emotions alert you.[3] A mechanism within your brain, the reticular arousal system, screens out competing stimuli so you can focus on the issues that are causing your feeling of overload. The messages reaching the hypothalamus via the reticular system and surrounding limbic portions of the brain become intense and urgent. The adrenal cortex releases floods of epinephrine, your hair stands erect, your eyes dilate, your heart pumps faster, your bronchial muscles relax to allow the intake of more oxygen, you breathe faster....you feel sick to your stomach. This is the classic *fight or flight* response, but there is no place to run, no one to fight...you sit at your desk and feel like you are going to explode. You are supraoptimally aroused, and well outside of the OPZ. You have entered the Zone of Dysfunction (ZOD).

   When the body is distressed, a series of hormonal events occur. These events are designed to enhance the survival of the individual. One of these hormonal events is the production of a hormone called cortisol. Cortisol has been somewhat vilified in the press recently, but the fact of the matter is that cortisol is absolutely essential for all metabolic functions; however, in times of distress it is produced at a higher than usual level. Should the distress continue unabated, cortisol production remains high. An excess of cortisol can have devastating effects on the human body. It can result in a depressed immune system, excessive weight gain, a decline in intellectual functioning, memory loss, and other undesirable consequences. In excess it becomes the hormone of dysfunction.

   Just as it is important to be alert for the early symptoms of supraoptimal arousal, it is equally important to be sensitive to the early signs of suboptimal arousal. Suboptimal arousal is associated with parasympathetic arousal, the so-called "rest and digest" response of the autonomic nervous system. When you feel more inclined to rest or eat than is normal for you, you might be shifting into a suboptimal level of arousal. Both circumstances link to the ZOD, and all of the negative consequences that result from being in this undesirable state. **Step one is learning to recognize when you are moving away from the OPZ and toward the ZOD.**

2. **The second step is to initiate actions that either reduce or increase the amount of stimulation associated with an activity, event, or situation, by selecting activities, events or experiences that promote personal growth and development.** As a rule of thumb remember this: When stimulation is too high, employ strategies that reduce stimulation. For example when there is too much novelty in your life, return to more familiar settings or activities. When there is too little stimulation, invoke strategies that elevate arousal or stimulation. For example, engage in activities that are challenging or innovative, activities that require behaviors that are different from your routine.[4]

   The OPZ lifestyle is about successful and effective living through systematic and sustained personal, professional, growth and development. When an activity becomes repetitious, boring, or predictable, we naturally are motivated to modify the activity or seek a new more stimulating activity. When activities

3. Listening to your body is something that is sometimes difficult to do. We find it easier to listen to others, and to ignore the messages emanating from our physical being. As a consequence, we often postpone taking steps to promote optimal performance until we have reached a point of near-collapse. The time to act is when we hear the first whisper of movement toward the ZOD.

4. In Chinese medicine, the most fundamental principle is that offered by "yin-yang theory." The essence of this theory is analogous to Western medicine's notion of homeostasis. The body is designed to function best when in homeostasis—in balance. Too much yang energy will produce burn-out; too much yin will drown a person in lethargy. Ideally, for every swing to the yang, there will be a balancing swing to the yin side. Without the complementary swing, the ZOD is inevitable.

exceed our level of development, we tend to simplify or return to more familiar environs. Too much simplicity or too great of familiarity and we are motivated to move toward greater complexity and novelty.

Understanding this process is critical for a successful lifestyle. Without understanding the OPZ philosophy, this process can result in unhealthy stimulation seeking (drugs, sensation-seeking, or entertainment), or stimulation avoidance (drugs, sensation-seeking, or entertainment). In order for one to enjoy the OPZ, the activities selected must do more than modulate sensory-stimulation and physiological arousal. OPZ activities, by definition, are those that modulate stimulation and arousal, but also contribute to personal growth and development, and by extension to a more effective, productive, and happier life.

The mechanisms that drive humans to seek optimal arousal are universal. Every healthy individual has a functioning peripheral nervous system, a reticular arousal mechanism, limbic system, and cerebral cortex. However, not everyone uses this drive to their advantage. Look around you and you will inevitably see individuals who are destroying their lives by seeking to find optimal arousal through unwise, and unhealthy, stimulus seeking. People lose themselves in mindless entertainment, gamble away their life savings, ingest foods that will ultimately kill them, and suck down drugs that rob them of their vitality and mental capabilities.

3. Once in the OPZ it is important that you stay there. The gains that come from being in the OPZ are so important that it is critical that you engage in behaviors that support continuation in the OPZ. For example, learning to be a risk taker may be helpful if you find yourself prone to suboptimal states, similarly, learning to be more creative can help as well. For those more inclined to supraoptimal states, learning to slow down, to balance work with leisure, and discovering simple pleasures are a few of the supportive behaviors that will contribute to an OPZ lifestyle.

The third step is to maintain your gains by practicing OPZ supporting behaviors.

Within recent years, there has been exciting research demonstrating an unexpected link between mind and body. It is now known that substances called "neuropeptides" have a profound impact on one's emotions and behaviors. In her book, *The Molecules of Emotion,* Dr. Candace Pert explains how old behaviors are reinforced by these "neuromodulators." The central idea of Pert's work is that the peptides that flood our bodies, in response to certain stimuli, produce both emotions and physical reactions. Old habits become linked to certain neuropeptides, which when released produce both a physical and mental reaction. When peptides associate with a positive emotion the chances of repeating that emotion are greatly enhanced. When the peptides produce a negative emotion, such as fear or guilt, the behavior tends to be avoided. For example, an embarrassing thought can produce an uncomfortable emotion along with causing the blood vessels of the face to dilate. This relationship appears to work in both directions, when certainin neuropeptides accumulate to a certain threshold, the desire to engage in an activity increases, or when the activity is engaged, neuropeptide levels increase. Dr. Pert suggests that because neuropeptides are found throughout one's anatomy, it might well be that the unconscious mind is in fact, one's body. The implication here is that by practicing OPZ behaviors, the body can begin to associate mood altering neuropeptides with the new behaviors. As this association builds, OPZ behaviors become easier and easier to demonstrate.[5] This gives new meaning to the idea that *practice* makes *perfect. It also explains why well learned responses tend to be satisfying.*

The third point cannot be overemphasized. When our bodies speak to us in the language of neuropeptides and other chemical messengers (acetycholine, biogenic amines, and amino acids),[6] the impact is profound and often enduring. Consequently, these molecules of mood have a very important function when it comes to optimal performance. The emotion or mood you experience when faced with a situation is an indica-

5. For more see Candace Pert, *The Molecules of Emotion*, NY: Scribner, 1997.

6. When a chemical transmits a message from one neuron to another via electrical current, it is called a "neurotransmitter." When it flows through the blood, it is called a hormone. Many chemicals are both hormones and neurotransmitters. Many are associated with specific emotional responses.

tor as to where your are in relationship to the OPZ. In short, those feelings that seem to arise from the unconscious mind are there for a very important reason. They are there for our survival. If a certain behavior produces feelings of anxiety, guilt or fear, those feelings are telling us something important. They associate with being unprepared, or taking too big of a risk, or having insufficient skills for a given task, or lacking sufficient experience for the situation at hand. In situations where you are clearly up to the task, have had adequate experience to meet a challenge, and possess the necessary skills to do so successfully, your mood will be substantially different and much more positive.

Ultimately, the release of chemical messengers is determined by a triggering mechanism—a form of stimulus that stimulates the production of, for example, a particular peptide.[7] The burst of energy a runner gets after a period of sustained running is the result of sustained aerobic exercise triggering the release of endorphin.[8] This accounts for the so-called *runner's high*. But, as any runner knows, if you run too long, you lose the high and begin to experience pain. When the body becomes distressed, another neuropeptide begins to accumulate to the point that it overwhelms the effects of the endorphin. This neuropeptide, called *substance P,* uses pain to remind the body that it is moving toward the ZOD. By paying attention to the message communicated by substance P a runner can avoid serious injury.

Chemical messengers can be triggered by simply thinking about an activity or an object. Try this experiment: Visualize a fresh, bright yellow lemon.

1. Now visualize cutting the lemon in half.
2. In your mind, study the freshly cut lemon.
3. Visualize taking a deep breath. Can you smell the aroma of the lemon.
4. Now see yourself bringing the lemon to your mouth.
5. Imagine squeezing the fresh lemon juice onto your tongue.

How does your mouth feel? Can you feel a tingling in your cheeks? Did you salivate? Most people get a profound biological response when going through this exercise. Thinking about any forthcoming challenging experience can also have an effect on one's biology. Visualizing any activity for which one is not prepared can produce anxiety, stomach discomfort, and distraction. Conversely, seeing yourself succeed in some activity will produce chemical messengers that link to positive emotions. **Learning to view yourself as a successful accomplished person is one of the fundamental principles of achieving an OPZ lifestyle**, which another way of saying a **healthy leisure lifestyle**. It is an essential precursor to actual engagement in the direct learning or behavior change process.

Think of the various conversations you have had with yourself in the last twenty-four hours. How many times did you convince yourself not to try something new, accept a challenge or opportunity, or disqualify yourself from an experience because you didn't feel up to the task? Probably more than you care to admit. These negative thoughts tend to be self-reinforcing because they stimulate the production of messenger chemicals that associate with negative emotions until the challenging idea is rejected and replaced with messenger chemical that produces the "whew, I'm glad I'm not going to have to do that" response. With repetition these kinds of thoughts become easier and easier, and avoidance of growth producing activities less likely. On the other hand, entertaining positive thoughts in a logical and increasingly complex manner enhances the probability of producing moods that motivate and support growth and development.

In building an OPZ lifestyle, we need to learn to develop OPZ skills, attitudes, and behaviors. These in turn need to associate with chemical messengers that have the capacity to reinforce and encourage the new behaviors. To accomplish this one must have a vision of what is to be accomplished, and the willingness to invest time and energy in slowly developing the appropriate knowledge, skills, and behaviors. When the pace

7. Peptides are essentially chains of amino acids. Relatively short in molecular terms, they contain between three and forty amino acids. "Neuropeptides" are amino acid chains that are associated with the transmission of an action potential (a weak electrical charge) between neurons. When serving in this function, neuropeptides are classified as neurotransmitters.

8. Endorphins work by blocking Substance P which stimulates the perception of pain.

is right, the development will occur within the OPZ, and the experience will be self-reinforcing. For, example, new behaviors and attitudes are analogous to learning a new language. If the pace is appropriate, and the learning schedule followed, the new language will be learned. Move too quickly and frustration will result, too slowly and boredom follows.

Whenever anyone sets out to change a behavior, acquire a new skill, or information set, there is always the possibility of becoming discouraged. This can be a direct result of failing to stay within the OPZ, but it also can be related to unrealistic expectations, lack of motivation, or lack of self-discipline. Each of these are critical elements in the development of an OPZ lifestyle. **You must want to succeed, have a vision of that means, and have the self discipline to engage in OPZ supporting internal dialogues and practical behaviors (the practice part).**

In life, you are either moving forward or falling back,
there is no such thing as standing still. —Louise Williams

CHAPTER 15

A Leisure Lifestyle

Everyone has a lifestyle. The transient lifestyle centers on travel, austere living circumstance, and occasional brushes with the law. On the other extreme, we find people like Rush Limbaugh and Oprah whose lifestyles center around travel, luxurious living, and occasional brushes with commoners. Most lifestyles fall in between these two extremes. One thing is certain, whether rich or poor, everyone has a lifestyle.

Lifestyle is essentially a social science concept. It refers to the amalgamation of one's beliefs, dreams, values and behaviors. It summarizes the characteristic approach that one takes to life. It is both a psychological and sociological concept. On one hand it may refer specifically to an individual, on the other, to the group that an individual is most closely associated. William D. Wells summarizes this notion thusly:

> Lifestyle is a social science concept connecting the totality of behaviors which comprise the characteristic approach of life of a particular individual or group (22).
>
> The psychological variable—essentially, what kind of an individual a person is, how he sees himself—are the other side of the coin of the sociological concept (23).

A leisure lifestyle, of course, refers to a pattern of behavior that is a manifestation of one's respect for and commitment to leisure values. A leisure lifestyle is, in many respects, the antithesis of a work-ethic lifestyle, which espouses values of hard work and self-sacrifice. As to which lifestyle is best is ultimately a philosophical issue. However, as was pointed out earlier, there are many important scientific findings to commend the leisure lifestyle. For example, it can be demonstrated that people who embrace a leisure lifestyle tend to be more productive, healthier, happier, and age more successfully, than people who subscribe to a work-oriented lifestyle.

If the heart of lifestyle is values, then the extent that you are able to alter your values, is the extent that you will alter the nature of your lifestyle. Certainly, early in one's life, lifestyle is largely a product of other people. As you mature and gain increasing control of your life's path, control of your own lifestyle increasingly becomes a matter of choice. Ultimately, regardless of the circumstances of your youth, you are responsible for your lifestyle.

Some people claim that change is something difficult to control Some even argue that change in basic lifestyles seldom occurs. Arthur Mitchell, following an extensive study of lifestyles in America, challenges this belief. He contends that people change constantly, and that they control the direction of change through the values and beliefs they choose to adopt. As he puts it:

> More than anything else, we are what we believe, what we dream, what we value. For the most part, we try to mold our lives to make our beliefs and dreams come true. And in our attempts to

> reach our goals, we test ourselves again and again in diverse ways, and in so doing, we grow. . . Most experience one or two periods when what is most important, most beautiful, most compelling shifts from one comprehensive pattern to another. These are times when a person's values change—and lifestyles are transformed (19).

A leisure lifestyle is a way of living characterized by intrinsic motivation and perceived freedom. It does not imply idleness nor laziness, but rather is likely to place value on creativity and self-actualization. As previously shown in other units, lifestyles based on leisure values are associated with health, productivity, happiness, and successful aging.

Change

The ultimate decision as to lifestyle choice rests with you. There is no reason to continue to embrace values and beliefs that are founded on misinformation and that are clearly to your detriment. The precursor to change is knowledge, but education alone will not produce a lifestyle change. Clare Graves (1967) argues that change in lifestyle only occurs when the following three conditions are met:

1. **Deep dissatisfaction.**
2. **Physical and psychological energy.**
3. **Insight as to what change will help.**

Graves also points out that there are certain **categories of influence** governing whether people change or do not change. These include **events and circumstances** that alter lives such as accidents or windfalls. **Age** produces certain biological changes, values shift, and in many cases financial resources increase, and of course as these variables change so do lifestyles. For some people, **family history and cultural traditions** prove obstacles to change. **Unresolved childhood issues** may also serve to make it difficult to change certain behaviors and/or attitudes. As society evolves, so to the paradigms (models) valued by society. **Changing paradigms** often lead to change in lifestyle.

The Christmas Season is a repeating **circumstance** which invariably alters my behavior. At Christmas I eat more empty calories than at anytime of the year. It is a family **tradition**. Invariably my weight goes up a pound or two and by New Year's Day I'm ready to alter my behavior in order to lose the holiday pounds. Changing paradigms play a role too. I have noticed that my interest in computers and particularly electronic communication competes with my interest in pursuing more physically challenging activities. The net (perhaps that should be "Internet") result is that the pounds seem to come on more easily, and activity requires more discipline. I can understand how some people can give up the "active lifestyle" for one more sedentary, but thus far, I have managed to offset the inactivity associated with computer use and the consumption of Christmas splurging by programming physically active events into my lifestyle. Usually, by February I am back on track.

A more dramatic example of change is found in the life of a friend of mine who changed his lifestyle from that of a drug addict to that of a successful and responsible citizen. He changed **paradigms**. He was a young father, and although he professed love for his daughters, he rarely demonstrated it. One day following a particularly woeful weekend of drug induced debauchery, he realized how far he was away from being the kind of father he wanted his children to have. He decided to change. He joined a support group, enrolled in a job training program, found a job, became active in a church group, and started a fitness program. Today he is clean, successful, and a wonderful father to his two teenage daughters. He will tell you that a lifestyle is something you can change. It is entirely up to you.

The American Lifestyles

Mitchell conducted a major survey of contemporary American lifestyles. Following his analysis, he identified nine distinct typologies. These typologies provide us with a useful frame of reference to begin our discussion on lifestyles. It can be seen that some of them lend themselves to leisure more than others, some are far removed from what might be considered a leisure lifestyle, others come quite close to meeting the criteria of perceived freedom and intrinsic motivation. Although Mitchell published his study in 1983, it still provides a useful model from which to launch a discussion of lifestyles in the United States. Some of the percentages may have changed, but it is likely that many of the categories persist. Following is a summary of Mitchell's findings.

The Value and Lifestyle Typology

Need-Driven Groups

1. **Survivor Lifestyle:** just make it from day-to-day . . . survive. Old intensely poor, fearful . . . about 4% of the adult U.S. population.
2. **Sustainer Lifestyle:** Sustain and solidify gains from survivor phase. Angry resentful, street-wise, edge of poverty . . . about 7%

Outer-Directed Groups

3. **Belonger Lifestyle:** Central concern . . . fitting in with clearly defined group or social network. Conventional middle Americans . . . about 35%.
4. **Emulator Lifestyle:** Central concern . . . breaking free of the local network or system, to make it as an individual in the greater system, emulating leaders of the system. Young, ambitious . . . flashy . . . about 9%.
5. **Achiever Lifestyle:** Central concern . . . achievement, success, leadership, and power in the major system. Middle aged, prosperous, self-assured . . . about 22%.

Inner-Directed Groups

6. **I-Am-Me:** Concerned with breaking free of outer-directed patterns. Usually young, narcissistic, impulsive, exhibitionist. A transitional state to Inner Direction . . . 5% of the population.
7. **Experimental:** Concerned with living intensely, vividly, and experimentally, so as to deepen the inner experience . . . about 7%.
8. **Societally Conscious:** Concerned with social issues, primarily of a non-material nature. Mission-oriented, mature, successful, out to change the world . . . about 8% of the adult U.S. population.

The Combined Outer and Inner-Directed Group

9. Psychologically mature, tolerant, understanding, flexible, able to see the "big picture." Concerned with melding outer and inner perspective so as to combine the best of the two into higher order views . . . 3%.

By evaluating each of Mitchell's typologies using Neulinger's criteria of leisure (perceived freedom and intrinsic motivation) we can hypothesize the extent to which Mitchell's typologies relate to a leisure lifestyle. For example, it can be reasonably assumed that an individual who is living on a survival basis will have little opportunity for discretionary experiences, will have fewer opportunities for flow experiences, will have a limited sense of perceived freedom, and will experience little intrinsic satisfaction. On the other hand the individual who has the resources, status, education, and opportunities necessary for self-directed activity will have more opportunities to experience significant intrinsic satisfaction and perceived freedom. The following chart is a summary of the presumed relationship between nine American lifestyles and leisure.

A Conceptual Relationship of Leisure to Mitchell's Nine American Lifestyles

	Lifestyle	Motivation		Perceived Freedom	
		Intrinsic	Extrinsic	Freedom	Constraint
1.	Survivor	Very low	Very high	Very low	Very high
2.	Sustainer	Low	High	Low	High
3.	Belonger	Low/Moderate	High/Moderate	Low/Moderate	High/Moderate
4.	Emulator	High/Moderate	High	High/Moderate	Moderate
5.	Achiever	High/Moderate	High	Very High	Low/Moderate
6.	I-Am-Me	High	Moderate	High	Low
7.	Experimental	High	Low	High	Low
8.	Societally	Very High	Low	High	Low
9.	Integrated	Very High	Low	Very High	Low

This exercise serves two important functions: (1) it illustrates that all lifestyles possess elements of leisure, and (2) it demonstrates that the concept of a leisure lifestyle can overlap other lifestyle models. In regards to the idea that all lifestyles possess some leisure, it should be noted that as a state of mind, leisure may be experienced in even the most demanding or austere lifestyles; however, the probability is good that where circumstances limit one's options, perceived freedom is usually limited. In addition, research suggests that even though money is not a strong predictor of happiness, too little money predisposes one to feelings of dissatisfaction and helplessness. Furthermore, current research shows an inverted relationship between free time and life satisfaction. (Iso-Ahola, 386) i.e., where an individual has either too many demands on his time or too little, the net result is feelings of dissatisfaction or unhappiness. If a transient's lifestyle is characterized by minimum demands on his/her time, it can be assumed that the net result would be feelings of boredom and dissatisfaction. As George Bernard Shaw said, "a perpetual holiday, is a working class definition of hell."

In regards to the second point, it is important to recognize that what from one prospective might legitimately be viewed as a leisure lifestyle, that same lifestyle when measured against other criteria might be categorized differently. For example, when I was a college student, I would buy gasoline from Crouch's Service Station. Every week for a year I stopped in at Crouch's Station to fill up. Gas was only 19 cents for a gallon, and in those days they checked your tires, your oil, and shined your windows. And, everytime I stopped at the station I would visit with Mr. Crouch. He was well into his 70's, and he loved visiting with customers. He particularly seemed to enjoy sharing his philosophy of life with younger generations, which meant almost everyone. Although, some might have referred to him as a workaholic or as having succumbed to the Puritan work ethic, (something not uncommon to his generation), from my perspective he was living a leisure lifestyle. He worked at his own pace, he clearly received intrinsic satisfaction from serving others, his customers provided him with stimulating conversations and occasional opportunities for creative problem solving.

Whether Mr. Crouch viewed his lifestyle as one of leisure, only he could answer. Were he here, I am certain he would love to discuss it. Without his input, I can only rely on my perceptions, which lead me to believe that Mr. Crouch lived a lifestyle rich in perceived freedom and intrinsic motivation—the fundamental ingredients to the leisure lifestyle. The critical point here is that the leisure lifestyle is more a function of one's state of mind than any other single ingredient (Neulinger 23). However, it also must be pointed out that there are several credible ideas as to what factors contribute to the probability of a person developing such an outlook. In the next section we will explore some of these ideas.

Nash's Pyramid: Creativity and Action—The Keys to Leisure

In a discussion of the leisure lifestyle, I think it is important to re-examine J.B. Nash's "Pyramid." As you may recall from an earlier chapter, Nash was a philosopher and educator who viewed leisure as characterized by activities ranging from the mundane to the sublime. According to Nash, the highest order of leisure is manifest by involvement in creative activity. This relates well to Neulinger's notion that associates pure leisure with high levels of perceived freedom and intrinsic reward. The least effective use of leisure is found in spectator activities. Nash also includes in his model activities that are harmful to self and society. These he refers to as negative leisure and argues that when society fails in socializing people for leisure, negative behaviors result. One of my professors, Israel Heaton, termed these negative leisure behaviors "wreckreation."

In developing a leisure lifestyle, Nash would have us evaluate our leisure activities in terms of the extent to which they lead to creativity. The fundamental assumption is that creative activities promote greater life satisfaction and happiness than lower order activities. Furthermore, we should be reminded that creative activities are not limited to recreational activities. Creativity is possible in almost any human activity. If Nash is correct, then the application of creative thinking to any task can enhance the probability of such an experience acquiring the characteristics of leisure. When we find ourselves thinking that we can find happiness through spectator activities or inactivity, we would be advised to remember the following message from John W. Gardiner:

> Storybook happiness involves a bland idleness; the truer conception involves seeking and purposeful effort. Storybook happiness involves every form of pleasant thumb-twiddling; true happiness involves the full use of one's powers and talents (121).

When people think of a leisure lifestyle they often visualize a life of luxury, a life characterized by limited responsibility, their needs well met and their cares few. Such a life may be pleasant for a short period of time, but soon it would grow boring (Morris, 147). Far greater satisfaction comes from a commitment to a lifestyle which, instead of insulating one from life, places value on making life more satisfying through creative engagement with it in all of its diverse aspects. Nash argued that life can only be fully enjoyed when it is being fully lived. In many respects this notion is similar to Maslow's idea of self-actualization—a theory that argues that people have an inherent need to organize their lives in such a manner as to achieve their highest potentials. As Maslow put it, "What a man can be, he must be" (46). In the next section we examine self-actualization as a contributing element in the leisure lifestyle.

Self-Actualization: A Function of Intrinsic Motivation in a Perceptually Free Context

The concept of human needs as an underlying motivator of human behavior is a clearly established psychological concept (Iso-Ahola 23). One of the most widely held theories regarding human needs and behavior is that of Abraham Maslow. His classification of human needs appears as a five-fold hierarchy. These needs are: (1) physiological needs, (2) safety needs, (3) social needs, (4) ego needs, and (5) the need for self-actualization. The needs are ranked in order of primacy with physiological needs placed at the bottom of the hierarchy. Physiological needs refer to food, air, water, and the protection of the body from the elements. Safety needs relate to the need for self-preservation and self-protection. Safety needs include both emotional needs for safety as well as the more apparent physical needs. Attacks on one's emotional self may actually be more devastating than a physical attack, and sometimes can have consequences of greater duration (254). Safety and physiological needs are considered the **primary needs**.

Social needs are those that are rooted in the interrelationship with others. They include love, affection, acceptance, belonging, and respect. "Ego needs" relates to how an individual is perceived by others. Maslow believed that people needed not only to look good to others, but most importantly, people need to look good to themselves. When one's self-esteem is attacked or twarted, the end result can be damaging. Feelings of inferiority, weakness, and helplessness can result. By developing a strong self-image, one is likely to experience feelings of self-worth, self-confidence, strength, capability, and a general feeling of satisfaction (255).

Self-actualization refers to an individual's need to evolve forward in a way that increases the likelihood of achieving one's potentials. To be self-actualized is to have become what one is best suited for. Naturally, what constitutes self-actualization varies from one person to another and is not limited to one field of endeavor. It spans all aspects of life, work, interpersonal relationships, leisure, recreation and so on. In addition to this need for self-actualization Maslow believed that we have other needs. These he named **metaneeds.** Metaneeds refer to an individual's desire to understand his/her environment and life experiences. It explains why some people use their free time to go back to school, read, and do independent research. Although not essential to survival, Maslow argued that the satisfaction of metaneeds brought more profound happiness than lower needs.

Implicit in Maslow's theory is the idea that the higher one moves up the hierarchy the less one experiences dissatisfaction. In other words personal happiness, according to Maslow is directly tied to the extent that one is able to achieve self-actualization. It can be inferred from the epigenetic nature of the hierarchy, that as one moves progressively up the "needs-ladder" one acquires greater perceived freedom and potential for intrinsic activity. Thus, we see a strong connection between the leisure lifestyle, self-actualization, and the fulfillment of metaneeds. Of course, this idea draws our attention to the connection between leisure and happiness.

> Happiness is the interval between periods of unhappiness.
>
> —Don Marquis

Boyfriend: Oh, sweetheart, I will be so unhappy and miserable all the while I am away from you this semester. . . .

Girlfriend: Oh, my darling, if I could only be certain of that it would make me so happy.

Understanding Happiness: Clues to a Leisure Lifestyle

What is happiness? Everyone seems to know what it is, everyone seems to want it, but how do you define it? The dictionary defines it as "the state of being happy," which then can be defined as the state of being "delighted, pleased or glad." Albert Schweitzer defined it as, "nothing more than good health and a poor memory." To Margaret Lee Runbeck happiness is "not a state to arrive at, but a manner of traveling." To Thomas Jefferson it meant to "not be pained in body or troubled in mind." To Mark Twain it was ". . . a good book, good friends and a sleepy conscience." Regardless of how one defines it, most of us would agree, without it, a leisure lifestyle is impossible. In this section, we turn our attention to studies dealing with happiness in hopes that we can further our understanding of the leisure lifestyle.

In 1975 Angus Campbell and his associates conducted a national survey to determine how people felt about the quality of their lives. Following is a summary of Campbell's findings:

1. Among the more revealing findings of the study was the fact that of those surveyed *single women of all ages were happier and more satisfied than single men.*
2. Fewer than 10% of all those surveyed described their lives in negative terms.
3. *Married people generally showed higher levels of satisfaction than the unmarried.* Of all Americans, married couples in their twenties were the happiest. However, this does not mean that marriage makes people happy, rather it might be the result of happy people tending to marry. We'll examine this idea shortly.

4. Young wives reported less stress after marriage than before, while young husbands showed an increase in stress. Divorced women with children showed the lowest levels of satisfaction.
5. Childless husbands showed higher satisfaction than other men in their age range; while their wives showed satisfaction equal to that of women of the same age who did have children.

It is clear through Campbell's study that companionship is an important ingredient to happiness. As Ernest Jones said, "A person can't be happy without a companion, that's why God created the dog." But companionship is not the only ingredient to happiness, other studies have suggested additional relationships.

In 1985 Johnathon Freedman, social psychologist, reviewed empirical data regarding happiness and life satisfaction. His findings in many respects support Campbell's findings as well as dispel some of the more common ideas about happiness. Wayne Weiten summarizes Freedman's findings as follows:

> Many factors that were commonly believed to be crucial to one's sense of well-being appear to bear only a slight relation to general happiness.
>
> **Money.** Money is important only when you don't have it. People at the very bottom of the economic ladder are relatively unhappy. However, once you ascend above the poverty level, there is little relation between income and happiness. In this modern era of voracious consumption, most of us find a way to spend all of our money. Wealthy people are no happier than the middle classes.
>
> **Health.** The situation is essentially the same in regard to physical health. Very poor health makes it difficult (although not impossible) to be happy, but good health does not, by itself, produce happiness. It appears that most people take their good health for granted.
>
> **Age.** It has been suggested that adolescence is both a time for fun and a period of turmoil, self-doubt, and misery. Neither of these assertions can be confirmed. Generally, age and happiness are found to be unrelated. The only exception involved old age, and here the findings were mixed. After age 65 the number of people who report themselves as unhappy increases. Surprisingly however, so does the number of people who say they are **very happy**.
>
> **Parenthood.** Although children can be a tremendous source of joy and fulfillment, they can also be a tremendous source of headaches and hassles. Apparently, the good and bad aspects of parenthood cancel each other out, because the evidence indicates that having children does not appreciably influence the happiness of most people.
>
> **Community.** When asked where they would most like to live, people showed a clear preference for the stereotype of the tranquil, pastoral life believed to exist in rural areas. However, when actual reported happiness was related to community type, it was found people living in urban suburban and rural areas were equally happy.
>
> **Religion.** Although members of the clergy reported themselves as exceptionally happy, religious convictions were not a major determinant of happiness for most people. Atheists were as happy as conventional religious believers. Moreover, even the belief in an afterlife did not enhance people's happiness.

However, a more recent study by Ellison (1991) suggests that religiousity does have an impact on a person's level of happiness. It was demonstrated that people with strong religious convictions generally express greater levels of personal happiness. It can be hypothesized that religiousity might lessen the impact of otherwise disorganizing events in a person's life. This notion is supported by Larson's 1989 study on the relationship of internal control and happiness. Larson found that individuals who reported "being in control of their lives" also reported higher than average levels of happiness. It is reasonable to assume, that for some people, religion provides a sense of direction and the ability to accept trauma and disorganizing events in a philosophical and peace inducing fashion. For others, religion may make little contribution to feelings of happiness. And, for others, religion might be so restrictive and demanding that it detracts from one's feelings of being in control. In short, the data on this point is conflicting, and as such it is difficult to make a firm statement regarding the relationship of religion to happiness. I won't try to advise you here, this is a very personal matter. The relationship of happiness and religion in your life is one that only you can explore.

> The more complex a religion, the more human imagination went into it.
>
> —O'Brien's Rule

Sex. Generally, sex is like money; it has a significant impact on your happiness only if you don't have any. Frequency of sexual encounters and number of sexual partners were unrelated to level of happiness. Running counter to the idea that sex is essential to happiness is the fact that many people choose abstinence. Heymann (1991) estimates that over 40,000,000 American adults practice celibacy. The data suggests that the quality of one's sex life is more important than quantity (at least for women). Among females, the report of specific sexual problems (mostly the inability to achieve orgasm) was related to being less happy. However, reports of males and their specific sexual problems were not related to lower levels of happiness. Homosexuals were found to be just as happy as heterosexuals (Weiten 24–25).

Freedman's findings counter many of the common notions regarding happiness. Money is a good example. Many people structure their lifestyle around the acquisition of money with the misguided idea that one can buy happiness. Years ago, I reminded a materialistic friend of this by saying, "Remember, money can't buy happiness." He responded quickly, "That may be true, but more important is the fact that happiness can't buy money." He was one of those people who subscribed to the idea that the person who dies with the most toys wins, naturally his lifestyle reflected that philosophy. He worked hard, acquired many material possessions, but rarely did I see him enjoy the fruits of his labors. As Hobart Brown said, "Money can't buy you happiness, but it can buy you the misery you prefer."

Well, if money, health, age, parenthood, community, and religion were not viewed by Freedman as very good predictors of happiness, what is? Freedman identified three factors which showed a strong positive correlation to happiness: (1) love, (2) marriage, and (3) work.

While sex may be of only marginal importance when it comes to happiness, love, is viewed by almost everyone as very important. Weiten points out that the single thing that would most contribute to their lives was love (25). Once the domain of poets and writers, love has recently come under the province of social science. Although, not easily defined or investigated, it appears that the human need for intimacy is very strong, and when denied it produces feelings of stress and unhappiness (Santrock 514). So strong is the need for intimacy that people in unhealthy relationships are often afraid to leave their partner for fear of being alone. In order for a love relationship to be healthy and fulfilling, Santrock says that it must include emotional security, respect, communication, help, play behaviors, sexual intimacy, and loyalty (515). If these are the ingredients for a successful love relationship, and if love is an important factor in general happiness and life satisfaction, then it is important that we learn how to develop and nourish loving relationships. Robert Browning the famous poet said, "Take love away and our earth is a tomb." Franklin Jones put it this way, "Love doesn't make the world go round. Love is what makes the ride worthwhile."

Marriage appears to be a significant determinant of happiness. A 1995 study by Nock supports these findings. In Nock's study, he found that married couples reported greater levels of happiness than unmarried cohabiting couples. Quality of one's marriage was also shown to be a powerful predictor of happiness in a 1994 study by Russell and Wells. In spite of the large number of people getting divorced; overall, marriage is a strong predictor of general happiness. This is not surprising when one considers that the essential element in the marriage relationship is love. People possessing a healthy relationship can learn to live together in a mutually fulfilling fashion. Naturally, couples who fail to communicate effectively, fail to demonstrate loyalty, and/or fail to provide emotional security for one another—may ultimately find their marriage leading to divorce. As Raymond Hull once said, "All marriages are happy. It's the living together that causes all the trouble." Couples who have learned how to love effectively are quite likely also capable of learning how to live together. These are couples who have learned the great secret of a successful marriage, which according to Harold Nicholson ". . . is to treat all disasters as incidents and none of the incidents as disasters." (Peters 321)

The following notes on the "Ties that Bind" were excerpted from an article by Dr. Diane Colansanto and James Shriver, "Marriage and Divorce American Style," in *The Sacramento Bee*, Saturday, May 6, 1989:

> If you've ever been married, the odds are now 50-50 that you've either been divorced, separated or seriously close to separation. If you're between the ages of 35 and 54, those odds increase to two out of three because you are part of a generation that ushered in the largest increase in divorce ever recorded. These are among the most disturbing findings of an in-depth Gallup study of marriage and divorce in America.
>
> Gallup studied the experience and beliefs of a nationally representative sample of 1,000 adults who have been married at some point in their lives. The survey portrays a nation in which marital disruption is almost as common as marital stability, and in which divorce and separation have become endemic. Key findings include:
>
> - Women are more likely than men to be unhappy in their marriages and are much more likely to initiate the process of separation that leads to divorce.
> - Religion enhances marital stability for adults at all ages. Individuals who claim that religion plays a very important role in their lives are much less likely to experience severe marital discord.
> - Personality differences and incompatibility are the leading causes of divorce. Specific problems such as drug and alcohol abuse, infidelity, physical mistreatment and financial disputes are far less often cited as causes of divorce.
> - Doomed marriages typically reveal themselves within the first few years of marriage, but premarital educational courses don't seem particularly effective in forestalling divorce.
> - Trial marriages do not appear to affect rates of marital harmony. But couples who had a long dating period are more likely to have stable marriages.
> - Despite the obvious emotional strain involved in going through a divorce, the overwhelming majority of divorced people feel they made the right choice, rejecting the idea that things would have been better for them if they had stayed married. Similarly, people who weathered a period of severe discord in their marriages and stayed together also affirm their decision.

Job Satisfaction and Happiness

Job satisfaction also appears important to general happiness. It is interesting to note that although work was viewed as related to happiness by all people, work was less correlated with married people than single people. In other words, single people rely more on their jobs for feeling of satisfaction than married people. Similarly, single people tend to value their leisure activities more than married people (Iso-Ahola 388). Freedman reports a high correlation between job status and happiness. However, he also points out that some professions associated with high status were inversely related to happiness. His research suggests that physicians and lawyers may be less happy than other high status professionals. Although one's job holds the potential for feelings of satisfaction, it should be noted that jobs that are relatively devoid of perceived freedom and intrinsic motivation are generally viewed as dull and unrewarding. Furthermore, in highly competitive organizations, the constant need to improve, to do better than one's colleagues, can contribute to frustration and anxiety. Happiness on the job may only occur when one is freed from having to constantly compete for ever decreasing positions (there can only be one chief executive officer). J. Laurence Peter may have the solution to this problem. In his book, *The Peter Principle*, he examines how an overly competitive environment can lead to unhappiness. In summarizing this book he says the following:

> I showed how an individual within a hierarchy tends to rise to his or her level of incompetence. I called this concept a principle, not a law, because it was neither universal, immutable, nor inevitable. It only described a tendency of an individual to climb or be pushed from one level of competence to the next until arrival at the level of incapacity. Unfortunately, this is where he or she usually remains, frustrating co-workers, eroding efficiency, or at the highest level, leading the country into one disaster after another (16).

The Peter Principle gives added strength to the old adage, "Quit while you are ahead." Peter actually suggests that rather than quitting you practice **creative incompetence** (132). Here the strategy is to give the appearance of having already achieved your level of incompetence, thus preventing any further promotions, but without the negative side of actual incompetence. Actual incompetence is a key ingredient to unhappiness whereas perceived competence is viewed as a critical ingredient to perceived freedom (Iso-Ahola 197) and thus the leisure lifestyle. What the Peter Principle advocates is creative incompetence, that is the ability to learn to conduct your work responsibilities in a way that places the focus on the quality of the work, not the extrinsic reward associated with it.

The importance workers hold for perceived competence is suggested in the work of Renwick and Lawler (1978) who following an extensive survey of workers' perception of factors contributing to job satisfaction identified the following factors as most important:

1. Opportunities to do things that contribute to one's self-esteem.
2. Opportunities to accomplish something worthwhile.
3. Opportunities to acquire new knowledge and/or skill.
4. Opportunities for perceived freedom on the job.
5. Opportunities to do things you do best.

Godbey (1985) citing the work of Parker points out that job satisfaction was linked with the following six elements:

1. The opportunity to create a product of some sort,
2. Demonstrating a skill,
3. Working at one's own pace and not being arbitrarily slowed,
4. Being able to demonstrate initiative and responsibility,
5. Socializing with others,
6. Working with competent people.

The same study revealed five factors associated with unhappiness on the job:

1. Too much repetition,
2. Too much specialization,
3. Doing useless tasks,
4. A sense of insecurity,
5. Too much scrutiny and supervision. (96)

In a 1995 study by Noor, it was demonstrated that work support and locus of control has a significant impact on the extent to which women experienced job satisfaction. It further suggested that when commensurate to ability, job challenge interacted favorably with locus of control and work support in predicting feelings of happiness. It appears that jobs which are characterized by appropriate challenge, support and locus of control contribute to one's feelings of happiness and well-being.

Central to all of the above regarding job satisfaction is the notion of **competence**, which is defined essentially as **the ability to bring about a desired change in one's environment**. The extent to which one perceives himself or herself free to demonstrate competence in the workplace is dependent upon such factors as the following: the skills possessed by the worker, the demands of the task, and the social constraints imposed upon the worker by the organization. When these factors coalesce in such a way as to **create an optimum work environment**, one critical result is a feeling of satisfaction. These are the essential conditions if one's work is to contribute to his or her personal happiness.

Choosing a career is one of the most important things you will do. You will be at it for a long time, and a very large percentage of your life will be spent doing it. It is important to choose a career that you enjoy and one that will produce feelings of happiness and satisfaction.

> "Work is the refuge of those who have nothing better to do."
>
> —Oscar Wilde

The Freedman Study Summarized

In putting Freedman's study into perspective, Weiten draws the following conclusions:

1. **There is no simple recipe for happiness.**

   > "Alas, the one overwhelming finding of all the research is there is no easy solution for finding it. I can suggest no religious beliefs, mystical practices. . . meditative exercises. . . strange diets, biofeedback or system of philosophy that will produce happiness" (26).

2. He further concludes that happiness is largely a matter of **attitude or perspective**. He says that people who tend to compare their status against those of slightly higher status will invariably feel lacking. Rarely do we compare ourselves with those less fortunate than ourselves. Rather, we tend to constantly try to keep up with the Joneses. Furthermore we constantly compare ourselves against our expectations. When we exceed our expectations we tend to feel satisfied, when we fall short we feel unhappy (26).

3. The good news is that Freedman believes that happiness is never hopeless. As Weiten states:

   > There is nothing, short of terminal illness—no setback, shortcoming, difficulty, or inadequacy—that makes happiness impossible. The evidence indicates that some people find happiness in spite of seemingly insurmountable problems. Unhappy children often become happy adults. Although Freedman was unable to discover any simple shortcuts to happiness, he did find that this important goal is not beyond the grasp of any of us. No matter how unhappy you might be presently, you can still realistically nurture the hope that someday your pursuit of happiness will bring fulfillment (27).

Myers, and Diener in 1995 reviewed a large number of studies and drew a similar conclusion—happiness is available to most people, regardless of their circumstances. They observed four inner traits that seem to relate to happiness: (1) self-esteem or feelings of self-worth, (2) sense of personal control, (3) an optimistic attitude, and (4) extroversion. Also in 1995, Greenwald and Schwartz surveyed the literature and concluded that there were six elements essential to happiness: (1) self-knowledge, (2) self-esteem, (3) positive thinking, (4) personal control, (5) healthy social relations, and (6) spirituality and transcendence.

Happiness is a goal universally sought by humanity. So important was it to our founding fathers that it was declared an "inalienable right." Born in the midst of political revolution, this notion is a guiding principle in our modern republican form of government. It remains an essential element in the philosophy of "democratic idealism" and is the **most fundamental manifestation** of the leisure lifestyle.

Other Research Findings on Happiness

Personality and Happiness

Some people seem to weather tough times better than others. Some people just seem born to be happy. In a study of the relationship of personality to happiness, Brebner, Kirby, Donaldson, and Ward found that there was a significant relationship between extraversion and happiness, and a significant relationship between unhappiness and neuroticism. Their results confirm other studies which suggest that basic personality structure is related to a person's tendency to be happy. People who are extraverted seem to report more happiness than introverted or neurotic individuals.

Special Events Don't Affect General Happiness

The "if only" events of life don't seem directly related to long term happiness. Even though most of us think happiness would be ours if we could win the lottery, own a certain type of car or look a certain way, evidence to the contrary is rather convincing. The most telling study involved 22 lottery winners, 22 controls and 29 accident victims. Both groups represented people who had experienced major unexpected changes in their lives. The accident victims were disabled by their accidents; the winners became rich overnight. A year after their winning or their accident, these people were asked questions about their present and expected future happiness. The researchers found no significant difference between the winners and controls, and no difference between the three groups in terms of expected happiness (Brickman, Coates and Janoff-Bullman 1978). In a study conducted in 1991, Diener, Colvin, Pavot, and Allman found evidence that support these earlier findings. In trying to understand why intense positive experiences are not greater contributors to happiness, they concluded that intense positive events may have consequences and costs that counterbalance the positive outcomes. They observed that the key to happiness or "affective-well being" seems not to be in intensity, but rather in the frequency of positive experiences.

People Generally View Themselves as Happy

Findings dating back as far as 30 years (Goldings, 1954) support the idea that under most circumstances, people tend to see themselves as relatively happy. Even disabled or severely injured people tend to look for the positive as demonstrated in the study cited above. It appears that happiness is not only the preference of most people, but an entirely normal condition.

A Good Night's Rest Contributes to Happiness

Most of us didn't need a researcher to tell us this. Your mother probably was the first person to apprise you of this important relationship. She might have put it this way, "If you don't get to sleep soon, you will be cranky all day." Aron and Aron in their exhaustive study of the literature on happiness conclude that "moods of happiness are associated with being rested" (260). According to Shakespeare, "Sleep is sore labor's bath, balm of hurt minds, great nature's second course, chief nourisher in life's feast." So rest, and be happy.

What about that morning cup of coffee? David Warburton studied the affect of caffeine on mood and cognition and found that 75-150 mg of caffeine has a positive effect on both mood and cognition. For mood, there was significant improvement in feelings of clarity, calmness, and happiness (1995).

Happiness May Be a Perceptual Set

Aron and Aron argue that the best explanation for happiness may be found in the research examining the relationship of self-reported happiness and variables designed to isolate a happiness set. Following extensive research on the relationship of meditation to happiness they concluded that the "background or 'neutral gear' of the nervous system may be happiness" (262). The evidence that happiness is not a product of external factors such as time, money, sex, etc., tends to support Aron and Aron's notion that happiness is a perceptual set which tends to filter out the undesirable and emphasize the positive. Aron and Aron cite several studies that suggest that internal locus of control (perceived freedom) may be critical to accessing one's natural reservoir of happiness (256). If this is true, then it should be clear that leisure and happiness are integrally connected. It might well be that the neurophysiological mechanism that produces happiness is also responsible for what we have been calling intrinsic satisfaction. Indeed, happiness may just be another word for intrinsic reward. Although the evidence is not conclusive, the work of Aron and Aron give added credence to the importance of developing a leisure lifestyle.

A Philosophical Note on Unhappiness

Everyone experiences unhappiness. The loss of a loved one can produce intense unhappiness. Accident or injury can cause unhappiness. The failure to achieve an important goal can make one unhappy. Almost any kind of rejection produces unhappiness. Can any good come from unhappiness? I believe unhappiness is an essential step in recovery, it is a natural part of the grieving process. During such times, people often gain insight and understanding that cannot be gained in any other way. In addition. unhappiness gives meaning to happiness. You wouldn't recognize happiness were it not for its opposite. Kahlil Gibran said it far more eloquently than I.

Your joy is your sorrow unmasked.
And the selfsame well from which your laughter rises
was oftentimes filled with your tears.
And how else can it be?
The deeper that sorrow carves into your being,
the more joy you can contain. (28)

Leisure and the Leisure Lifestyle

Throughout this book, we have looked at leisure as a state of mind. But, what of leisure from the traditional perspective? What of leisure as free time? How important is one's free time activity in the leisure lifestyle? Diversions, recreation, and play have long been recognized as contributing to the quality of one's life. Implicit in the term *recreation* is the idea of recreating spent energies, buoying up one's spirit through play. This is nicely illustrated in the book, *Zen and Motorcycle Maintenance* (1974). Where we pick up the text, Robert Persig, the author, has just finished explaining why he is attracted to the seldom used word "gumption." A word which he describes as essentially meaning "to be filled with enthusiasm" from the root "enthusiasmos," which Persig says literally means to be filled with "God or Quality."

> You see it often in people who return from long quiet fishing trips. Often they are a little defensive about having put so much time to "no account" because there's no particular justification to what they have been doing. But the returned fisherman usually has a peculiar abundance of gumption, usually for the very same things he was sick to death of a few weeks before. He hasn't been wasting time. It's only our limited cultural viewpoint that makes it seem so (297).

Sports and active games make an important contribution to one's physical well being. Music unleashes our creative energies and soothes our souls. Play has long been viewed as a means of releasing pent-up tensions: an antidote to stress. Art and drama have long been a popular means of self-expression. Laughter is touted as the best medicine. As Cicero stated nearly 2,000 years ago, "Leisure consists of all those virtuous activities by which a man grows morally, intellectually, and spiritually. It is that which makes life worthwhile." Iso-Ahola comments that "perhaps the most common theme running through the literature is the assumption of the positive affect of leisure behavior on life satisfaction" (383). The following comment from Dr. William Menninger is representative of this idea.

> Mentally healthy people participate in some form of volitional activity to supplement their required daily work. . . their satisfaction from this activity meets deep-seated psychological demands, quite beyond the superficial rationalizations of enjoyment. . . There is considerable scientific evidence that the healthy personality is one who not only plays, but who takes play seriously (Kraus 321).

In considering the role of "free time activities" in the leisure lifestyle one should recall our earlier discussion regarding the value of intrinsic motivation in the recreational experience. It was noted then, as it is now, that a leisure activity increases in value to the participant in proportion to the extent that it is engaged in for its own sake. That is to say, free time activities rich in intrinsic motivation yield greater satisfaction than those where the motivation is largely of an external nature. Thus, it is clear that not all "free time activities" hold the same potential for life satisfaction. Iso-Ahola makes this point in the following statement.

> Leisure satisfaction cannot be improved merely by increasing the number of and variety of services available. It is the individual who, either by himself or with the help of others, has to make the available service personally meaningful before they can contribute to leisure satisfaction. Only intrinsically motivated leisure activities can become personally meaningful ones (384).

Martin adds clarity to this idea by pointing out that in contemporary society, "external" leisure resources can be found in such rich abundance that it becomes easy for an individual to lose touch with the richer and more meaningful inner resources. Unlimited options for diversion and entertainment create a type of cognitive noise that can flood an individual's senses to the extent that the subtle and sensitive components of the leisure state of mind are incapable of surfacing (101).

There is little argument that a leisure state of mind is central to the leisure lifestyle. It also appears that leisure activities, when endowed with intrinsic rewards, are important to feelings of satisfaction and happiness. But what can one do to enhance the quality of such activities? Chester McDowell argues that the extent to which one is capable of enjoying leisure activities is dependent upon having first developed an effective **leisure style**. This is a condition wherein leisure values and benefits flourish, which in turn is a function of a condition he refers to as *leisure wellness*.

McDowell views leisure wellness as an interplay between four distinct variable: (1) awareness and understanding, (2) coping, (3) knowledge, and (4) assertion. In essence he suggests that to attain leisure wellness, you must be aware of the value that leisure can hold for you. Your ability to cope with events and forces that interfere with your leisure wellness is also an important factor in maintaining a healthy and satisfying leisure lifestyle. Under the heading knowledge, McDowell suggests that you should be knowledgeable in three areas: (1) interest and desire, (2) resources, and (3) fitness and general wellness. Finally, McDowell argues that it is ultimately your responsibility to assert and affirm your personal leisure lifestyle (6–11).

Although, I find value in McDowell's work, I take exception to one idea. The notion of asserting one's leisure lifestyle may not be an accurate reflection of the philosophy of the type of leisure lifestyle I have presented here. An individual functioning from the cognitive framework of perceptual freedom will behave in accordance with his or her perception of correct behavior. And, such behavior will be evaluated in accordance with its intrinsic potential. External locus of control factors will have little impact on the practitioner of the leisure lifestyle. His or her fundamental course of behavior will be rooted in the internal locus. Consequently, a person possessing a leisure lifestyle will demonstrate independent and confident behavior, will be self-directed and in touch with his/her inner resources. Such a person will have little need to assert his or her individuality; every action will represent the commitment to principles of leisure in a natural and unfettered manner.

Elements of the Leisure Lifestyle

People often ask me what characterizes a leisure lifestyle. I tell them an abundance of perceived and perceptual freedom, intrinsic satisfaction, optimal arousal, and flow experiences. Invariably that is too esoteric or academic because they then ask for specifics. I don't like to give specifics because there is no such thing as the perfect leisure lifestyle. What may be a perfectly legitimate expression of leisure in one person's lifestyle may not be for another. Nevertheless, this is a question that I have long pondered, and on a personal level I have drawn some conclusions. So, for me, a leisure lifestyle will include, to varying degrees, the following elements:

1. Behaviors and experiences that contribute to my self-esteem.
2. Behaviors that demonstrate and attitudes that support internal locus of control.
3. Behaviors that demonstrate and attitudes that support perceived freedom.
4. Experiences that allow for perceptual freedom (the state of being essentially so focused on a pleasurable experience that one loses awareness of all other competing stimuli; flow experiences do this.)
5. Behaviors and experiences that provide intrinsic satisfaction.
6. Behaviors, experiences, and attitudes that maximize optimal arousal and diminish the probability of supraoptimal and suboptimal arousal.
7. Behaviors and attitudes that promote my physical and emotional health, minimize disease, and promote wellness.
8. Behaviors and attitudes that enable me to minimize distress.
9. Coping behaviors that limit the harmful potential of stressful circumstances.
10. Behaviors that generate novelty and arousal (a continual series of discovery events will do this).
11. A career that is rich in job satisfaction, security, and provides me with adequate financial resources.
12. Effective time management.
13. Self-programmed opportunities for self-expression.
14. Experiences that allow me to experience self-actualization.
15. Opportunities for creativity and divergent thinking.
16. Behaviors and circumstances that meet my need for affiliation and interaction with others.
17. Familial experiences that allows my needs for intimacy and sharing with significant others.
18. A healthy sense of humor.
19. The capacity to experience play frequently and easily.
20. A spiritual theme which allows me to find unity with the universe.

This last notion is one which gets little press in textbooks, but one which I think has some merit and on a personal level is an important element in my version of the leisure lifestyle. It is strictly philosophical and based on my own metaphysical experiences. It is different from religion and it has nothing to do with faith. It is based on the notion that most people want to believe that life has a purpose that goes beyond the physical and temporal, and that on an intuitive level people can find support for this belief. It goes beyond the psychological notion of intrinsic satisfaction or perceived freedom. It is more than flow or optimal arousal. It is more of an intuitive and artful blending of the known with the unknown. It is a sense of being more than a random occurrence in a chaotic universe, it is the feeling of belonging, to being part of an orderly unknown. This feeling of connection is demonstrated when you feel enthusiasm for a sunset, when you marvel at the colors of nature, when you stare into the night sky and feel embraced by it. Spirituality, in my leisure lifestyle, affords me a feeling of comfort when faced with unknown forces. It transforms fear of the unknown into wonderment, confusion into curiosity, and despair into strength. It is spirituality that, for me, binds together all the other elements of my leisure lifestyle.

In our modern world, it is often difficult to get in touch with the spiritual side of life. We are bombarded by constant stimuli, products of our technical world, which in effect provide a synthetic-temporal barrier between the physical and the metaphysical. It is hard to entertain spiritual thoughts while driving the freeways, watching television, talking on the phone, or surfing the net. That is why, I suppose, many people turn to the outdoors, for it seems that in nature, free from the intervention of technology, people are more receptive to the spiritual. Ruth Russell puts it this way:

> Early writers frequently used the descriptive language of spirituality, mysticism, or emotional transcendence to describe their experiences in the wilderness. They viewed the wilderness as a source of psychic energy. Today, perhaps more than ever, people consider the wilderness as a place for the human spirit. To many people, natural areas are important settings for answering the deepest questions of human existence and for contemplating the unifying power behind life and things. Through history, we have gone to the woods, oceans, plains, deserts, and rivers to discover the spiritual riches within ourselves. The outdoors is a place were we cannot escape the fundamental truth of what we are. (66)

In the depth of your hopes and desires lies your silent knowledge of the beyond.
And like seeds dreaming beneath the snow your heart dreams of spring.
Trust the dreams, for in them is hidden the gate to eternity.

—Kahlil Gibran from The Prophet

Closing Note...

Lifestyle is essentially a social science concept. It may be viewed from one of two perspectives: (1) societally or (2) psychologically. Essentially, a lifestyle is a pattern of behaviors that define the personal characteristics of an individual or the characteristics of a group. As a student, you share in the student lifestyle, but you also possess characteristics that are not reflected in the larger group. It is important to realize that there are numerous factors that influence the extent to which people can orchestrate their lifestyles. These include such factors as age, tradition, values, and beliefs, natural development, and unresolved childhood issues. Ultimately what determines the degree of control that a person assumes over his or her lifestyle, is the extent to which the person feels dissatisfied with elements in his life and has the energy and knowledge required to change.

A leisure lifestyle is associated with happiness, a condition described by Aron and Aron as the background state of the nervous system. Since happiness is such an important characteristic of leisure, understanding happiness may be essential to learning how to create a leisure lifestyle. Recent research suggests that most external events have little bearing on happiness; rather, it appears that happiness is more a function of internal factors. This conforms with findings which show that love and intimacy, as well as job satisfaction, are better predictors of happiness than such external factors as money, time, status, possessions, etc. Research on happiness shows a strong connection between perceived freedom, intrinsic reward, and happy moods. Although, there is no such thing as a perfect leisure lifestyle, an individual can incorporate behaviors and attitudes, which will lead one toward a lifestyle that promotes a sense of perceived freedom, increased levels of intrinsic satisfaction, optimal arousal, and flow experiences. Such a lifestyle can be considered a leisure lifestyle.

But taken all together, happiness appears to consist of pursuing, and if possible, achieving all or some of the desires referred to previously—to be healthy, to be free, to be wanted, to be useful, and to find our place in the universe. These lead to the enjoyment of living, to a kind of happiness. Not the narrow happiness of being cheerful, glad or gleeful, nor the limited happiness of pleasurableness, but rather the happiness of abundant, rewarding, and enriched life, the full, expressive existence which brings with it great personal satisfactions.

—Charles Brightbill (18)

REFERENCES

Aron, El. and A. Aron. "The Influence of Inner-State on Self-Reported Long-Term Happiness." *Journal of Humanistic Psychology* 27.2 (1987): 248–270.

Bammel, G. and L.L Burrus-Bammel. *Leisure and Human Behavior*. William C. Brown, 1982.

Brebner, J., J. Donaldson, N. Kirby and L. Ward. "Relationships between Happiness and Personality." *Personality and Individual Differences* 19.2 (1995): 251–258.

Brickman, P., Coates, D. and J. Bullman. "Lottery Winners and Accident Victims: Is Happiness Relative?" *Journal of Personality and Social Psychology* 3618 (1978): 917–927.

Brightbill, C.K. *Man and Leisure: A Philosophy of Recreation*. Englewood Cliffs: Prentice-Hall, 1961.

Campbell, A. *The Quality of American Life*. Ann Arbor: Institute for Social Research, 1975.

Ellis, M. *Why People Play*. New York: Prentice-Hall, 1973.

Ellison, C.G. "Religious Involvement and Subjective Well-Being." *Journal of Health Social Behavior*, 32.1 (1991): 80–99.

Freedman, J.L. *Social Psychology*. Englewood Cliffs, N.J., Prentice-Hall, 1985.

Gardner, J.W. *Self-Renewal*. New York: Harper and Row, Publishers, 1968.

Gibran, K. *The Prophet*. New York: Alfred A. Knopf, 1953.

Godbey, G. *Leisure in Your Life*. State College: Venture Publishing, 1985.

Graves, C. *On the Theory of Value*. Stanford, Mimeographed Paper, 1967.

Greenwald, M. and R. Schwartz. "What Does Bring Happiness?" http://www.happiness.com/quest/keys.html, (Oct. 15, 1996).

Heymann, T. *The Unofficial U.S. Census: What the U.S. Census Doesn't Tell You*. New York: Fawcett, 1991.

Iso-Ahola, S.E. *The Social Psychology of Leisure and Recreation*. Dubuque, Iowa: Wm. C. Brown Company Publishers.

Kraus, R. *Recreation and Leisure in Modern Society*. New York: Scott Foresman Company, 1986.

Larson, R. "Is Feeling in Control Related to Happiness in Daily Life?" *Psychology Reports* 64.3.1 (1989): 775–84.

Maslow, Abraham. *Motivation and Personality*. New York: Harper and Row, 1954.

McDowell, C.F. "Leisure Wellness: An Introduction," *Leisure Wellness Concepts and Helping Strategies*. Eugene, Oregon: Sun Moon Press, 1983.

Mitchell, A. *Nine American Lifestyles*. New York: Macmillan Publishing Co., 1983.

Morris, D. *The Human Zoo*. New York: Dell Publishing, 1974.

Myers, D.G. and E. Diener. "Who Is Happy?" *Psychological Science*. 6.1 (1995) 10–19

Nash, J.B. *Philosophy of Recreation and Leisure*. St. Louis: The C.V. Mosby Co., 1953.

Neulinger, J. *To Leisure: An Introduction*. State College: Ventura, 1984.

Neulinger, J. *The Psychology of Leisure*. Springfield IL: Charles C. Thomas, 1974.

Nock, S. "A Comparison of Marriages and Cohabiting Relationships." *Journal of Family Issues* 16.1 (1995): 53–76.

Noor, N.M. "Job Role Quality and Women's Psychological Well-Being: Locus of Control and Social Support as Moderators." *Journal of Community and Applied Social Psychology* 5.4 (1995): 259–272.

Persig, R.M. *Zen and the Art of Motorcycle Maintenance*. New York: Morrow, 1974.

Peter, J.L. *The Laughter Prescription*. New York: Ballantine, 1978.

Renwick, P.A. and Lawler, E.E., "What You Really Want from Your Job." *Psychology Today*. 11 (1978) 53–65, 118.

Russell, R.J. and P.A. Wells, "Predictors of Happiness in Married Couples." *Personality and Individual Differences* 17.3 (1994): 313–321.

Santrock, John W. *Development Psychology: A Life-Cycle Perspective*. Dubuque, Iowa: W.C. Brown, 1986.

Shoestrom, Everett. *Man the Manipulator*. New York: Bantam Books, 1972.

Tepperman, I. and J. Curtis. "A Life Satisfaction Scale for Use with National Adult Samples from the USA, Canada, and Mexico." *Social Indicators Research* 35.3 (1995): 255–270.

Warburn, D. "Effects of Caffeine on Cognition and Mood without Caffeine Abstinence." *Psychopharmacology* 119.1 (1995): 66–70.

Weiten, W. *Psychology Applied to Modern Life*. Monterey: Brooks/Cole Publishing Co., 1986.

Wells, W.D. *Lifestyle and Psychographics*. Chicago, American Marketing Association, 1974.

Witt, P. and G.D. Ellis. "Development of Short Form to Assess Perceived Freedom in Leisure." A final report of a study funded by grant from the U.S. Department of Education, 1982.

CHAPTER 16

Self-Directed Lifestyle Change

As I write this unit, I cannot help but reflect on the fact that I have spent my entire vacation working on material for this book. It has been a costly project, both in personal finances and in time. "I would much prefer to be somewhere else," I hear myself saying, yet I persist at hammering out this collection of notes. In defending my commitment to this project, I hear myself arguing that I am doing it because it fills a much needed literary gap, that it will be beneficial to its readers, and that it will contribute to student learning. But, echoing somewhere in the background, is a quiet and persistent voice that reminds me that there are intrinsic motives at play as well. I enjoy creating, learning, and studying. Putting this collection of material together has met that need. I like doing this.

Is Change Possible?

Some people argue that we as human beings are not meant to make dramatic changes in our lives, then there are others who sing praise to self-determination. Richard Bach and Wayne Dyer would have us believe that the sky is the limit, that we can be more than what we are. Others are more cautious and suggest that the parameters in which we operate are dictated by heredity and to a lesser extent, environment, and that any changes are limited by these factors. Wherein lies the truth? My personal belief falls somewhere between these points of view. I suppose it most closely relates to the thinking of Abraham Maslow. We should strive for self-actualization in all aspects of our lives, and certainly within that which is perhaps most personal, our leisure. Self-actualization means becoming the best that you can be. It means recognizing your limitations and reaching them, expanding them and reaching again. You may not be a world class athlete, but you can be the best athlete you can be. You may not be the most attractive person in the world, but you can emphasize your good points and be the most attractive you can be. For most of us, change is not really a major undertaking, but rather a series of minor adaptations and modifications. Is change possible? It occurs all the time. A better question is "What can one do to bring about desirable changes"

There Are Some Things That You Can't Readily Change

Before going any further with this discussion, there is an important point that needs to be made: **Unfortunately, there are some characteristics that resist change**. For example, there are some who would say that anything rooted in your genetic structure is relatively resistant to change. It is difficult to alter your body type for example. Yes, there are surgical procedures that one can try, but the truth is that the body type is essentially immutable to change. You can't change your race, your age, or your sexual orientation (Seligman 36). Such characteristics as artistic talent (or the lack of it), intelligence, or personality, may resist change. And, there are those characteristics that you probably cannot change without help from a qualified therapist. For example emotional and psychological characteristics rooted in the experiences of early childhood, depression, anxiety, phobias, obsessive-compulsive disorder, jealousy, anger, posttraumatic stress disorder, and the like. Addiction to smoking, alcohol, or drugs may resist self-directed attempts at change.

In short, there are some things we can change on our own, there are some things we can change through therapy, and there are some things that we simply cannot change. Learning to recognize what you can change, what you can change with assistance, and what you cannot change is vitally important. By placing emphasis on those elements that are least likely to change can result in disappointment and frustration, not to mention proving to be a waste of time and energy—all counter to a leisure lifestyle. Martin Seligman says it much better than I:

> *I want to provide an understanding of what you can and what you can't change about yourself so that you can concentrate your limited time and energy on what is possible. So much time has been wasted. So much needless frustration has been endured. So much of therapy, so much of child rearing, so much of self-improving, and even some of the great social movements in our century have come to nothing because they tried to change the unchangeable. Too often we have wrongly thought we were weak willed failures, when the changes we wanted to make in ourselves were just not possible. (36–37)*

Small Changes—Great Outcomes

The benefits of reading this book will vary from reader to reader, but my purpose in writing has been to acquaint you with some of the philosophies and theories regarded as most central to the study of leisure. In addition, I have tried to motivate you to further explore the role that leisure can have in your personal growth and development. If you are like me, as you looked at the different ideas presented in this book, you found some more attractive than others. For these you might feel a special enthusiasm, and as a result feel inclined to make them part of your life. A former student, for example, found value in the discovery event concept. She has since made it a point to have one major discovery each year. Now these discoveries are reported to her friends in the form of an annual newsletter and Christmas card. She never ceases to amaze me with her enthusiasm for discovery and her letters are always entertaining. This year's Christmas card included a photo of her standing in front of the Kremlin! Another student was impressed with the information on fitness and health, and decided to become a more healthy person. Her weight had been a serious obstacle in her life, and in fact had prevented her from pursuing the career of her dreams. She seriously set out to change, and today she is 60 pounds lighter and the flight attendant she had dreamed of becoming. Another student was impressed with information about careers, she decided she wanted a career that offered variety, a chance to work with people, and offered opportunities for adventure. Today she is a professor of outdoor recreation. Another student, for a discovery event, entered a standup comedy contest, today he is a famous comic, you may have seen him on MTV! Each of these, and there are others I could tell you about, found something in the concepts presented in this book that made sense to them, ideas that seemed to offer something missing from their lives, something that if applied might make their lives richer. And, that is what this book is about, helping people have richer, happier lives. The essence of leisure is to be free. That means to be free to self-actualize, free to discover, free to self-express, free to laugh and play, and to be free from sorrow, stress, disease, loneliness, and poverty. All of the ideas in this book were selected because they in one way or another relate to this goal.

In a sense this book is about self-directed change for the better. It is not about therapeutic change, global change, personality change, or social change. It is about behavior change, and principally those behaviors that will most contribute to the quality of one's life. It is about the kinds of things you can do on your own to enrich your life. If attitudes are improved, if therapeutic results accrue, or personalities shift, so much the better, but that is not what this book has been about. Therapy should come from a therapist, and there are times when all of us could benefit from a few hours on the couch. I am not a therapist, rather, I see myself as a coach and a cheerleader, standing on the sidelines of your life, suggesting strategies and giving encouragement, which if accepted and applied might bring a little more joy and happiness into your world. This book has provided the medium through which I can say, "Here, try this idea, it has worked for others." And, you decide whether it is worth trying. You might find you like the idea of a vegetarian diet, and much to the surprise of your carnivore friends, change your diet to that of a vegetarian. You decide that self-expression has been lacking from your life, and so you start writing poetry, or short stories, or you begin painting, and your lifestyle becomes more creative and expressive. You decide that you need to see more of the world, and so you begin traveling, and in the process become more cosmopolitan and universal in perspective. You decide your current career choice is not where you want to spend 1/3 of your life, and so you shift from accounting to antique repair. You feel that you need more social activities in your life and so you take a dance class and make social dancing an important part of your lifestyle. These are the types of changes in behavior that I am talking about in this book, and generally they may appear far from monumental, but in the long term very simple changes can have extraordinary consequences.

If you decide to be a more effective time manager, the consequences can be significant. Take the lost *key syndrome*, by changing your *key behavior* so that you spend less time looking for lost keys, you will have more time to do the things you need to do or desire. If you, on the average spend 15 minutes a day looking for your keys, that can, over a 12 month period, amount to a large amount of time—about 90 hours! In ten years that amounts to 900 hours or about 37 days. See what I mean, a simple change in behavior can have far reaching implications. Change your eating behavior so that you consume 100 fewer calories per day. Providing that you make no other changes in your lifestyle, at the end of one year, you will have lost between 10 and 12 pounds. Don't change your diet, but change your behavior so that you take the stairs to your office. Providing that you get about 20 minutes of such exercise a day, you will lose between 10 and 12 pounds at the end of the year. Some changes and their consequences are more difficult to measure. Laughing twenty times a day will no doubt have positive outcomes, but it may be difficult to assess them. Allowing a few minutes a day to send an e-mail or "snail mail" message to just one person a day will result in 365 communications a year, and more goodwill than you could begin to measure. Meditating for 10 minutes a day might go a long way toward helping you cope with distress, practicing autogenics might have a similar impact. Changes don't have to be great to have great significance in one's life.

As you know, one of my favorite themes relates to the importance of discovery. Giving yourself permission to have new experiences and adventures is an important element in my notion of the leisure lifestyle. By giving one's self permission to try something new at least once a week can have a significant long term impact on a person. The key here is finding activities that are new to you. As was pointed out in an earlier chapter, novelty is closely related to optimal arousal, thus, by programming new events into your life, you can increase the amount of optimal arousal you experience. Make a commitment to yourself to experience discovery at least once a week, and watch your life become more interesting. Such discoveries don't have to be complex or expensive. They can be as simple as visiting a museum, walking along the river, seeing an unusual movie, communicating with someone new to you, wearing a fashion style different from your usual choice, etc. Do this once a week for one year, and you will have 52 discoveries to reflect on, talk about, and repeat. Now, extrapolate that to a lifetime.

Sometimes, even the simplest of behaviors may be difficult to change. Habits die hard, and new behaviors can easily be extinguished. But it is within our ability to change many common behaviors. A few simple changes can help us become better organized, more relaxed, more effective, more attractive, and generally happier.

Leisure Attitudes and Interests

If leisure is a state of mind, then attitudes must have a great deal to do with our decisions regarding leisure. For some people, the mere concept of leisure produces a negative response. Other people long for leisure and place great value on it. This is a function of one's attitudes regarding leisure. An attitude can be either positive or negative; interests, on the other hand, are always positive. You have an interest in soccer, in sports, in fitness, in art, and so on.

An attitude is a learned predisposition to react in certain ways to ideas, events, objects or people. Interests tend to be more directed than attitudes, while attitudes tend to be more general. Interests and attitudes may not always be congruent. It is possible that you have an attitude about leisure involvement that is contrary to your actual interests. For example, you may find that working out in public is undesirable to you, but your interest in fitness compels you to work out at a health club. This type of situation results in an internal conflict and is manifest by feelings of frustration. Such feelings are clearly detrimental to a leisure lifestyle. Consequently, attempts to change are usually directed toward changing one's attitudes about various aspects of leisure in such a manner as to encourage the probability of an increase in an individual's perceived freedom and intrinsic motivation. Sometimes it is helpful to seek professional assistance from a therapist when trying to change an attitude, sometimes it helps to take courses related to the object of the attitude, sometimes you can do it on your own.

Harmful Emotions

Often, when you ask people how they would like to change in order to have a more leisure oriented lifestyle, they will tell you that they would like to be less angry, less jealous, less guilty or less worried. These are universal emotions that seem to prevent many of us from fully enjoying life. Munn tells us that emotion comes from the Latin word "emovere," which means to agitate, to stir up, or excite. He clarifies this by saying:

> Sometimes emotion not only stirs us up, but. . . when emotion is intense, there are widespread changes which embrace every aspect of one's body and its activity. Physiological and neural processes are altered. Thoughts and actions are affected. Marked disorganization may be disturbed. In an emotion provoking emergency, we may exhibit unusual energy or we may be 'rooted to the spot' or we may 'lose our heads' (156).

Not all emotions are bad, for emotions range from ecstasy to agony. It is only the negative ones that cause us grief and detract from a leisure lifestyle. Because of the depth and complexity of certain emotions, it is a good idea to seek assistance from a therapist. The good news here is that many of our most common negative emotions are amenable to therapy (Seligman 36). If you are chronically angry, jealous, or anxious, help is available.

Time

In many respects, leisure is a function of time. As I type this manuscript, I am well aware that this project is taking longer than I had planned and consequently cutting into other activities that I value. Learning to effectively manage one's time so that you don't feel like you are on a treadmill is an important aspect of learning to live in a leisurely manner. For most of us, a little planning and reflection can result in significant changes in how we "manage our time." And, of course, as has been pointed out, it isn't time that we manage, it is behavior that we manage. By learning how to be more efficient and effective, we give the appearance of being good time managers. In reality, we are just good managers.

Health

All of us are familiar with the notion that health is central to happiness. But most of us take it for granted, paying attention only to health and fitness when we are ill. To have a leisure lifestyle, one must learn to maximize wellness and minimize illness. In addition, I think it is important to develop an attitude which enables us to be aware and appreciate those times when we are healthy. Too often we fail to appreciate good health until it is gone. There are definitely some behaviors that we can do on our own to help ensure good health. This is one area where change can produce extremely important results.

Money

Some would argue that you cannot have leisure without money. I do not think that it is entirely true, but I do agree that money and other resources can contribute to a successful leisure lifestyle. A quick look at Maslow's hierarchy shows where you are when you are constantly worried about sustenance. Generating and managing money, is another area where we have a great deal of control. If you need more money, marshal your resources and generate more, or modify your attitude toward money so that you can comfortably accept having less.

Coping with Stress

Coping with stress may require some changes. A change in behavior, a change in job, a change in location, etc. often are needed to minimize stress in one's life. Dealing with stress often requires creative problem solving and the application of coping techniques.

Humor

Many people can benefit from exercising their funny bone. This is another area where you can make some changes that will contribute to leisure. Look back at the chapter on humor and review some of the simple changes that help you enjoy a richer sense of humor.

Recreation, Discovery and Play

As we get older, it seems that we get further away from playful behavior, discovery gets more difficult, and recreation occurs with less frequency. Generally, the blocks to enjoyable activity are self-imposed and without any pathogenic origin. For most of us, it is simply a matter of scheduling some time for fun, and giving ourselves permission to relax and enjoy. If this is an area needing change in your life, go for it. Block in some time for play and give yourself permission to participate in something fun!

Strategies for Change

How does one go about improving attitudes, minimizing jumbled emotions, managing time, practicing healthier habits, and acquiring more money? Although there is no easy answer, following are some suggestions that might help you get started.

> He who aims at nothing is bound to hit.
>
> —Lars Bishop

Where Does One Begin?

Common sense, practical experience, and social science all show that you cannot begin a program of selfdirected change until you have an idea as to what changes are appropriate, desirable, and possible.

Change begins with determining what it is you want to accomplish. Without some clear-cut goals and objectives to direct your efforts, it will be impossible to systematically eliminate undesirable behavior and increase more leisure-related activity and attitudes.

Determining what it is you need/want to change usually requires some introspection. True, most of us do not have to think very long to determine that we would like to be happier, healthier, wealthier, wiser, more attractive, etc. But, these are very general goals. They are **long-range goals**, they are end goals, they might even be referred to as the ultimate goals of life. Some of them might be impossible to achieve. Achieving long-range goals requires the successful completion of many **short-term** and **mid-range goals**. It is to the short-term and mid-range goals that we should direct our attention when deciding what changes we should undertake in order to develop a more leisure based lifestyle.

Change begins when you decide to evaluate your leisure style, to look for behaviors that fail to contribute to the important goals of life, and to identify behaviors that you do not currently demonstrate which seem directly related to a leisure lifestyle. This type of introspection should take some time. It should not be spontaneous, but should be systematically undertaken over a period of time. You cannot begin to change something of which you are not consciously aware, or do not see as a problem. It might require several days of careful evaluation to determine just what it is that you feel requires modification. Upon conclusion of this initial introspection, you should have a fairly good idea as to the kinds of change you would like to undertake. **Generally, such changes fall under two headings: (1) attitudes and behaviors that you perform which detract from your leisure lifestyle; and (2) behaviors and attitudes you believe would contribute to a leisure lifestyle that you do not currently experience.**

Attitudes, Behavior and Learning

Attitudes, interests, and behaviors are basically learned. It is true that some people may exhibit behaviors that are the result of physiological imbalances caused by disease, diet, or congenital problems, but these are the exception. For most people, the behaviors and attitudes that disrupt one's leisure are the product of prior experiences, the product of learning. Consequently, self-directed change generally involves learning some new attitudes and behaviors and unlearning others.

It has been fairly well established that attitude and behavior are closely connected. Thus, if you wish to change a specific behavior, it is important to look at the attitude that predisposes you toward that behavior. Similarly, if you wish to engage in certain behaviors, it follows that the necessary antecedent attitudes need to be developed. Take, for example, the man who says that he is interested in learning to be more social with women, but has strong prejudices about men who dance. In order for him to develop the social skill of dancing, he first must replace old attitudes with new ones that favor dancing as a recreation activity.

Iso-Ahola has clearly demonstrated that leisure related attitudes can be changed. Furthermore, steps necessary to bring about an attitude of change have been suggested by a variety of authors. As Fishbein and Ajzen put it, "in the final analysis, attitude change involves changing a person's beliefs, whether they are beliefs about the object or beliefs about its attributes" (Iso-Ahola 216).

In changing an attitude, two approaches can be considered. First, one can attack the "salient beliefs" about the attributes or characteristics of the object of the attitude to be changed. The second is to consider the beliefs one has about the attributes themselves (Iso-Ahola 260). For example, if the object of the attitude is aerobic exercise, and the offending attribute is exertion and its side effects, perspiration and exhaustion, then one cannot attack or discredit the salient beliefs, for that would lead to a misrepresentation of the facts. Indeed, people do perspire and are exhausted following aerobic exercise. Consequently, the appropriate strategy here would be to alter beliefs about the attributes. By looking at perspiration as being natural and desirable, fatigue as important to rest, and exertion essential to wellness—the necessary attitudes would evolve.

In addition to modifying your attitudes through systematically exposing yourself to information that supports an attitude change, there is research to indicate that actual involvement in an activity may help bring about an attitude change. Of course, it is important that the activity selected reinforce the desired change, otherwise the change process may be hindered.

So, essentially, this unit suggests that if you want to change an attitude, you have two basic tactics available:

1. you can cognitively work on the attitude through increasing your exposure to information which discredits or strengthens the salient features or attributes of the attitude; and/or
2. you can experientially acquire new beliefs about the object or attributes of the attitude.

Using Reinforcers

The concept of reinforcing behavior is not new. Essentially, the notion underlying reinforcement is that behavior which is rewarding tends to be repeated. Behavior for which there is little reward or that is met with punishment tends not to be repeated. Consequently, one can view learning as a change in behavior that is due to prior experience, which leads one to expect certain responses from various behaviors. Consequently, I believe that self-administered reinforcers can contribute to the change process. This is particularly true of leisure behavior, where the intrinsic reward of participation may allow the activity itself to serve as a reinforcer.

Developing a Plan for Change

In order to bring about attitude change and the resultant change in behavior, one must devise a step-by-step plan, otherwise it is quite likely that attempts to change will only result in the spinning of cognitive and behavioral wheels. Attitudes and behaviors are rooted in childhood. It has taken years of socialization to get attitudes where they are today. Although it would be nice, it is not likely that they will change overnight. It usually takes weeks of concentrated effort to bring about even small changes. Learning a new behavior is analogous to learning a new language. It takes time and practice.

For years, I heard myself saying, "Where are those darned keys?" (Yes, I know all the jokes about absent-minded professors). I decided it was time to bring about an attitudes change. I needed to view myself as a person who did not lose his keys, who was very organized when it came to his keys, and who could put his hands on his keys readily. The beliefs were clear, the underlying attitudes of organization and efficiency were obvious, and I understood the value of the beliefs, but the problem, of course, was to find a way to actually change the behavior.

My plan was very simple. I did three things: (1) I installed a very large hook by my outside door. It was located so it actually touched the door as it was opened. It was also located immediately above the light switch. (2) I bought a notebook, labeled "Key Behavior," and placed it near the hook. (3) Perhaps the most important thing I did was to assume full responsibility for my behavior and agree with myself to alter this time wasting problem.

For one week, I kept track of the times I forgot to use the key hook and noted my reactions to those times. It was clear to me that finding my keys easily and quickly was a strong reinforcer. In this case, the behavior was reinforcing itself. Within two weeks, I had recorded a tremendous drop in the number of times the keys were misplaced. Today, I seldom misplace my keys. In behavioral terms, the key losing behavior is now extinct, and my life is better for the change. This small and seemingly insignificant change has had many positive effects. I seldom waste time looking for my keys, my self-image has been strengthened and the old myth about absent-minded professors clearly refuted. Now, what was I saying. . . .

Most plans for change have the following elements:

1. **Clearly Established Goals.** This is terribly important. You must have a goal that you can achieve, one that is measurable and one that can be achieved through the successful completion of shorthand mid-range objectives. It is far better to have a few small goals than one major goal that is too difficult to achieve.
2. **Some Baseline Data.** It is a good idea to collect some data about what you want to change before you undertake your self-directed change program. This serves two functions: (1) you acquire some data to help you evaluate your progress, and (2) you can acquire insight into any behavioral pattern that is at work.
3. **Contingencies and Reinforcers.** In altering behaviors, it is good to make clear to yourself under what circumstances you will reward behavior. What are the contingencies that will lead to reinforcement? What type of reinforcement will be used? Some argue that you can expedite change by coupling positive reinforcement with punishment. My sense is that most of the behaviors that we try to extinguish carry with them a built-in punishment system. To add upon that only adds insult to injury,

and may, in the long run, have such a negative effect on one's self-confidence that it ends up reinforcing the undesirable behavior. So the emphasis here is on positive reinforcement.

One of the problems associated with this approach to change is finding good reinforcers. Remember, a positive reinforcer is anything that you can view as a reward, contingent upon demonstrating a change in behavior. In searching for reinforcers, you do not need to limit reinforcers to things that make you feel good. You can use any behavior that you regularly perform. You may use these essential and regular behaviors much in the same way that you would use pleasurable reinforcers.

4. **The Power of Suggestion.** For a number of years, I worked as a hypnotist for law enforcement agencies. My job was to hypnotize people in order to help them recall information about crimes they had witnessed. Occasionally, I would suggest that the subject draw a picture of the suspect. Normally, if this suggestion were made prior to hypnosis, the subject would argue that he/she was not able to draw. Once hypnotized, they forgot that they could not draw and in many cases produced fairly descriptive sketches. The power of suggestion can be a useful tool in bringing about self-directed change. However, in your case, you are both hypnotist and subject.

   One way of implementing suggestions on a personal level without having to understand self-hypnosis is through *affirmations*. An affirmation is nothing more than a positive statement about the changes you are making in your life. For example, if you are working on feeling less guilt about leisure, you might regularly affirm to yourself that you are changing. This might take the form of notes to yourself, a daily debriefing where you verbally state how you are changing, and in the course of day-to-day conversations you might allude to the changes you are making. Try saying something like, "I used to have difficulty enjoying my free time, but I am changing, feeling less guilt and more freedom."

5. **Desensitization.** Watson and Thorp define desensitization as a process of reconditioning a person's reactions "so that stimuli that previously elicited an unpleasant emotion will, instead, come to elicit a different, tolerable emotional reaction" (171). Desensitization is appropriate in situations where something triggers an unfavorable, emotional response. Snakes do this to some people. Although, it is a good idea to seek a therapist's assistance when faced with a phobia, there are some steps you can take on your own.

   Desensitization is closely related to affirmations, but differs in that the process primarily requires the active use of your imagination. Within the context of a safe environment and while in a relaxed state, you visualize successfully encountering the anxiety producing situation. The example of the man who wants to learn to dance, but is burdened by considerable anxiety when confronted with the possibility of dancing is a good example. By gradually viewing himself as a dancer, in dancing situations, and being watched by others while dancing, his fears may begin to diminish. Eventually, he may be able to actually further his desensitization by gradually becoming physically involved in settings where dancing occurs; taking basic dancing lessons, etc. The important thing to remember when applying desensitization is to establish a logical series of imaginary or physical encounters ranging from the very safe to the most anxiety producing, all within a safe and relaxed context.

6. **Record Keeping.** Earlier, I suggested that you spend some time early in the project collecting "baseline data." This gives you a basis for evaluating your progress. One of the best ways of doing this is to maintain a "change diary." At the end of every day, spend a few minutes and review your successes and failures. Analyze why you succeeded and why you failed. Keep this diary faithfully and it will prove a valuable tool in helping you direct the course of your life.

   Another useful tool is the "cumulative graph" (Foster 50–55). Normally, this type of graph is constructed so that the abscissa (the horizontal line) represents a measure of time in days, hours, etc. and the ordinate (the vertical line) represents the measure of the behavior either in terms of frequency or intensity. This approach, faithfully followed, gives you an excellent and easily interpreted record of your progress. Both techniques have the added advantage of serving as a reinforcement for the new behavior.

7. **Maintenance.** A friend of mine was dieting. During the course of a conversation she said, "I can hardly wait until I reach 120 lbs. I'm going to really pig out." It was clear to me that she had failed to make a significant change in her underlying attitudes and values. She viewed a diet as a means to an end, not as an end in itself. In order to maintain her desirable weight, she would have to alter her values so that her lifestyle promoted her ideal weight; otherwise, her life would be an endless battle with her weight marked by endless diets. In that event, no significant change would have occurred. Before her weight loss would remain stable, she would have to change her attitude about fattening foods and exercise. A healthier diet and a positive attitude about exercise would enable her weight change to be considered permanent.

It is far better to recognize that change requires a total commitment, and that it is a never-ending process. We either progress or regress, and we seldom, if ever, simply maintain. The whole point of change is to: grow, to get closer to our ultimate goals, to continually improve, to continually identify new short term and mid-range goals, and to continually strive to achieve a leisure lifestyle. It is also important to recognize that there are some things about ourselves that we cannot change, these we must accept.

Closing Note. . .

This chapter is about change. The underlying assumption of the material presented here is that, in order to more fully experience the leisure lifestyle, most of us can benefit from some self-directed change in our attitudes and behavior. Can people change? This chapter pointed out that not only can people change, change is in a sense a constant—it happens continuously. A more pertinent question relates to the extent to which people can control the change that occurs in their lives.

Generally change that promotes a leisure lifestyle will take two forms (1) eliminating those things that detract from a leisure lifestyle, and (2) embracing those things that contribute to the leisure lifestyle.

In order to bring about change, one must have an idea as to what needs to be done. The old saying, "He that aims at nothing is bound to hit," applies here. Long-term goals, and short-range and mid-range objectives need to be identified. Once you have a sense of direction, then you need to develop a strategy to enable you to achieve your goals. Essential to successful change is record keeping. A change diary is valuable too in the process of self-directed discovery and development. Other tools that you can use in the change process include self-hypnosis, contingencies and reinforcers, and desensitization.

REFERENCES

Dyer, Wayne. *Your Erroneous Zones*. New York: Avon Books, 1976.

Foster, C. *Developing Self-Control*. Kalamazoo. MI: Behaviordelia, Inc., 1974.

Iso-Ahola, S.E. *The Social Psychology of Leisure and Recreation*. Dubuque, IA: Wm. C. Brown, 1980.

Karoly, P. and F.H. Kanfer, Ed. *Self-Management and Behavior Change, From Theory to Practice*. New York: Pergamon Press, 1982.

McDowell, C.F. *Leisure Wellness, Concepts and Helping Strategies*. Booklet 8, "Managing Attitudes, Affirmation and Assertion." Eugene, OR: Sun Moon Press, 1983.

Munn, N. *Introduction to Psychology*. Boston: Houghton-Mifflin, 1962.

Pelletier, K.R. *Mind a Healer, Mind a Slayer*. New York: Delta Publishing, 1976.

Persig, R.M. *Zen and the Art of Motorcycle Maintenance*. New York: Bantam Books, 1976.

Seligman, M.E.P. "What You Can Change, What You Cannot" *Psychology Today*. 27.3 (1994): 34–84.

Watson, D.L. and R.G. Tharp. *Self-Directed Behavior, Self-Modification for Personal Adjustment*. Monterey, CA: Brooks/Cole Publishing, 1972.

CHAPTER 17
Leisure and Love

We can do no great things; only small things with great love.

—Mother Theresa

Leisure textbooks don't talk about love. I have never understood that. If anything has the capacity to free a person from monotony and boredom, it is love. Love lifts the spirit and heals the heart. Love stimulates perceived freedom, perceptual freedom, and intrinsic satisfaction. In fact, in my opinion, if love is absent from one's life, it is impossible for a person to experience a leisure lifestyle.

My granddaughter, three-year-old Samantha, called me yesterday. Her little voice coming to me from nearly 1000 miles away. She called to tell me about the death of Moe, her little box turtle. She quietly told me how Moe had been left with a neighbor while she and her family vacationed. When they returned, Moe was very ill. She described how she tried to make him well by wrapping him in her doll's blanket, how she gave him water, and how she hid him in a quiet place. But nothing she did made Moe well. And, one day, as she put it, "Poof, just like magic, Moe was gone." She was very sad, because she had loved her little turtle. Her tiny voice, flowing with sincerity and emotion, pulled at my heart. She had no experience with death, this was something new to her, and in her own way she was trying to make sense out of it, "Poof, just like magic, Moe was gone."

As I listened to her, I futilely tried to think of something to make it all okay for her. I would buy her another turtle, I would sing her a song, I would tell her a story. . . . but I knew there was nothing that I could do to take the hurt away. As I listened to her tell her story, I felt my love for her swell inside and spill out in the form of tears. Somehow I managed to change the subject to her preschool, and from there we went to a song. I sang to her "Down by the Station," and she sang to me her version of "Twinkle Twinkle Little Star," and then she said she was sleepy. "Goodnight grandpa, sweet dreams. I love you." "I love you too, Samantha." I hung up the phone, my mind filled with the image of a blue-eyed, blond haired, precocious little girl.

I've always felt grandparents have a special kind of love, and this was my first time to be on the grandfather end. I reflected on my own grandparents and how I had always felt very cared for by them, and how I never doubted that they loved me. Their love for me was a special gift. It made me feel safe, secure, and hopeful. I think there may have been times, particularly as an adolescent, that I doubted my parents' love, but I never doubted my grandparents' love. I never questioned my love for my grandparents, it was simply a given. When my Grandma Williams was in her last few weeks, I spent as much time as I could with her. Unable to feed herself, I arranged my schedule so that I could be with her at dinner time. She had lost most of her faculties, and sometimes she didn't recognize me. But, I could tell she still loved me, and that knowledge seemed to give me strength to face her death, and my love seemed to give her courage. As I reflected on these thoughts, a chilling reality struck me, it had become my turn to be the grandparent. Little Sammie had called me because she needed the kind of love a grandparent specializes in. I was flattered, humbled, and grateful all in one.

To love someone deeply gives you strength.
Being loved by someone deeply gives you courage.

—Lao Tzu

A grandpa's love is just one kind of love. There are other kinds of love, too. I once fell in love with a beautiful girl, I was in high school (okay, it might have been infatuation). I remember mustering enough courage to say those three magic words—"I love you." She looked at me sweetly and said, "I love you too—like, like a brother." Not what I had in mind. And, what about our love for things? A friend of mine had a beautiful car. He worked on it regularly, maintained it properly, and kept it waxed with a brilliant shine. It was a convertible. He and his date took the car to the local Fourth of July fireworks show. Unfortunately, one of the fireworks went awry and landed in the convertible. When I heard about the accident I called to ask how he was doing, The car had been destroyed by the fire started by the fireworks. He and his date had escaped uninjured, but all he could mutter was, "I really loved that car, I really loved that car."

Our pets are another category. Several years ago my brother, a game warden, lost his favorite dog to an accident. He brought the dog's body home for burial. As he approached the house, his entire family came out to comfort him. His wife touched his arm and looked him in the eyes and said, "Remember, you've got your family, and we all love you." He responded, "I know, but no one quite loved me like this dog."

One of the reasons we seem to love our pets so much is because they love us unconditionally. They put no restrictions on us. I have never had a dog that said to me, "If you don't give me a dog biscuit, I won't love you anymore." Pets love us without condition, without strings or expectations. They accept us as we are, something most people have difficulty doing. I suppose that's why we say, "A dog is a human's best friend." We might want to add to that ". . . and pretty good role model, too."

When a person is deprived of love, regardless of the form, it leaves an aching. Our need to be loved and to love is just as real as our need for food, shelter, air, and water. Without love, we focus on filling the need to the extent that the quality of life is compromised. As Charlie Brown said, "Nothing takes the taste out of peanut butter like unrequited love." A more scholarly perspective is found in Coleman, Butcher and Carson (1980). Here love is described as "—crucial to healthy personality development and adjustment" (98). They go on to point out that when a child feels loved, "many conditions that might otherwise impair development—may be largely neutralized" (98). Conversely when a child is deprived of love, social and personality development will be distorted.

We need it all, we need love in every form, from a grandpa's love to a best friend's love to a lover's love. Without love the ache can be unbearable, and no matter how successful we are at life's other endeavors, failure to love and be loved is a failure for which no other success can compensate.

The most terrible poverty is loneliness and the feeling of being unloved.

—Mother Theresa

How Hate Compromises Leisure

I really enjoy talking about romantic love, you know the kind of slippery, gushy kind of love that attaches a rocket booster to your heart and sends you spinning into orbit. And, I am going to get to that kind of love in just a moment, but first I want to talk about a more general kind of love, the kind often spoken of as "brotherly love." This kind of love can be described as "goodwill in action," or perhaps "generalized kindness." It is the kind of love that brings out the best in people, disarms anger and extinguishes hatred. This is the kind of love that Sonny and Cher were singing about in the 70's. This is the kind of love that allows people to walk streets freely, express themselves freely, give to one another freely, to worship freely, to philosophize freely, to explore and discover freely. I suppose that a society is capable of experiencing leisure to the extent that it is capable of this kind of love. It is the kind of love that not only makes the "world go around," but makes the ride worthwhile.

The antithesis of this kind of love is hate. Where hate surpasses love, serenity gives way to fear, anger supplants peace, and hope gives way to despair. Where there is hate, perceptions become narrow, people become targets, and friendship is less important than alliances. A world filled with hate is a world devoid of the two critical dimensions of leisure—perceived freedom and intrinsic satisfaction. I recently heard a noted radio personality talk about how if he were wronged by someone he would do whatever was necessary to destroy the offending person. He spoke with the venom and intensity of someone who had not learned how to love. Everyday, we read in the news of people who literally gave up their lives in order to strike out at another human being in a hateful manner. They become so limited in their thinking that they give up their freedom for a self-imposed constraint. They lose their capacity to enjoy simple satisfactions. They become driven by hate, and their pathway becomes increasingly narrow, converging on a point of no return. This week in Sacramento, a husband and father of two children killed his wife and then turned the gun on himself. Where had his love gone? How could he leave his children both fatherless and motherless? Hate destroyed a presumably once loving family. One day later the newspaper reported a similar story, but the players were different. Next week there will be more such stories. More lives will be ruined, more pain will be inflicted on people who should be enjoying the fruits of love, not the agony of hate.

> Love looks at life through a telescope; hate through a microscope.
>
> –Anonymous

Hate magnifies slights into monumental offenses even capital offenses. When a perceived offense is viewed as sufficiently serious, then vengeance, getting even, retribution, is easily justified. When you set out to ruin someone, you are in effect allowing someone else to control your behavior. "Hey, he cut me off! I'll get even with him!" And so the focus becomes getting even, and when that happens a cloud of ugliness descends, the light of love is dimmed and in some cases completely extinguished. Recently, I read where an angry motorist pursued a young couple for over thirty-miles for some perceived wrong. When he caught them he fired his revolver into the car killing the couple's two-year old daughter. His anger and hate had placed him on that ever narrowing pathway which leads to a point from which there is neither redemption nor return. *Hatred makes leisure impossible.*

> Hatred paralyzes life; love releases it.
> Hatred confuses life; love harmonizes it.
> Hatred darkens life; love illumines it.
>
> —Martin Luther King, Jr.

Romantic Love

Romantic love is sort of like the other kind of love, but with hormones. It is the kind of love that leads to marriage, children, and grandchildren. It is the kind of love that can bring the very best out in people, and endures a lifetime. It's the kind of love that happens when you feel you have found your soul-mate.

It is different from infatuation, and has very little to do with sex. You can have sex with a person without being in love, and you can be infatuated without being in love. But, when you have found love in a relationship with another person, you transcend the physical and enter into the spiritual. You accept another unconditionally, you don't impose unrealistic expectations on your love, you see each other as complementary parts of a whole, and yet you recognize your individuality and protect your partner's independence as your own. Infatuation is based on fantasy, love in reality. Judith Viorst distinguishes infatuation and love in the following way:

> Infatuation is when you think that he's as sexy as Robert Redford, as smart as Henry Kissinger, as noble as Ralph Nader, as funny as Woody Allen, and as athletic as Jimmy Conners. Love is when you realize that he's as sexy as Woody Allen, as smart as Jimmy Conners, as funny as Ralph Nader, as athletic as Henry Kissinger, and nothing like Robert Redford.[11]

Romantic love differs from other kinds of love in a very important way. It has a powerful physical component. Recent studies have shown that when the chemistry between two people is sufficiently rich, a chemical is secreted in the brain. It has an effect similar to epinephrine! That explains phrases like, "She makes me feel like I am floating on a cloud." This kind of natural high is what makes romantic love so exciting. It also explains why ending a relationship is so painful. When the chemistry dies, the production of phenylethylamine declines and the net effect is a physical "withdrawal." Sometimes the withdrawal is so intense that the couple comes back together for a "fix." This only prolongs the agony.

Some broken-hearted lovers salve the ache of a broken heart by eating anything and everything with chocolate in it. It seems that chocolate contains large amounts of phenylethylamine. This fact gives added meaning to what one of my friends once said to me, "Love is what people seek when they run out of chocolate."

Love is a really strange game. It is the only game where there are either two winners or two losers.

—Anonymous

Enhancing Both Kinds of Love

It would be nice if we could snap our fingers, and "poof, just like magic" make everyone more loving, but we can't. What we can do is try to make ourselves more loving. Just like hate, love is contagious. Demonstrate love and it will come back to you, and as love grows the world becomes a little less hectic. Here are some ideas worth exploring:

Five Things a Person Can Begin to Do Right Now to Promote Love

1. **Random Acts of Kindness.** Do something nice for someone without expecting something in return. I recently was the recipient of such an act. It was approaching rush hour and people were hurrying to exit the downtown parking garage where my car had spent the afternoon. Traffic was bumper to bumper, and this made it difficult for cars to enter from any of the aisles that lined the main exit route. At one point, I allowed a car to slip in front of me. When I got to the cashier's booth, I was surprised to learn that the woman in the car that I had allowed in line had paid for my parking toll.

   The world is a more gentle place thanks to people like my unknown benefactor. Make it a practice, both in your primary love relationships and in general, to practice random acts of kindness.

11. You can update this quote by inserting the names of current celebrities.

Right now, stop for a moment and think of different things you might do that would qualify as random acts of kindness. Here are some examples:

- Send someone flowers for no particular reason.
- Write a letter to someone complimenting them for something well done.
- Do another family member's most disliked chore.
- Give a street person a dollar instead of a scowl.
- Give your partner an unconditional foot massage.

2. **Demonstrate Respect.** What this means is to allow a person to *be*. The real test of respect is in traffic when you are not the driver. Can you relax and avoid telling the other party how to drive? "Watch out for that car, don't ride the clutch, you are the worst driver." Extend this notion to food, clothing, entertainment etc. Respect validates another person, allows them to enjoy a feeling of integrity and self-respect, and creates an environment that encourages growth and development. It also allows them to respect you!

   Here are five ways to demonstrate respect.

   - Don't stereotype others.
   - Don't ignore the expressed wishes of another person.
   - Don't be unreasonably critical of another's beliefs or values.
   - Don't judge another's way of doing things as incorrect just because he or she does them differently than you.
   - Don't mock or ridicule a person because he or she is different from you.

3. **Be Attentive.** "What was that?" My daughter told me of an experience she had with a counselor. During her appointment her counselor kept dozing off. I asked her how that made her feel. She said, "Not very important." She paused, brightened, and said, "Some good came of it, at least I got a good chuckle. I started talking nonsense, and the counselor kept responding as if I were talking sense." Being attentive serves to validate another person.

   Think of some ways in which you can be more attentive to the needs and interests of those people who are most important to you. Here are five ideas:

   - Look directly at people when they are talking to you; give them your undivided attention.
   - Remember special likes and dislikes of people close to you and reflect this awareness in how you relate to them.
   - Don't discuss issues that you know make another person uncomfortable.
   - Be alert for nonverbal communication.
   - Don't put a person in a situation that you know will disturb that person.

4. **Be Available.** One common complaint of couples in trouble is that they no longer have time for one another. If you love someone you will be available. It may require some effort to arrange your schedule, but one hallmark of a loving relationship is reliability. Be there for your daughter on those special occasions, be there for your partner on those times when you are most needed, attend your son's football game. Being available is different from being present. We have all been around people who were physically present, but emotionally or psychologically somewhere else. People can live together, sleep together, eat together and yet be emotionally light years apart. Being available means being open, accessible, responsive, and efficacious. Be available to those you love.

   What are some things that you can do to make yourse1fmore available to those you love? Here are five ideas along these lines:

   - Make certain your loved ones know how to reach you.
   - Inform others of your work schedule.
   - Stay abreast of special events in the lives of your family and friends in order that you can arrange your schedule accordingly.

- Surprise someone by attending an event that is important to them.
- Take time to eat together as a family.

5. **Be Communicative.** Communication is the art of expressing and listening. It is one of the most important skills in building and maintaining loving relationships.

   It involves more than just talking at someone, the expressing part, it also involves making certain you understand what the other person is saying, as well as confirming that what you are saying is understood.

   What are some things that you can do to be more effective in your communication with others that you love? Here are five ideas:

   - Say these words more often, "I love you."
   - Openly accept it when someone says, "I love you."
   - Never use the pronoun "you" when you are being critical of someone.
   - Don't just rely on words, employ actions (they speak louder than words).
   - Hug someone you care about.

Five Principles That Support Love

1. **Love Is Unmeasurable.** Learn from your pets, put no conditions or strings on your love. There may be some behaviors that you can't support, but never base your love on your partners performance, or your children's behavior, or your friends' actions. Love is not conditional, nor is it limited.
2. **Love Thrives on Honesty and Trust.** Deceit will destroy a relationship as quickly as anything. But do you need to tell your partner everything? Opinions are divided here, but my feeling is that once a relationship has commenced, honesty is the best policy. If it's history, let it be.
3. **Love Generates Tenderness.** Love brings out nurturing qualities in people, and there isn't a person alive who can't benefit from a little nurturing. Nurturing and enabling are two different things. Sometimes people enable self-defeating behavior in the name of love, but to enable someone to engage in self-defeating behavior is not consistent with the true nature of love. Love nurtures and in so-doing promotes growth and development.
4. **Love Promotes Growth and Development.** When people are surrounded by unconditional love and acceptance they tend to take the steps necessary to grow and develop. People feel comfortable learning new things, taking risks, and changing their lives when they are supported by those who love them. A loving environment is the best gift you can give your children.
5. **Love Is Fun.** It is fun to be with people who love you, for in their love they create an environment that brings out the best in you, and allows you to feel free. Where there is love there is often laughter, play, and humor. Love is fun.

What about Sex?

> The world would be a better place if love were as easy to keep as it is to make.
>
> –Anonymous

By not having said anything about sex, I am not suggesting it isn't important. It is important, and you should exercise creativity and care in maintaining a healthy sexual relationship. But, sex is not love. Where there are sexual problems, there are probably other problems that interfere with a loving relationship. To have a successful sexual life, it is important to have an abundance of love and all that goes along with it. When you have love in a relationship you hold one another with sensitivity and tenderness. When you have love in a relationship you are free to pleasure one another without inhibition. When you have an abundance of love in a relationship you are free to discover one another again and again.

Finding Love

I once had a friend who had a loving family, a wonderful job, and good health. By all outward appearances he was happy, but he lacked one important thing. He lacked romantic love. He really wanted a girl friend, a significant other, but the harder he looked the more hopeless it seemed. In the process of seeking romantic love he came to depreciate himself. "Why can't I get a date?" evolved to "Why would anyone want to date me?" which led to "I wouldn't want to date anyone who would date someone like me." He started to avoid the very places where he was most likely to meet a romantic partner. The net effect was depression, pessimism and unhappiness. And, of course, no one wanted to date him.

I relocated and lost touch with my friend. But time is circular and eventually our paths crossed again. When chance put us together again seven years later, many things had happened to my friend. The first thing that I noticed was how positive and happy he seemed. The second thing I noticed was his apparent physical health. The third, and most surprising thing I noticed—there was a wedding band on his ring finger!

Over dinner he told me a wonderful story. His depression drove him to seek professional help, and through therapy and Prozac, he was able to turn his life around. In the period that followed, he made an effort to apply two principles. (1) When you are alone, think of it as a time for self-improvement so that you have more to offer a potential partner, and (2) before you can effectively love someone else, you first must love yourself. By using his free time to develop new skills and knowledge, he became a more interesting and confident person. As he learned to love and appreciate himself, he gradually developed a strength of character that made him more attractive to others. When he met his wife, she found him irresistible and he found her to be the girl of his dreams.

In talking about his wife, he described her in glowing terms. He even said, "I never thought I would find a woman like her." I couldn't resist saying, "The old you probably never would have. . . you would have rejected yourself so she wouldn't have to!"

Romantic love comes and goes, relationships end and begin, some last longer than others, and a few last forever. A break from romantic love is not a bad thing. It is an opportunity to grow and develop and get better acquainted with yourself. A new love will likely come along, and its important that you are ready to participate when love is proffered. If you are lost in negativity, self-loathing, and pessimism, you can be certain, romantic love will be hard to find.

A Final Note on Love

A few years ago I asked my students to write love poems. A student by the name of Derek Trent Jones penned these words (I share them with his permission):

Once I sat all alone
Without a love to call my own
My heart was hid behind a curtain
Without a love my soul was hurtin'.

And then I looked into a mirror
And knew why no one called me "dear."
I was a droopy, sad old grump.
I'd even give myself the dump.

And so I set out to change my style,
And although it took a little while,

Optimism, happiness became my life,
And, now I have a loving wife!

Agreed, Derek is no Robert Frost, but the sentiment is right on the mark. Without love we miss out on a very important part of life. To find love, we must start with ourselves, and if we persist in developing loving qualities, love will grow.

Love is like cool sheets in the summer and a comforter in the winter.

—Marie Huff

Closing Note. . .

Love's highly personal and private nature make it a difficult topic for leisure writers and scholars to explore. Consequently, it is rarely discussed in textbooks on leisure. It is generally thought to be a topic for poets and artists. Nevertheless it is also a legitimate area of discussion for students of leisure. Without love, life neither sparkles nor glows. When one is lost in longing for love, leisure can only be a dream.

REFERENCES

Coleman, J.C., J.N. Butcher and R.C. Carson. *Abnormal Psychology and Modern Life*. 6th Edition. Palo Alto, CA: Scott Foresman and Company, 1980.

CHAPTER 18

Applying Leisure Principles

Boredom doesn't just happen, it takes some effort!

—Derek Jones

I can't begin to tell you the number of times I have heard people say, "There is nothing fun to do in this town." I suppose that even if you lived in Disneyland, the happiest place on earth, there would be those who would say, "Nope, nothing to do here." I recently surveyed my students, and in the questionnaire I included the question, "What is your favorite fun thing to do in this town?" The most common response was, "Leave." Some responded, "Sleep." One even said, "Are you kidding—THIS town!"

This complaint isn't unique to Sacramento, California. I've heard similar comments from people in Houston, Phoenix, St. Louis, and Salt Lake City. And of course, in all of these communities there is at least one or two things to do for fun. People come from all over the world to visit Sacramento. They come to see the seat of California state government, to visit historic "Old Town," to float the American River, to attend the Jazz Festival, and visit the Rail Road Museum. Yet, there are numerous people who live here for years and never once visit any of these places. Why? They will tell you without hesitation, "There is nothing to do in this town!"

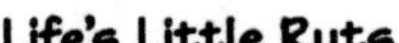

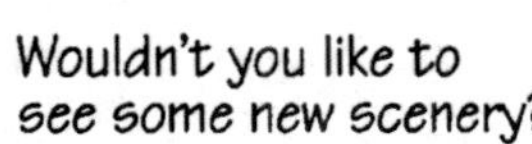

You spend a lot of time in your town. It is in a sense your backyard, and just as your backyard has its own distinct landscape, your community has a leisure landscape. There are places to go, people to see, and things to do—all part of the leisure landscape. There is the old adage of the man who searched the world for wealth only to find that there were diamonds all the time in his own backyard, but when he finally found them he was too old to enjoy them! The same thing can happen to those of us who believe that we have to travel over the hill to the greener pasture in order to find something fun to do. There are lots of opportunities for recreation and leisure involvement, all around us. We merely have to open our eyes to the opportunities and then take the steps necessary to enjoy them.

If You Don't Know It's Available, It's Not!

One of the reasons that people often find it hard to find recreation in their own environment is because we operate from a misconception about what can be a leisure activity. We limit ourselves by thinking that recreation or leisure activities are confined to sports or entertainment. In addition, we sometimes get trapped into thinking that the bigger and louder the event, the more recreational it is. We forget that a great deal of satisfaction can derive from hobbies, crafts, fitness, inventing, music, writing, drama, gardening, and so on.

Mitchel and Mason in 1934 recognized that "the motive of the player determines the character of the play" (114). After considerable research they identified five fundamental motivations that influenced the kind of activities people choose during leisure. I've mentioned these "wishes" earlier, but let's look at them again.

A wish for new experiences
Competition, adventures, learning, creative expression, travel
A wish for security
Family fun, religion, spiritual pursuits, home-based recreation
A wish for response
Friendship, socializing, social groups, courtship, dating
A wish for recognition
Participation in social groups, advocating a cause, politics
A wish for the aesthetic
Exposure to beauty in the form of color, movement, rhythm, motion, sound

It can be Montana or Maine, New Jersey or Nevada, it really doesn't matter where a person is, we all can enjoy activities that are aesthetic in nature, or that provide new experiences, or engender a feeling of security, or that provide socializing and recognition. These are common to all places and all people. You don't need to go to Disneyland, or Las Vegas, or New Orleans to find activities that meet these needs. You just need to be motivated to look in your own backyard and aware enough to find the diamonds lying easily within reach.

Let's revisit the work of Carlson, Deppe and Maclean who suggest you might look in any one of the following eleven categories of activities for something of interest:

Arts and Crafts. You can do arts and crafts anywhere—your garage or the community center, the community college or the community park.

Dance. You can always find someone who would love to teach you to dance, or if you already dance you can always find a church social, a community dance, a night club, or your own living room to waltz, fox trot, folk dance, or boogie woogie.

Drama. Every community has a theater group, and they always are recruiting, but you don't have to perform, you can write, study drama, or become technically skilled in lighting, props, or stage management.

Mental, Linguistic and Literary. Some of the great writers of our time came from small communities, and almost every community has a book club, or a poetry corner, or some other special interest group. And, if you can't find what you are looking for in your local community, you can always try the cyber-community.

Music. Learn to play an instrument, join a choral group, study music theory, collect a certain kind of music, become part of a music appreciation club.

Outdoor Recreation. Camping, picnicking, hiking, backpacking, rafting, climbing, and sightseeing are outdoor activities that most of us can easily enjoy.

Social Recreation. People have a need for affiliation, we like to be in the presence of others. Every community offers a number of social groups in which you can find membership, everything from church groups to nudists.

Sports and Games. It is true that as people get older, there seem to be fewer opportunities for participation in active games and sports, but when you are young there is an abundance. And, what is stopping you from starting a league of seniors if your community doesn't have one?

Hobbies. Hobbies bring people a great deal of pleasure. Some people are collectors and others inventors. Some are creative and some just organize things. The best electric trains are owned and operated by adults.

Service Activities. I read in the newspaper yesterday that a retired teacher, a woman well into her sixties, routinely walks along the American River Parkway picking up debris. That's impressive! I was equally impressed by the senior woman who I met at the MedClinic Health Library who told me she volunteers her time there for fun. I was also impressed by the college engineering student who volunteered his time to help 3rd graders with their science projects. People often forget that there is great recreational value in giving your time and talents in the service of others.

Special Events. Every town has a founders day, not to mention national and state holidays. Families have reunions, anniversaries, and birthday parties. Every region of the country sponsors fairs, jubilees, and festivals. There are auctions, displays, exhibits and showcases almost everywhere one goes.

Now what do you mean, there is nothing to do in this town?

If you don't know that an opportunity exists, then for you it does not. A person committed to developing a leisure lifestyle pays attention to leisure opportunities. A person who is committed to a leisure lifestyle values discovery.

Do Your Interests Match Your Actual Behavior?

Sometimes the wake-up call comes when you realize that there are lots of activities in which you have an interest, but few that you actually experience. Try this exercise:

For each of the following recreational activities answer two questions. Choose the appropriate response for each item and note the numerical value. The questions are:

A. How **interested** are you in this activity?	B. How OFTEN do you participate in this activity?
Very = 5	Quite Frequently
Quite = 4	Often = 4
Somewhat = 3	Occasionally = 3
Not much = 2	Rarely = 2
Not at all = 1	Never = 1

		A	B
1.	Going to movies that appeal to me.	_____	_____
2.	Playing team sports.	_____	_____
3.	Hanging out, socializing with friends at a bar or coffee shop.	_____	_____
4.	Playing card or table games with friends.	_____	_____
5.	Doing things in nature like hiking, camping or picnicking.	_____	_____
6.	Playing with my computer.	_____	_____
7.	Working on my hobby.	_____	_____

		A	B
8.	Going dancing.	_____	_____
9.	Doing something really risky, wild, crazy or adventurous.	_____	_____
10.	Volunteering my time for a cause I believe in.	_____	_____
11.	Participating in some special event like a community event, concert, fair, or public spectacle.	_____	_____
12.	Spending quality time with my family, significant other or friends.	_____	_____
13.	Taking a road trip to some nearby place of interest.	_____	_____
14.	Having a sensuous or sexual experience.	_____	_____
15.	Having a spiritual or aesthetic experience.	_____	_____
16.	Doing something creative.	_____	_____

Compare your answers for each question. If you are like most people, you will find some disparity between your interests and your behaviors. The greater the disparity the louder the alarm. "But, Dr. Olson, there is only so much time." That's true, but the time you spend in recreation will come back to you in a number of very important ways—you will be refreshed, you will be more positive, you will be physically healthier, you will be more pleasant to be around, and you will be more productive. In school we had recess, as adults we sometimes don't even take lunch. One of the most important elements of the leisure lifestyle is the concept of recess—scheduled time for fun.

Some Practical Tips for Getting More Time

Throw Away Your Television. I got rid of my television for several months and was amazed at how much free time I had!

Don't Double Back. Plan your day so that you don't have to waste time driving back to a point you passed earlier in the day.

Don't Drive during Rush Hour. An ideal time for recess is when everyone else is rushing home. Spend the time you would otherwise spend steaming in traffic doing something fun, and then drive home leisurely in half the time.

Stop Losing Things. We spend too much time trying to find keys, socks, and billfolds. I have a friend who had a terrible time keeping track of her eye glasses. She solved the problem by buying 20 different pair. If she loses one, there is always another lying around. I also use that technique.

Learn to Say NO. Derek Jones designed something he calls a "NOte Pad." He found that it was hard for him to say no to someone even if he really didn't want to do what was being asked of him. This in the long run cost him a lot of time. He rarely did the task on time and when he did do it he often did it poorly and had to do it again. He knew he had to learn to say no.

NOTE PAD

In response to your request . . .

_____ I apologize, but I am unable to answer in the affirmative.
_____ Thank you for asking me, but I won't be available.
_____ Nice try, but I'll be doing something I actually want to do at that time.
_____ Right now I'm feeling pretty good, but if I say yes, I'll be miserable.
_____ I'll put your request on my priority list right below root canal.
_____ Sorry, but your request falls right in the middle of my recess time.

Learn to Delegate. If someone else is doing it, you don't have to. There are a lot of people who wouldn't know what to do with their own time if someone like you didn't tell them what to do. They feel important and you have more time for recess. By delegating, you are doing them and you a favor!

Use the KISS Principle. You've heard of the KISS Principle—"Keep it simple, stupid." People often make things too complicated. We acquire too many things, try to accept too many responsibilities, and opt for the grand over the merely functional. I just recently talked to someone who had spent two weeks on vacation. She complained that she was miserable the whole time. Why? They tried to do too much, see too much, go too many places. They needed a vacation from their vacation. As my old Welsh grandmother observed, "Too many pots on the stove makes for a tasteless dinner."

Write It Down. Dora Clarke is never without her list. It is the first thing she attends to in the morning and the last thing she puts down at night. Her list is broken down in logical categories, grouped together in such a manner as to allow her to get the most done in the shortest period of time. Included on her list are her daily recesses—a break in the morning, a relaxing lunch, and a workout in the afternoon—during rush hour.

Make Your Daily Recess Important. When you prioritize your day, include something fun. Make going to the movie, having a muffin and coffee, reading the newspaper, taking a swim, dancing after work, etc. just as important as going to the store, paying your bills, picking up your room.

Schedule Some Discovery Time. Discovery events are essential to a leisure lifestyle because they stimulate those much desired neurotransmitters. Block in time to try new activities, give yourself permission to explore new leisure horizons. Commit yourself to doing this.

Set Aside Some Cash for Recreation. Just as you save for the proverbial rainy day, save for the recreational day.

Competence and Leisure Skills

Time is a significant barrier to our engaging in leisure activities, but it is not the only one. Some leisure activities require a certain degree of skill. As has been pointed out earlier, in order for a person to derive satisfaction from a leisure activity, there must be a reasonable match between the demands of the activity and the individual's capacity to meet these demands. When the activity demands more than the participant can deliver, the quality of the experience diminishes quickly. Competence is a combination of innate ability and training. Some people are well suited for high risk-recreation such as skiing or ski diving, but to actively engage in risk-recreation one must possess the necessary skills. A certain inherent athletic ability coupled with adequate training is essential if a person is to get the most out of many such leisure activities.

For many activities early training is desirable. Young people learn more quickly, and also recover more quickly from injuries. Consequently, it is a good idea for young people to learn as many recreational skills as possible. Unfortunately, many of our educational systems seem to be eliminating some of the very programs that offer the most in terms of lifetime leisure skills. Public and semi-public recreation programs may help pick up the slack, but the most logical place for people to learn leisure skills is in the public schools.

Just because learning occurs most efficiently during one's youth doesn't mean that older people shouldn't try to learn new recreational skills. As discussed in Chapter 6, recent research demonstrates that the brains of older people may be able to reorganize themselves in response to adult experiences. Whether this is the result of the production of new neural connections or an adaptation of existing neural structures is not clear. What is clear is that older people can learn new skills. When an adult sets out to learn a new recreational skill, two benefits result (1) The new skill leads to new recreational opportunities, and (2) the process of learning the new skills leads to a healthier brain. The emphasis here is on the "new" skill. The mere reinforcement of old pathways may not stimulate the brain to greater health. Consequently, it is important to apply the discovery concept, and try something different from the types of leisure activities with which you have the greatest familiarity. What follows are four ideas to help you develop new leisure interests, skills, and competencies.

Explore Special Interests. Every community has various special interest groups, most of which offer training in their area of interest. Look to see what your community offers and then give yourself permission to try something entirely new. If it makes you feel uncomfortable to think about doing a certain activity, it may just be what the doctor ordered.

Take a Class. Most communities are reasonably close to a community college. Look into the possibility of taking a course that interests you. If you are taking it just for fun, the homework might qualify for a hobby. More and more people are studying over the Internet.

Learn on Your Own. Your library is a wonderful leisure resource. If you are near a university, there will be more than enough resources to pique your interests and enhance your leisure skills.

Give Yourself Permission. Give yourself permission to experience the learning process. Too many times we disqualify ourselves from learning a new skill because we don't feel that we will excel. Learning a leisure activity does have something to do with excelling, but not in a competitive sense. Leisure is about excelling in the living sense. Give yourself permission to experience new activities. Give yourself permission to be as good as you are. Give yourself permission to enjoy the process of learning something new.

As your repertoire of leisure skills grow, so will your opportunities for leisure. It is amazing how a person can find time to do something they have come to really enjoy.

There is always something to do for fun no matter where you are. It is fundamentally a function of attitude, knowledge, and interests. In a world where the chaotic seems to prevail, it is essential that we make time for recreation and leisure. It not only provides a contrast to the disorder, it helps restore our energies and fortify our attitudes and abilities to hang loose in an uptight world.

Finding Leisure During Non-Leisure Time

Much of this book has been about developing an approach to life that enables you to experience leisure in any number of non-leisure environments. For many people this is the ultimate challenge—finding enjoyment in activities that are relatively devoid of perceived freedom.

For some people work is drudgery, for others it is a joy. How can a person make his work his leisure?

Choose Wisely

As was pointed out in Chapter 9, finding the right job is one of the most important things you will ever do for yourself. Some people aren't willing to pay the price to acquire the skills that will enable them to hold a job that brings them joy. Consequently, finding leisure in their work may be very difficult. I have an acquaintance who frequently talks about how much he dislikes his current job, and how he would like to acquire skills for another job, but he never takes the steps necessary to acquire the necessary skills. My own experience is a contrast to his. I have the best job in the world, but getting here didn't come easy. I had to study long and hard, for years I had to live in uncomfortable circumstances, and during many of the years I was in graduate school I didn't even have a car. Discretionary money was a fantasy. This may shock you, but for years I didn't even have a television! But, I persevered, and today I am enjoying a wonderful life. My friend tells me how lucky I am, but luck had nothing to do with it. But, even if you didn't choose wisely or haven't found the perfect job, you can still find leisure in your work. It depends on your frame of mind.

Attitudes, Interests and Perceptions Make the Difference

The difference between those who really seem to find fun in everything they do and those who live rather dull and colorless lives is likely a function of interests and attitudes. For some people there is no job so daunting that they can't find something exciting, interesting, or fun to do. For these people, almost any job seems to hold potential for optimal arousal. Individuals with a less optimistic attitude and more prosaic interests might find it difficult to enjoy themselves even in what appears to others as exciting and rewarding jobs. It is all a function of attitude, interest, and perception.

The nasty thing about negative thoughts is that they can feed upon themselves. When people begin to operate under the proverbial dark cloud a biochemical response follows that leads them into a rather dark and often deep emotional pit. This process (discussed in Chapter 5) involves the diminution of powerful mood elevators, neurotransmitters such as dopamine, epinephrine, and seratonin. As these important chemicals become less potent, interests diminish further, leading to an increased negative attitude and a further reduction of the chemicals associated with positive moods. Depressed people find it very hard to find something fun to do.

When people are saying, and believing, that their work is unpleasant, they will continue to say and believe that until they begin to look at things more positively. Found in the lyrics of an old song, sometimes sung in grade school, is the secret to improving any situation it goes like this:

> If you chance to meet a frown
> Do not let it stay.
> Quickly turn it upside down
> And, smile that frown away!

Philosophers knew it before scientists, the scriptures even before the philosophers, and you have known it since your youth—the mind and body have an incredible capability of influencing one another. I have a friend who is an elementary school teacher. One day she discovered that one of her students had lice. For the next twenty-four hours her head itched. No lice, just the power of suggestion. Remember the example of how visualizing a lemon can produce a physical response (Chapter 14) illustrates the mind/body duality. Visualize the image in each line.

1. Visualize a fresh, bright, yellow lemon.
2. Visualize slicing the lemon, notice the juice oozing from the cut.
3. Visualize taking one slice and sniffing its aroma.
4. Visualize tasting the freshly cut lemon.

Now, if you are like most people, the mere image of a fresh lemon invoked a physical response. You salivated, perhaps puckered your lips, and felt a tingling in your cheeks. I often remind my students, that as the brain leads, the body follows. The converse is also true: As the body leads, the brain will follow. That's why you always feel better after exercising, and why my Father always feels better after thinking about exercising.

As simplistic as it sounds, to clear the clouds and let the sunshine through, turn that frown upside down and smile that frown away. In the process you will stimulate the production of catecholamines—those mood elevators that help you find fun things to do—regardless of where you work. So, for starters, if you want work to be more enjoyable, begin practicing at work those behaviors that are associated with pleasant responses. Remember, in Chapter 10, we were encouraged by Dr. Peter to laugh at least twenty-times daily, particularly if we had nothing to laugh at.

If one's work yields an optimal level of arousal, we know from Chapter 5 that the net outcome will be increased productivity and feelings of satisfaction. We also learned from Chapter 9 that perceived competence, just as with leisure activities, is vital to enjoying one's work. If you don't have adequate job skills the result will likely be supraoptimal arousal manifested by feelings of anxiety. Of course where your skills exceed the demand of your job, the results will likely be suboptimal arousal and boredom. Where the job requirements nicely fit with your skills, it is likely that you will find yourself slipping into periods of what I call perceptual freedom, the absence of awareness of competing stimuli. This is one of the characteristics of optimal arousal and a manifestation of being in what I call the "optimal performance zone."[12] It is also correlated with feelings of satisfaction. When you find yourself so involved in your work that you forget about time or other interests, it is similar to being so absorbed in a recreational activity that you are similarly unaware of competing interests. If you measure leisure in terms of perceptual freedom and intrinsic satisfaction, you can say that both circumstances have produced leisure. "Time flies when you are having fun."

To increase the probability of experiencing leisure at work a person can employ the following strategies:

1. If work is supraoptimally arousing, lower arousal by reducing stimuli (less responsibilities, more time to do tasks, familiar work partners, etc.)
2. If work is suboptimally stimulating, increase arousal by increasing stimulation (increased responsibilities, more complex tasks, more novel tasks, different work settings, etc.)
3. Develop attitudes that serve to reduce stimuli or enhance stimuli (learn to see the task from a more positive perspective, develop more positive interactions with co-workers, view the experience as a growing experience, etc.)
4. Develop job skills while on the job that will enable you to move to a more enriching environment.
5. Finally, if your job is making you sick and it is beyond your ability to improve the working environment or the tasks you are required to do, call in well.

Finding the right job is very important. If you choose wisely you will find leisure in both your work and free-time.

Simple Pleasures

Robert Ornstein and David Sobel begin their book, *Healthy Pleasures*, by talking about "The Pleasure Principle." They present a convincing argument that pleasure has a purpose. They present evidence that the human desire for pleasure evolved to "enhance our survival." Pleasure responses are linked to survival needs such as eating and drinking; reproduction, recuperation, exercise, and so on. Pleasure responses are also linked to our needs for affiliation, self-esteem, and competence. Consequently, as humans, it can be said that we are designed to experience pleasure, and that the degree to which we experience it in everyday life is an indication of whether or not we are on the "right track" (4). They put it this way:

> Although there are exceptions in the modern world, pleasure—enjoying food, sex, friends, work, and family—is the universal innate guide to health. People recognize what is healthful by the joys of life, by their pleasurable feelings—a delicious nap, a sated stomach, or the satisfaction of sexuality. These sensations signal our brain that we are on the right track (4).

They in no way suggest that people give themselves up to unbridled passions or uncontrolled self-indulgence. Rather, they encourage an approach to living that counters the sterile emphasis society places on work and challenges "archaic religiosity" that condemns all forms of pleasure seeking. They argue in effect for a middle ground. They are talking about simple pleasures. Again, turning to the authors' own words:

> The idea of napping, lovemaking, going for a walk, sitting idly and watching the natural world, or just playing catch with a child somehow seems unproductive. This view is needlessly shackling in twentieth-century society. In truth, simple pleasures can contribute to real productivity as well as to genuine health (11).

---

12. The term "flow" is attributed to Mihaly Csikszentmihalyi and is discussed in Chapter 5. Flow is similar to the optimal performance zone (OPZ).

Simple pleasures can occur at anytime, and should. Simple pleasures are as broad as life, and as the name implies uncomplicated and unpretentious. Ornstein and Sobel categorize pleasures in essentially the following manner:

Sensual Pleasures—touch and being touched, exposure to pleasant temperatures, exposure to light, pleasant tastes and aromas, looking at nature and natural environments, listening to music.

Mental Pleasures—play, happiness, optimism, humor, self-improvement, time-off, altruism.

Most of us overlook the little pleasures in lieu of the grandiose. We plan for the big vacation, the special theatrical presentation, the ski trip etc. But in reality, when you evaluate what brings you the most "pleisure" it is the combination of simple pleasures. This was illustrated by Ed Diener (and colleagues) in a study (1987) where he found the best predictor of happiness was simple events that produced a positive affect. It was clear from this study that it isn't the momentous events that bring happiness, but rather the accumulation of lots of simple pleasures. These findings are similar to the studies on microflow (discussed in Chapter 5) where it was shown that people have constant need to modulate arousal through simple, routine behaviors such as chewing gum, playing with a lock of hair, humming, or massaging one's forehead.

In completing this book, it is important to me that you feel comfortable with the value of simple pleasures in your life. I often hear people say things like, "I don't have time or money for leisure activities." This is offered as an excuse for being grumpy, exhausted, or overly serious. Intense moments of pleasure are delightful and valuable, but not nearly as important as the cumulative effect of many small pleasure producing experiences.

Closing Note. . .

Many books on recreation and leisure conclude with a discussion on the future of recreation. I'm not going to do that because if you have read this book carefully, you know that it has been written with the future in mind. The future is always peering through the window trying to get our attention. We can't shut it out, but we can fail to prepare for it. This book has been about learning to use leisure in such a manner as to make the future as pleasant as possible: learning to live in the present, learning to develop positive attitudes and behaviors, and learning how to enjoy simple pleasures. This book has been about using leisure now to make your future one of continued growth, development, and discovery.

REFERENCES

Ornstein, R. and D. Sobel. *Healthy Pleasures.* New York: Addison-Wesley, Publishing Company, Inc. 1990.

Larsen, R.J., E. Diener and R.S. Cropanzano. "Cognitive Operations Associated with Individual Differences in Affect Intensity." *Journal of Personality and Social Psychology.* 53.4 (1987): 767–74.

Appendix

Name: ______________________________ Date: ____________________ Section: ___________

The Leisure Profile Packet

The Leisure Profile Packet (LPP) consists of eight separate questionnaires (scales). These scales are designed to measure factors generally viewed by leisure educators as important to effective leisure functioning. The first two scales are designed to measure leisure awareness and leisure knowledge. These scales are referred to as "Cognitive Scales." The next four scales fall under the heading "Affective Scales." These scales measure leisure values, attitudes, and beliefs. The third set of scales is labeled "Behavioral Scales," and is designed to measure one's actual as well as desired leisure behaviors. The final scale is a measure of one's perceptions of obstacles to leisure. This final scale is referred to as the "Temporal Scale."

Only the first scale is a test of one's knowledge, and as a consequence is the only test for which there are correct answers. All of the remaining scales ask you to select a response valued form one to five (in one case one to four). By totaling these numerical values one can derive a score for each scale.

The scores derived for each scale are viewed to be a quantitative reflection of the attribute or factor measured. For example, high scores on the LPP Affective Scales are believed to be an indication of a positive orientation to leisure; conversely, low scores would indicate a negative outlook toward leisure. A high score on the Cognitive Scales are believed to indicate a relatively high level of leisure awareness and leisure knowledge. A high score on the LPP Behavioral Scales indicates the extent to which one is involved and desires to be involved in leisure activities. The LPP Temporal Scale provides an indication of the extent to which an individual perceives him or herself free of barriers to leisure. Each scale has a potential score of 100 and is designed to be self-scoring. As already mentioned, all of the scales are tabulated by simply adding the numerical values of the responses selected. Cognitive Scale 1 is scored using the answers found at the end of the scale.

For convenience, the LPP and all other worksheets are designed for easy removal. However, students are reminded to staple multiple sheets together. In addition, it is always a good practice to make certain your name, date and section number appear on any worksheets that are submitted for grading.

This edition of the Leisure Profile Packet is a research edition and should only be used for heuristic purposes. Although possessing face validity and reliability, its predictive capabilities remain uncertain. Consequently, its primary value is in stimulating an interest in self-discovery as related to leisure, exploration of the roles that leisure can play in one's life, and the interests and values one holds for leisure.

Name: ______________________________ Date: ____________________ Section: ___________

I. Cognitive Scale: Knowledge

Read each question carefully, then circle the correct answer from the choices provided.

1. Most people are likely to use which of the following definitions when speaking of leisure?
   a. Leisure is free or discretionary time.
   b. Leisure is a positive attitude marked by intrinsic satisfaction and perceived or perceptual freedom.
   c. Leisure is a physical activity engaged in for fun.
2. Which of the following is most likely true of play among children?
   a. Play is unimportant to a child's development.
   b. Play among children is a meaningless time filler.
   c. Play is an important contributor to healthy development.
3. The word "leisure" comes from an ancient Greek word meaning which of the following?
   a. To have fun.
   b. To be permitted.
   c. Lot relax.
4. To what extent did the philosopher Aristotle examine leisure?
   a. Leisure as a concept didn't exist during Aristotle's time.
   b. Aristotle was too busy to contemplate leisure.
   c. Aristotle placed great social and philosophical value on the concept of leisure.
5. From a psychological perspective, leisure is viewed as what?
   a. A state of mind.
   b. An attitude characterized by perceived freedom and intrinsic motivation.
   c. Both a and b.
6. Play is a behavior characterized by which of the following?
   a. A high degree of organization.
   b. Clear cut objectives.
   c. Spontaneity.
7. Recreation differs from play in what way?
   a. Recreation usually costs more in time and money than play.
   b. Recreation is usually less goal-oriented than play.
   c. Recreation tends to be more spontaneous than play.
8. Which of the following is true of play among adults?
   a. They entirely cease to play.
   b. They have no further need to play.
   c. Play continues to have an important role in their lives.
9. The claim that leisure activity can contribute to one's longevity is . . .
   a. wishful thinking.
   b. supported by scientific investigations.
   c. logical but wholly unsupported by science.
10. What are the negative consequences of restricting normal play patterns among children?
    a. Physical growth may be retarded.
    b. Emotional problems may develop.
    c. Both of the above (a and b) may occur.

11. What does science tell us about the influence of television on a child's play behavior?
   a. Children have a tendency to model their behavior after what they see on t.v.
   b. Watching television has no influence on a child's behavior.
   c. There is no evidence to support either position.
12. Overemphasis on extrinsic rewards as an adult may result from which of the following?
   a. Too much emphasis on winning during competitive sports as a child.
   b. Too little exposure to competitive and artistic activities as a child.
   c. Involvement in creative and artistic activities as a child.
13. What is the relationship between physiological arousal and feelings of satisfaction?
   a. Too little arousal makes a person feel dissatisfied.
   b. Too much arousal makes a person feel dissatisfied.
   c. Both of the above conditions produce dissatisfaction.
14. What of the following is likely to be the most serious problem associated with boredom?
   a. Lethargy and disinterest.
   b. Watching television?
   c. Self-generated problems.
15. To what extent can leisure activity help a person cope with stress?
   a. It is usually not helpful.
   b. It helps by relieving tension.
   c. It usually eliminates the underlying problems.
16. How does play affect one's immune system?
   a. It weakens it.
   b. It strengthens it.
   c. It has no effect.
17. What is the highest academic degree a person can receive in the leisure studies field?
   a. B.A. or B.S.
   b. M.A. or M.S.
   c. Ph.D.
18. What is the relationship of recreation/leisure to c linical/medical settings?
   a. Recreation and leisure have been shown to hinder the healing process.
   b. Recreation and leisure have no effect on the treatment of disease.
   c. Recreation and leisure are viewed as having therapeutic potential.
19. What organization represents professionals in the field of recreation and leisure?
   a. The American Play Association.
   b. The National Recreation and Leisure Association.
   c. The National Park and Recreation and Association.
20. What is the National Education Association's position on leisure?
   a. Every school should have a physical education program.
   b. Leisure education is one of the primary responsibilities of modern education.
   c. Every school should have at least two recess periods daily.

Self-scoring: Compare your answers with the following correct answers. Every correct answer is worth 5 points. Write your score here: _______.

Answers: la, 2c, 3b, 4c, 5c, 6c, 7a, 8c,9b, 10c, 11a, 12a, 13c, 14c, 15b, 16b, l7c, 18c, 19c, 20b

Name: ______________________________ Date: ____________________ Section: ___________

2. Cognitive Scale II: Practical and Pragmatic

In answering the following questions, you are to use a four point scale. In the space provided, indicate where your answer falls on the following scale:

STRONG YES = 4 Yes = 3 Weak Yes = 2 Very Weak Yes = 1 **No**=0

________ 1. If you were interested in learning how to do oil painting, do you know where or who to contact for information on how to get started?

________ 2. Do you feel you maintain a healthful lifestyle, including proper nutrition, exercise and stress reduction?

________ 3. Could you advise someone as to how he/she could get involved in a dance class?

________ 4. Do you have a collection that you maintain (trains, stamps, records, etc.)?

________ 5. Are you aware of any opportunities for people in your community to attend or participate in live theater performances?

________ 6. Do you participate in hobbies or crafts which involve using your hands (pottery, car repair, sewing etc.)?

________ 7. Have you attended a community event in the past 6 months (attend a concert, museum, art show, etc.)?

________ 8. Could you teach someone how to play a card game?

________ 9. Do you know how to operate a computer?

________ 10. Are you familiar with the basics of vegetable or flower gardening?

________ 11. Do you know how to playa musical instrument?

________ 12. Have you participated in a nature experience in the past 6 months (hiking, camping, bird watching etc.)?

________ 13. Would you know where to take classes in gourmet cooking or baking?

________ 14. If you wanted to go to an outdoor recreational area to camp for the weekend, do you know where you would go?

________ 15. Do you know how to reserve a campsite at a state or national park?

________ 16. Do you have basic skills in a recreational sport such as water skiing, snow skiing, surfing, or some other sport done individually?

________ 17. Do you know the basic rules of such sports as football, baseball or volleyball?

________ 18. Do you know the basic principles of aerobic fitness conditioning?

________ 19. If you wanted to attend a professional sporting event, would you know how to obtain tickets?

________ 20. Are you a good conversationalist?

________ 21. If a single friend needed help in meeting new people, could you advise him or her?

________ 22. Are you satisfied with your love life?

________ 23. Have you participated in a board game in the past 6 months (Monopoly, Scrabble, etc.)?

________ 24. Have you read a book in the past 6 months just for fun?

________ 25. Do you know what recreational services are provided in your area by the city, county, state or federal governments?

Self-scoring: To determine your score add the numerical values you entered for each questions. The sum of these values is your score. Write your score here: ______.

Name: ______________________________ Date: ____________________ Section: ___________

3. Affective Profile: Perceived Freedom

Read each statement carefully, then use the appropriate numerical value from the following scale to indicate the extent of your agreement with the statement.

STRONGLY AGREE = 5   Agree = 4   Undecided = 3   Disagree = 2   **STRONGLY DISAGREE** = 1

________ 1. I can usually make time to do the things I really want to do.

________ 2. I can usually schedule my work and other commitments to enable me to participate in leisure.

________ 3. I usually have enough money to do the things I really want to do.

________ 4. When activities are expensive, I can usually arrange to meet the expense.

________ 5. I can usually say "no" to people in order to allow time to participate in leisure activities.

________ 6. There are lots of fun things to do in this town.

________ 7. I usually have someone to participate in leisure activities with me.

________ 8. Even when I don't have a leisure companion, I usually participate in activities in which I have an interest.

________ 9. People like to do things with me.

________ 10. I actively seek to participate in leisure activities that will make me laugh.

________ 11. I consciously encourage myself to be playful and even silly sometimes.

________ 12. I am capable of delegating work in order to participate in leisure activities.

________ 13. I purposely schedule time specifically for leisure.

________ 14. I am capable of postponing work in order to participate in leisure activities.

________ 15. I enjoy activities that others might perceive as risky.

________ 16. I actively create and coordinate leisure activities for me and my friends.

________ 17. I am not afraid to try new or novel activities.

________ 18. I am pretty good at thinking of fun things to do.

________ 19. I rarely feel guilty for participating in leisure activities.

________ 20. I don't worry what other people think of me when it comes to leisure activities.

Self-scoring: To determine your score add the numerical values you entered. The sum of these values is your perceived freedom score. Write your score here:______.

Name: ______________________________ Date: ____________________ Section: ___________

4. Affective Profile II: Leisure Values

Read each statement carefully. Use the following five point scale to indicate the extent to which you agree with each statement.

STRONGLY AGREE = 5 Agree = 4 Undecided = 3 Disagree = 2 **STRONGLY DISAGREE** = 1

________ 1. Leisure is an important part of one's lifestyle.

________ 2. Leisure activities contribute to one's physical health.

________ 3. Being at leisure contributes to one's mental health.

________ 4. Leisure activities help make life more worthwhile.

________ 5. Leisure activities are important to family togetherness.

________ 6. Leisure activities are a good place to meet other people.

________ 7. Leisure activities provide opportunities for personal growth.

________ 8. People should feel good about their leisure involvement.

________ 9. Leisure activities help people live longer.

________ 10. Leisure activities can help workers be more productive.

________ 11. When I am at leisure, I am generally quite happy.

________ 12. Time really flies when I am at leisure.

________ 13. I really look forward to participating in leisure activities.

________ 14. I think it is important for me to participate in leisure activities as frequently as possible.

________ 15. I find my leisure activities tend to refresh me.

________ 16. I personally value my leisure time.

________ 17. I would like to have more leisure time.

________ 18. I don't think a person should feel guilty about participating in leisure activities.

________ 19. Leisure activities help reduce stress in people's lives.

________ 20. I highly value my leisure opportunities.

Self-scoring: To determine your score add the numerical values you entered. The sum of these values is your leisure values score. Write your score here:______.

Name: ______________________________ Date: ____________________ Section: ___________

5. Affective Profile III: Leisure Satisfaction

Use the following five point scale to indicate the extent to which you agree with each of the following statements:

STRONGLY AGREE = 5   Agree = 4   Undecided = 3   Disagree = 2   **STRONGLY DISAGREE** = 1

________ 1. My leisure activities provide laughter in my life.

________ 2. My leisure activities provide me with a network of friends.

________ 3. I can always count on being around friendly people at my leisure activities in which I participate.

________ 4. My leisure activities definitely contribute to my physical health.

________ 5. I usually feel refreshed after participating in leisure.

________ 6. Leisure activities help me stay in shape.

________ 7. My leisure activities contribute to my sense of well-being.

________ 8. My leisure activities help me stay intellectually sharp.

________ 9. My leisure involvement helps keep me emotionally healthy.

________ 10. My leisure activities usually leave me with a feeling of accomplishment.

________ 11. My leisure involvement usually helps me relax.

________ 12. My leisure activities help me deal with stress.

________ 13. Many of my leisure activities help me learn new skills.

________ 14. My leisure activities help me feel good about myself.

________ 15. My leisure activities provide me with an opportunity to express myself in creative ways.

________ 16. I find myself trying out new and adventurous leisure activities.

________ 17. I am rarely bored.

________ 18. Leisure provides me with opportunities to see, hear and experience beautiful things and places.

________ 19. My leisure activities never result in a bad experience.

________ 20. Overall, I am satisfied with the quality of my leisure.

Self-scoring: To determine your score add the numerical values you entered. The sum of these value is your leisure satisfaction score. Write your score here:______.

Name: ______________________________ Date: ____________________ Section: ___________

6. Affective Profile IV: Playfulness

Use the following five point scale to indicate the extent to which you agree with each of the following statements:

STRONGLY AGREE = 5   Agree = 4   Undecided = 3   Disagree = 2   **STRONGLY DISAGREE** = 1

________ 1. I rarely take things too seriously.
________ 2. I can generally find a funny side to most things.
________ 3. I am pretty creative.
________ 4. I seldom get bored.
________ 5. I enjoy teasing my friends.
________ 6. It is easy for me to talk to strangers.
________ 7. People view me as a fun person.
________ 8. I can express myself in novel ways.
________ 9. I find it easy to have fun in public places.
________ 10. It is easy for me to be silly.
________ 11. I like being spontaneous.
________ 12. I enjoy solving problems in creative ways.
________ 13. I am frequently able to laugh at myself.
________ 14. I enjoy the reaction I get from other people.
________ 15. I have a good sense of humor.
________ 16. I often enjoy being around strangers.
________ 17. It is easy for me to get others to have fun.
________ 18. People seem to like to be around me.
________ 19. I think of myself as a playful person.
________ 20. Being playful makes me feel good.

Self-scoring: To determine your score add the numerical values you entered. The sum of these value is your playfulness score. Write your score here: ______.

Name: ______________________ Date: __________________ Section: __________

7. Behavioral Profile 7 A and 7B

Behavioral Profile 7 A: In this scale you are to identify the extent to which you currently participate in various leisure activities. Read each statement carefully and circle the most appropriate response.

Behavioral Profile 7B: In this scale you are to indicate the extent to which you would like to participate in the activities listed. Read each statement carefully and then circle the most appropriate response.

Frequently = 4 Sometimes = 3 Rarely = 2 Never = 1

	BEHAVIORAL 7A	BEHAVIORAL 7B
1. Activities that are entertaining such as movies, theater, videos, concerts, etc.	4 3 2 1	4 3 2 1
2. Activities that involve competition: sports, contests, other competitive activities.	4 3 2 1	4 3 2 1
3. Activities that focus attention on me: activities that put me in front of others.	4 3 2 1	4 3 2 1
4. Activities that affect me emotionally: that excite me or cause me to feel deeply.	4 3 2 1	4 3 2 1
5. Activities that I perceive as risky or adventurous.	4 3 2 1	4 3 2 1
6. Activities that are novel or different: unusual events or special programs.	4 3 2 1	4 3 2 1
7. Activities that require and challenge a skill	4 3 2 1	4 3 2 1
8. Activities that are spontaneous and playful.	4 3 2 1	4 3 2 1
9. Activities that allow me to relate to nature and the "out-of-doors."	4 3 2 1	4 3 2 1
10. Activities that are self-enriching or promote personal development and growth.	4 3 2 1	4 3 2 1
11. Activities that allow me solitude or privacy.	4 3 2 1	4 3 2 1
12. Activities that are intellectually stimulating.	4 3 2 1	4 3 2 1
13. Activities that are sexually satisfying.	4 3 2 1	4 3 2 1
14. Activities that stimulate the senses: i.e. activities that affect my visual, tactile, auditory, olfactory and kinesthetic senses.	4 3 2 1	4 3 2 1
15. Activities that allow me to volunteer my time to help others.	4 3 2 1	4 3 2 1
16. Activities that allow me to interact with other people.	4 3 2 1	4 3 2 1

17. Activities that allow me to be creative.	4	3	2	1	4	3	2	1
18. Activities that involve rhythm or sound.	4	3	2	1	4	3	2	1
19. Activities that allow me to appreciate something that I find beautiful.	4	3	2	1	4	3	2	1
20. Activities that are physically challenging.	4	3	2	1	4	3	2	1
21. Activities that help me relax.	4	3	2	1	4	3	2	1
22. Activities that I view as being safe.	4	3	2	1	4	3	2	1
23. Activities that require cooperation with others.	4	3	2	1	4	3	2	1
24. Activities that involve travel to new and interesting places.	4	3	2	1	4	3	2	1
25. Activities that permit me to be expressive in an artistic or creative way.	4	3	2	1	4	3	2	1

Self-scoring: Compare your actual with your desired behavior. Do this by totaling up the number of points in each category (Behavioral 7 A and Behavioral 7B).

Enter your scores here: Behavioral 7 A ______ Behavioral 7B______

Name: ______________________________ Date: ____________________ Section: ___________

8. Temporal Scale: Obstacles to Leisure

Use the following five point scale to indicate the extent to which you agree with each of the following statements:

STRONGLY AGREE = 5 Agree = 4 Undecided = 3 Disagree = 2 **STRONGLY DISAGREE** = 1

________ 1. I simply don't know how to say "no" to some of the things I'm doing.

________ 2. My work schedule prevents me from doing many fun things.

________ 3. Because of my work, it is important that I maintain an image that de-emphasizes leisure.

________ 4. I simply don't have time to participate in leisure activities.

________ 5. Most of the things I want to do as part of my leisure cost too much money.

________ 6. I can't justify spending money for leisure activities.

________ 7. My family responsibilities take up most of my free time.

________ 8. Getting to and from leisure events is hard for me.

________ 9. I would do more leisure, but I don't have many friends who like to do the things I enjoy.

________ 10. It is hard for me to do things with other people.

________ 11. Being around groups of people makes me feel uneasy.

________ 12. The most important people in my life don't approve of my participating in leisure activities.

________ 13. There really isn't much to do in this town.

________ 14. I would participate in more leisure activities, but I am not very good at anything.

________ 15. I usually find out about fun things to do after it is too late to participate in them.

________ 16. I am embarrassed to ask for help so I can participate in leisure.

________ 17. I don't think leisure activities are very important.

________ 18. I have more important things to do than participate in leisure activities.

________ 19. I have a hard time deciding what to do in my free time, and usually end up not doing anything.

________ 20. I am afraid to try new leisure activities.

Self-scoring: To determine your score add the numerical values you entered. Write your score here:______.
NOTE: On this scale a low score is desirable.

Name: ______________________________ Date: ____________________ Section: ___________

9. Leisure Profile Background Information

Please answer the following questions. The information you provide will be helpful in evaluating the Leisure Profile Packet as well as helping your instructor interpret the results of each of the scales to which you have responded. The information you provide will be held in the strictest confidence.

1. What is your ethnic background? ____
2. What is your gender? _____ 3. How old are you? _____ 4. What is your marital status? _____ If you are married, do you have children? _____ How old are they? ______________________________
5. Are you a U.S. citizen? _____ 6. If you are employed, how many hours do you work per week? _______
7. As a child, in what country did you spend your youth?________ 8. Did you grow up in a rural or urban setting? _____
9. How many siblings (brothers and sisters) do you have? _____ 10. Did your parents divorce during your childhood? _____ If yes, how old were you at the time of divorce? _____

The following questions can be answered using the following scale:

VERY HIGH = 5 Somewhat high = 4 Average = 3 Somewhat low = 2 **VERY LOW** = 1

________ 11. Rate the extent to which your parents or guardians encouraged participation in recreation activities.

________ 12. Rate the extent to which your parents were active in recreation.

________ 13. Rate the extent to which your family participated, as a unit, in recreation.

________ 14. Rate the extent to which television filled your leisure time.

________ 15. Rate the level of stress in your life today.

________ 16. How would you rate your present level of satisfaction with your job or career?

________ 17. How would you rate your present level of satisfaction with your school experience?

________ 18. How would you rate your present level of satisfaction with your "love life?"

________ 19. How would you rate your present level of satisfaction with your social life?

________ 20. How would you rate your present level of activity in recreation and leisure activities?

21. If you are enrolled in a college or university, what is your major? ______________________________
22. If you are enrolled in a college or university, what is your GPA? _____
23. If you are enrolled in a college or university, what year are you? ______________________________
24. What career are you seeking? ____

Evaluation of the Scales

These scales are constantly being updated and improved. Do you have any suggestions for the next generation of the LPP. Please share your ideas in this space.____

____

____

____

Name: ______________________________ Date: ____________________ Section: ___________

Summary Chart

Leisure Profile Packet Scores

	Cognitive				Affective		Behavioral	Temporal	
Value	1	2	3	4	5	6	7A	7B	8
100									
95									
90									
85									
80									
75									
70									
65									
60									
55									
50									
45									
40									
35									
30									
25									
20									

Scale 1 = Test of knowledge about the subject of leisure.
Scale 2 = Measure of level of awareness of leisure activities.
Scale 3 = Measures the degree to which a person is free to engage in leisure.
Scale 4 = Measures the degree a person values leisure.
Scale 5 = Measures to what degree one finds satisfaction in leisure.
Scale 6 = Measures the degree to which a person is playful.
Scale 7 A = Measures one's depth of involvement in leisure activity.
Scale 7B = Measures one's desire for involvement in leisure activity.
Scale 8 = Measures obstacles to leisure. Low score desirable.

Even though this is a heuristic exercise, you might want to know how you compare to other students. The most recent normative data derived from this scale is found in the appendix. Many instructors require students to write an essay on the insight gained from the LPP. Sample insight statements are also included in the appendix.

For a graphic representation of your scores, below each scale's number write your score for that scale. Now color in the column for each score. This creates a bar graph visually reflecting your scores for each scale. Remember a low score on Scale 8 is desirable. The highest score you can receive on any scale is 100 and the lowest score possible is 20. In the case of Scale 8, a score of 20 corresponds to a score of 100 on the other scales.

Name: ______________________________ Date: ____________________ Section: ___________

Autobiography of a Student of Leisure

This section is for instructor use only and will be held in confidence.

Birthday: _________ What is your cumulative GPA? ____________________

Your mailing address: ____

____E-mail ____________________________________

Telephone Numbers __________________________________Hours on job per week ____________

1. What is your major?__________________________________ Minor?________________________
2. What career do you wish to pursue?____
3. If you have a job, describe it:
4. If you could have lunch with anyone from the past, who would that be? ____________________
   Why?____
5. If you were locked in a room for one month and could only have one food and water, what would your food selection be? ____
6. What are your five all-time favorite movies _______________________________________

   ____

   What is the worst movie you have ever seen? ____

   What is your favorite TV show?____
7. What is the last book you read for fun?
8. What animal are you most alike? ____

   What is your personal theme song? ____

   What is your personal motto?____

   What is your personal symbol? ____
9. How much money do you need in order to be happy? _________________________________
10. Describe your ideal mate: ____

    Now what will you settle for: ____
11. In general what is your favorite fun thing to do?____________________________________

    In this town? ____
12. What is your greatest recreational accomplishment?___________________________________
13. What is your greatest recreational ambition?____
14. What word would you choose to use in place of the word "leisure"? ______________________

    How do you define "leisure"?____
15. What is the number one thing that interferes with your personal happiness? _______________

Now on the reverse side of this sheet, please draw a portrait of yourself. Use bold strokes! Be creative, be descriptive

Making Discovery a Regular Occurrence: The Discovery Event

Central to this book is the idea that discovery is important. Indeed, as you read in the first chapter, there are numerous studies that support the importance of continued leisure exploration throughout one's life. To further your personal exploration you are encouraged to make discovery events a frequent occurrence, but what to discover? In trying to answer this question, 120 college students enrolled in a general education class at California State University were asked to identify their favorite recreational activities as well as those new activities they most wanted to experience. The activities identified were then organized into a survey instrument called the Activity Preference Questionnaire (APQ). The APQ has been adapted to the theme of this book and is presented here as a means of helping you identify some recreational activities that you might want to explore. Once you have completed the APQ, you will find that there are many activities that you have already experienced. What should you be interested in are those with which you have little experience.

Select a few activities that are either entirely new to your or activities with which you have limited familiarity. Make these the objects of discovery.

In evaluating a discovery event, you might want to address the following:

1. What was the event, when did it occur, and where?
2. Why did you choose this particular activity?
3. What were your expectations prior to the activity?
4. What emotional responses did you experience as the event approached?
5. Briefly describe the actual event.
6. What emotional responses did you experience during the event?
    a. To what extent did you experience optimal arousal?
    b. to what extent did you experience perceived or perceptual freedom?
    c. To what extent did you experience intrinsic satisfaction?
7. How could the event have been better?
8. To what extent will this event be part of your leisure in the future.

A worksheet is provided to help you document your discovery events. This form can be copied and used to report your discoveries to your instructor. Some instructors want proof of participation such as a ticket stub or event program. Documenting the discovery event can be a discovery in itself. For example, some people have discovered joy in photography from having taken photos of a discovery event. Some students have videotaped their discovery events. Your instructor will give you specific information regarding this exercise. As with all writing assignments, it is important to express your ideas clearly and logically. Good grammar and spelling are important. Be careful with "spell check," your computer won't know whether you wanted "their" or "there."

Name: ______________________________ Date: ____________________ Section: ___________

Activity Preference Questionnaire (APQ)

Please answer: **"Do you like to do these activities?"**

Please use a five point scale:

STRONG YES = 5, yes = 4, undecided = 3, no = 2, **STRONG NO** = 1

❐ 1. bowl
❐ 2. bicycle
❐ 3. play tennis
❐ 4. play racquetball
❐ 5. play flag football
❐ 6. play table tennis
❐ 7. run or jog
❐ 8. swim
❐ 9. ski, downhill
❐ 10. water ski
❐ 11. roller skate
❐ 12. play golf
❐ 13. cross-country ski
❐ 14. ride horses
❐ 15. go rafting
❐ 16. go hiking
❐ 17. go sailing
❐ 18. go caving
❐ 19. go scuba diving
❐ 20. go hunting
❐ 21. go surfing
❐ 22. go kayaking
❐ 23. draw or paint
❐ 24. do calligraphy
❐ 25. do needlepoint
❐ 26. do macrame
❐ 27. do model making
❐ 28. woodworking
❐ 29. do sculpture
❐ 30. make jewelry
❐ 31. make pottery
❐ 32. jazz dance
❐ 33. do ballet
❐ 34. go social dancing
❐ 35. attend dance concerts
❐ 36. attend live theater
❐ 37. attend music concerts
❐ 38. go to the movies
❐ 39. visit museums
❐ 40. go to the mall
❐ 41. go out to dinner
❐ 42. visit with friends
❐ 43. read novels
❐ 44. read poetry
❐ 45. write poetry
❐ 46. write stories
❐ 47. play video games
❐ 49. computer play
❐ 50. Internet surfing
❐ 51. play table games
❐ 52. play chess
❐ 53. play checkers
❐ 54. play cards
❐ 55. collecting things
❐ 56. travel places
❐ 57. drive around town
❐ 58. drink alcohol
❐ 59. inline skate
❐ 60. skateboard
❐ 61. view pornography
❐ 62. play an instrument
❐ 63. listen to music
❐ 64. garden
❐ 65. cook
❐ 66. decorate my house
❐ 67. sew
❐ 68. go out on dates
❐ 69. flirt
❐ 70. be romantic
❐ 71. be with my boyfriend/girlfriend
❐ 72. have sex
❐ 73. go to parties
❐ 74. work on my car
❐ 75. take courses
❐ 76. go for walks
❐ 77. attend church services
❐ 78. meditate
❐ 77. attend church services
❐ 80. to relax—do nothing
❐ 81. volunteer to help others
❐ 82. target shoot with guns
❐ 83. casino gambling
❐ 84. do crafts
❐ 85. be with family
❐ 86. do aerobics
❐ 87. go bird watching
❐ 88. baking/cooking
❐ 89. attend professional sports
❐ 90. ropes course participation
❐ 91. visit the zoo
❐ 92. visit museum
❐ 93. visit amusement parks
❐ 94. visit state parks
❐ 95. bungee jump
❐ 96. go fishing
❐ 97. martial arts
❐ 98. mountain biking
❐ 99. snowboarding
❐ 100. go to strip clubs/ nudie bars
❐ 101. watch television
❐ 102. sunbathe
❐ 103. kick boxing
❐ 104. crossword puzzles
❐ 105. singing
❐ 106. playing bridge
❐ 107. playing table games
❐ 108. playing poker
❐ 109. spiritual experience
❐ 110. yoga
❐ 111. write in a diary
❐ 112. ceramics
❐ 113. backpacking
❐ 114. camping
❐ 115. miniature golf
❐ 116. laser tag
❐ 117. paintball game
❐ 118. horseback riding
❐ 119. attend rodeo
❐ 120. badmiton
❐ 121. folk dancing
❐ 122. hang gliding

- ❒ 123. sail plane
- ❒ 124. riverboat cruise
- ❒ 125. ship cruise
- ❒ 126 karaoke
- ❒ 127. hypnosis
- ❒ 128. do magic
- ❒ 129. watch magic
- ❒ 130. do cartooning
- ❒ 131. invent something
- ❒ 132. computer graphics
- ❒ 133. paint a picture
- ❒ 134. photography
- ❒ 135. video production
- ❒ 136. massage
- ❒ 137. reflexology
- ❒ 138. acupuncture
- ❒ 139. stamp collecting
- ❒ 140. archery
- ❒ 141. darts
- ❒ 142. flower arranging
- ❒ 143. decoupage
- ❒ 144. pet training
- ❒ 145. visit national park
- ❒ 146. amusement park
- ❒ 147. weight lifting
- ❒ 148. kite flying
- ❒ 149. acting
- ❒ 150. antique hunting
- ❒ 151. flying
- ❒ 152. cross-cultural activity
- ❒ 153. square dancing
- ❒ 154. call a talk-show
- ❒ 155. ice skating
- ❒ 156. aqua-aerobics
- ❒ 157. origami
- ❒ 158. political campaign
- ❒ 159. opera
- ❒ 160. leather craft

Generally I like to...

- ❒ 161. do activities by myself
- ❒ 162. do activities with others
- ❒ 163. do competitive
- ❒ activities
- ❒ 164. do noncompetitive activities
- ❒ 165. do intellectual activities
- ❒ 166. do physical activity
- ❒ 167. be a spectator
- ❒ 168. take risks
- ❒ 169. be creative
- ❒ 170. do self-directed activities
- ❒ 171. do relaxing activities

APPLICATION. To get the most out of this questionnaire, review each item and select those that received scores of 3 or less.

Those receiving a 3 are good candidates for discovery. For those receiving a 1 or a 2, ask yourself if your lack of interest in the activity is due to an informed evaluation or simply bias. Gender bias, for example, might influence you away from an activity that you might enjoy. If bias is the reason for a negative response, you might consider exploring the activity to see of your bias is justified. Now, continue this exercise by going to APQ part 2: Discover Analysis.

Now to complete this exercise go to part 2. →

Name: ______________________________ Date: ____________________ Section: ___________

APQ Part 2: Discovery Analysis

So what did you learn from this exercise? To help you analyze your findings complete the following: As you went through the exercise, were you reminded of activities not included in the APQ that you might want to investigate? If so list them here: ____

____

____

↓

In reference to the activities included in the APQ, what were the activities about which you were uncertain (activities receiving a 3)? List them here: ____

____

____

____

↓

Now review those receiving a score less than 3. Are any of these the product of bias as compared to a reasoned judgment? For example, gender bias might prevent you from selecting activities that you view as limited to members of the opposite sex. Age bias might prevent you from selecting activities that you view as specific to either older or younger populations, etc. List those activities that are the product of such bias: ___

____

↓

Review your findings as presented in above lists. How many of these activities are you willing and able to explore? Write your top ten selections in the space below.

POTENTIAL DISCOVERY EVENTS for (name) __________________ Date______________Section _

1. ______________________________ 6. ______________________________
2. ______________________________ 7. ______________________________
3. ______________________________ 8. ______________________________
4. ______________________________ 9. ______________________________
5. ______________________________ 10. ______________________________

From this list your instructor will ask you to identify a certain number to experience and evaluate. Following completion of a discovery event you will complete and submit to your instructor a Discovery Event Report. A form is provided. If you require more, you may copy a blank form.

Name: ______________________________ Date: ____________________ Section: ___________

Time Survey

How much time do yo spend in activities that promote growth and development? How much time do you spend engaging in negative behaviors or experiencing unpleasant emotions? In this exercise we try to answer these and similar questions.

During the next seven day period, you are to keep an accurate record of how you spend your time, how you feel during different activities, and reasons for negative emotions. To accomplish this you will need to keep a "time diary" in which you make note of the amount of time spent on an activity, the affective response (how you felt during the activity) and an explanation for any negative emotions experienced.

Then, using the following code, you will record your daily findings. At the end of the week, you will total the number of hours per activity, the affective response produced by each activity, and the number of hours associated with negative emotions. The categories and subcategories to be considered in this exercise are as follows:

CODE	CATEGORY AND SUBCATEGORIES
	TIME SPENT IN PERSONAL ACTIVITIES
01	grooming or personal hygiene
02	eating
03	night seeping
04	napping or resting
05	medical, dental, or counseling
06	other personal matters
	TIME SPENT IN HOUSEHOLD DUTIES OR CHORES
07	cleaning or tidying the house
08	doing laundry
09	other inside chores
10	working on the car
11	gardening or doing yardwork
12	shopping or running errands
13	paying bills or doing bookkeeping
14	time spent doing other household tasks not listed
	TIME SPENT WITH FAMILY
15	alone with grandparents
16	alone with parents
17	alone with siblings
18	alone with children
19	time spent with other family members or family as a group
	TIME SPENT TRAVELING
20	to and from work
21	to and from school
22	traveling for recreation or fun (Sunday drives, sightseeing, etc.)
23	to and from recreation or leisure activities
24	other types of traveling

TIME SPENT IN OBLIGATION

25 at work
26 at school
27 professional meetings, civic duties, religious responsibilities
28 doing homework
29 other obligatory activity

TIME SPENT IN ENTERTAINMENT

30 at the movies
31 live theater
32 watching television
33 watching sports
34 playing on the Internet or computer
35 video games
36 watching adult (sexually related) movies, videos, WWW sites
37 other entertainment

TIME SPENT IN SOCIAL ACTIVITY

38 visiting friends
39 talking with friends on the phone
40 organized parties or social gatherings
41 dating
42 social dancing
43 socializing in bars or night clubs
44 time spent in other social activity

TIME SPENT IN PHYSICAL ACTIVITY

45 weight training
46 aerobic dance
47 jogging or running
48 cycling
49 walking
50 active sports
51 time spent on other physical activities

TIME SPENT IN MENTAL, ARTISTIC, LINGUISTIC OR SPIRITUAL ACTIVITIES

52 reading for pleasure
53 music for pleasure
54 time spent producing or enjoying visual art
55 attending museums or exhibits
56 meditating or worshipping
57 writing poetry, stories, etc. for personal satisfaction
58 time spent in other mental, artistic, linguistic or spiritual activities

TIME SPENT IN OUTDOOR RECREATION

59 hiking, backpacking, camping
60 hang-gliding, sky diving, scuba diving, or sailing
61 rafting, canoeing, kayaking
62 skiing (water or snow)
63 swimming outdoors, sunbathing
64 surfing, skim boarding, sail boarding
65 other outdoor activities

Name: ______________________________ Date: ____________________ Section: ___________

TIME SPENT IN MISCELLANEOUS ACTIVITIES

66 volunteer service to others
67 writing letters or sending email
68 working on a hobby
69 engaging socially unacceptable or illegal recreation
70 under the influence of alcohol
71 time spent on hold or waiting for another person (on the phone, in line, in traffic etc.)
72 Other ____________________________

Evaluation System

01 agony
02 pain
03 discomfort
04 neutral
05 comfortable
06 pleasure/joy
07 ecstasy

Reasons for Negative Responses

01 jealousy
02 frustration
03 guilt
04 distrust
05 boredom
06 anger
07 open conflict
08 feelings of inferiority/inadequacy
09 worry
10 disappointment
11 aloneness
12 physical illness
13 anxiety
14 fear

How to Report Your Findings

After your study week has ended, total up the hours per category, the hours per affective response, and the number of hours per reason for negative responses. You may round to the nearest 1/4. What about situations where you were involved in two activities simultaneously? Here you make a judgment call. One activity will generally be the primary activity and the other activity will be secondary. You are talking on the phone while doing your ironing. One is dominant, one affects your mood more than the other. You have to choose. In making your report, you can include both primary and secondary activities.

For most people this is a very interesting exercise. Most of us are unaware of just how much time we spend in activities that contribute little to our personal growth and development. Generally people are amazed at just how much time they spend watching television or attending to boredom. Many people are unaware of how much time they spend eating, sleeping, and doing household chores. Similarly, people are surprised to find how much time they spend "on hold . . ." Time is a precious commodity that we sometimes take for granted. *Following this activity, you might want to contemplate ways to budget your time more effectively.*

The report form you are to use to report your time survey findings follows.

Name: ______________________________ Date: ____________________ Section: ___________

Time Survey Report

Gender ________________________Age ________ Major __________________________________

Note: Column A is for the primary activity, column B is for the secondary activity.

CODE	COLUMNS a	b
Personal Activities		
01	____	____
02	____	____
03	____	____
04	____	____
05	____	____
06	____	____
Total	____	____
Household Duties		
07	____	____
08	____	____
09	____	____
10	____	____
11	____	____
12	____	____
13	____	____
14	____	____
Total	____	____
Family Involvement		
15	____	____
16	____	____
17	____	____
18	____	____
19	____	____
Total	____	____
Time Spent Traveling		
20	____	____
21	____	____
22	____	____
23	____	____
24	____	____
Total	____	____

CODE	COLUMNS a	b
Obligations		
25	____	____
26	____	____
27	____	____
28	____	____
29	____	____
Total	____	____
Entertainment		
30	____	____
31	____	____
32	____	____
33	____	____
34	____	____
35	____	____
36	____	____
37	____	____
Total	____	____
Social Activity		
38	____	____
39	____	____
40	____	____
41	____	____
42	____	____
43	____	____
44	____	____
Total	____	____
Physical Activity		
45		
46	____	____
47	____	____
48	____	____
49	____	____

CODE	COLUMNS a	b
50	____	____
51	____	____
Total	____	____
Mental, Spiritual etc.		
52	____	____
53	____	____
54	____	____
55	____	____
56	____	____
57	____	____
58	____	____
Total	____	____
Outdoor Recreation		
59	____	____
60	____	____
61	____	____
62	____	____
63	____	____
64	____	____
65	____	____
Total	____	____
Miscellaneous Recreation		
66	____	____
67	____	____
68	____	____
69	____	____
70	____	____
71	____	____
Total	____	____

Total up the time associated with each item on the pain-pleasure scale.

01	_____	agony
02	_____	pain
03	_____	discomfort
04	_____	neutral
05	_____	comfortable/satisfied
06	_____	pleasure/joy
07	_____	ecstasy

Now total up the time associated with a negative response:

01	_____	jealousy
02	_____	frustration
03	_____	guilt
04	_____	distrust
05	_____	boredom
06	_____	anger
07	_____	conflict
08	_____	inadequacy
09	_____	worry
10	_____	disappointment
11	_____	aloneness
12	_____	illness
13	_____	anxiety
14	_____	fear

Pause for Reflection:

Take a few minutes and reflect on the result of the time budget study. What did you learn about your use of time? Will you make any changes in your daily schedule?

Name: ______________________________ Date: ____________________ Section: ___________

Discovery Event Report Form

Please respond to the following:

1. What was the event, when did it occur, and where?

2. Why did you choose this particular activity?

3. What were your expectations prior to the activity?

4. What emotional responses did you experience as the **event approached**?

5. Briefly describe the actual event.

6. What emotional responses did you experience **during the event**?

    a. To what extent did you experience optimal arousal?

    b. To what extent did you experience perceived or perceptual freedom?

    c. To what extent did you experience intrinsic satisfaction?

7. What emotional responses did you experience **following the event**?

8. How could the event have been better?

9. To what extent will this event be part of your leisure **in the future**?

10. What potential for your **personal growth and development** does this activity hold for you?

Name: ______________________________ Date: ____________________ Section: ___________

Coming to Terms

Identifying Leisure Behaviors

Early in this textbook we discussed the nature of play, recreation and leisure. We also contrasted recreational games to interpersonal games. In this exercise you are demonstrate you ability to distinguish between these five terms. Over the next twenty-four hour period, you are to watch the behavior of other people, with the intention of finding examples of play, recreation, leisure, interpersonal and recreational games. You may include your own behavior in this exercise. For each observation, describe the behavior, explain when and where it occurred and with whom. Explain why you view the behavior as representing the category in which you have placed it. What criteria did you use in evaluating the behaviors you observed? You may use additional paper if necessary.

Example of play or playfulness: ____

____

____

Example of recreation: ____

____

Example of interpersonal game: ____

____

____

Example of recreational game: ____

____

____

Example of leisure: ____

____

____

NOTE: *Drawing accurate inferences from the behavior of other people is a difficult task. In the case of the example of a person at leisure, how were you able to ascertain the subject's state of mind? In making observations of the behavior of other people, we look for certain observable variables that are believed to be related to the construct in question. Smiling, laughing, and focus all may indicate a leisure state of mind. But, how can you be certain?*

Name: ______________________________ Date: ____________________ Section: ___________

Philosophy Worksheet

Your Philosophy of Leisure

As pointed out in the textbook and in lecture, philosophy is essentially a collection of ideas. It is basically what you believe to be true about something. In this assignment, you are to examine and briefly write about your personal philosophy of leisure. To help you express your leisure philosophy, the following questions are offered as a guide.

1. What does the word leisure mean to you? ____

____

____

2. Epistemology: From what sources have your drawn your conclusions regarding leisure? How valid are these sources? ____

____

____

3. Metaphysics: What role does metaphysics play in your philosophy? ____________________________

____

____

4. Axiology: Generally speaking, just how much value do you place on leisure. What role does leisure play in your life, what is its function? ____

____

____

   a. Aesthetics: In your philosophy of leisure, what constitutes beauty? ______________________

   ____

   ____

   ____

   b. Ethics: In your philosophy of leisure, what constitutes ethical leisure behavior? _____________

   ____

   ____

   ____

   ____

5. Logic: What are some of the fundamental premises that provide the foundation for your leisure philosophy? Is their a logical relationship between these premises and your axiology? Are your fundamental premises epistemologically sound? ____

____

____

____

Name: ______________________________ Date: ____________________ Section: ___________

Anti-leisure Behavior: Interpersonal Games

Players: Interpersonal games require two or more people.
Goal: One player attempts to manipulate another player into a situation that yields some gain to the manipulator. In other words, in an interpersonal game, player A attempts to put player B into a situation that is clearly advantageous to A. Whether or not B is harmed is of little concern to A.
Rules: There are no rules (not at least as we think of them); the interpersonal dynamic is one of conflict as compared to recreational games where the dynamic is primarily one of a contest.
Transactions: The interpersonal transactions that occur between A and B (with A initiating the game) are characterized by deceit (dishonesty) and manipulation (leading one through deception to some desired, but generally unwise, outcome).
Motivation: Some psychologists argue that motivations are generally not known to the player. Some motivations are viewed as rooted in the subconscious mind. However, other experts think that most games are initiated on the conscious level, particularly in first-degree games. (Interpersonal games can be ranked by degree of harm; first-degree, second-degree, and third-degree—the most damaging.) Game playing often involves the denial of an unhealthy need, issue, or attitude.
Outcome: When a desired (conscious or un conscious) need has been met, the games comes to its conclusion; however, it usually spawns a follow-up game. The outcome is an indication of the motivation.
Anti-leisure: Anti-leisure occurs when a situation produces constraint (as opposed to perceived freedom); is characterized by negative perceptual-freedom (the focus is on some disturbing or disorganizing influence), and yields uncomfortable feelings.
Describe an Interpersonal Game You Have Seen or Experienced (Use additional paper if necessary.)
Name Your Game: ______________________________

Who are the players?

____

____

What is the outcome being sought?

____

____

What is the motivation (the outcome gives you a hint)?

____

____

Describe the transactions that player A is likely to employ to achieve the desired outcome.

____

____

____

____

If A achieves his/her desired outcome, what are the consequences to B? Are there any undesirable consequences to A?

____

____

____

What would be a desirable alternative to this game? (What course of actions would be more in keeping with a leisure philosophy?) If the game has commenced, what might be a reasonable strategy to prevent a negative outcome?

___

___

___

Name: ______________________________ Date: ____________________ Section: ___________

Mirthwhile Humor

Making humor an important part of your lifestyle is a twofold proposition. First you need to develop a sense of humor so that you can increase your ability to find humor in otherwise stress producing situations. Second, it is important that you learn to share your humorous ideas and experiences with others in order to help create a more pleasant world in which to live. In this crazy, hectic, and sometimes frightening world, humor is something from which we all can benefit.

Your Funny Bone Exercise: During the next 24 hours, look for opportunities to practice finding humor in situations that otherwise might be viewed as distressing. Experiment with the effect that humor has on your mood during anxiety producing situations. To what extent was humor helpful to you in coping with anxiety or distress? How did it affect others? Summarize your findings. ____________________________________

____

____

____

____

____

____

____

____

____

____

Again, looking back over the past 24 hours, did you note any occasions when humor might not have been appropriate? In using humor, what are your personal guidelines for ensuring that your use of humor is appropriate? Do your guidelines address the role humor can play in your personal growth and development?

____

____

____

____

____

____

____

Sharing: Learning to share humor in a positive and sensitive manner is an important skill. In the space below or on the reverse side of this sheet, share a story, riddle or joke that you enjoy sharing. ________________

____

____

____

Name: ______________________________ Date: ____________________ Section: ___________

Creativity Exercise

Using the suggestions found in the chapter on creativity, try your hand at coming up with a creative response to the following problem.

A new planet was recently discovered. It was decided that a random sample of earthlings would be selected to design the life forms that would inhabit the new planet. Thanks to the marvels of genetic engineering all you have to do is draw a rough sketch of one life form that you would like to see created, and the engineers will do the rest. In addition you will want to include any notations to explain to the engineers what your creation will be like. Name your creation.

____

____

____

____

____

____

____

____

____

Here's one that is a little more down to earth. As a parent, list five things you can do to help your child approach his or her creative potential:

1. ____
2. ____
3. ____
4. ____
5. ____

What's one thing you can do to help yourself become more creative? (Explain) ________________

____

____

____

____

____

____

____

____

____

____

____

____

Name: ____________________ Date: ______________ Section: ________

Time Bandits

ELIMINATING TIME BANDITS

Pay attention to the things in your life that rob you of precious time. If you look closely, you will find that most of these time bandits are really nothing more than inefficient behavior. Lose your keys and you lose precious time. Fail to get adequate rest and spend the next day moping about. Plan poorly and get caught in traffic and you lose more time! Write down, in the space below, the prominent time bandits in your life.

Time bandits in my life:

____

____

____

____

Now in the space provided, identify one time bandit you intend to eliminate from your life. Personify this time enemy in a drawing or cartoon.

Describe the behavior that you hope to eliminate.

What specific steps do you intend to take in order to arrest this undesirable behavior? Identify at least four actions that you can take to render this time bandit harmless.

1. ______________________________

2. ______________________________

3. ______________________________

4. ______________________________

Allow yourself one-week to arrest this time bandit. Report your results here.

WANTED FOR CRIMES AGAINST TIME

Name: ______________________________ Date: ____________________ Section: ___________

My Prescription for Stress Relief

In this exercise, you are asked to identify specific problems that produce distress in your life. Following the identification of the leading stressors in your life, you are to write a prescription for a leisure activity or activities that might help you COPE with the stressor while you work on overcoming the source of the distress.

Sources of distress in my life are:

1. Physiological elements in my life that cause distress: ____

   ____

2. Psychological elements in my life that cause distress: ____

   ____

3. Environmental elements in my life that cause distress: ____

   ____

4. Specific events in my life that cause distress: ____

   ____

Of the items listed above, what is the most significant stressor?

My **BIG** stressor is:____

Relaxing activities such as listening to music, going for a stroll, playing, or meditating might be helpful. Physical activities such as jogging, swimming, cycling, aerobics etc. also might help. Ponder the type of activities that will help relieve some of your distress. Remember this is just for immediate relief. Resolving the problem will require application of the principles provided in the text

.

PRESCRIPTION
DR. I.M. RELAXING, M.D.

Activity description:____

____

Specific time and dosage:____

____

____

____

____

____

Name: ______________________________ Date: ____________________ Section: ___________

Worksheet on Work

J.B. Nash observed that "If you don't want to work, you have to work to earn enough money so that you won't have to work." It's ironic isn't it. We spend a good share of our life working to earn money so that we won't have to work. And, yet if that were our only purpose in working, what an unhappy world this would be. Indeed, for many people, work provides far more than monetary rewards.

1. In the space below, list some of the important intrinsic values that you hope to find in your first job following graduation: ____

2. How can leisure contribute to one's work? Are there times when one's work and leisure become indistinguishable? Can you give an example? ____

3. How important is location in seeking a job? Where would you not accept employment under any circumstance? When does salary become more important than locale? ____

4. Describe your ideal job. Explain how it will contribute to your leisure lifestyle? What are you doing to make this dream come true? ____

Name: ______________________________ Date: ____________________ Section: ___________

Leisure Socialization

Within recent years, there has been more and more interest in the effect that television has on children.

The famous "Bobo Doll" study, cited in the text, dramatically demonstrates that children model their behavior after that which they see in adults—even adult actors in a movie. Subsequent studies support these early findings and present persuasive evidence that television is a powerful socializing influence in today's society. In this exercise, you are to select a children's television program and evaluate it as a socializing influence. Look carefully for behaviors that might be inappropriate for children to model.

Identify the principle values communicated by the program. Do the values demonstrated conflict with values stated (does the program meet its stated objectives, if any)? Was violence promoted in any manner? Was gender bias promoted? What messages were communicated by the commercials? Overall, what kind of developmental effect might the program have on a young child? What effect did it have on you?

TV Observation

Program observed__________________________ Station______________ Day and time _____________
Length of program ______________________Commercial sponsors ______________________________
Using the questions in the paragraph above, write a brief statement regarding the likely impact this program would have on a young child.

____
____
____
____
____
____
____
____
____
____
____
____
____
____
____
____
____
____

Would you want your child to watch this program? If so, would you impose any special conditions?

____
____

Alternative Activity

Instead of watching television, select a popular video game and play the game as an objective observer. Ask yourself the same questions as above.

What video game did you play? ____

where did you play the game and when: ______________________ Day and time ______________________

Write your analysis in the space provided above.

Name: ______________________________ Date: ____________________ Section: ___________

Parenting

It has been demonstrated that effective leisure functioning and self-esteem are both associated with perceived freedom (related to internal locus of control), intrinsic satisfaction (related to perceived competence), and optimal arousal (related to productivity and satisfaction). As a parent, what can you do to help your child develop internal locus of control, perceived freedom, the appreciation of intrinsic rewards, a sense of competence, and the capacity to generate optimal arousal in socially productive ways?

What I Can Do as a Parent to Encourage the Development of These Attributes

PERCEIVED FREEDOM

INTERNAL LOCUS OF CONTROL

INTRINSIC SATISFACTION

PERCEIVED COMPETENCE

OPTIMAL AROUSAL

Name: ______________________________ Date: ____________________ Section: ___________

Change

Some people might think that human development ceases when you reach adulthood. This of course is not entirely true. People continue to learn new concepts, acquire skills, refine old skills, and alter their behavior. It is true that some attributes and behaviors resist change, but there are many things we can do to change our lives in a positive way. We can continue to develop. Identifying areas in which we can grow and develop is an important ability. In this exercise you are to think carefully about things you can change in your life and things you cannot change. After identifying some areas in which you can change, ask yourself, "How can I change these things in order to develop a more leisure oriented lifestyle—a lifestyle characterized by optimal arousal, perceived freedom, and intrinsic satisfaction?"

Things about Me That I Can't Change	→	Things about Me That I Can Change
____________________		____________________
____________________		____________________
____________________		____________________
____________________		____________________
____________________		____________________

Three Changes That I Can Make in Order to Have a More Leisure Oriented Lifestyle

1. ______________________________
2. ______________________________
3. ______________________________

How Will You Bring about These Changes?

____

____

____

Classroom Research Project #1
A Summary of Leisure Profile Packet Scores Among RLS 100 Students

Prepared by E. Olson
Fall, 1996

The LPP[1] is routinely used for heuristic purposes in courses such as RLS 100. Normative data for a sample of college students was collected during the Fall Semester, 1996, and is reported here.

Sample: 400 students enrolled in three sections of RLS 100 at CSUS filled out the eight scale instrument.

Analysis

Scale 1: Measure knowledge regarding recreation and leisure. The average score on this scale was 80.86.

Scale 2: Measures practical knowledge regarding recreation and leisure activity. The average score on this scale was 71.56.

Scale 3: Measures perceived freedom.[2] Average score is 72.14.

Scale 4: Measures leisure values. Average score is 91.69. This score is noteworthy because it is the highest average score among the eight scales. Among the subjects surveyed, it appears that leisure is highly valued.

Scale 5: Measures leisure satisfaction. Average score is 80.8.

Scale 6: Measures playfulness. Average score is 74.52. Anecdotal data suggest that most people find it difficult to be as playful as they would like. Similar data suggest that some subjects question the validity of certain items on this scale.

Scale 7A: Measures "current" leisure behavior: Average score is 69.

Scale 7B: Measures "desired" leisure behavior. Average score is 87.

Scale 8: Measures obstacles to leisure. This score is adjusted from the raw data to conform to the foregoing scales. The adjusted score is 75.

1. The Leisure Profile Packet consists of nine separate scales or questionnaires. These scales are designed to measure factors generally viewed as important to leisure functioning. Each scale has a potential score of 100 and is designed to be self-scored.
2. The term "perceived freedom" is associated with John Neulinger and is in reference to the mental state of "feeling" free. It should not be confused with the term "perpetual freedom" that I use in lectures to denote an element often referred to in discussion of flow–the mental state where one is so highly focused as to be oblivious to any stimuli except that central to the experience.

Commentary

The scores between men and women were remarkably similar, except for Scale 3: Perceived Freedom. It is interesting to note that men scored seven points higher than women, no other differences were judged significant. This finding follows cultural expectations regarding gender. Women are typically viewed as less independent and given less recreational opportunities than men; furthermore, women of the age group studied are often counseled to always be vigilant.

There was relatively little variance between ethnic groups; correlation by gender, ethniciety, and age revealed no significant variance.

Index

J

K

L

M

N

O

P

Q

R

S

T

U

V

W

Z